Spain
& Portugal
The most in-depth campsite guides

Alan Rogers

INSPECTED
CAMPSITES
& SELECTED

Compiled by: Alan Rogers Guides Ltd

Designed by: Paul Effenberg, Vine Design Ltd

Additional photography: T Lambelin, www.lambelin.com

Maps created by Customised Mapping (01769 540044)
contain background data provided by GisDATA Ltd
Maps are © Alan Rogers Guides and GisDATA Ltd 2009

Published by: Alan Rogers Guides Ltd,
Spelmonden Old Oast, Goudhurst, Kent TN17 1HE
www.alanrogers.com Tel: 01580 214000

British Library Cataloguing-in-Publication Data:
A catalogue record for this book is available
from the British Library.

ISBN 978-1-906215-15-6

Printed in Great Britain by J H Haynes & Co Ltd

Contents

The Alan Rogers approach

Alan Rogers Guides were first published over 40 years ago. Since Alan Rogers published the first campsite guide that bore his name, the range has expanded and now covers 27 countries in five separate guides. No fewer than 20 of the campsites selected by Alan for the first guide are still featured in our 2009 editions.

There are many thousands of campsites in Spain and Portugal of varying quality: this guide contains impartially written reports on over 270 of the very finest, each being individually inspected and selected. All the usual maps and indexes are included, designed to help you find the choice of campsite that's right for you. We hope you enjoy some happy and safe travels – and some pleasurable 'armchair touring' in the meantime!

A question of quality

The criteria we use when inspecting and selecting sites are numerous, but the most important by far is the question of good quality. People want different things from their choice of campsite so we try to include a range of campsite 'styles' to cater for a wide variety of preferences: from those seeking a small peaceful campsite in the heart of the countryside, to visitors looking for an 'all singing, all dancing' site in a popular seaside resort. Those with more specific interests, such as sporting facilities, cultural events or historical attractions, are also catered for.

The size of the site, whether it's part of a chain or privately owned, makes no difference in terms of it being required to meet our exacting standards in respect of its quality and it being 'fit for purpose'. In other words, irrespective of the size of the site, or the number of facilities it offers, we consider and evaluate the welcome, the pitches, the sanitary facilities, the cleanliness, the general maintenance and even the location.

" ...the campsites included in this book have been chosen entirely on merit, and no payment of any sort is made by them for their inclusion."

Alan Rogers, 1968

INSPECTED SINCE 196. & SELECTED

Expert opinions

We rely on our dedicated team of Site Assessors, all of whom are experienced campers, caravanners or motorcaravanners, to visit and recommend sites. Each year they travel some 100,000 miles around Europe inspecting new campsites for the guide and re-inspecting the existing ones. Our thanks are due to them for their enthusiastic efforts, their diligence and integrity.

We also appreciate the feedback we receive from many of our readers and we always make a point of following up complaints, suggestions or recommendations for possible new sites. Of course we get a few grumbles too – but it really is a few, and those we do receive usually relate to overcrowding or to poor maintenance during the peak school holiday period. Please bear in mind that, although we are interested to hear about any complaints, we have no contractual relationship with the campsites featured in our guides and are therefore not in a position to intervene in any dispute between a reader and a campsite.

Independent and honest

Whilst the content and scope of the Alan Rogers guides have expanded considerably since the early editions, our selection of campsites still employs exactly the same philosophy and criteria as defined by Alan Rogers in 1968.

'telling it how it is'

Firstly, and most importantly, our selection is based entirely on our own rigorous and independent inspection and selection process. Campsites cannot buy their way into our guides – indeed the extensive Site Report which is written by us, not by the site owner, is provided free of charge so we are free to say what we think and to provide an honest, 'warts and all' description. This is written in plain English and without the use of confusing icons or symbols.

HIGHLY RESPECTED BY SITE OWNERS AND READERS ALIKE, THERE IS NO BETTER GUIDE WHEN IT COMES TO FORMING AN INDEPENDENT VIEW OF A CAMPSITE'S QUALITY. WHEN YOU NEED TO BE CONFIDENT IN YOUR CHOICE OF CAMPSITE, YOU NEED THE ALAN ROGERS GUIDE.

- SITES ONLY INCLUDED ON MERIT
- SITES CANNOT PAY TO BE INCLUDED
- INDEPENDENTLY INSPECTED, RIGOROUSLY ASSESSED
- IMPARTIAL REVIEWS
- OVER 40 YEARS OF EXPERTISE

Written in plain English, our guides are exceptionally easy to use, but a few words of explanation regarding the layout and content may be helpful. In Spain we have used the 16 official administrative regions, whilst in Portugal we use the five regions defined by the Portuguese Tourist Board. A full page introduction to each region highlights its main areas of interest, places to visit and the local cuisine.

The Site Reports – *Example of an entry*

Site Number Site name

Postal address (including county)

Telephone number. Email address

alanrogers.com web address

A description of the site in which we try to give an idea of its general features – its size, its situation, its strengths and its weaknesses. This section should provide a picture of the site itself with reference to the facilities that are provided and if they impact on its appearance or character. We include details on pitch numbers, electricity (with amperage), hardstandings etc. in this section, as pitch design, planning and terracing affect the site's overall appearance. Similarly we include reference to pitches used for caravan holiday homes, chalets, and the like. Importantly at the end of this column we indicate if there are any restrictions, e.g. no tents, no children, naturist sites.

Facilities

Lists more specific information on the site's facilities and amenities and, where available, the dates when these facilities are open (if not for the whole season). Off site: here we give distances to various local amenities, for example, local shops, the nearest beach, plus our featured activities (bicycle hire, fishing, horse riding, boat launching). Where we have space we list suggestions for activities and local tourist attractions.

Open: Site opening dates.

Directions

Separated from the main text in order that they may be read and assimilated more easily by a navigator en-route. Bear in mind that road improvement schemes can result in road numbers being altered.

GPS: references are provided as we obtain them for satellite navigation systems (in degrees and minutes).

Charges 2009 (or a general guide)

Indexes

Our three indexes allow you to find sites by their number and name, by region and site name or by the town or village where the site is situated. See also the Quick Reference sections at the back of the guide.

Campsite maps

The maps will help you to identify the approximate position of each campsite within its region. The colour of the campsite number indicates whether it is open all year or not. You will certainly need more detailed maps and we have found the Michelin atlas to be particularly useful.

Facilities

Toilet blocks

We assume that toilet blocks will be equipped with a reasonable amount of British style WCs, washbasins with hot and cold water and hot showers with dividers or curtains, and will have all necessary shelves, hooks, plugs and mirrors. We also assume that there will be an identified chemical toilet disposal point, and that the campsite will provide water and waste water drainage points and bin areas. If not the case, we comment. We do mention certain features that some readers find important: washbasins in cubicles, facilities for babies, facilities for those with disabilities and motorcaravan service points. Readers with disabilities are advised to contact the site of their choice to ensure that facilities are appropriate to their needs.

Shop

Basic or fully supplied, and opening dates.

Bars, restaurants, takeaway facilities and entertainment

We try hard to supply opening and closing dates (if other than the campsite opening dates) and to identify if there are discos or other entertainment.

Children's play areas

Fenced and with safety surface (e.g. sand, bark or pea-gravel).

Swimming pools

If particularly special, we cover in detail in our main campsite description but reference is always included under our Facilities listings. We will also indicate the existence of water slides, sunbathing areas and other features. Opening dates, charges and levels of supervision are provided where we have been notified.

Leisure facilities

For example, playing fields, bicycle hire, organised activities and entertainment.

Dogs

If dogs are not accepted or restrictions apply, we state it here. Check the quick reference list at the back of the guide.

Off site

This briefly covers leisure facilities, tourist attractions, restaurants etc. nearby.

Charges

These are the latest provided to us by the sites. In those cases where 2009 prices are not given, we try to give a general guide.

Reservations

Necessary for high season (roughly mid-July to mid-August) in popular holiday areas (e.g. beach resorts). You can reserve many sites via our own Alan Rogers Travel Service or through other tour operators. Or be wholly independent and contact the campsite(s) of your choice direct, using the phone or e-mail numbers shown in the site reports, but please bear in mind that many sites are closed all winter.

Telephone numbers

All numbers assume that you are phoning from within Spain or Portugal. To phone Spain from outside that country, prefix the number shown with the relevant International Code '00 34' and then the number indicated. To phone Portugal prefix the number shown with the International Code '00 351'.

Opening dates

Are those advised to us during the early autumn of the previous year – sites can, and sometimes do, alter these dates before the start of the following season, often for good reasons. If you intend to visit shortly after a published opening date, or shortly before the closing date, it is wise to check that it will actually be open at the time required. Similarly some sites operate a restricted service during the low season, only opening some of their facilities (e.g. swimming pools) during the main season; where we know about this, and have the relevant dates, we indicate it – again if you are at all doubtful it is wise to check.

Sometimes, campsite amenities may be dependant on there being enough customers on site to justify their opening and, for this reason, actual opening dates may vary from those indicated.

Some campsite owners are very relaxed when it comes to opening and closing dates. They may not be fully ready by their stated opening dates – grass and hedges may not all be cut or perhaps only limited sanitary facilities open. At the end of the season they also tend to close down some facilities and generally wind down prior to the closing date. Bear this in mind if you are travelling early or late in the season – it is worth phoning ahead.

The Camping Cheque low season touring system goes some way to addressing this in that participating campsites are encouraged to have all key facilities open and running by the opening date and to remain fully operational until the closing date.

Mobile homes page 182

Our Accommodation section

Over recent years, more and more campsites have added high quality mobile home and chalet accommodation. In response to feedback from many of our readers, and to reflect this evolution in campsites, we include a separate section on mobile homes and chalets.

If a site offers this accommodation, it is indicated above the site report with a page reference where full details are given. We have chosen a number of sites offering some of the best accommodation available and have included full details of one or two accommodation types at these sites. Please note however that many other campsites listed in this guide may also have a selection of accommodation for rent.

Whether you're an 'old hand' in terms of camping and caravanning or are contemplating your first trip, a regular reader of our Guides or a new 'convert', we wish you well in your travels and hope we have been able to help in some way. We are, of course, also out and about ourselves, visiting sites, talking to owners and readers, and generally checking on standards and new developments.

We wish all our readers thoroughly enjoyable Camping and Caravanning in 2009 – favoured by good weather of course!

THE ALAN ROGERS TEAM

Regions

Galicia

Asturias

Cantabria

Pais Vasco-Euskadi

Navarra

Porto & North

Castilla y León

Aragón

Catalunya

Beiras & Centre

Madrid

Castilla La Mancha

Balears

Lisbon & Vale do Tejo

Comunidad Valenciana

Extremadura

Alentejo

Murcia

Algarve

Andalucia

The Alan Rogers Awards

The Alan Rogers Campsite Awards were launched in 2004 and have proved a great success.

Our awards have a broad scope and before committing to our winners, we carefully consider more than 2,000 campsites featured in our guides, taking into account comments from our site assessors, our head office team and, of course, our readers.

Our award winners come from the four corners of Europe, from southern Portugal to Slovenia, and this year we are making awards to campsites in 13 different countries.

Needless to say, it's an extremely difficult task to choose our eventual winners, but we believe that we have identified a number of campsites with truly outstanding characteristics.

In each case, we have selected an outright winner, along with two highly commended runners-up.

Listed below are full details of each of our award categories and our winners for 2008.

Our warmest congratulations to all our award winners and our commiserations to all those not having won an award on this occasion.

THE ALAN ROGERS TEAM

Alan Rogers Progress Award 2008

This award reflects the hard work and commitment undertaken by particular site owners to improve and upgrade their site.

WINNER

PO8202 Turiscampo, Portugal

RUNNERS-UP

DE3202	Grav-Insel, Germany
IT60450	Marina di Venezia, Italy

Alan Rogers Welcome Award 2008

This award takes account of sites offering a particularly friendly welcome and maintaining a friendly ambience throughout reader's holidays.

WINNER

FR05000 Princes d'Orange, France

RUNNERS-UP

FR71110	Du Lac, France
DK2022	Vikær Diernæs, Denmark

Alan Rogers Active Holiday Award 2008

This award reflects sites in outstanding locations which are ideally suited for active holidays, notably walking or cycling, but which could extend to include such activities as winter sports or water sports

WINNER

FR07120 L'Ardéchois, France

RUNNERS-UP

SV4210   Sobec, Slovenia

AU0265   Park Grubhof, Austria

Alan Rogers Motorhome Award 2008

Motorhome sales are increasing and this award acknowledges sites which, in our opinion, have made outstanding efforts to welcome motorhome clients.

WINNER

UK0220 Trevornick, England

RUNNERS-UP

BE0655   De Lilse Bergen, Belgium

CZ4840   Oase Praha, Czech Republic

Alan Rogers 4 Seasons Award 2008

This award is made to outstanding sites with extended opening dates and which welcome clients to a uniformly high standard throughout the year.

WINNER

AU0440 Schluga, Austria

RUNNERS-UP

NL6520   BreeBronne, Netherlands

ES92950 Don Cactus, Spain

Alan Rogers Seaside Award 2008

This award is made for sites which we feel are outstandingly suitable for a really excellent seaside holiday.

WINNER

NL5735 Tempelhof, Netherlands

RUNNERS-UP

UK1070   Woolacombe Bay, England

CR6732   Polari, Croatia

Alan Rogers Country Award 2008

This award contrasts with our former award and acknowledges sites which are attractively located in delightful, rural locations.

WINNER

FR23030 Creuse Nature, France

RUNNERS-UP

ES90260 El Burro Blanco, Spain

IT62090 Vidor, Italy

Alan Rogers Rented Accommodation Award 2008

Given the increasing importance of rented accommodation on many campsites, we feel that it is important to acknowledge sites which have made a particular effort in creating a high quality 'rented accommodation' park.

WINNER

IT60370 Jesolo International, Italy

RUNNERS-UP

FR33300 La Jenny, France

NL5560   De Wijde Blick, Netherlands

Alan Rogers Unique Site Award 2008

This award acknowledges sites with unique, outstanding features – something which simply cannot be found elsewhere and which is an important attraction of the site.

WINNER

FR34070 Sérignan, France

RUNNERS-UP

IT60030 Pra' delle Torri, Italy

DE3182   Teutoburger Wald, Germany

Alan Rogers Family Site Award 2008

Many sites claim to be child friendly but this award acknowledges the sites we feel to be the very best in this respect.

WINNER

FR32010 Camp de Florence, France

RUNNERS-UP

ES80350 L'Amfora, Spain

IT62630   Bella Italia, Italy

Alan Rogers Readers' Award 2008

We believe our Readers' Award to be the most important. We simply invite our readers (by means of an on-line poll at www.alanrogers.com) to nominate the site they enjoyed most.

The outright winner for 2008 is:

WINNER

IT60200 Union Lido, Italy

Alan Rogers Special Award 2008

A special award is made to acknowledge sites which we feel have overcome a very significant setback, and have, not only returned to their former condition, but have added extra amenities and can therefore be fairly considered to be even better than before. In 2008 we acknowledged two campsites, which have undergone major problems and have made highly impressive recoveries.

UK2885   Warner Farm, England

FR32080 Le Talouch, France

Crossing the Channel

One of the great advantages of booking your ferry-inclusive holiday with the Alan Rogers Travel Service is the tremendous value we offer. Our money-saving Ferry Deals have become legendary. As agents for all major cross-Channel operators we can book all your travel arrangements with the minimum of fuss and at the best possible rates.

Just call us for an instant quote

01580 214000

or visit
www.**alanrogers**.com/travel

Let us price your holiday for you

instantly!

The quickest and easiest way is to call us for advice and an instant quote. We can take details of your vehicle and party and, using our direct computer link to all the operators' reservations systems, can give you an instant price. We can even check availability for you and book a crossing while you're on the phone!

Please note we can only book ferry crossings in conjunction with a campsite holiday reservation.

It's all on-line

www.alanrogers.com is a website designed to give you everything you need to know when it comes to booking your Alan Rogers inspected and selected campsite, and your low cost ferry.

Our friendly, expert team of travel consultants is always happy to help on

01580 214000 – but they do go home sometimes!

Visit **www.alanrogers.com** and you'll find constantly updated information, latest ferry deals, special offers from campsites and much more. And you can visit it at any time of day or night!

Campsite Information

- ☑ Details of all Travel Service campsites - **instantly**
- ☑ Find latest special offers on campsites - **instantly**
- ☑ Check campsite availability - **instantly**

Ferry Information

- ☑ Check ferry availability - **instantly**
- ☑ Find latest ferry deals - **instantly**
- ☑ Book your ferry online - **instantly**
- ☑ Save money - **instantly**

One of the largest countries in Europe, with glorious beaches, a fantastic sunshine record, vibrant towns and laid back sleepy villages, plus a diversity of landscape, culture and artistic traditions, Spain has all the ingredients for a great holiday.

Tourist Office

Spanish National Tourist Office
22/23 Manchester Square
London W1U 3PX

Tel: 020 7486 8077
E-mail: info.londres@tourspain.es
Fax: 020 7486 8034
Internet: http://www.tourspain.es

Spain has a huge choice of beach resorts to choose from. With charming villages and attractive towns, the Costa Brava boasts spectacular scenery with towering cliffs and sheltered coves. There are plenty of lively resorts, including Lloret, Tossa and Calella, plus several quieter ones. Further along the east coast, the Costa del Azahar stretches from Vinaros to Almanzora, with the great port of Valencia in the middle. Orange groves abound. The central section of the coastline, the Costa Blanca, has 170 miles or so of silvery-white beaches. Benidorm is the most popular resort. The Costa del Sol lies in the south, home to more beaches and brilliant sunshine, whilst in the north the Costa Verde is largely unspoiled, with clean water, sandy beaches and rocky coves against a backdrop of mountains.

Beaches and sunshine aside, Spain also has plenty of great cities and towns to explore, including Barcelona, Valencia, Seville, Madrid, Toledo and Bilbao, all offering an array of sights, galleries and museums.

Population
39.5 million

Capital
Madrid

Climate
Spain has a very varied climate. The north is temperate with most of the rainfall; dry and very hot in the centre; subtropical along the Mediterranean.

Language
Castilian Spanish is spoken by most people with Catalan (northeast), Basque (north) and Galician (northwest) used in their respective areas.

Telephone
The country code is 00 34.

Currency
The Euro (€).

Banks
Mon-Fri 09.00-14.00. Sat 09.00-13.00.

Shops
Mon-Sat 09.00-13.00/14.00 and 15.00/16.00-19.30/20.00. Many close later.

Public Holidays
New Year; Epiphany; Saint's Day 19 Mar; Maundy Thurs; Good Fri; Easter Mon; Labour Day; Saint's Day 25 July; Assumption 15 Aug; National Day 12 Oct; All Saints Day 1 Nov; Constitution Day 6 Dec; Immaculate Conception 8 Dec; Christmas Day.

Flanked by the Pyrenees mountains and bathed by the Mediterranean Sea, Catalunya occupies the northeastern part of the Iberian peninsula. It has a strong identity, with a unique culture and language all of its own.

CATALUNYA IS COMPRISED OF FOUR PROVINCES: BARCELONA, TARRAGONA, LLEIDA AND GIRONA

THE REGIONAL CAPITAL IS BARCELONA

Barcelona is the historical capital of Catalunya and Spain's second leading city in both size and importance, after Madrid. The beautiful city has an impressive architectural heritage that includes the Gothic Quarter, with its cathedral, the old City Hall Building, the Episcopal Palace and the splendid Palace of the Generalitat. The city also boasts the work of the incomparable modernist architect Antonio Gaudí. In the centre of the fertile plain of the river Segre sits Lleida, capital of the province of the same name. Prominent atop a hill in the historic quarter of the city is the old cathedral or Seu Vella. The Costa Brava is the coastal zone that begins about 40 km. north of Barcelona and includes the entire shoreline of the province of Girona. It is an area of great natural beauty, formed by a succession of steep cliffs and small coves with finely grained sand. Some of its towns have been massively exploited for tourism but others, such as Tossa de Mar, still maintain their original size and fishing-village charm. The principal tourist centres on the coast include Roses, Sant Pere Pescador, L'Escala, L'Estartit, Palamós, Palafrugell, Platja d'Aro, S'Agaro, Sant Feliu de Guixols, Lloret de Mar and Blanes. There are daily boat services which operate along the coast for most of the year.

Places of interest

Empúries: Greco-Roman city.

Figueres: birthplace of Salvador Dali, museum displaying his finest work.

Girona: one of the oldest and most beautiful Catalan cities, 14th century cathedral.

La Costa Dorada: stretches south from the Costa Brava to Tarragona, with beautiful, open, well maintained beaches.

Parque Natural de Aigüamolls de L'Empordà: park made up of three reserves, with wildlife and over 320 bird species.

Sitges: attractive beach town, museum of Cau-Ferrat featuring paintings by El Greco.

Tarragona: Roman remains of Tarraco, the original Roman city.

Cuisine of the region

Mediterranean influence with lots of tomatoes, garlic, fresh herbs, olive oil, onions, fish. Wild mushrooms in the autumn. Locally produced wines from Penedés, Conca de Barberá, Pla de Bages and Alella.

Calçots: green onions grilled on a barbecue.

Cod esqueixada: cod soaked in cold water then mixed with tomatoes, olives and onion.

Escalivada: vegetable stew with roasted aubergine and peppers.

Fuet, llonganisa, butifarra: local sausages.

Suquet: seafood casserole.

Recao de binefar: rice cooked with white beans, potatoes and chorizo.

FRANCE

ANDORRA

ARAGON

CATALUNYA

- BENASQUE

91240

91190

91430
91440
91420

91400
91390

91380

17

91230

16

N260

N240

C25

LLEIDA/
LERIDA

N11

A7

A2

BARCELONA

85020

85060

84200 84100

84860
84800 84850
84790
84810
84780
85400
85300
85370 85350
84820
84700

85330

83900
84020

83920
SITGES
83930

TARRAGONA

84830

85080

N420

85360

85550

MORELLA
COMUNIDAD
VALENCIANA

Red text = all year opening

0   20   40   60 kms

For campsites in North East Catalunya please see the map on the following page.

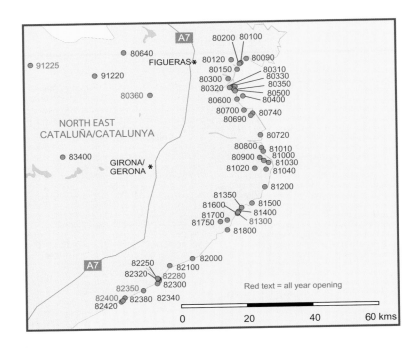

ES91190 **Frontera Park**

Ctra Seo d'Urgell - Andorra N145 km 8, E-25799 Farga de Moles (Lleida)

Tel: **973 355 830**. Email: **info@fronterapark.com**   www.alanrogers.com/ES91190

Frontera Park lives up to its name, as it is situated on the border with Andorra and makes an ideal base for visiting this small Principality. The site is strung out along the bank of a small river with no reported problems with flooding. There are 230 fairly small grass pitches, 50 for touring, with mountain views, trees giving some shade and 10A electricity. Spacious chalets are situated in the northern part of the site, away from the camping area. During the winter this is a good area for skiing in the Pyrenees. In summer there are hiking trails and possibilities for wild water canoeing.

Facilities

Two very clean toilet blocks have separate areas for ladies and men. Baby washroom but no facilities for campers with disabilities. Small bar with terrace. Cosy restaurant. The catering facilities, open all year, closed on Wednesdays. Swimming pool and paddling pool (July/Aug) with grassy sunbathing area. Multisport field. Play area. Off site: Fishing. Riding. Golf. Lake with beach and sailing 8 km. Hiking trails. During the ski season many pistes 13 km.

Open: All year.

Directions

Site lies about 8 km. north of Seu d'Urgell and south of Andorra. From Seu d'Urgell take N145 towards Andorra. After 8 km. sign look out for site sign on the left mountain wall. Turn right to make a sharp left turn across the main road into the access road of the site. GPS: N42:25.683 E01:27.783

Charges guide

Per unit incl. 2 persons and electricity (10A)	€ 20,00
extra person	€ 4,10
Camping Cheques accepted.	

Check real time availability and at-the-gate prices...

www.alanrogers.com

ES91230 Camping El Solsones

Ctra Sant Llorenc km 2, E-25280 Solsona (Lleida)

Tel: 973 482 861. Email: info@campingsolsones.com

www.alanrogers.com/ES91230

Situated on a hillside, 2 km. from Solsona, this all year site has pleasant views of the hills on three sides and lots of mature trees giving a pleasant green shady appearance. With a lovely Spanish feel, it would be a pleasant spot for a short stay during any season. There are many weekend units here, and although only 72 of the 269 pitches are for touring (22 for caravans or motorcaravans and 50 for tents), we were told that finding a pitch was unlikely to be a problem. They are in separate sections of the site and are slightly sloping, with shade and 4/10A electricity.

Facilities

Modern sanitary facilities are in two buildings, with free hot water. Motorcaravan services. Large supermarket. Restaurant and bar (24/6-15/9 and winter weekends). Simple meals and snacks served indoors and outside on the terrace. Swimming pool with lifeguard (24/6-12/9). Excellent sports complex. Minigolf. Tennis. Bicycle hire. Play area. Petanque. Aviary. Picnic area. WiFi. Dogs are not accepted. Off site: Golf, riding and skiing nearby. Solsona is interesting with good bars, restaurants and cafés.

Open: 10 January - 10 December.

Directions

Solsona is 45 km. northwest of Manresa, along the C55 and is on the C26 Lleida/Andorra - Barga road. Site is 2 km. out of town on the LV4241 signed to Sant Llorenc de Morunys and Ski Port del Comte. GPS: N42:00.799 E01:31.035

Charges guide

Per person	€ 5,90
pitch incl. car	€ 10,50 - € 11,80
electricity (4-10A)	€ 3,90 - € 7,50

Plus 7% VAT. No credit cards.

ES91240 Camping Caravaning Bedurá Park

Era Bordeta - Val d'Aran CN230 km 174,4, E-25551 Lleida (Lleida)

Tel: 973 648 293. Email: info@bedurapark.com

www.alanrogers.com/ES91240

Bedurá Park lies in the Val d'Aran at a height of 900 metres, surrounded by wonderful panoramic views. The surrounding woods are alive with a wide variety of wildlife, including deer, wild boar, capercaillies and pine martens. This is a perfect place for a quiet, yet active holiday. With 173 small, well shaded, stony/grass pitches set out on terraces, there are 150 for touring, all with 5A electricity. Access for large units may be difficult due to the low trees. This is a haven for nature lovers.

Facilities

One large and one small toilet block provide some washbasins in cabins plus facilities for campers with disabilities. Shop (1/6-30/9). Bar, restaurant and takeaway. Heated swimming and paddling pools (15/6-15/9). Miniclub (July/Aug). Games/TV room. Play area. Barbecues are only permitted on a communal area. Dogs and other animals are not accepted. Off site: Adventure sports, cycling, hiking, fishing. Riding 12 km. Skiing 20 km. Vielha ice palace with ice rink, indoor pool, sauna 10 km.

Open: All year.

Directions

Site is on the N230, 12 km. from the French border and 10 km. north of Vielha. Leave A60 (French) autoroute at exit 17 and take N125 south to border. Continue on N230 through Bossost then 4 km. to site at la Bordeta. GPS: N42:45.017 E00:41.882

Charges guide

Per person	€ 5,25
pitch	€ 10,00 - € 18,00
electricity	€ 4,25

No credit cards.

ES91420 Camping Solana del Segre

Ctra N260 km 198, E-25720 Bellver de Cerdanya (Lleida)

Tel: 973 510 310. Email: sds@solanadelsegre.com

www.alanrogers.com/ES91420

The Sierra del Cadi offers some spectacular scenery and the Reserva Cerdanya is very popular with Spanish skiers. This site is situated in an open, sunny lower valley beside the River Segre where the far bank is a National Park (unfenced so children will need supervision). The site is in two sections, the lower one nearer the river being for tourists, mainly flat and grassy with 200 pitches of 100 sq.m. or more, shaded by trees with 15A electricity. The upper area is taken by permanent units.

Facilities

Modern sanitary facilities are in a central building on the lower level, with extra 'portacabin' style units (unisex toilets/showers). Facilities for disabled campers are on the upper level (wheelchair users will experience problems). Laundry facilities. Motorcaravan services. Shop, bar and restaurant. Swimming and paddling pools. Indoor pool. Two play areas. Games room. River fishing. Dance area. Barbecue areas. Internet. Torches required. Off site: Village has a range of shops bars and restaurants. Riding 2 km. Bicycle hire and golf 10 km. Skiing. Superb walking area.

Open: 1 July - 15 September.

Directions

Site is on left at the 198 km. marker on the N260 from Puigcerda to La Seu d'Urgell, well signed just beyond Bellver le Cerdanya. GPS: N42:22.352 E01:45.629

Charges guide

Per unit incl. 1 person and electricity	€ 28,50
extra person	€ 6,00
child (2-9 yrs)	€ 5,50
dog	€ 4,75

Plus 7% VAT.

ES80090 Camping Salatá

Port Reig s/n, Platja Salatá, E-17480 Roses (Girona)

Tel: 972 256 086. Email: info@campingsalata.com

www.alanrogers.com/ES80090

Situated in the heart of Roses, in one of the most attractive areas of the Costa Brava, Salatá is a short walk from the magnificent seafront promenade with its bars, restaurants and shops. Opposite the site entrance there is a pretty landscaped sea inlet. There are 288 grass pitches with 16A electricity and some shade (80-110 sq.m). Buildings and amenities are well maintained. The campsite is part of a complex that includes apartments and the Hotel Terraza where a spa centre, indoor pool and other amenities can be enjoyed by campers in low season. The bar/restaurant may be used at all times.

Facilities

Very clean toilet blocks have British style toilets and very good showers. Facilities for disabled visitors, babies and children. Washing machines. Gas supplies. Bar with snacks. Swimming pool. Playground. Limited animation programme in high season. Internet. Barbecue area. Bicycle hire. Off site: Extra facilities at hotel (under the same ownership). Tennis 300 m. Riding 5 km. Golf 15 km.

Open: February - December.

Directions

From the AP7/E15, take exit 3 south or exit 4 north (there is no exit 3 northbound) and then the N11 to the C260 and on to Roses. Site is well signed before you enter the town. GPS: N42:15.953 E3:09.457

Charges guide

Per person	€ 4,40 - € 6,25
pitch	€ 13,00 - € 26,10
incl. services	€ 15,00 - € 29,00

ES80100 Camping Castell Mar

Platja de la Rubina, E-17486 Castelló d'Empúries (Girona)

Tel: 972 450 822. Email: cmar@campingparks.com

www.alanrogers.com/ES80100

This friendly site is 350 metres from one of the very pleasant Gulf of Roses beaches, and within the large Aiguamolls de l'Empordá nature reserve. It is also convenient for (but quite separate from) the latest tourist development and facilities at Empuria Brava. With some 300 pitches, it is smaller than many sites in this part of Spain and is particularly suitable for families. The pitches, most with electricity, are of average size for the Costa Brava and are on level ground with some artificial shade mainly for tents, and natural shade from the trees and hedges.

Facilities

The large, well maintained, modern toilet block is of a high standard. Some washbasins in cabins. Facilities for disabled visitors. Laundry facilities. Bar, restaurant/pizzeria and takeaway. Supermarket. Play area. Swimming pools. Many activities and entertainment over a long season. ATM. Security boxes. Torches required in some areas. Off site: Boat launching 500 m. Riding and bicycle hire 1 km. Golf 10 km. Discounts at local attractions.

Open: 23 May - 20 September.

Directions

Castello d'Empuries is north of Girona and east of Figueres on the coast. From AP7/E15 take exit 3 south or exit 4 north (note there is no exit 3 north) and then N11 to the C260 towards Roses. Site signed on right at km. 40.5, just after second turn for Empuriabrava; follow road for about 1.5 km. GPS: N42:15.310 E03:08.196

Charges 2009

Per person	€ 4,50
pitch incl. electricity	€ 8,00 - € 37,00
No credit cards.	

ES80200 Camping Internacional de Amberes

Playa de la Rubina, E-17487 Empúriabrava (Girona)

Tel: 972 450 507. Email: info@campingamberes.com

www.alanrogers.com/ES80200

Situated in the 'Venice of Spain', Empuriabrava is interlaced with inland waterways and canals, where many residents and holidaymakers moor their boats directly outside their homes on the canal banks. Internacional Amberes is a large friendly site 50 m. from the wide, sandy beach, which is bordered on the east and west by the waterway canals. The site has 700 touring pitches, most enjoying some shade from strategically placed trees. All have electricity and water connections.

Facilities

Toilet facilities are in five fully equipped blocks. Washing machines. Motorcaravan services. New modern supermarket, bakery and shop. Restaurant/bar. Disco bar. Takeaway. Pizzeria. Watersports with windsurfing school. Organised sports activities, children's programmes and entertainment. Swimming pool. New playground. Petanque. Tennis. Internet café and WiFi. Dog Shower. Apartments. Off site: Beach 200 m. Fishing 300 m. Bicycle hire and boat launching 500 m. Riding 1 km. Golf 3 km.

Open: 1 April - 15 October.

Directions

Empuriabrava is north of Girona and east of Figueres on the coast. From AP7/E15 take exit 3 south or exit 4 north (note there is no exit 3 north), then N11 to the C260 towards Roses. At Empuriabrava follow camping signs to site. GPS: N42:15.160 E03:07.902

Charges 2009

Per person (over 3 yrs)	€ 3,60 - € 4,00
pitch incl. electricity and water (85 sq.m)	€ 14,50 - € 31,50
No credit cards.	

ES80120 Kawan Village Mas Nou

Ctra Mas Nou no. 7, E-17486 Castelló d'Empúries (Girona)

Tel: **972 454 175**. Email: **info@campingmasnou.com**   www.alanrogers.com/ES80120

Some two kilometres from the sea on the Costa Brava, this is a surprisingly tranquil site in two parts on either side of the access road. One part contains the pitches and toilet blocks, the other houses the impressive leisure complex. There are 450 neat, level and marked pitches on grass and sand, a minimum of 70 sq.m. but most 80-100 sq.m. and 300 with electricity (10A). The leisure complex is across the road from reception and features a huge L-shaped swimming pool with a paddling area. A formal restaurant has an adjoining bar, pleasant terrace crêperie and rotisseria under palms. A barbecue/rotisseria in another part of the site offers takeaway meals (in season). The site owns the large souvenir shop on the entrance road. There are many traditional bargains here and it is worth having a good look around as the prices are extremely good. Lots of time and money goes into the cleanliness of this site and it is good very for families. Ask about the origin of the site coat of arms. The Bay of Roses and the Medes islands have a natural beauty and a visit to Dali's house or the museum (the house is fascinating) will prove he was not just a surrealist painter.

Facilities

Three excellent, fully equipped sanitary blocks include baby baths, good facilities for disabled visitors. Washing machines. Supermarket and other shops. Bar/restaurant. Takeaway. Swimming pool with life guard (from 1/5). Tennis. Minigolf. Miniclub (July/Aug). Play area. Electronic games. Off site: Riding 1.5 km. Fishing or bicycle hire 2 km. Beach 2.5 km. Aquatic Park. Romanica tour of famous local churches.

Open: 4 April - 27 September.

Directions

From A7 use exit 3. Mas Nou is 2 km. east of Castelló d'Empúries, on the Roses road, 10 km. from Figueres. Do not turn left across the main road but continue to the roundabout and return.
GPS: N42:15.935 E03:06.150

Charges 2009

Per person	€ 2,50 - € 4,80
child (4-11 yrs)	free - € 3,40
pitch	€ 14,70 - € 28,00
electricity	€ 3,20 - € 4,50
dog	free - € 2,20
Camping Cheques accepted.	

ES80150 Camping Caravaning La Laguna

Apdo 55, E-17486 Castelló d'Empúries (Girona)

Tel: **972 450 553**. Email: **info@campinglaguna.com**   www.alanrogers.com/ES80150

La Laguna is a relaxed, spacious site on an isthmus within a Catalan national maritime park, on the migratory path of many different birds. It has direct access to a sandy beach and the estuary of the river Muga. The owners continue to spend much time and effort on improvements. The double lagoons are a most attractive feature. The 773 pitches (with just 40 mobile homes) are shaded and clearly marked on grass and sand, all with 6/10A electricity. There are also 37 fully serviced pitches. An attractive bar/restaurant overlooks the lagoons and there are two swimming pools (one is heated in low season). A disco operates across the road from reception, keeping the noise away from the main site. A large riding school operates (May - Sept) and there are many other activities. The beach frontage is large and has a sailing school. It is said to be possible to cross over to Empuria Brava when the tide is out. There are many pleasant walks in this area and this a good site for family holidays.

Facilities

Five toilets blocks, placed to avoid long walks. All have been completely rebuilt and provide solar heated water. Laundry room. Bar, restaurant and takeaway. New supermarket. Swimming pools (1/4-26/10). Football. Tennis (free in low seasons). ATM. Minigolf. Windsurfing and sailing schools (July/Aug). Fishing. Miniclub. New play area. Bicycle hire. Riding. Animation programme and competitions. Satellite TV. Internet access and WiFi. Off site: Boat launching. Golf 15 km. Birdwatching.

Open: 29 March - 25 October.

Directions

Castelló d'Empuries is north of Girona and east of Figueres on the coast. From AP7/E15 take exit 3 south or exit 4 north (note there is no exit 3 north) and then N11 to the C260 towards Roses. At Castelló d'Empuries follow camping signs and a 4 km. unmarked road will take you to the site.
GPS: N42:14.238 E03:07.284

Charges 2009

Per person	€ 5,15 - € 8,95
child (3-10 yrs)	€ 4,15 - € 6,65
pitch	€ 9,55 - € 17,90
motorcaravan	€ 4,00
Discounts for longer stays and pensioners in low season. No credit cards.	

ES80300 Camping Nautic Almata

Ctra Giv 6216, km 11,6, E-17486 Castelló d'Empúries (Girona)

Tel: **972 454 477**. Email: **info@almata.com**   www.alanrogers.com/ES80300

In the Bay of Roses, south of Empuriabrava and beside the Parc Natural dels Aiguamolls de l'Empordá, this is a site of particular interest for nature lovers (especially bird watchers). Beautifully laid out, it is arranged around the river and waterways, so will suit those who like to be close to water or who enjoy watersports and boating. It is worth visiting because of its unusual aspects and the feeling of being on the canals, as well as being a high quality beachside site. A large site, there are 1,109 well kept, large, numbered pitches, all with electricity and on flat, sandy ground. There are some pitches right on the beach. As you drive through the natural park to the site watch for the warning signs for frogs on the road and enjoy the wild flamingos alongside the road. The name no doubt derives from the fact that boats can be tied up at the small marina within the site and a slipway also gives access to a river and thence to the sea. Throughout the season there is a varied entertainment programme for children and adults. The facilities on this site are impressive. Some tour operators use the site.

Facilities

Toilet blocks of a high standard include some en-suite showers with basins. Good facilities for disabled visitors. Washing machines. Gas supplies. Excellent supermarket. Restaurant and bar. Two separate bars by beach where discos held in main season. Water-ski, diving and windsurfing schools. 300 sq.m. swimming pool. Tennis, squash, volleyball and 'fronton'. Minigolf. Games room. Extensive riding tuition with own stables and stud. Children's play park (near river). Fishing (licence required). Car, motorcycle and bicycle hire. Hairdresser. Torches are useful near beach. Off site: Canal trips 18 km. Aquatic Park 20 km.

Open: 16 May - 20 September, including all facilities.

Directions

Site is signed at 26 km. marker on C252 between Castelló d'Empuries and Vildemat, then 7 km. to site. Alternatively, on Sant Pescador - Castelló d'Empuries road head north and site is signed.
GPS: N42:12.750 E03:05.166

Charges 2009

Per pitch incl. up to 6 persons	€ 22,00 - € 44,00
extra person (over 3 yrs)	€ 2,40 - € 4,75
dog	€ 4,90 - € 6,40
boat or jetski	€ 8,90 - € 12,00

No credit cards.

ES80320 Camping Riu

Ctra de la Platja s/n, E-17470 Sant Pere Pescador (Girona)

Tel: **972 520 216**. Email: **info@campingriu.com**   www.alanrogers.com/ES80320

Camping Riu is an established campsite which has been purchased by the Sènia group and is being comprehensively upgraded. The pool and gym areas are brilliant for such a small site. There are 200 pitches of which 190 are for tourers with 5/10A electricity on flat ground and are shaded by mature trees. The bungalows are in a separate area away from the touring pitches. The bar restaurant and terrace are very pleasant overlooking the floodlit pool and children's area, where some animation is held in high season. Riu is on the Fluvia river, 1.5 km. from the sea. The site has an attractive private jetty where it is possible to launch small boats and kayaks directly into the river to gain access to the Bay of Roses. Riu is a short walk across the river bridge to charming Sant Pere Pescador with its street markets and restaurants, and also has easy access to the plethora of cultural and historical areas of interest nearby. The friendly Director Rosa and her staff speak excellent English and Dutch and are very keen that you enjoy their family campsite.

Facilities

Two toilet blocks are clean and well positioned with good showers. Almost all WCs are British style. Facilities for disabled visitors. Baby room. Washing machines. Gas supplies. Supermarket. Pleasant bar and restaurant. Swimming pool and new pool for children. Adventure playground. Internet. Gym. Bicycle hire. Animation programme including entertainment for children (high season). Kayaking. Fishing. Barbecue area. Excursions. Torches useful. Off site: Public transport 400 m. Golf 20 km. Road train to beach from site in high season.

Open: 1 April - 16 September.

Directions

Sant Pere Pescador is on the coast between Roses and L'Escala. From AP7/E15 exit 4 take N11 north towards Figueres and then the C31 towards Torroella de Fluvia. Take Vilamacolum road east and continue to Sant Pere Pescador. Site is well signed in the town.
GPS: N42:11.247 E03:05.340

Charges 2009

Per unit incl. 2 persons and electricity	€ 14,40 - € 38,00
extra person	€ 2,95 - € 4,35
child (1-9 yrs)	free - € 3,40

No credit cards.

See advert on page 39

1ª Cat

E 3° 05' 10"
N 42° 12' 45"

Camping Nautic Almata
Ctra. Giv-6216
17486 Castelló d'Empuries
Costa Brava-Girona-España
Tel:(34)972 454477
Fax:(34)972 454686
info@almata.com
www.almata.com

La Jonquera → Figueres → Castelló d'Empuries → Sant Pere Pescador

ES80400 Camping Las Dunas

Ctra San Marti - Sant Pere, E-17470 Sant Pere Pescador (Girona)

Tel: **972 521 717**. Email: **info@campinglasdunas.com**   www.alanrogers.com/ES80400

Las Dunas is an extremely large, impressive and well organised site with many on site activities and an ongoing programme of improvements. It has direct access to a superb sandy beach that stretches along the site for nearly a kilometre with a windsurfing school and beach bar. There is also a much used swimming pool with large double children's pools. Las Dunas is very large, with 1,700 individual hedged pitches (1,479 for tourers) of around 100 sq.m. laid out on flat ground in long, regular parallel rows. All have electrical connections and 180 also have water and drainage. Shade is available in some parts of the site. Pitches are usually available, even in the main season. Much effort has gone into planting palms and new trees here and the results are very attractive. The large restaurant and bar have spacious terraces overlooking the swimming pools and you can enjoy a very pleasant more secluded cavern styled pub. A magnificent disco club is close by in a soundproof building (although people returning from this during the night can be a problem for pitches in the central area of the site). With free quality entertainment of all types in season and positive security arrangements, this is a great site for families with teenagers. Everything is provided on site so you don't need to leave it during your stay. Member of Leading Campings Group.

Facilities

Five excellent large toilet blocks (with resident cleaners 07.00-21.00) have British style toilets, controllable hot showers and washbasins in cabins. Excellent facilities for youngsters, babies and disabled people. Laundry facilities. Motorcaravan services. Extensive supermarket and other shops. Large bar with terrace. Large restaurant. Takeaway. Ice cream parlour. Beach bar in main season. Disco club. Swimming pools. Playgrounds. Tennis. Minigolf. Sailing/windsurfing school and other watersports. Programme of sports, games and entertainment, partly in English (15/6-31/8). Exchange facilities. ATM. Safety deposit. Internet café. WiFi. Dogs taken in one section. Torches required in some areas.

Open: 19 May - 2 September.

Directions

L'Escala is northeast of Girona on coast between Palamós and Roses. From A7/E15 autostrada take exit 5 towards L'Escala on GI 623. Turn north 2 km. before reaching L'Escala towards Sant Marti d'Ampurias. Site well signed.
GPS: N42:09.659 E03:08.087

Charges guide

Per person	€ 3,50 - € 5,00
child (2-10 yrs)	€ 3,00 - € 3,25
standard pitch incl. electricity	€ 14,00 - € 42,00
water and drainage	€ 17,50 - € 51,00
dog	€ 3,20 - € 4,40
All plus 7% VAT.	

ES80360 Camping Caravaning Esponellá

E-17832 Esponellá (Girona)

Tel: **972 597 074**. Email: **informa@campingesponella.com**   www.alanrogers.com/ES80360

This large campsite has a lovely setting alongside a slow flowing river. The last 10 km. of the route here is well worth the trip, but careful driving is necessary with large motorhomes. There are 240 medium sized pitches, 140 for touring, many fully serviced, all with 5A electricity and shaded by trees. The better pitches are behind the reception office which is in a newer building. The site is very popular with Spanish campers who keep their caravans with large awnings here. An older part of the campsite houses a well stocked shop, a bar/restaurant adjacent to the swimming pools. One smaller pool is heated and partly covered. A new toilet block is in the same building as reception. There is a communal barbecue area near the older toilet blocks. A small stream runs along the lower side which can be seen from the pool and restaurant area, which faces the swimming pool complex. In summer children's club activities are run from here and this is definitely the part of the campsite with a lot going on.

Facilities

Two old toilet blocks, a smaller one with only toilets and washbasins near the rental accomodations, and a newer one at the front part of the site. Some washbasins with only cold water. Small shop (Easter - Sept). Traditional restaurant, snacks and bar (all year). Three swimming pools. Play area. Boules. Minigolf. Children's activities. Small disco. Internet access. Barbecues are not permitted in summer. Off site: Hydrotherapy and massage centre next to site gate (April - Aug). Bus stop in the village. Beaches at L'Escala 30 km. Good lake for rowing and fishing at Banyoles nearby.

Open: All year.

Directions

From Figueres towards Olot via the N260. Continue for 4 km. past Navata. Turn left in 12 km. over a smaller road to entrance of the site. Site is southeast of the village and well signed.
GPS: N42:10.900 E02:47.700

Charges guide

Per unit incl. 2 persons and electricity (5A)	€ 20,25 - € 26,90
extra person	€ 5,20 - € 6,95
child (3-10 yrs)	€ 3,85 - € 5,20

ES80350 Kawan Village L'Amfora

2 avenida Josep Tarradellas, E-17470 Sant Pere Pescador (Girona)

Tel: **972 520 540**. Email: **info@campingamfora.com**

www.alanrogers.com/ES80350

This super, spacious site is family run and friendly. It has a Greek theme which is manifested mainly in the restaurant and pool areas. The site is spotlessly clean and well maintained and the owner operates in an environmentally friendly way. There are 830 level, grass pitches (730 for touring) laid out in a grid system, all with 10A electricity. Attractive trees and shrubs have been planted around each pitch. There is good shade in the more mature areas and these pitches include 64 large pitches (180 sq.m), each with an individual sanitary unit (toilet, shower and washbasin). The newer area is more open with less shade and you can choose which you would prefer. Three excellent sanitary blocks (one heated) are fully equipped and offer free hot water, each with staff on almost permanent duty to ensure very high standards are maintained. There is extra provision near the pool area. Access is good for disabled visitors. To the right of the entrance, an inviting terraced bar and two restaurants overlook a smart pool complex that includes pools for children and two water slides. In high season (from July) there is ambitious evening entertainment (pub, disco, shows) and an activity programme for children. Right beside the site, the magnificent sandy beach on the Bay of Roses offers good conditions for children and a choice of high season watersport activities.

Facilities

Three main toilet blocks, one heated, provide washbasins in cabins and roomy free showers. Baby rooms. Laundry facilities. Motorcaravan services. Supermarket. Terraced bar, self-service and waiter service restaurants. Pizzeria/takeaway. Restaurant and bar on the beach with limited menu (high season). Disco bar. Swimming pools (1/5-30/9). Petanque. Tennis. Bicycle hire. Minigolf. Play area. Entertainment and activities. Windsurfing. Boat launching and sailing. Fishing. Exchange facilities. Games and TV rooms. Internet room and WiFi. Car wash. Torches required in beach areas. Off site: Riding 4 km. Golf 15 km.

Open: 4 April - 30 September.

Directions

From the north on A17/E15 take exit 3 onto the N11 towards Figueres and then shortly onto the C260 towards Roses. At Castello d'Empuries turn right onto the GIV-6216 to Sant Pere. From the south on the A17 use exit 5 (L'Escala) and turn to Sant Pere in Viladamat. Site is well signed in the town towards the beach.
GPS: N42:10.888 E03:06.243

Charges 2009

Per person	€ 3,70 - € 5,00
child (2-9 yrs)	free - € 4,00
pitch	€ 16,00 - € 65,00

Children free low season. Senior citizens specials. Electricity (10A) included. No credit cards.

Camping Cheques accepted.

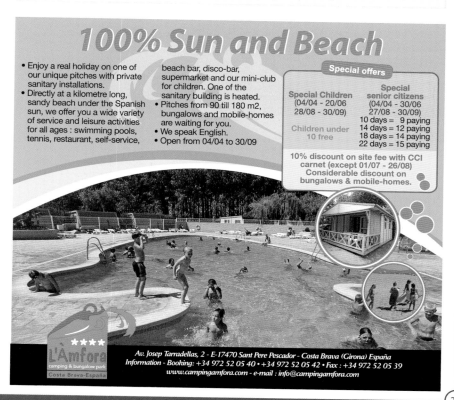

Check real time availability and at-the-gate prices...
www.alanrogers.com

ES80330 Camping Las Palmeras

Ctra de la Platja, E-17470 Sant Pere Pescador (Girona)

Tel: **972 520 506**. Email: **info@campinglaspalmeras.com**   www.alanrogers.com/ES80330

A very polished site, the pleasant experience begins as you enter the palm bedecked site and are greeted at the air conditioned reception building. The 230 pitches are flat, very clean and well maintained, with some shade and 5A electricity. A few pitches are complete with water and drainage. 26 smart mobile homes are placed unobtrusively around the site. A very pleasant pool complex has a lifeguard and the brightly coloured play areas are clean and safe. The very pleasant beach is a 200 m. walk through a gate at the rear of the site. A full animation programme allows parents a break during the day and there is organised fun in the evenings in high season. The owner Juan Carlos Alcantara and his wife have many years experience in the campsite business which is clearly demonstrated. You will enjoy a stay here as there is a very happy atmosphere.

Facilities

Two excellent, very clean toilet blocks include first class facilities for disabled campers. Baby rooms. Facilities may become a little busy at peak periods. Washing machines. Motorcaravan services. Supermarket. Restaurant/bar (children's menu). Swimming pools (heated). Play areas. Tennis. Gym. Barbecue. Bicycle hire. Miniclub. Animation. Satellite TV. Internet access. ATM. Torches useful. Off site: Beach and fishing 200 m. Sailing and boat launching 2 km. Riding 4 km. Golf 7 km.

Open: 4 April - 17 October.

Directions

Sant Pere Pescador is south of Perpignan on coast between Roses and L'Escala. From the AP7/E15 take exit 4 onto N11 north towards Figueres and then C31 towards Torroella de Fluvia. Take the Vilamacolum road east and continue to Sant Pere Pescador. Site well signed in town. GPS: N42:11.283 E03:06.162

Charges 2009

Per unit incl. 2 persons	
and electricity	€ 21,70 - € 47,90
extra person	€ 2,50 - € 4,00
child (2-10 yrs)	€ 2,30 - € 2,30
pet	€ 2,50 - € 4,00

C A M P I N G
LAS PALMERAS
COSTA BRAVA

- Small and cosy family site in quiet situation
- In midst of nature
- Near the beach
- Heated swimming pool, bungalows...
- Facilities for babies and small children

E-17470 Sant Pere Pescador (Girona)

Tel.: (34) 972 52 05 06
Fax: (34) 972 55 02 85

Open: 04.04 - 17.10

www.campinglaspalmeras.com · info@campinglaspalmeras.com

ES80310 Camping La Gaviota

Ctra de la Platja s/n, E-17470 Sant Pere Pescador (Girona)

Tel: **972 520 569**. Email: **info@lagaviota.com**   www.alanrogers.com/ES80310

La Gaviota is a delightful, small, family run site at the end of a beach access road. This ensures a peaceful situation with a choice of the pleasant L-shaped pool or direct beach access to the fine clean beach and slowly shelving access to the water. Everything here is clean and smart and the Gil family are very keen that you will enjoy your time here. There are 165 touring pitches on flat ground with shade and 6A electricity supply. A lush green feel is given to the site by many palms and other semi-tropical trees and shrubs. English is spoken.

Facilities

One smart and clean toilet block is near reception. All WCs are British style and the showers are excellent. Superb facilities for disabled visitors. Two excellent family rooms plus two baby rooms. Washing machine. Gas supplies. Supermarket. Pleasant bar and small, delightful restaurant. Swimming pool. Playground. Games room. Limited animation. Beach sports and windsurfing. Internet. Torches useful. Off site: Boat launching 2 km. Riding 4 km. Golf 15 km.

Open: 20 March - 25 October.

Directions

From the AP7/E15 take exit 4 onto the N11 north towards Figueres and then the C260 towards Roses. At Castelló d'Empuries take the GIV 6216 and continue to Sant Pere Pescador. Site is well signed in the town. GPS: N42:11.341 E3:06.506

Charges 2009

Per person	€ 2,60 - € 3,70
child (under 10 yrs)	€ 1,20 - € 2,60
pitch	€ 13,00 - € 38,00
electricity (5A)	€ 3,70

ES80600 Camping La Ballena Alegre 2

E-17470 Sant Pere Pescador (Girona)

Tel: **902 510 520**. Email: **infb2@ballena-alegre.com**

www.alanrogers.com/ES80600

La Ballena Alegre 2 is partly in a lightly wooded setting, partly open, and has some 1,800 m. of frontage directly onto an excellent beach of soft golden sand (cleaned daily). They claim that none of the 1,432 pitches is more than 100 m. from the beach. The site has won Spanish tourist board awards and is keen on ecological fitness. The grass pitches are individually numbered and there is a choice of size (up to 100 sq.m). Electrical connections (5/10A) are available in all parts and there are 91 fully serviced pitches. It is a great site for families. There are restaurant and bar areas beside the pleasant terraced pool complex (four pools including a children's pool). For those who wish to drink and snack late there is a pub open until 03.00 hrs. The well managed soundproof disco is popular with youngsters. A little train ferries people along the length of the site and a road train runs to local villages. Plenty of entertainment and activities are offered, including a well managed watersports centre, with sub-aqua, windsurfing and kite surfing, where equipment can be hired and lessons taken. You can also use a comprehensive open air fitness centre near the beach. A full animation programme is provided all season.

Facilities

Seven well maintained toilet blocks are of a very high standard. Facilities for children, babies and disabled campers. Launderette. Motorcaravan services. Gas supplies. Supermarket. New 'Linen' restaurant. Self-service restaurant and bar. Takeaway. Pizzeria and beach bar in high season. Swimming pool complex. Jacuzzi. Tennis. Watersports centre. Fitness centre. Bicycle hire. Playgrounds. Sound proofed disco. Dancing twice weekly and organised activities, sports, entertainment, etc. ATM. Dogs allowed in one zone (dog showers). WiFi. Torches useful in beach areas. Off site: Go-karting nearby with bus service. Fishing 300 m. Riding 2 km.

Open: 15 May - 20 September.

Directions

From A7 Figueres - Girona autopista take exit 5 to L'Escala GI 623 for 18.5 km. At roundabout take sign to Sant Marti d'Empúries and follow site signs. GPS: N42:09.194 E03:06.749

Charges guide

Per unit incl. 2 persons	
and electricity	€ 24,50 - € 54,00
extra person	€ 3,75 - € 4,50
child (3-9 yrs)	€ 2,70 - € 3,25
dog	€ 2,25 - € 4,70

All plus 7% VAT. Discount of 10% on pitch charge for pensioners all season. No credit cards.

ES80720 Camping Les Medes

Paratge Camp de L'Arbre, E-17258 L'Estartit (Girona)

Tel: **972 751 805**. Email: **campinglesmedes@cambrescat.es**

www.alanrogers.com/ES80720

Les Medes is different from some of the 'all singing, all dancing' sites so popular along this coast and the friendly family of Pla-Coll are rightly proud of their award wining site and provide a very warm welcome. With just 172 pitches, the site is small enough for the owners to know their visitors and, being campers themselves, they have been careful in planning their top class facilities and are aware of environmental issues. The level, grassy pitches range in size from 60-80 sq.m. depending on your unit. All have electricity (5/10A) and the larger ones (around half) also have water and drainage. All are clearly marked in rows, but with no separation other than by the deciduous trees which provide summer shade. A cheery children's pool with fountains is behind the unusually shaped pool ringed by palms. This is part of an attractively landscaped feature with a false island, producing a relaxing atmosphere in front of the old Catalan farmhouse buildings. The open air dance floor has music twice weekly (in season). A classy indoor pool (heated) with sauna and solarium and good access for disabled campers is a great option out of high season. Set back from busy L'Estartit itself, it is only 800 m. to the nearest beach and a little train runs from near the site (June - Sept) to the town. The Medes islands are very pretty and worth exploring or a bad weather day could be used to visit Salvador Dali's amazing house.

Facilities

Two modern spacious sanitary blocks can be heated and are extremely well maintained. Washbasins in cabins, top class facilities for disabled people and baby baths. Washing machines and dryer. Motorcaravan services. Bar with snacks (all year). Good value restaurant (1/4-31/10). Shop. Swimming and paddling pools (1/5-15/9). Indoor pool with sauna, solarium (15/9-15/6). Play area. TV room. Internet access and WiFi. Excursions (July/Aug). Diving activities. Bicycle hire. Dogs only accepted at certain times – check with the site. Torches are useful. Off site: Riding 400 m. Fishing 800 m. Nearest beach 800 m. Medes Natural Reserve 1.5 km. Strait 2 km. Golf 8 km.

Open: All year excl. November.

Directions

Site is signed from the main Torroella de Montgri - L'Estartit road GE641. Turn right after Camping Castel Montgri, at Joc's hamburger/pizzeria and follow signs. GPS: N42:02.900 E03:11.273

Charges 2009

Per unit incl. 2 persons	
and electricity	€ 21,05 - € 37,95
extra person	€ 3,95 - € 7,90
child (0-10 yrs)	€ 2,50 - € 5,60
dog	€ 2,35

Discounts outside high season and special offers for low season longer stays. No credit cards.

ES80690 Camping Neus

Cala Montgó, E-17130 L'Escala (Girona)
Tel: **972 770 403**. Email: **info@campingneus.cat**

www.alanrogers.com/ES80690

Camping Neus is a mature site which is undergoing an ongoing renovation programme. It is set on the edges of a forest under mature pines with 190 pitches arranged on sets of terraces. The pitches vary in size and 160 have 4A electricity. The site facilities are mainly close to the reception building. A small pool with a circular paddling pool is welcome after a hot days sightseeing and other site amenities include a tennis court and bar/restaurant. The nearest beach at Cala Montgó is 850 m. away and easily accessible on foot. A range of activities is on offer there, including sea kayaking and diving (introductory courses available in the site's pool).

Facilities

Bar. Restaurant. Takeaway. Shop. Play area. Swimming pool. Paddling pool. Entertainment and activities in peak season. Club for children. Off site: Nearest beach 850 m. Fishing. Kayaking. Diving.

Open: 29 May - 13 September.

Directions

Take exit 5 from the AP7 and the GI 623 to L'Escala. Continue to Riells and Montgó. Site is on the right shortly before reaching Cala Montgó. GPS: N42:06.294 E3:09.490

Charges 2009

Per unit incl. 2 persons	
and electricity	€ 21,00 - € 40,50
extra person	€ 3,00 - € 5,00
child (5-10 yrs)	€ 1,00 - € 3,50
dog	€ 1,60

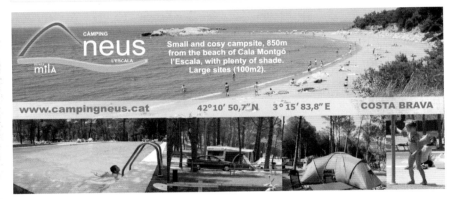

CAMPING neus L'ESCALA
PUNTA mila

Small and cosy campsite, 850m from the beach of Cala Montgó l'Escala, with plenty of shade. Large sites (100m2).

www.campingneus.cat   42°10' 50,7"N   3° 15' 83,8" E   COSTA BRAVA

ES80640 Camping Bassegoda Park

Camí Camp de l'illa, E-17733 Albanya (Girona)
Tel: **972 542 020**. Email: **info@bassegodapark.com**

www.alanrogers.com/ES80640

Surrounded by mountains alongside the Muga river, Bassegoda Park is a place to experience Spain in a natural environment but with a touch of luxury. This totally rebuilt site is in Albanya on the edge of the Alta Garrotxa National Park in an area of great beauty. In their own area, the 106 touring pitches are level and well shaded, all with electricity, water and drainage. Tents are dotted informally in the terraced forest areas. Particular care has been taken in the landscaping, layout and design of the whole site, but especially the most attractive pool, bar and restaurant, the hub of the site. These, with al fresco dining and night entertainment complement the natural setting. Regional wines and dishes are available in the reasonably priced restaurant.

Facilities

A new main toilet building includes facilities for babies and disabled visitors. It is supplemented by three refurbished, clean blocks which are well positioned. Facilities for disabled visitors. Washing machine. Gas supplies. Supermarket. Pleasant bar and restaurant. Swimming pool. Playground. New leisure area with outdoor relaxation area and minigolf. Animation programme including children's entertainment. Walking, trekking and bicycle hire. Barbecue areas. Torches useful. Air conditioned bungalows to rent. Off site: Sailing 5 km. Riding 15 km. Golf 20 km. Beach 35 km. Limited public transport.

Open: March - November.

Directions

Site is north of Girona, west of Figueres. From Barcelona on AP7/E15, take exit 4 and the N11 towards France. Then the GI 510 to Llers and GI 511 to St Llorenc de la Muga and Albanya. Site is well signed where the road ends. From France take exit 3 then the GI 510 to Llers. There is NO exit 3 northbound on the AP7/E15. GPS: N42:18.406 E02:42.533

Charges guide

Per person	€ 5,35 - € 5,90
child (0-4 yrs)	€ 4,30 - € 4,85
pitch incl. 3A electricity	€ 10,50 - € 13,10
10A electricity	€ 5,65

Check real time availability and at-the-gate prices...

alanrogers

ES80500 Camping Aquarius

Playa s/n, E-17470 Sant Pere Pescador (Girona)
Tel: **972 520 003**. Email: **camping@aquarius.es**

www.alanrogers.com/ES80500

A smart and efficient family site, Aquarius has direct access to a quiet sandy beach that slopes gently and provides good bathing (the sea is shallow for quite a long way out). One third of the site has good shade with a park-like atmosphere. There are 435 pitches with electricity (6/16A). Markus Rupp and his wife are keen to make their visitors experience a happy one and even issue flags to denote the number of years they have stayed at the site. The site is ideal for those who really like sun and sea, with a quiet situation. Mr Rupp has a background in architecture and a wealth of knowledge on the whole Catalan area and culture. He has written a booklet of suggested tours (available from reception). The family is justifiably proud of their most attractive site which they continually upgrade and improve. The fountain at the entrance, the fishponds and the water features in the restaurant are soothing and pleasing. A small stage close to the restaurant is used for live entertainment in season. The spotless beach bar complex with shaded terraces, satellite TV and further evening entertainment, has marvellous views over the Bay of Roses. The 'Surf Center' with rentals, school and shop is ideal for enthusiasts and beginners alike.

Facilities

Attractively tiled, fully equipped, large toilet blocks provide some cabins for each sex. Excellent facilities for disabled people, plus baths for children. Superb new block has under-floor heating and features family cabins with showers and basins. Laundry facilities. Gas supplies. Motorcaravan services. Full size refrigerators. Supermarket. Pleasant restaurant and bar with terrace. Takeaway. Children's play centre (with qualified attendant), playground and games hall. TV room. 'Surf Center'. Minigolf. Bicycle hire. Barbecue and dance once weekly when numbers justify. ATM. Internet access. WiFi. Dogs are accepted in one section. (Note: no pool). Off site: Fishing and boat launching 3 km. Riding 6 km. Golf 15 km.

Open: 15 March - 31 October.

Directions

Sant Pere Pescador is south of Perpignan on coast between Roses and L'Escala. From the AP7/E15 take exit 4 onto N11 north towards Figueres and then the C31 towards Torroella de Fluvia. Take the Vilamacolum road east and continue to Sant Pere Pescador. Site well signed in town.
GPS: N42:10.614 E03:06.478

Charges guide

Per person	€ 3,00 - € 3,85
child (under 12 yrs)	free - € 2,65
pitch acc. to season and facilities	€ 8,05 - € 38,70
electricity	€ 3,15 - € 6,30
animal	€ 2,80 - € 3,70

All plus 7% VAT. No credit cards.
Discounts for pensioners on longer stays.

ES80740 Camping Illa Mateua

Avenida de Montgó 260, E-17130 L'Escala (Girona)

Tel: **972 770 200**. Email: **info@campingillamateua.com**

www.alanrogers.com/ES80740

If you prefer a quieter site out of the very busy resort of L'Escala then this site is an excellent option. This large, family run site has a dynamic owner Marti, who speaks excellent English. The site is divided by the beach access road and has its own private access to the very safe and unspoilt beach. There are 358 pitches, all with electricity (10A), some on sloping ground although the pitches themselves tend to be flat. Established pine trees provide shade for most places with more coverage on the western side of the site. Non-stop maintenance ensures that all facilities at this site are of a high standard. There are three swimming pools, the largest with an idyllic and most unusual setting on the top of a cliff overlooking the Bay of Roses. A CCTV security system monitors the pools and general security from a purpose built centre.

Facilities

Modern, fully equipped sanitary blocks are kept very clean. Washing machines and dryers. Shop, extensive modern complex of restaurants, bars and takeaways (all open all season). Swimming pools (1/5-20/9). Pool bar. Play areas. Fishing. Kayak hire. Organised activities for children in high season. ATM. Private access to beach. Off site: Cala Montgó beach 100 m. with a charming bay of soft sand offering all manner of watersports, pretty restaurants and a disco in season. Road train service to town centre from outside site. Riding 2 km. Golf 10 km.

Open: 18 March - 15 October.

Directions

Leave autopista A7 at exit 5 heading for Viladimat, then L'Escala. Site is well signed from town centre. Follow signs for Montgó and site is south of town beside the coast. GPS: N42:06.631 E3:09.925

Charges guide

Per person	€ 3,10 - € 5,60
child (3-10 yrs)	€ 2,20 - € 3,90
pitch	€ 15,50 - € 30,00
electricity	€ 3,40
Plus 7% VAT.	
No credit cards.	

ES80800 Camping El Delfin Verde

Ctra de Torroella de Montgrí, E-17257 Torroella de Montgrí (Girona)

Tel: **972 758 454**. Email: **info@eldelfinverde.com**

www.alanrogers.com/ES80800

A large, popular and high quality site in a quiet location, El Delfin Verde has its own long beach stretching along its frontage. A prime feature of the site is an attractive large pool in the shape of a dolphin with a total area of 1,800 sq.m. This is a large site with 1420 touring pitches and around 6,000 visitors at peak times. It is well managed by friendly staff. Level grass pitches nearer the beach are marked and many are separated by small fences and hedging. All have electrical connections (5/6A) and access to water points. A stream runs through the centre of the site. There is shade in some of the older parts and a particularly pleasant area of pine trees in the centre provides marked but not separated pitches (sandy and not so level). The pool has two island areas, one containing a huge fountain which can be lit at night. In the main season an elevated area with a large bar, full restaurant and a separate takeaway give wonderful views over the huge pool. There is a further restaurant with slightly cheaper, good value food in the main complex with an open air arena for entertainment. El Delfin Verde is a large, cheerful holiday site with many good facilities, sports and a free family entertainment programme in season. It is well worth considering for your Costa Brava holidays. Used by British tour operators (60 pitches).

Facilities

Six excellent large and refurbished toilet blocks plus a seventh smaller block, all with resident cleaners, have showers using desalinated water and some washbasins in cabins. Laundry facilities. Motorcaravan services. Supermarket and shops. Swimming pools (with lifeguard). Two restaurants, grills and pizzerias. Three bars. 'La Vela' barbecue and party area. Large sports area. 2 km. exercise track. Dancing and entertainment weekly in season. Excursions. Bicycle hire. Minigolf. Playground. Trampolines. Fishing. Hairdresser. Car servicing. Gas supplies. Internet access. Dogs are not accepted in high season (11/7-14/8). Off site: Golf 4 km. (20% discount). Riding 4 km.

Open: 4 April - 27 September.

Directions

Torroella de Montgri is close to the coast east of Girona. From A7/E15 take exit 6 and C66 (Palafrugell). Then the GI 642 east to Parlava and turn north on C31. GPS: N42:00.718 E03:11.284

Charges 2009

Per unit incl. 2 person and electricity	€ 30,50 - € 55,00
extra person	€ 4,75 - € 5,50
child (2-9 yrs)	€ 4,00 - € 5,00
dog (excl 11/7-14/8)	€ 4,00
Special offers on long stays in low season.	

ES81010 Camping Playa Brava

Avenida del Grau 1, E-17256 Platja de Pals (Girona)
Tel: 972 636 894. Email: info@playabrava.com

www.alanrogers.com/ES81010

This is a pleasant site with an open feel which has access to a large sandy beach and a freshwater lagoon. On both you can enjoy watersports and you may launch your own boat. The ground is level and very grassy with shade provided for the 500 pitches by a mixture of conifer and broad-leaf trees. Electricity is provided (5A) and about a third of the pitches (75-85 sq.m) have water and drainage. The air of spaciousness continues around the large swimming pool. There are no fences but huge grass sunbathing areas, the whole being overlooked by the restaurant terrace. The restaurant is very pleasant and offers a most reasonable menu of the day including wine. An energetic entertainment programme runs during July and August. There are many interesting things to explore in the area including La Bisbal – famous for the ceramics, Dali's Museum, the Roman ruins at Empuries Girona and many more. This is a green and pleasant family site.

Facilities

Five modern, fully equipped toilet blocks include facilities for disabled visitors. Washing machines and dryers. Motorcaravan service point. Bar/restaurant. Takeaway. Supermarket. Swimming pool. Tennis. Minigolf. Play area on grass. Fishing. Watersports on river and beach, including sheltered lagoon for windsurfing learners. Internet access. Satellite TV. ATM. Gas supplies. Torches required in some areas. Dogs are not accepted. Off site: Two 18 hole golf courses 1 km. Bicycle hire 3 km. Riding 5 km.

Open: 14 May - 18 September.

Directions

From the AP7/E15 at Girona take exit 6 towards Palamós on the C66. This road changes number to the C31 near La Bisbal. 7.5 km. past La Bisbal, exit to Pals on the GI 652. Follow signs for Platja de Pals. At El Masos take the 6502 east to the coast. Travel through Sa Piera (site signed). Site on left just before road ends at beach car park.
GPS: N42:00.106 E03:11.621

Charges guide

Per person	€ 2,00 - € 3,00
child (2-9 yrs) or senior (60+ yrs)	free - € 3,00
pitch incl. electricity	€ 23,00 - € 38,00

All plus 7% VAT. No credit cards.
Discount for longer stays in low season.

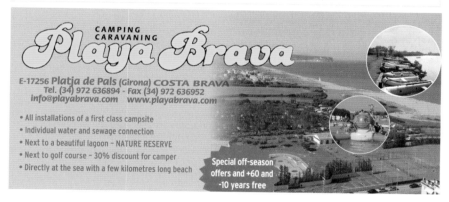

ES80700 Camping L'Escala

Cami Ample, E-17130 L'Escala (Girona)
Tel: 972 770 084. Email: info@campinglescala.com

www.alanrogers.com/ES80700

Under the same ownership as Las Dunas (no. ES80400), but a complete contrast in terms of size, this is a small, traditional site with limited facilities. The site has a canopy of fir trees giving excellent shade. There are 140 pitches of which 90 are for touring units, so reservation is essential. All pitches have electricity, water and drainage. In season there is a bar and restaurant offering very good food with a pleasant enclosed terrace with a retractable candy-striped canopy. There is some road noise despite the very high wall between the site and the busy road alongside.

Facilities

The central toilet block is basic but clean, with British style toilets, washbasins (two in cabins for ladies), free hot water and 25 free showers. Dishwashing and laundry sinks with hot water. Shop, bar and restaurant (all high season). Basic play area. Satellite TV. Off site: Public transport 500 m. Beach 100 m. Bicycle hire 500 m. Riding 3 km. Golf 15 km.

Open: Easter - 25 September.

Directions

From A7/E15 autostrada take exit 5 towards L'Escala on GI 623. Turn north 2 km. before reaching L'Escala towards Sant Marti d'Ampurias. Site well signed on north side of town and beach. Watch for site name high on wall. GPS: N42:07.260 E03:08.087

Charges guide

Per person	€ 2,80 - € 3,50
pitch incl. electricity	€ 16,25 - € 23,00

ES81000 Camping Inter-Pals

Avenida Mediterrania, E-17256 Platja de Pals (Girona)

Tel: **972 636 179**. Email: **interpals@interpals.com**

www.alanrogers.com/ES81000

Set on sloping ground with tall pine trees providing shade and about 500 metres from the beach, Inter-Pals has 625 terraced pitches. It is sister site to no. ES81700 Valldaro. Arranged on level terraces, mostly with shade, some of the terraced pitches have views of the sea through the trees. The main entrance and its drive resembles a pretty village street as the bungalows are set on both sides of the street which is lined with traditional lamp posts. Continuing the village theme is a row of shops where you will find most camper's needs. The formal restaurant with good value menu and choice of takeaway overlooks the pools. The site is close to Platja de Pals which is a long sandy unspoilt stretch of beach, a discreet area, part of which is now an official naturist beach. The pretty town of Pals is close by along with a good golf course. The site will assist with touring plans of the area.

Facilities

Three well maintained toilet blocks include facilities for disabled campers. Laundry facilities. Gas supplies. Fridge/TV rental. Shops. Restaurant/bar. Pizzeria with dancing and entertainment area. Café/bar by entrance. Swimming pool. Tennis. Playground. Organised activities and entertainment in high season. Excursions. Watersports arranged. ATM. Internet access. Some breeds of dog are excluded (check with site). Mini adventure park. Medical centre. Torch useful. Off site: Fishing 200 m. Bicycle hire 500 m. Golf 1 km. Riding 10 km.

Open: 1 April - 27 September.

Directions

Site is on the road leading off the Torroella de Montgri - Bagur road north of Pals and going to Playa de Pals (Pals beach).
GPS: N41:58.520 E03:11.590

Charges 2009

Per person	€ 4,15 - € 6,30
child (3-12 yrs)	€ 3,00 - € 3,70
pitch	€ 19,10 - € 33,20

Discounts for long stays in low season. No credit cards. Camping Cheques accepted.

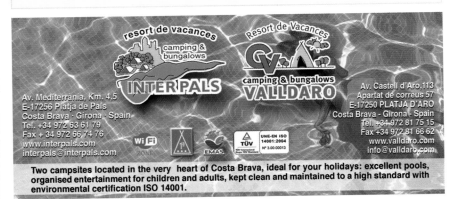

ES81030 Camping El Maset

Playa de Sa Riera, E-17255 Begur (Girona)

Tel: **972 623 023**. Email: **info@campingelmaset.com**

www.alanrogers.com/ES81030

A delightful little gem of a site in lovely surroundings, El Maset has 107 pitches, of which just 20 are slightly larger for caravans or motorcaravans, the remainder suitable only for tents. The owner of some 40 years, Sr Juan Perez is delightful and his staff are very helpful. The site entrance is steep and access to the caravan pitches can be quite tricky. However, the owner's son will tow your caravan to your pitch. All these pitches have electricity, water and drainage with some shade. Tent pitches are more shaded on attractive rock-walled terraces on the hillside. Access to these seems quite straightforward, with parking for cars not too far away – of necessity the pitches are fairly small. All steep terraced pitches are safely fenced for children.

Facilities

Good sanitary facilities in three small blocks are kept very clean. Baby facilities. Washing machines and dryers. Unit for disabled campers but the ground is steep. Bar/restaurant, takeaway (all season). Shop. Swimming pool (all season). Solarium. Play area. Area for football and basketball. Excellent games room. Internet access and free WiFi. Dogs are not accepted. Off site: Beach and fishing 300 m. Golf and bicycle hire 1 km. Riding 8 km.

Open: Easter - 24 September.

Directions

From the C31 Figueres - Palamós road south of Pals, north of Palafrugell, take GI653 to Begur. Site is 2 km. north of the town; follow signs for Playa de Sa Riera and site (steep entrance).
GPS: N41:58.116 E03:12.601

Charges guide

Per person	€ 5,35 - € 7,49
pitch incl. electricity	€ 15,28 - € 19,28

Discount in low season for 7 day stay.

ES81700 Camping Valldaro

Apdo 57, avenida Castell d'Aro 63, E-17250 Platja d'Aro (Girona)

Tel: 972 817 515. Email: info@valldaro.com

www.alanrogers.com/ES81700

Valldaro is 600 m. back from the sea at Platja d'Aro, a small, bright resort with a long, wide beach and plenty of amusements. It is particularly pleasant during out of peak weeks and is popular with British and Dutch visitors. Like a number of other large Spanish sites, Valldaro has been extended and many pitches have been made larger, bringing them up to 85 sq.m. There are now almost 1,200 pitches with 544 for touring units. The site is flat, with pitches in rows divided up by access roads. You will probably find space here even at the height of the season. The newer section has its own vehicle entrance (the nearest point to the beach) and can be reached via a footbridge; it is brought into use at peak times. It has some shade and its own toilet block, as well as a medium-sized swimming pool of irregular shape with a grassy sunbathing area and adjacent bar/snack bar and takeaway. The original pool (36 x 18 m.) is adjacent to the attractive Spanish style restaurant which also offers takeaway fare. There are 400 permanent Spanish pitches and 150 mobile homes and chalets to rent, but these are in separate areas and do not impinge on the touring pitches.

Facilities

Four sanitary blocks are of a good standard and are well maintained. Child-size toilets. Washbasins (no cabins) and adjustable showers (temperature perhaps a bit variable). Two supermarkets and general shops. Two restaurants. Large bar. Swimming pools. New outdoor jacuzzi. Tennis. Minigolf with snack bar. Playgrounds. Sports ground. Children's club. Organised entertainment in season. Hairdresser. Internet. WiFi area (charge to use). Satellite TV. Gas supplies. Off site: Beach 1.5 km. Fishing, bicycle hire and golf 1 km. Riding 4 km.

Open: 3 April - 27 September.

Directions

From Girona on the AP7/E15 take exit 7 to Sant Feliu on C65. On C65 at km. 313 take exit to Platja d'Aro (road number changes here to C31). In 200 m. at roundabout take GI662 towards Platja d'Aro. Site is at km. 4. If approaching from Palamós, access is via Platja d'Aro centre, exit on the GI662 as the GI662 cannot be accessed from the C31 southbound. GPS: N41:48.856 E03:02.622

Charges 2009

Per unit incl. 2 persons	€ 20,00 - € 44,60
extra person	€ 4,10 - € 6,75
child (3-12 yrs)	€ 2,70 - € 3,80
dog	€ 2,80

Discounts in low seasons. No credit cards. Camping Cheques accepted.

ES80900 Camping Cypsela

Ctra de Pals - Platja de Pals, E-17256 Platja de Pals (Girona)

Tel: 972 667 696. Email: info@cypsela.com

www.alanrogers.com/ES80900

This impressive, de-luxe site with lush vegetation and trees is very efficiently run. The main part of the camping area is pinewood, with 569 clearly marked touring pitches of varying categories on sandy gravel, all with electricity and some with full facilities. The 228 'Elite' pitches of 120 sq.m. are impressive. Cypsela is a busy, well administered site, only 2 km. from the sea, which we can thoroughly recommend, especially for families. The site has good quality fixtures and fittings, all kept clean and maintained to a high standard. All your needs will be catered for here. The site has many striking features, one of which is the sumptuous complex of sports facilities and amenities near the entrance. This provides a fine large swimming pool, a good children's pool and playgrounds, two excellent squash courts, a tennis court, fitness room, and other entertainment rooms. These include a children's playroom with miniclub and organised entertainment (including video screen), an amusements room with pool tables, football tables, video games, and a luxurious air conditioned lounge. The 'Les Moreres' is a pleasant al fresco restaurant offering a varied menu plus good wines (it can become very busy). If you wish to travel to the beach there is a regular free bus service from the site. The gates are closed at night. Several tour operators use the site (257 pitches).

Facilities

Four sanitary blocks are of excellent quality with comprehensive cleaning schedules and solar heating. Three have washbasins in cabins and three have amazing children's rooms. Superb facilities for disabled people. Serviced launderette. Supermarket and other shops. Restaurant, cafeteria and takeaway. Bar. Hairdresser. Swimming pools. Tennis. Squash. Minigolf. Skating rink. Fitness room. Solarium. Air conditioned social/TV room. Barbecue and party area. Comprehensive animation programme in season. Games room. Business and internet centre. Gas supplies. ATM. Dogs are not accepted. Off site: Bicycle hire 150 m. Golf 1 km. Fishing 2 km.

Open: 15 May - 21 September.

Directions

Platja de Pals is southeast of Girona on the coast. From the AP7/E15 at Girona take exit 6 towards Palamós on the C66. This road changes number to the C31 near La Bisbal. 7.5 km. past La Bisbal, exit to Pals on the GI 652. Follow signs for Platja de Pals. At El Masos take the 6502 for 1 km. Main entrance for Cypsela is on the left between the white metal fencing. GPS: N41:59.100 E03:10.740

Charges guide

Per person	€ 6,00
child (2-10 yrs)	€ 4,60
pitch acc. to season and services	€ 22,80 - € 61,50

ES81040 Camping Begur

Ctra d'Esclanya km 2, E-17255 Begur (Girona)

Tel: **972 623 201**. Email: **info@campingbegur.com**

www.alanrogers.com/ES81040

The owners here have made a massive investment in making the site a pleasant place to spend some time. There are some good supporting facilities including a new pool complex at its centre which has been well designed with terraces and sunbathing area. The touring areas are protected from the sun by mature trees which are all numbered. The 317 pitches are informally arranged on sloping sandy ground (chocks useful). Most pitches have electricity (10A), water and drainage. There a few mobile homes and apartments scattered around the slopes. Environmental activities are encouraged including visits to the revolutionary water cleansing plant deep in the woods. There are many sporting facilities including a well equipped weight training room (free). A huge supermarket is just outside the gate, used by locals and on site there is a restaurant and a very pleasant outdoor café and bar overlooking the pool. The bays of the Costa Brava are just 1.5 km. away.

Facilities

Two modern toilet blocks are fully equipped and include really large showers. Excellent facilities for disabled campers. Baby bath. Laundry facilities. Motorcaravan services. Bar and snacks. Swimming pools. Boules. Weight training room. Play area. Some animation and children's entertainment in high season. Little farm with ponies, goat and chickens. Internet access. Off site: Restaurant and supermarket just outside gate. Beaches 1.5 km. Fishing 3 km. Golf 10 km. Riding 15 km.

Open: 3 April - 27 September.

Directions

From Girona take road east to La Bisbal and Palafrugell then Begur. Turn south towards Fornells, the site is well signed 3 km. south of Begur. GPS: N41:56.998 E03:11.934

Charges 2009

Per person	€ 3,30 - € 6,20
child (3-10 yrs)	€ 1,60 - € 3,30
pitch incl. electricity	€ 11,80 - € 20,00
fully serviced	€ 13,70 - € 22,60

No credit cards.

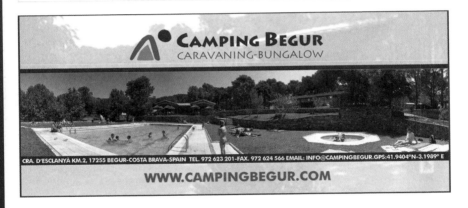

CRA. D'ESCLANYA KM.2, 17255 BEGUR-COSTA BRAVA-SPAIN TEL. 972 623 201-FAX. 972 624 566 EMAIL: INFO@CAMPINGBEGUR.GPS:41.9404°N-3.1989° E

WWW.CAMPINGBEGUR.COM

ES81200 Kim's Camping

Font d'en Xeco, E-17211 Llafranc (Girona)

Tel: **972 301 156**. Email: **info@campingkims.com**

www.alanrogers.com/ES81200

This attractive, terraced site (to which the owner has been welcoming guests for 50 years) is arranged on the wooded slopes of a narrow valley leading to the sea and there are many trees including huge eucalyptus. There are 350 grassy and partly shaded pitches, 240 used for touring units, all with electricity (5A). Many of the larger pitches are on a plateau from which great views can be enjoyed. The terraced pitches are connected by winding drives, narrow in places. This is a pleasant place for holidays where you can enjoy the bustling village and beach, while staying in a quieter environment.

Facilities

All sanitary facilities are spotlessly clean and include a small new block and excellent toilet facilities for disabled visitors. Laundry facilities. Motorcaravan services. Gas supplies. Well stocked shop. Bar. Bakery and croissanterie. Café/restaurant (15/6-10/9). Swimming pools. Play areas. Children's club. TV room. Excursions. Visits arranged to sub-aqua schools (high season). Torches required. WiFi. Mobile homes to rent. Off site: Beach, fishing, sailing and bicycle hire 500 m. Riding 3.5 km. Golf 9 km.

Open: Easter - 30 September.

Directions

Llafranc is southeast of Palafrugell. Turn off the Palafrugell - Tamariu road at turn (GIV 6542) signed Llafranc, Club de Tennis. Site is on right 1 km. further on. GPS: N41:54.032 E03:11.361

Charges guide

Per person	€ 2,67 - € 6,42
child (3-10 yrs)	€ 1,07 - € 3,21
pitch incl. electricity	€ 12,84 - € 27,80

Discounts for long stays and for senior citizens.

Check real time availability and at-the-gate prices...

www.alanrogers.com

ES81020 Camping Resort Mas Patoxas Bungalow-Park

Ctra C31 Palafrugell - Pals km 339, E-17256 Pals (Girona)

Tel: **972 636 928**. Email: **info@campingmaspatoxas.com**

www.alanrogers.com/ES81020

This is a mature and well laid out site for those who prefer to be apart from, but within easy travelling distance, of the beaches (5 km.) and town (1 km). It has a very easy access and is set on a slight slope with wide avenues on level terraces providing over 400 grassy pitches of a minimum 72 sq.m. All have electricity (5A) and water; many have drainage as well. There are some very pleasant views and shade from a variety of mature trees. Both bar and restaurant terraces give views over the pools and distant hills. The air-conditioned restaurant/bar provides both waiter service meals and takeaway food to order (weekends only mid Sept - April) and entertainment takes place on a stage below the terraces during high season. The restaurant menu is varied and very reasonable. We were impressed with the children's miniclub activity when we visited. There is a large, supervised irregularly shaped swimming pool with triple flume, a separate children's pool and a generous sunbathing area at the poolside and on the surrounding grass.

Facilities

Three modern sanitary blocks provide controllable hot showers, some washbasins with hot water. Baby bath and three cabins for children. No specific facilities for disabled people. Laundry facilities. New supermarket (15/3-30/9). Restaurant/bar, pizzeria and takeaway (all 15/3-30/9). Swimming pool (1/5-30/9). Tennis. Entertainment in high season. Fridges for rent. Gas supplies. Torches useful in some areas. Off site: Bus service from site gate. Bicycle hire or riding 2 km. Fishing or golf 4 km.

Open: 12 January - 16 December.

Directions

Site is east of Girona and about 1.5 km. south of Pals at km. 339 on the C31 Figueres - Palamós road, just north of Palafugel.
GPS: N41:57.311 E03:09.478

Charges guide

Per unit incl. 2 persons and electricity	€ 15,00 - € 42,00
extra person	€ 3,60 - € 5,75
child (1-7 yrs)	€ 3,00 - € 4,00
dog	€ 2,10 - € 3,20

Plus 7% VAT. Special low season offers.

ES81350 Eurocamping

Avinguda Catalunya 15, E-17252 Sant Antoni di Calonge (Girona)

Tel: **972 650 879**. Email: **info@euro-camping.com**

www.alanrogers.com/ES81350

This large campsite on the Costa Brava near Girona is attractively landscaped, with lawns, flowers and pretty features around the site, and 615 grass and gravel pitches (475 for touring). The size of the pitches varies, with some of good size and others that would struggle with larger units. Older areas of the campsite are shaded by tall trees creating a cooler zone, while the new areas have good size trees but are not yet under the same shade canopy. There are two pool complexes.

Facilities

Four refurbished, clean toilet blocks vary in size and are well positioned. Almost all WCs are British style in cabins with shower and basin. 11 private cabins for rent. Good facilities for disabled visitors. Rooms for babies and families. Washing machines. Gas supplies. Supermarket just outside gate. Bars and good restaurant. Swimming pools. Playgrounds. TV in bar. Weight training room. Full animation programme including children's entertainment. Internet and WiFi. ATM. Excursions. Beach train (July/Aug). Torches useful. Off site: Bicycle hire 100 m. Beach 300 m. Fishing 300 m. Golf 6 km. Riding 15 km.

Open: 4 April - 20 September.

Directions

The town of Sant Antoni de Calonge is southeast of Girona on the coast. Leave the AP7/E15 at exit 6. Take the C66 towards Palomós which becomes the C31. Use the C31 (Girona - Palamós) road to avoid Palomós town. Take the C253 coast road. Site well signed at northern end of Sant Antoni de Calogne. GPS: N41:50.793 E03:05.945

Charges 2009

Per person	€ 2,70 - € 6,80
pitch	€ 18,95 - € 31,65

ES81400 Camping Treumal

Ctra 253 km 47.5, E-17250 Calonge (Girona)

Tel: **972 651 095**. Email: **info@campingtreumal.com**

www.alanrogers.com/ES81400

This very attractive terraced site has been developed on a hillside around the gardens of a large, spectacular estate house which is close to the sea. The site's excellent facilities, include a superb restaurant with terraces overlooking two tranquil beaches, protected in pretty coves. There are 550 pitches on well shaded terraces, 447 of which are accessible to tourers and there are some 50 pitches on flat ground alongside the sea. Electrical connections are available in all parts (5/16A).

Facilities

Four well maintained sanitary blocks have free hot water in the washbasins (with some private cabins) and controllable showers. New beach block. Washing machines. Motorcaravan services. Gas supplies. Supermarket, bar and takeaway (all season). Restaurant (1/6-15/9). Fishing. Play area. Sports area. Games room. Satellite TV. Internet access and WiFi. ATM. Dogs are not accepted. Off site: Bicycle hire 2 km. (delivered to site). Riding, golf 5 km.

Open: 15 March - 30 September.

Directions

Site is southeast of Girona on the coast 3 km. south of Palamós. It is best to avoid the town centre by using C31 (Girona - Palamós) road, leave at km. 320, and take road south to Sant Anthoni de Calonge. Take C253 south towards Platja d'Aro. Site is well signed. GPS: N41:50.185 E03:05.235

Charges guide

Per person	€ 4,10 - € 7,50
pitch incl. electricity	€ 14,40 - € 28,40

Plus 7% VAT. No credit cards.

ES81500 Camping Internacional de Palamós

Apdo 100, E-17230 Palamós (Girona)

Tel: **972 314 736**. Email: **info@internacionalpalamos.com**

www.alanrogers.com/ES81500

This is a comfortable site which is clean, welcoming and useful for exploring the local area from a peaceful base. Traditional in style, it is open for a long season and has a range of facilities. It might have space when others are full and has over 453 moderate sized pitches. The majority are level and terraced with some less defined under pine trees on a gentle slope. All pitches have a sink and variable shade, with electrical connections (6A) available in most parts.

Facilities

Two refurbished toilet blocks and one smart new one are fully equipped. Some washbasins in cabins. Facilities for disabled people. Laundry room. Small shop. Bar (1/4-29/9). Snack bar serving simple food and takeaway (from 1/6). Swimming pool (36 x 16 m.) with paddling pool. Torches necessary. Off site: Nearest beach 400 m. Fishing 500 m. Town 1 km. with hourly bus service. Bicycle hire or riding 1.5 km.

Open: 15 March - 30 September.

Directions

Central Palamós is too narrow for caravans. Turn off C255 road just outside Palamós. Continue north by large garage signed Kings Camping and La Fosca. Turn right just before Kings and follow Camping Internacional Palamós signs (not another site called Camping Palamós). GPS: N41:51.433 E03:08.283

Charges guide

Per person	€ 3,00 - € 3,65
pitch incl. electricity	€ 26,50 - € 42,00

All plus 7% VAT. No credit cards.
Camping Cheques accepted.

ES81300 Camping Internacional de Calonge

Ctra San Feliu/Guixols - Palamós, E-17251 Calonge (Girona)
Tel: **972 651 233**. Email: **info@intercalonge.com**

www.alanrogers.com/ES81300

This spacious, well laid out site has access to the fine beach by a footbridge over the coast road, or you can take the little road train as the site is on very sloping ground. Calonge is a family site with two good sized pools on different levels, a paddling pool plus large sunbathing areas. The site's 800 pitches are on terraces and all have electricity (5A) with 167 available for winter use. A large proportion are suitable for touring units (the remainder for tents) being set on attractively landscaped terraces. Access to some pitches may be a little difficult. There is good shade from the tall pine trees and some views of the sea through the foliage, although the views from the upper levels are taken by the tour operator and mobile home pitches. The swimming pools are overlooked by the restaurant terrace which has great views over the mountains. A nature area within the site is used for walks or picnics. A separate area is set aside for visitors with dogs (including a dog shower!)

Facilities

Generous sanitary provision in new or renovated blocks include some washbasins in cabins. One block is heated in winter. Laundry facilities. Motorcaravan services. Gas supplies. Shop, Bar/restaurant, Patio bar (pizza and takeaway) (all 15/3-19/10). Swimming pools (15/3-12/10). Playground. Electronic games. Rather noisy disco two nights a week (but not late). Bicycle hire. Tennis. Hairdresser. ATM. Internet. Torches necessary in some areas. Off site: Fishing 300 m. Supermarket 500 m. Golf 3 km. Riding 10 km.

Open: All year.

Directions

Site is on the inland side of the coast road between Palamós and Platja d'Aro. Take the C31 south to the 661 at Calonge. At Calonge follow signs to the C253 towards Platja d'Aro and on to site which is well signed. GPS: N41:50.000 E03:05.050

Charges guide

Per person	€ 3,65 - € 7,55
child (3-10 yrs)	€ 1,85 - € 4,25
pitch incl. electricity and water	€ 14,80 - € 33,25

All plus 7% VAT. No credit cards.
Discounts for longer stays Oct - end May.

ES81600 Camping Cala Gogo

Ctra San Feliu - Palamós km 46.5, Platja d'Aro, E-17251 Calonge (Girona)
Tel: **972 651 564**. Email: **calagogo@calagogo.es**

www.alanrogers.com/ES81600

Cala Gogo is a large traditional campsite with a pleasant situation on a wooded hillside with mature trees giving shade to most pitches. The 619 shaded touring pitches varying in size are in terraced rows, some with artificial shade, all have 10A electricity and 250 have water and drainage. There may be road noise in eastern parts of the site. Some pitches are now right by the beach, the remainder are up to 800 m. uphill, but a tractor train takes people between the centre of site and beach.

Facilities

Seven toilet blocks are of a high standard and are continuously cleaned. Some washbasins in private cabins. Two private cabins for hire. New laundry room. Motorcaravan services. Gas supplies. Supermarket. General shop. Restaurants and bars. Swimming and paddling pools (lifeguards). New playground. Crèche and babysitting service (charged). Sports centre. Sports and entertainment. Bicycle hire. Kayaks. Fishing. Internet access and WiFi. Dogs are not accepted mid June - end August. Off site: Golf 5 km. Riding 10 km. Aqua Park.

Open: 25 April - 27 September.

Directions

The town of Sant Antoni de Calonge is southeast of Girona. Leave the AP7/E15 at exit 6. Take C66 towards Palomos which becomes the C31. Use the C31 (Girona - Palomos) road to avoid Palomas town. Take the C253 coast road. Site is at km. 46.5 (4 km. south of Palomas). GPS: N41:49.850 E03:04.948

Charges 2009

Per unit incl. 2 persons and electricity (5A)	€ 18,20 - € 46,15
extra person	€ 3,60 - € 7,15
child (3-12 yrs)	€ 1,10 - € 3,60

ES81750 Yelloh! Village Mas Sant Josep

Ctra Santa Cristina - Platja d'Aro km 2, E-17246 Santa Cristina d'Aro (Girona)

Tel: **04 66 73 97 39 (FR)**. Email: **info@yellohvillage-mas-sant-josep.com**   www.alanrogers.com/ES81750

This is a very large well appointed site in two parts. The main side is centred around charming historic buildings, including a beautiful, but mysterious, locked and long unused chapel. Nearby are excellent lagoon style pools with a palm decorated island and a large complex including a bar, restaurant, takeaway foods and entertainment areas. The sporting facilities and fitness areas across the minor road are superb. Here there is another swimming pool and many sport and training possibilities. There are 868 pitches with 200 for touring units in a separate area with shade from established trees.

Facilities

Three older style toilet blocks and the facilities for tourers are better than the long stay areas but all had graffiti when seen. Facilities for disabled visitors and baby rooms. Motorcaravan services. Supermarket. Bars, restaurant, snack bar and takeaway. Swimming pools. Playgrounds. Tennis. Squash. Minigolf. Spa room and gym. Animation programme. Internet. ATM. Bicycle hire. Torches useful. Off site: Riding 2 km. Nearest beach 3 km.

Open: 29 February - 7 December.

Directions

Site is at Santa Christiana d'Aro, 3 km. from the sea at San Feliu. From AP7 E15 (Girona - Barcelona) take exit 7 and C65 San Filiu road. Site is well signed at the Sant Christina d'Aro roundabout 3 km. from San Filiu. GPS: N41:48.670 E03:01.093

Charges guide

Per unit incl. 2 persons and electricity	€ 17,00 - € 44,00
extra person (over 1 yr)	€ 6,00 - € 7,00

ES82000 Camping Cala Llevadó

Ctra GI-682 de Tossa a Lloret pk. 18,9, E-17320 Tossa de Mar (Girona)

Tel: **972 340 314**. Email: **info@calallevado.com**   www.alanrogers.com/ES82000

For splendour of position Cala Llevadó can compare with almost any in this book. A beautifully situated cliff-side site, it has fine views of the sea and coast below. It is shaped something like half a bowl with steep slopes. High up in the site with a superb aspect, is the attractive bar/restaurant with a large terrace overlooking the pleasant swimming pool. There are terraced, flat areas for caravans and tents (with electricity) on the upper levels of the two slopes, with a great many individual pitches for tents scattered around the site. Some of these pitches have fantastic settings and views. Many of the 577 touring pitches are available for caravans with 10/16A electricity.

Facilities

Four very well equipped toilet blocks are immaculately maintained and well spaced around the site. Baby baths. Laundry facilities. Motorcaravan services. Gas supplies. Fridge hire. Large supermarket. Restaurant/bar (5/5-28/9). Swimming and paddling pools. Three play areas. Botanic garden. Entertainment for children (4-12 yrs). Sailing, water ski and windsurfing school. Fishing. Excursions. Internet access and WiFi. Torches definitely needed in some areas. Off site: Bicycle hire 3 km. Large complex adjacent for sports, activities and swimming.

Open: 1 May - 30 September, with all services.

Directions

Leave the AP7/E15 at exit 7 to the C65 Sant Feliu road and then take C35 southeast to the GI 681 to Tossa de Mare. Site is signed off the GI 682 Lloret - Tossa road at km. 18,9, about 3 km. from Tossa. Route avoids difficult coastal road. GPS: N41:42.769 E02:54.374

Charges 2009

Per person	€ 5,65 - € 9,45
child (4-12 yrs)	€ 3,25 - € 5,05
pitch incl. car	€ 9,55 - € 19,45
electricity	€ 4,55 - € 5,00

ES91220 Camping Montagut

Ctra Montagut - Sadernes km 2, E-17855 Montagut (Girona)

Tel: **972 287 202**. Email: **info@campingmontagut.com**   www.alanrogers.com/ES91220

This is a delightful, small family site where everything is kept in pristine condition. Jordi and Nuria, a brother and sister team, work hard to make you welcome and maintain the superb appearance of the site. Flowers and shrubs abound, with 90 pitches on attractively landscaped and carefully constructed terraces or on flat areas overlooking the pool. A tranquil atmosphere pervades the site and drinks on the restaurant terrace are recommended, along with sampling the authentic menu as you enjoy the views over the Alta Garrotxa. There is much to see in the local area.

Facilities

The modern sanitary block has free hot showers, washing and laundry facilities plus a modern section for babies and disabled campers; everything was spotless when seen. Motorcaravan services. Restaurant and bar (1/7-31/8; weekends only in low season). Supermarket. Medium sized swimming pool with large sunbathing area (1/7-31/8). Playground. Petanque. Barbecue area. Free WiFi area. Torches useful in some areas.

Open: 16 March - 19 October.

Directions

Going west from Figueres take the N260 Olot road which becomes the A26. Take exit 75, turn right towards Montagut. At end of village turn left towards Sadernes and site entrance is 3 km. GPS: N42:14.814 E02:35.826

Charges 2009

Per person	€ 5,00 - € 6,80
child (2-10 yrs)	€ 4,20 - € 5,70
pitch incl. electricity	€ 14,40 - € 18,10

Ctra de Blanes - Lloret, E-17310 Lloret de Mar (Girona)

Tel: **972 369 965**. Email: **info@campingtucan.com**

www.alanrogers.com/ES82100

Situated on the busy Costa Brava near Lloret de Mar, Camping Tucan is well placed to access all the attractions of the area. Views over the mountains are mixed with views of the nearby town. The 250 good size pitches all have electricity, and are laid out in a herring-bone pattern with areas dedicated to singles, families with young children and couples who enjoy the quiet. Pitches are on terraces, flat surfaced with gravel and many are shaded. Tucan is a lively site with a variety of activities including an animation programme for children and modest entertainment in the evenings. Activities on the site centre around the pleasant pool, bar, restaurant and terrace all of which are close to reception. There is a separate, largely independent facility for young people at the rear of the site. Tucan is part of the Sènia group.

Facilities

Two modern toilet blocks include washbasins with hot water and facilities for disabled visitors, although access is difficult. All very clean when seen. Washing machine. Gas supplies. Shop. Busy bar and good restaurant. Takeaway. Swimming pools and indoor solarium. Playground and fenced play area for toddlers. TV in bar. Bicycle hire. Animation in high season. Miniclub. Off site: Town 500 m. Nearest beach 600 m. Riding 1 km. Golf 4 km.

Open: 3 April - 27 September.

Directions

From A7/E4, A19 or N11 Girona - Barcelona roads take an exit for Lloret de Mar. Site is 1 km. west of the town, well signed and is at the base of the hill off the roundabout. The entrance can get congested in busy periods. GPS: N41:41.832 E02:49.310

Charges 2009

Per person	€ 4,95 - € 8,50
child (1-9 yrs)	€ 3,50 - € 5,70
pitch incl. electricity	€ 12,90 - € 21,95

ES82250 Camping La Masia

Ctra Colon 44, E-17300 Blanes (Girona)

Tel: **972 331 013**. Email: **info@campinglamasia.com**

www.alanrogers.com/ES82250

A large resort site, La Masia has 757 pitches with 300 for touring units. These pitches are flat, shaded by trees and in rows with some mobile homes inserted here and there. There is something for everyone in La Masia and the resort town is just outside the gate, as is the fine beach. A large, central building houses the bar and restaurant. Below this you can enjoy an indoor heated pool, spas, massage, plunge and exercise pools, and pamper yourself in a 'Roman bath' type setting (charged).

Facilities

Six well maintained toilet blocks provide basic facilities with facilities for disabled campers and a well equipped baby room (key at reception). Motorcaravan services. Laundry facilities. Supermarket. Bakery. Restaurants. Snack bars. Swimming pools. Spa centre. Play areas. Boules. Bicycle hire. Barbecue area. Entertainment programme. Internet. WiFi. ATM. Security boxes. Torches useful. Off site: Resort town and beach outside the gate. Fishing. Boat launching 200 m. Bicycle hire 0.5 km. Riding 3 km. Golf 5 km.

Open: 9 January - 10 December.

Directions

La Masia is on the southwest side of Blanes. From exit 9 on the AP7 Girona - Barcelona road follow the N11 to the B600 towards Blanes. Before entering Blanes turn southwest following site signs at the roundabouts which will direct you to La Masia avoiding Blanes town which has narrow roads and is best avoided by large units.
GPS: N41:39.786 E2:46.494

Charges 2009

Per unit with 2 persons, car and electricity	€ 24,60 - € 40,50
extra person	€ 5,00 - € 6,00

Camping Cheques accepted.

ES82280 Camping Blanes

Avenida Villa de Madrid 33, Apdo 72, E-17300 Blanes (Girona)

Tel: **972 331 591**. Email: **info@campingblanes.com**

www.alanrogers.com/ES82280

Camping Blanes is the first of the sites which edge the pedestrian promenade here and probably the smallest. Open all year, it is family owned and run and indeed has been in the hands of the Boix family for 40 years. Antonio the son runs the site now with pride and care, speaking good English. With only 206 pitches, no bungalows or mobile homes and only 5 seasonal vans, there is a comfortable atmosphere. Shade is provided by tall pines and because of this, some of the pitches are a bit irregular in shape and average between 60-80 sq m.

Facilities

Traditional but well equipped sanitary block with provision for disabled visitors (by key). Baby changing unit. Washing machine and dryer. Shop (15/6-15/9). Bar (1/4-12/10). Restaurant and takeaway (7/7-25/8). Swimming pool. Play area. No organised entertainment. Beach alongside site. Gate closed at night. Off site: Town is within walking distance (500 m). Golf and riding 5 km.

Open: All year.

Directions

Site is south of the town beside the beach before Camping Bella Terra and El Pinar. Follow signs for 'campings' until individual site signs appear.
GPS: N41:39.600 E02:46.800

Charges 2009

Per person	€ 5,00 - € 6,90
pitch incl. electricity	€ 14,60 - € 20,40

Less 10% in low season. No credit cards.

ES82300 Beach Camp El Pinar

Ctra Villa de Madrid, s/n, E-17300 Blanes (Girona)

Tel: **972 331 083**. Email: **camping@elpinarbeach.com**

www.alanrogers.com/ES82300

A long established campsite, El Pinar enjoys an excellent location on the southern edge of Blanes with direct access to the superb beach. The site is in two halves, arranged on either side of a large road that terminates just past the site entrance gates where it meets the very clean, sandy beach. One side of the site is more modern than the other with a degree of shade from young trees. All the 450 touring pitches are on level sandy grass and all have 5A electricity.

Facilities

Sanitary facilities in two large blocks (one older but refurbished) include some private washbasins. Facilities for disabled visitors. Baby room. Cleaning is continual through the day. Laundry facilities. Shop. Bar/restaurant and takeaway. Swimming and paddling pools (from 1/5). Multisport area. Bicycle hire. Simple play area. Miniclub (late June - early Sept). Beach. Off site: Bicycle hire 1.5 km. Riding 8 km. Golf 15 km. Marina and harbour. Blanes is a walk along the promenade.

Open: 15 March - 30 September.

Directions

From AP7 or C-32 motorways follow signs for Blanes. Site is the last travelling south from Blanes town centre. Follow camping signs in Blanes until you see the El Pinar sign.
GPS: N41:39.330 E02:46.717

Charges guide

Per person	€ 5,40 - € 6,60
child	€ 4,30 - € 5,70
pitch incl. electricity	€ 15,90 - € 20,45

ES81800 Camping Sant Pol

Carrer del Doctor Fleming No.1, E-17220 Sant Feliu de Guíxols (Girona)

Tel: **972 327269**. Email: **info@campingsantpol.cat**

www.alanrogers.com/ES81800

Sant Pol is a small, family owned site and Anna Genover speaks excellent English, with a firm understanding of campers needs. On the Costa Brava, this hillside site is on the edge of Sant Feliu, only 350 m. from the beach (there may be some road noise on one side of the site). An attractive pool, bar and restaurant are the central focus of the site with shaded terraces and pitches of differing sizes curving down the slope. Higher terraces have the chalets and bungalows. There are 100 pitches for tourers and the pleasant small terraces take 37 tents. The on site restaurant features regional dishes based on the best local produce available. San Feliu is an attractive seaside village with lots of cafés, restaurants and a crescent shaped white sandy beach. The local area has museums and archaeological sites. Dali's house is within driving distance (book ahead). A great small family site for exploring the area or just to relax and enjoy the ambience.

Facilities

The clean and modern sanitary block has British style WCs and hot water. WC for disabled campers, but no shower (terrain would be difficult for wheelchairs). Washing machines and dryer. Motorcaravan services. Small supermarket. Restaurant/bar. Solar heated swimming pools. Play area. Animation for children in high season. Minigolf. Internet point and WiFi. Excursions. Torches needed in some areas. Off site: Large supermarket 300 m. Beach 350 m. Regular bus service into town. Riding 1 km. Golf 5 km.

Open: 27 March - 1 November, also 1-10 December.

Directions

Via the C65 (Girona - Palamós) road. Leave this at km. 312 signed to S'Agaró. Then proceed towards Sant Feliu to outskirts of village. Site signed from first roundabout and is directly off second roundabout. Caution as entrance is up very steep slope marked with small green camping triangles. GPS: N41:47.196 E03:02.492

Charges guide

Per person	€ 4,00 - € 7,00
child (5-10 yrs)	€ 2,00 - € 4,00
pitch incl. electricity and water	€ 15.00 - € 36.00

Very competitive low season offers available on request.

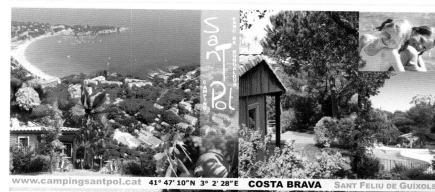

www.campingsantpol.cat 41° 47' 10"N 3° 2' 28"E **COSTA BRAVA** SANT FELIU DE GUÍXOLS

ES91225 Camping Vall de Camprodon

Ctra C38 Ripoll a Camprodon, E-17867 Camprodon (Girona)

Tel: **972 740 507**. Email: **info@valldecamprodon.net**

www.alanrogers.com/ES91225

This large holiday village is attractively situated in a wooded valley with cows grazing to one side, their pleasant bells often to be heard. A stream runs between the site and the road and the site lies a few yards above. There are 200 grass and gravel pitches many with shade, with just 40 for touring units, all with 4-10A electricity. There are some fully serviced pitches near the entrance. The Gomes family, who also own the nearby 'Els Roures' site, took over this complex a few years ago and since then have done all they can to turn it into a pleasant holiday destination.

Facilities

One centrally placed, fully equipped and well maintained toilet block. Very large en-suite bathroom for disabled visitors. Washing machines, dryers and ironing board (iron from reception). Shop. Bar/restaurant with simple menu (July/Aug). Swimming pool (July/Aug). Fishing. Tennis. Multisport court. Boules. Miniclub (July/Aug). WiFi. Off site: Golf and bicycle hire 2 km. Riding 6 km. Valley station of the railway to Nuria 40 km. Skiing 20 km.

Open: All year.

Directions

From the N260 after Olot continue towards Ripoll. Take C26 north via Valley of Bianya. After the tunnels turn right on C-38 to Camprodon. Site is halfway between St Pau de Seguries and Camprodon, on the right. GPS: N42:17.350 E02:21.817

Charges guide

Per person	€ 7,25
pitch incl. electricity	€ 13,60 - € 7,45

Camping Cheques accepted.

ES82320 Camping Bella Terra

Avenida Vila de Madrid 35-40, E-17300 Blanes (Girona)

Tel: **972 348 017**. Email: **info@campingbellaterra.com**

www.alanrogers.com/ES82320

Camping Bella Terra is set in a shady pine grove facing a white sandy beach on the Mediterranean coast. There are 906 pitches with 830 for touring units, the rest taken by bungalows to rent (75) and by Spanish 'residents' (200). All pitches have 5/6A electricity and 24 are fully serviced. The site is in two sections, each with its own reception, on either side of a road which leads to another campsite. The main reception is on the right as you approach, as are the restaurant with its own bar and the two swimming pools. With direct access to the beach, the older part of the site always fills up first.

Facilities

The older sanitary blocks are just acceptable with provision for disabled visitors and laundry. The block on the newer side is much more modern and spacious. It includes very good facilities for children. Shop, restaurant, bar and takeaway and outdoor swimming pool (all May - Sept). Playground. Fishing. Bicycle hire. Internet café. WiFi. Miniclub. Off site: Blanes town within walking distance. Sailing 3 km. Golf 8 km. Riding 12 km.

Open: 1 April - 30 September.

Directions

Camping Bella Terra is on the southwest side of Blanes. From exit 9 on the AP7 Girona - Barcelona road follow N11 to the B600 towards Blanes. Before entering Blanes turn southwest following site signs at the roundabouts which will direct you to Bella Terra avoiding Blanes town (best avoided by large units). GPS: N41:39.696 E02:46.567

Charges guide

Per person	€ 4,50 - € 5,80
pitch	€ 15,90 - € 37,90

ES91430 Camping Pirineus

Ctra Guils de Cerdanya km 2, E-17528 Guils de Cerdanya (Girona)

Tel: **972 881 062**. Email: **guils@stel.es**

www.alanrogers.com/ES91430

This is a sister site to nos. ES84200 and ES91440, with a well organised entrance and an immediate impression of space, green trees and grass. The pitches are neat, marked, of average size and organised in rows. Generally flat with some on a gentle incline, a proportion have water at their own sink on the pitch. Many trees offer shade but watch overhanging branches if you have a high unit. From the restaurant terrace you have fine views of the mountains in the background.

Facilities

Two fully equipped sanitary blocks of top quality and decorated with boxes of bright flowers, are kept spotlessly clean and can be heated. Laundry facilities. Motorcaravan service point. Shop, bar and restaurant. TV and games room. Snooker. Heated swimming pool and paddling pool. Boules. Outdoor sports. Play area and supervised clubhouse for youngsters. Excursions. Entertainment (high season). Dogs are not accepted. Off site: River fishing. Bicycle hire 2 km. Riding 4 km. Golf 6 km.

Open: 19 June - 13 September.

Directions

From Perpignan take N116 to Prades and Andorra. Exit at Piugcerda taking N250 signed Le Seu d'Urgell and almost immediately take second right for Guils de Cerdanya. Follow for 2 km. to site on right. GPS: N42:26.587 E01:54.350

Charges 2009

Per unit incl. 2 persons and electricity (7.5A)	€ 40,30
extra person	€ 6,40
child (3-10 yrs)	€ 5,25

ES91440 Camping Stel

Ctra N152 Ramal - Llivia s/n, E-17520 Puigcerdá (Girona)

Tel: **972 882 361**. Email: **puigcerda@stel.es**

www.alanrogers.com/ES91440

Sister site to ES84200 and ES91430, this is an extremely efficient, if pricey site. Part of a large, attractive building, the spacious entrance houses a modern reception (English is spoken). From here you will quickly be on your way to one of the flat, terraced pitches. Many of the pitches have shade and all are marked, clean and organised in rows with a water tap for each row. There is some road noise so, in order to avoid this and have views of the Cerdanya valley and the eastern Pyrenees, take one of the pitches on the upper terraces. It is worth the trouble.

Facilities

Sanitary facilities in the main building are of very high standard and are kept very clean. A small, smart block serves the upper terraces. Both can be heated. Separate modern unit with facilities for disabled campers. Laundry facilities. Shop. Bar/restaurant (all season). Swimming pool (June - Sept). Boules. Novel adventure style play frame (supervision needed). Adventure club (watersports and outdoor activities such as biking, tours, climbing, hang-gliding and many others). Animation (high season). Off site: Riding 5 km. Fishing and golf 7 km.

Open: 29 May - 27 September.

Directions

From Perpignan take N116 to Prades and Andorra. At roundabout at the border crossing at Puigcerdá take first right for Llivia (almost a turn back on yourself). Site is on left after 1 km. GPS: N42:26.492 E01:56.477

Charges 2009

Per unit incl. 2 persons and electricity	€ 40,30
extra person	€ 6,40
child (3-10 yrs)	€ 5,25
Camping Cheques accepted.	

ES83900 Camping Vilanova Park

Ctra de l'Arboc km 2.5, E-08800 Vilanova i la Geltru (Barcelona)

Tel: 938 933 402. Email: **info@vilanovapark.es**

www.alanrogers.com/ES83900

Sitting on the terrace of the bustling but comfortable restaurant at Vilanova Park, it is difficult to believe that in 1908 this was a Catalan farm and then, quite lacking in trees, it was known as 'Rock Farm'. Since then imaginative planting has led to there being literally thousands of trees and gloriously colourful shrubs making a most attractive, large campsite, with an impressive range of high quality amenities and facilities open all year. There are 344 marked pitches for touring units in separate areas. All have 6A electricity, 185 also have water and some larger pitches (100 sq.m) also have drainage. The terrain, hard surfaced and mostly on very gently sloping ground, has many trees and considerable shade. At present there are 786 pitches with a significant proportion occupied by bungalows and chalets carefully designed to fit into the environment. The site is used by tour operators (190 pitches). The really good amenities include a second pool higher up in the site with marvellous views across the town to the sea and an indoor pool, sauna, jacuzzi and gym. Here there is also a second, more intimate restaurant overlooking the twinkling evening lights. The original pool has water jets and a coloured floodlit fountain playing at night time, which complement the dancing and entertainment taking place on the stage in the courtyard overlooking the pool. An unusual attraction is a Nature Park and mini-zoo with deer and bird life, which has very pleasant picnic areas and views. There is a good excursion programme to Barcelona, Monserrat and Bodegas Torres for wine tasting. There is also a transfer service from Barcelona and Reus airports should you fancy taking advantage of the off season offers in the site's own accommodation.

Facilities

All toilet blocks are of excellent quality, can be heated and have washbasins (over half in cabins) with free hot water, and others of standard type with cold water. Serviced laundry. Motorcaravan services. Supermarket. Souvenir shop. Restaurants. Bar with simple meals. Swimming pools (outdoor 1/4-15/10, indoor all year). Wellness centre including sauna, jacuzzi and gym. Play areas. Sports field. Games room. Bicycle hire. Tennis. ATM and exchange facilities. Off site: Fishing 4 km. Golf 5 km. Vilanova town and beach are 4 km. (local bus).

Open: All year.

Directions

Site is 4 km. northwest of Vilanova i la Geltru towards L'Arboc (BV2115). From the A7 Tarragona - Barcelona take exit 29 onto C15 to Vilanova, then C31 El Vendrell road (Km. 153) then onto BV2115. GPS: N41:13.942 E01:41.455

Charges 2009

Per person	€ 4,00 - € 10,00
child (4-12 yrs)	€ 3,20 - € 6,00
pitch incl. electricity	€ 15,50 - € 28,00
dog	€ 4,00 - € 7,00

Camping Cheques accepted.

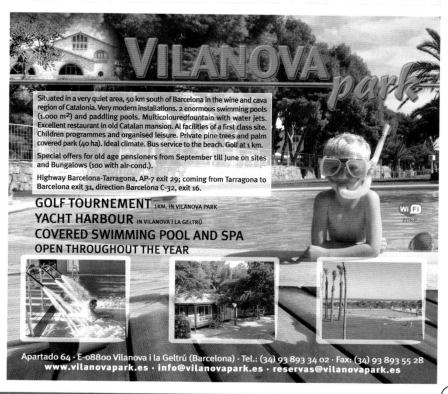

ES82340 Camping del Mar

Avenida Pomareda s/n, E-08380 Malgrat de Mar (Barcelona)

Tel: **937 653 767**. Email: **delmar@campingsonline.com**   www.alanrogers.com/ES82340

With such a wide choice of campsites along this part of the coast, standards have to be kept high and that is just what the Sisa family achieve at Camping del Mar. Beautifully manicured lawns and a well designed site help to create a relaxed atmosphere. All the facilities are kept immaculately clean. The 120 flat, grassy pitches all have electricity (6A) and easy access to a water point. The site is surrounded by a high hedge providing privacy and some shade to those pitches alongside.

Facilities	Directions
Modern, clean sanitary facilities are in the central building. Showers in large cubicles, open style washbasins and controllable hot water. Separate laundry room with washing machines. Small shop. Bar with TV and separate restaurant with varied menu. Games room. Swimming pool with separate children's pool. Multisport court. Tennis. Large play area. Minigolf. Children's club and entertainment (July/Aug). Off site: Boat launching 4 km. Riding 5 km. Golf 20 km.	From Malgrat de Mar town centre follow signs to 'zona campings'. Cross railway line and head north along beach front. Site is the second campsite on the left. GPS: N41:38.917 E2:46.368

Open: 1 April - 28 November.

Charges 2009

Per unit incl. 2 persons and electricity	€ 20,00 - € 34,00
extra person	€ 4,15 - € 5,85
child (4-10 yrs)	€ 2,95 - € 4,55

ES82350 Camping Bon Repos

Malgrat de Mar, E-08398 Santa Susana (Barcelona)

Tel: **937 678 475**. Email: **info@campingbonrepos.com**   www.alanrogers.com/ES82350

If you enjoy the hustle and bustle of the Costa Brava in summer, then Bon Repos is ideal. It is a long, narrow coastal site with many pitches along the length of the attractive fine sandy beach with direct access and no fence. The 500 pitches are of reasonable size, flat with a sand surface and lots of shade, and with 10A electricity. The railway runs close along one side of the site, which is good for train spotters but does create a noise problem. The beach is a strong point of the site having rocky outcrops and close by is the bar/restaurant with huge terrace.

Facilities	Directions
The two sanitary blocks are dated but clean. The number of showers is low and we suspect they are extremely busy at peak periods. Cold water at washbasins. Units for disabled campers. Baby room. Washing machines and dryers. Motorcaravan services. Supermarket. Restaurant. Chicken bar. Swimming pools (with lifeguard). Play area. Internet. Barbecue area. Tennis. Bicycle hire. Animation and happy hour. ATM. Torches useful. Off site: Resort town very close by. Boat launching 200 m. Bicycle hire 1 km. Riding 3 km. Golf 5 km.	From A7 exit 9 (A19 exit 22) take road to Malgrat de Mar. Then turn south on coast road for Santa Susanna. Follow obvious campsite signs – they lead to site through a high tunnel under the railway line on a minor beach road. GPS: N41:37.884 E2:43.194

Open: All year.

Charges guide

Per person	€ 1,63 - € 4,67
child	€ 1,31 - € 3,73
pitch incl. electricity	€ 11,45 - € 32,71

ES83400 Camping Rupit

Ctra de Vic - Olot km 31,5, E-08569 Rupit (Barcelona)

Tel: **938 522 153**. Email: **info@rupit.com**   www.alanrogers.com/ES83400

The approach road to the site from the coast is not for the faint hearted, but if a rural setting is what you're looking for, then this is the site for you – we loved it! The Morell family who own the site (and others on the coast) will welcome you warmly and speak English very well. The mostly level, grass pitches are slightly terraced and some have shade from mature trees. Long leads will be necessary as the electricity points are well spread out. Two beautiful stone buildings house the main facilities.

Facilities	Directions
The central toilet block provides open washbasins and shower cubicles with curtains only. Baby bath. Facilities for disabled visitors in the men's side only. Laundry room. No shop (essentials can be purchased from the bar). Bar and separate restaurant. Outdoor swimming pool and paddling pool overlooked by restaurant terrace. Games room. Play area. Communal barbecue area. Bicycle hire. Off site: Rupit town 1 km. Riding 5 km. Fishing 15 km.	From the AP7 exit 6 (Gerona), take the C66 to Olot. From Olot follow C153 for 31.5 km. This road is steep and winding in places. Site is 1 km. before the town of Rupit. The site entrance is on a sharp bend where extra care is required. GPS: N42:01.510 E02:27.530

Open: March - December.

Charges guide

Per person	€ 4,60 - € 6,50
pitch	€ 3,50 - € 5,10
electricity (3A)	€ 3,85

Check real time availability and at-the-gate prices...

www.**alanrogers**.com

ES82400 Camping Botánic Bona Vista Kim

Ctra NII km 665,8, E-08370 Calella de la Costa (Barcelona)

Tel: **937 692 488**. Email: **info@botanic-bonavista.net**

www.alanrogers.com/ES82400

While Calella itself may conjure up visions of mass tourism, this site is set on a steep hillside some 3 km. out of the town. Apart from perhaps some noise from the nearby coast road and railway, it is a quite delightful setting with an abundance of flowers, shrubs and roses (1,700, all planted by the knowledgeable owner Kim, who has won prizes for his roses). The site celebrated its 40th anniversary in 2006. Its design successfully marries the beautiful botanic surrounds with the attractive views of the bay. Of the 160 pitches, 130 are for tourers, all with electricity and on flat terraces on the slopes, with some shade. On arrival, park at the restaurant and choose a pitch – Kim is most helpful with siting your van. The access road is steep, with many of the pitches enjoying lovely views. The bar/restaurant is close to reception at the bottom of the site and is unusual in the attractive choice of Spanish décor and in having a circular, central open-hearth fire/cooker. There are two roof top terraces, the first terrace has service from the restaurant and bar and above that (for over 16 year olds), is the computer controlled sauna, jacuzzi with pool sized filter, a well equipped gymnasium and a sunbathing area, all enjoying views over the sea. There are quite good beaches just across the road and railway, accessible via a tunnel and crossing (including a naturist beach). The site has won environmental awards.

Facilities

The standard of design in the three sanitary blocks is quite outstanding for a small site (indeed for any site). Some washbasins in cabins in the newest block. Baby room. Washing machines. Motorcaravan services. Bar/restaurant, takeaway and shop (1/4-1/10). Outdoor pool (1/5-30/9). Large play area. Recreation park. Satellite TV. Internet point. Games room. Barbecue and picnic area. No cycling on site. Off site: Fishing 100 m. Bicycle hire 1 km. Riding and golf 3 km. Watersports near.

Open: All year.

Directions

From N11 coast road, site is signed south of Calella (km. 665), and is on right hand side of road. The road is busy and sign is almost on top of turn (entrance shared with Camping Roca Grossa). Entrance is very steep. From Barcelona, pass through Sant Pol de Mar, go into outside lane shortly after 'Camping 800 m.' sign and keep signalling left. Site entrance is just before the two lanes merge. GPS: N41:36.411 E02:38.551

Charges guide

Per person	€ 6,45
child (3-10 yrs)	€ 5,85
pitch incl. car	€ 13,00
electricity	€ 6,50
All plus 7% VAT.	

ES82420 Camping Roca Grossa

Ctra NII km 665, E-08370 Calella de la Costa (Barcelona)

Tel: **937 691 297**. Email: **rocagrossa@rocagrossa.com**

www.alanrogers.com/ES82420

Roca Grossa celebrated its 50th year in 2006. The owners, the Bachs family, are very friendly and there is a very happy atmosphere in the campsite. Very steep slopes predominate at this site and there is a 100 m. climb from reception to the swimming pool set at the top of the site. In high season a road train runs all day to ferry you to the amenities, but the site is unsuitable for disabled campers. The bonus is some great views over the sea from most of the terraced, but flat and reasonably sized pitches. Landrovers are used to site your unit. The permanent section of pitches is separated from the touring pitches and everything is kept very smart and clean. Clean and crisp, the pleasant pool enjoys fabulous views and the small restaurant/bar there is open all day. The sports facilities are also at this lofty point and if you wish to shop or use the main bar and restaurant, catch the train to the lower area near reception. The beach is just 50 m. across the road and the town is a short walk.

Facilities

An amazing array of clean sanitary blocks means there is not far to walk from any area of the site. Large and small, all blocks are well kept with hot water throughout. Washing machines. Gas supplies. Shop. Pleasant bar (with internet) and restaurant. Swimming pools (1/5-30/9). Playground. Road train. Tennis. Animation programme including children's entertainment. Excursions. ATM. Torches useful. Off site: Beach, boat launching and fishing 50 m. Town 100 m. Riding 1 km. Golf 2 km. Watersports nearby.

Open: 1 April - 30 September.

Directions

From A7 (Girona - Barcelona) take exit 9 or 10 for Malgrat del Mar on the N11. Turn south towards Calella and site is at 665 km. marker sharing an entrance with another campsite. Caravans are placed on pitches with site Landrover. GPS: N41:36.220 E02:38.200

Charges guide

Per person	€ 6,70
child (under 10 yrs)	€ 5,90
pitch incl. electricity	€ 12,20 - € 18,90
dog	€ 3,95
No credit cards.	

ES83920 Camping El Garrofer

Ctra 246 km 39, E-08870 Sitges (Barcelona)

Tel: 938 941 780. Email: info@garroferpark.com

www.alanrogers.com/ES83920

This large pine covered site, alongside fields of vines, is 800 m. from the beach close to the pleasant town of Sitges. This is an attractive resort with seaside entertainments and is well worth exploring. The site has over 500 pitches of which 380 with 6A electricity are for tourers, including 28 with water used for large motorcaravans. Everything is kept clean and the pitches are tidy and shaded. The amenity buildings are along the site perimeter next to the road which absorbs most of the road noise. The permanent pitches are grouped in a completely separate area.

Facilities

Two of the three sanitary blocks have been refurbished and provide roomy showers and special bright facilities for children. Separate baby room with bath. Good facilities for disabled campers. Laundry. Bar/restaurant. Shop (reception in low season). Swimming pool. Golf packages. Practice golf. Tennis. Play area for older children and fenced play area for toddlers. Bicycle hire. Boules. Off site: Bus from outside site to Barcelona. Golf, riding and fishing 500 m.

Open: 17 January - 17 December.

Directions

Sitges is 30 km. southwest of Barcelona. From the A16/C32 autopista take exit 26 towards Vilanova and St Pere Ribes. From Tarragona, go under the autopista, around roundabout and back to the roundabout on the other side to pick up site sign (towards Sitges). Follow C-246a to km. 39; site entrance is not too easy to see beside old large tree. Look for the flags. GPS: N41:14.011 E01:46.867

Charges guide

Per person	€ 2,85 - € 5,00
pitch incl. electricity	€ 14,98 - € 19,70
Plus 7% VAT.	

ES82380 Camping Caballo de Mar

Passeig Maritim 52-54, E-08397 Pineda de Mar (Barcelona)

Tel: 937 671 706. Email: info@caballodemar.com

www.alanrogers.com/ES82380

This is definitely a site for lovers of the seaside with its direct access to a lovely, sandy beach. Actually divided into two parts by the railway and dual-carriageway, the main part of the site is neatly arranged off a central access road with plenty of colourful shrubs and trees providing shade. In total there are 400 pitches, 200 taken by seasonal visitors and a few bungalows. On the beach side of the site the pitches are generally smaller (60-70 sq.m) with less shade (some artificial shade) but there is a bar and a toilet block on this side. All pitches have electricity (5/6A).

Facilities

Two toilet blocks, one in each area, are fully equipped and well maintained. En-suite units to rent (main side) with units for disabled visitors. Facilities for babies. Washing machines. Motorcaravan services. Shop (limited hours in low season). Main bar and restaurant. Swimming pool. Play area. Entertainment organised. Off site: Beach activities. Town with bars and restaurants within walking distance. Bicycle hire 500 m. Riding 3 km.

Open: 1 April - 30 September.

Directions

Site is between Pineda and Calella with access off dual carriageway linking the two places and runs parallel to the railway. GPS: N41:37.080 E02:40.603

Charges guide

Per person	€ 4,50 - € 7,45
child (1-9 yrs)	€ 3,20 - € 5,30
pitch	€ 4,50 - € 7,45
electricity (3/6A)	€ 3,60 - € 4,60

ES83930 Camping La Rueda

Ctra C31 km 146,2, E-08880 Cubelles (Barcelona)

Tel: 938 950 207. Email: info@la-rueda.com

www.alanrogers.com/ES83930

On arrival at La Rueda, you are met with an impressive security barrier opposite the reception building. The staff here speak good English and are very welcoming. Just inside the gate is a small pine forest where a more casual camping area is to be found offering plenty of shade. The remainder of the 300 flat, grassy pitches are set amongst young trees where some artificial awnings provide shade. At the far end of the site is a railway underpass (some noise) leading to a long sandy beach.

Facilities

Two identical sanitary blocks, one on each side of the site. Although dated, they offer adequate facilities and are kept very clean. Some washbasins in cabins. Baby cubicle. Laundry room. Shop (weekends only in low season). Bar and snack bar with takeaway pizzas. Formal restaurant. Swimming pool (July/Aug). Games room. Play area. Animation and entertainment (July/Aug). Off site: Fishing 200 m. Riding and bicycle hire 1 km. Golf 7 km.

Open: 4 April - 13 September.

Directions

La Rueda is very easy to find. It is on the C31 road at 146.2 km. west of Cubelles.
GPS: N41:11.992 E1:38.602

Charges 2009

Per unit incl. electricity	€ 24,60 - € 41,03
extra person	€ 4,10 - € 6,84
child	€ 2,87 - € 4,79
dog	€ 2,20 - € 3,66

ES91380 Camping Campalans

Ctra Sant Jaume de Frontanyá km. 1,5, E-08619 Borredá (Barcelona)

Tel: 938 239 163. Email: campalans@campalans.net   www.alanrogers.com/ES91380

With its wonderful location in a quiet river valley with views of the surrounding mountains, Camping Campalans is an excellent site for enjoying this beautiful area. Combining camping with chalets and a hostel, the site has 40 small, grass touring pitches (with 5A electricity). The terraced pitches are below an old, stone building housing reception, a bar, a restaurant and a small shop. The approach is by a steep, narrow, gravel mountain track and the site is 5 km. from the nearest village. However, for all but the largest units, the trip is well worth making. The site offers assistance with a 4x4 vehicle.

Facilities

One new toilet block, heated and with well equipped showers, washbasins and en suite cabins. Laundry room and drying room. Motorcaravan services. Shop (1/6-31/8). Bar (all season). Swimming pool (1/6-15/9). Play area. Large adventure trail next to site. Wooden bungalows and lodges to rent. Off site: Village of Borredá with cafés and small shops 5 km. Berga 22 km.

Open: 1 July - 31 August, (plus weekends only 1 February - 31 December.

Directions

From France via Puigcerda on the C-16, just before Berga turn left towards Ripoll. After Borredá turn left to Sant Jaume de Frontanyá. Site is east of the village, 1.5 km. on the left.
GPS: N42:08.750 E01:59.967

Charges guide

Per person	€ 5,35
child (under 12 yrs)	€ 3,21
pitch incl. electricity (5A)	€ 16,91

ES91390 Camping El Berguedá

Ctra B400 a Saldes km. 3,5, E-08694 Guardiola de Berguedá (Barcelona)

Tel: 938 227 432. Email: campingbergueda@gmail.com   www.alanrogers.com/ES91390

The short scenic drive through the mountains to reach the site is breathtakingly beautiful. Situated under trees this terraced campsite, in the area of the Cadi-Moixer Natural Park, is not far from the majestic Pedraforca mountain. A favourite for Catalan climbers and walkers. Access to the site is quite easy for large units. Of the 73 small grass gravel pitches there are 20 for touring with 6A electricity. The campsite owners will do what they can to make your stay here enjoyable.

Facilities

Two clean, well equipped, heated modern toilet blocks. Facilities for campers with disabilities. Three private cabins with washbasin, toilet and bidet. Washing machines and dryer. Small shop, restaurant and bar (w/ends only then 10/7-31/8). Outdoor pools (24/6-31/8). Play areas. Barbecues are not permitted except in communal area. Off site: Mountain biking. Artigas gardens designed by Gaudi. Picasso Museum. New adventure park 5 km.

Open: Easter - 30 November.

Directions

From France via Puigcerda take the C-16, towards Berga. After Guardiola de Berguedá turn right towards Saldes. Site is on right after 3.5 km.
GPS: N42:12.985 E01:50.215

Charges 2009

Per person	€ 5,35
child (1-10 yrs)	€ 4,20
pitch incl. car	€ 10,70
electricity (6A)	€ 4,60

ES91400 Camping Repos del Pedraforca

Ctra B400 km 13.5, E-08697 Saldés (Barcelona)

Tel: 938 258 044. Email: pedra@campingpedraforca.com   www.alanrogers.com/ES91400

Looking up through the trees in this steeply terraced campsite in the area of the Cadi-Moixero Natural Park, you see the majestic Pedraforca mountain. A favourite for Catalan climbers and walkers, its amazing rugged peak in the shape of a massive stone fork gives it its name. Access to the site is via a steep, curving road which could challenge some units. Pitches vary in size and accessibility, although there are excellent pitches for larger units. The long scenic drive through the mountains to reach the site is beautiful. The campsite owner, Alicia Font, is a charming hostess who speaks English.

Facilities

Two clean, modern sanitary blocks are fully equipped (but at peak periods there may be queues). Facilities for disabled campers. Separate family room with baby baths, etc. Washing machines and dryer. Small supermarket (w/ends all year, then 15/5-30/9). Restaurant/bar (1/6-30/9). Heated indoor swimming pool, gym and spa. Outdoor pool (15/5-30/9). Play areas. Animation in high season. Games and social rooms. Torches required. Off site: Motorcaravan service point close. Suggestions for excursions. Mountain biking. Artigas gardens designed by Gaudi. Museum of mines. New adventure park 5 km.

Open: All year.

Directions

Site is about 90 minutes from Barcelona. Access to the site is gained from the C-16 Berga road. 2 km. south of Guardiola de Berguedá turn west to Saldes and site is well signed. It is 13.5 km. to site from the C-16. GPS: N42:13.847 E01:45.147

Charges 2009

Per person	€ 4,90 - € 6,05
child (1-10 yrs)	€ 4,00 - € 4,95
pitch	€ 13,95 - € 17,20
electricity (3/5A)	€ 4,50 - € 5,40
Camping Cheques accepted.	

47

ES84780 Camping Joan

Passeig Maritim 88, E-43850 Cambrils (Tarragona)

Tel: 977 364 604. Email: info@campingjoan.com

www.alanrogers.com/ES84780

Camping Joan is a family site to the south of the popular resort of Cambrils and with direct access to the sandy beach. There are 200 touring pitches of two different types, some being suitable for larger units. Most are between 60-90 sq.m. in size with 5A electrical connections and there is good shade. The 160 remaining pitches are used for mobile homes and chalets to rent. The site has a swimming pool, but obviously the main attraction here will be the beach. This is a lively site in high season with a varied and comprehensive programme of entertainment and activities for adults and children. In the centre of the site, near the entrance, is the La Palmera restaurant and bar, with a further bar/restaurant (Maritim) located beside the beach, alongside a well stocked shop. These amenities are open for quite a long season (Easter - September).

Facilities

Six sanitary blocks of which only four are available for the touring pitches Bar, restaurant and takeaway meals. Supermarket. Swimming and paddling pools. Playground. Entertainment programme in high season, children's club. Direct access to beach. Off site: Cambrils 2 km. Golf 8 km. Port Aventura 8 km.

Open: 1 April - 1 October.

Directions

Heading south on the AP7 motorway, leave at exit 37 (Costa Daurada) and join the southbound N340. Leave this road at the service station in La Dorada. GPS: N41:03.320 E01:01.400

Charges guide

Per person	€ 2,80 - € 5,30
child (3-10 yrs)	€ 1,80 - € 4,40
pitch	€ 13,00 - € 23,25
electricity	€ 3,90

Camping Cheques accepted.

WiFi ZONE

www.campingjoan.com
info@campingjoan.com

E-43850 CAMBRILS (Tarragona)
COSTA DAURADA
Tel.: +34 97 736 4604
Fax: +34 97 779 42 14

Camping Joan
bungalow park

The quiet, small holiday site directly on the beach

Road AP-7, exit nr. 37, than the N-340 direction Valencia and turn off at km 1.141 (Hotel La Daurada). Situated at 2 km south of Cambrils and 6 km of the theme park 'PORT AVENTURA'.
• Bungalows and caravans • very clean and quiet • swimming pool • organized leisure for grown ups and children • modern sanitary installations with free hot water • ideal for families with children • nice, personal contact with the owner • large sites with lots of shade • Considerable discounts off-season • Wifi Zone

ES84700 Camping La Siesta

Calle Ctra Norte 37, E-43840 Salou (Tarragona)

Tel: 977 380 852. Email: info@camping-lasiesta.com

www.alanrogers.com/ES84700

The palm bedecked entrance of La Siesta is only 250 m. from the pleasant sandy beach and close to the life of the resort of Salou. The site is divided into 470 pitches which are large enough and have electricity (10A), with smaller ones for tents. Many pitches are provided with artificial shade and within some there is one box for the tent or caravan and a shared one for the car. There is considerable shade from the trees and shrubs that are part of the site's environment. In high season, the siting of units is carried out by the friendly management. Young campers are located separately to the rear of the site.

Facilities

Three bright and clean sanitary blocks provide very reasonable facilities. Motorcaravan services. Supermarket. Various vending machines. Self-service restaurant and bar with cooked dishes to take away. Dancing some evenings untill 23.00. Swimming pool (300 sq.m. open all season). Playground. Medical service daily in season. ATM point. Torches may be required. Off site: Many shops, restaurants and bars near. Port Aventura is close. Bicycle hire 200 m. Fishing 500 m. Riding and golf 6 km.

Open: 14 March - 3 November.

Directions

Leave A7 at exit 35 for Salou. Site is signed off the Tarragona - Salou road and from the one way system in the town of Salou. The site is in the town so keep a sharp eye for the small signs. GPS: N41:04.662 E1:08.334

Charges guide

Per person	€ 4,60 - € 8,80
child (4-9 yrs)	€ 3,40 - € 4,50
pitch	€ 3,40 - € 17,60
electricity	€ 3,25 - € 4,00

All plus 7% VAT. No credit cards.

Ctra N340 km 1136, E-43300 Montroig (Tarragona)

Tel: **977 810 486**. Email: **info@latorredelsol.com**

www.alanrogers.com/ES85400

A pleasant banana tree-lined approach road gives way to avenues of palms as you arrive at Torre del Sol. This is a very large site occupying a good position in the south of Catalunya with direct access to the soft sand beach. The site is exceptionally well maintained by a large workforce. There is good shade on a high proportion of the 1,500 individual, numbered pitches. All have electricity and are mostly of about 70-80 sq.m. Strong features here are 800 m. of clean beachfront with a special Mediterranean type of pitch, and the entertainment that is provided all season. Part of the site is between the railway and the sea so there is some train noise. The cinema doubles as a theatre to stage shows all season. A complex of three pools, thoughtfully laid out with grass sunbathing areas and palms has a lifeguard. There is wireless internet access throughout the site. There is usually space for odd nights but for good places between 10/7-16/8 it is best to reserve (only taken for a stay of seven nights or more). We were impressed with the provision of season-long entertainment and to give parents a break whilst children were in the safe hands of the animation team who ensure they enjoy the novel 'Happy Camp' and various workshops. There is a separate area where the team will take your children to camp overnight in the Indian reservation.

Facilities

Four very well maintained, fully equipped, toilet blocks include units for disabled people and babies. Washing machines. Gas supplies. Large supermarket, bakery and souvenir shops at entrance. Full restaurant. Takeaway. Bar with large terrace where entertainment is held daily. Beach bar. Coffee bar and ice cream bar. Pizzeria. Open roof cinema with seating for 520. 3 TV lounges. Sound-proof disco. Swimming pools (two heated). Solarium. Sauna. Large jacuzzi. Tennis. Squash. Language school (Spanish). Minigolf. Sub-aqua diving (first dive in pool free!) Bicycle hire. Fishing. Windsurfing school; sailboards and pedaloes for hire. Playground, crèche and Happy Camp. Fridge hire. Library. Hairdresser. Business centre. WiFi. No animals permitted. No jet skis. Off site: Theme parks. Beach fishing. Riding 3 km. Golf 4 km.

Open: Easter - 20 October.

Directions

Entrance is off main N340 road by 1136 km. marker, about 30 km. from Tarragona towards Valencia. From motorway take Cambrils exit and turn west on N340. GPS: N41:02.224 E00:58.487

Charges guide

Per unit incl. 2 adults

and electricity	€ 19,70 - € 61,15
extra person	€ 3,25 - € 9,35
child (0-10 yrs)	free - € 7,45

Discounts in low season for longer stays.
Camping Cheques accepted.

Check real time availability and at-the-gate prices...

www.**alanrogers**.com

ES84800 Camping & Bungalows Sanguli

Prolongacion Calle, Apdo 123, E-43840 Salou (Tarragona)

Tel: **977 381 641**. Email: **mail@sanguli.es**   www.alanrogers.com/ES84800

Sanguli is a superb site boasting excellent pools and ambitious entertainment. Owned, developed and managed by a local Spanish family, it provides for all the family with everything open when the site is open. There are 1,041 pitches of varying size (75-90 sq.m) and all have electricity. About 155 are used by tour operators and 205 for bungalows. A wonderful selection of trees, palms and shrubs provides natural shade. The good sandy beach is little more than 100 metres across the coast road and a small railway crossing (a little noise). Although large, Sanguli maintains a quality family atmosphere due to the efforts of the very keen and efficient staff. The owners are striving to achieve the 'Garden of Eden' that is their dream. There are three very attractive pool areas, one (heated) near the entrance with a grassy sunbathing area partly shaded and a second deep one with water slides that forms part of the excellent sports complex (with fitness centre, tennis courts, minigolf and football practice area). The third pool is the central part of the amphitheatre area at the top of the site which includes an impressive Roman style building with huge portals, containing a bar and restaurant with terraces. An amphitheatre seats 2,000 campers and treats them to very professional free nightly entertainment (1/5-30/9). All the pools have adjacent amenity areas and bars. A real effort is made to cater for the young including teenagers with a 'Hop Club' (entertainment for 13-17 year olds), along with an internet room. Located near the centre of Salou, the site can offer the attractions of a busy resort while still being private and it is only 3 km. from Port Aventura. This is a large, professional site providing something for all the family, but still capable of providing peace and quiet for those looking for it.

Facilities

The quality sanitary facilities are constantly improved and are always exceptional, including many individual cabins with en-suite facilities. A new block also has excellent facilities for babies. All are kept very clean. Launderette with service. Motorcaravan services. Bars and restaurant with takeaway. Swimming pools. Jacuzzi. Fitness centre. Sports complex. Fitness room (charged). Playgrounds including adventure play area. Miniclub, teenagers' club. Internet room. Upmarket minigolf. First-aid room. Gas supplies. Off site: Fishing and bicycle hire 100 m. Riding 3 km. Golf 6 km. Resort entertainment.

Open: 14 March - 2 November.

Directions

On west side of Salou about 1 km. from the centre, site is well signed from the coast road to Cambrils and from the other town approaches.
GPS: N41:04.500 E01:06.960

Charges guide

Per person	€ 6,00
child (4-12 yrs)	€ 4,00
pitch incl. electricity	€ 15,00 - € 44,00
incl. water	€ 15,00 - € 52,00

All plus 7% VAT.
Less 25-45% outside high season for longer stays.
Special long stay offers for senior citizens.

ES85020 Camping Caravaning Montblanc Park

Ctra Prenafeta km 1,8, E-43400 Montblanc (Tarragona)

Tel: **977 862 544**. Email: **info@montblancpark.com**   www.alanrogers.com/ES85020

Taking current trends into account, Montblanc Park may be described as a campsite of the future. Purpose designed, there are 200 terraced pitches for touring units and about 80 for wooden chalets, with more being developed, on the upper terraces. The restaurant and terrace enjoy views of the exceptionally large, lagoon-style pool and further across the valley, over the autoroute towards the town of Montblanc and the Prades mountains of the Serra del Prades. The pitches are on terraces so take advantage of the mountain views and gentle cooling afternoon breezes. They vary in size, with hedging and trees, and are sloping (chocks useful). Visitors have first class facilities, including the very high quality restaurant serving typically Catalan dishes along with dishes to suit any palate and a terrace area for those who would choose a less formal atmosphere. There is much emphasis on activities for children and an animation team keeps children amused during the day in July and August so parents can have a break. There is organised sport and live entertainment on Saturday nights. This is a very professional operation, ideal for a relaxing holiday or exploring the attractions of the local area. Medieval Montblanc itself is worth exploring and nearby Poblet with its monastery.

Facilities

Two purpose built toilet blocks feature en-suite facilities including superb facilities for disabled campers and a well equipped baby room. Washing machines and dryers. Supermarket. Restaurant. Snack bar. Swimming pool and large paddling pool. Play areas. Boules. Bicycle hire. Entertainment for children (weekends and main season).Tents for hire. Off site: Riding 4 km. Beach or golf 35 km. Mountain activities: climbing, caving, canyoning and orienteering. Quad biking and trips by 4x4.

Open: All year.

Directions

Site is 3 minutes off the autopista. From A2 (Barcelona - Lleida) take exit 9 and follow N240 (Reus - Tarragona), then road to Prenafeta and site stands out on the left. It is 1.8 km. out of Montblanc and signed in the town.
GPS: N41:22.360 E01:11.600

Charges guide

Per person	€ 4,50 - € 6,50
child (0-10 yrs)	free
pitch incl. electricity	€ 13,00 - € 21,00

CAMPING RESORT
Sangulí Salou
* * * * *

Paseo Miramar–Plaza Venus • SALOU
Camping   +34 977 38 16 41
Bungalow +34 977 38 90 05
Fax   +34 977 38 46 16
@ mail@sanguli.es
www.sanguli.es
Apartat de Correus 123
43840 SALOU • Tarragona • España

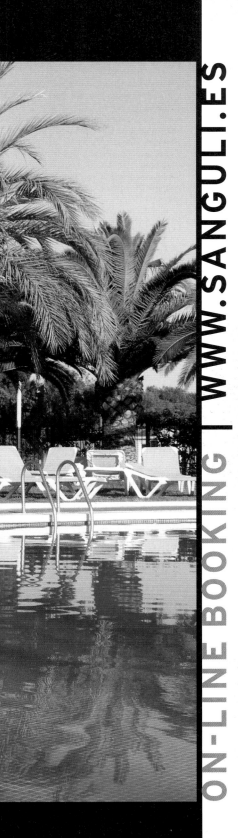

ON-LINE BOOKING | WWW.SANGULI.ES

ES84790 Camping Playa Cambrils Don Camilo

Ctra Cambrils - Salou km 1,5, E-43850 Cambrils (Tarragona)

Tel: 977 361 490. Email: camping@playacambrils.com

www.alanrogers.com/ES84790

Almost completely canopied by trees which provide welcome shade on hot days, the site is 300 m. from the beach across a busy road. It is mature and has had some recent renovations. The small (60 sq.m) pitches are on flat ground, divided by hedges. There are many permanent pitches and half the site is given up to chalet style accommodation. Large units are placed in a dedicated area where the trees are higher. The pool complex includes a functional glassed restaurant and bar with a distinct Spanish flavour reflected in the menu and tapas available all day. As this is a popular site with Spanish families it is a good place to practice your language. The pool is long and narrow with separate children's pool and a large paved area for soaking up the sun. Entertainment for children is organised by a good animation team. A big building at one end of the site consists of the supermarket, an attended electronic games room and a large play room.

Facilities

One modern sanitary building, and one large plus one small refurbished block offer reasonable facilities with British style WCs and free showers in separate buildings. Facilities for disabled campers. Laundry facilities. Supermarket (April-Sept). Bar/snacks and separate restaurant (April-Sept). Swimming pool. Playground. Animation in high season. Miniclub. Huge electronic games room. Torches useful. Off site: Resort town has a range of shops, bars and restaurants. Bicycle hire 500 m. Fishing and golf 1 km. Riding 1.5 km.

Open: 15 March - 12 October.

Directions

Leave AP7 autopista at exit 37 and head for Cambrils and then to the beach. Turn left along beach road. Site is 1 km. east of Cambrils Playa and is well signed as you leave Cambrils marina. GPS: N41:03.892 E01:05.021

Charges guide

Per person	€ 2,50 - € 4,80
child (under 9 yrs)	€ 1,70 - € 3,65
pitch	€ 11,60 - € 27,60
No credit cards.	

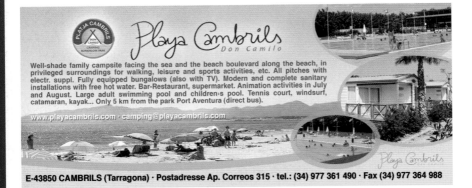

Playa Cambrils Don Camilo

Well-shade family campsite facing the sea and the beach boulevard along the beach, in privileged surroundings for walking, leisure and sports activities, etc. All pitches with electr. suppl. Fully equipped bungalows (also with TV). Modern and complete sanitary installations with free hot water. Bar-Restaurant, supermarket. Animation activities in July and August. Large adult swimming pool and children,s pool. Tennis court, windsurf, catamaran, kayak... Only 5 km from the park Port Aventura (direct bus).

www.playacambrils.com · camping@playacambrils.com

E-43850 CAMBRILS (Tarragona) · Postadresse Ap. Correos 315 · tel.: (34) 977 361 490 · Fax (34) 977 364 988

ES84020 Camping Vendrell Platja

Avenida del Sanatori s/n, E-43880 Coma-ruga - El Vendrell (Tarragona)

Tel: 977 694 009. Email: vendrell@camping-vendrellplatja.com

www.alanrogers.com/ES84020

In the popular Calafell area, this site is set back from the beach across a minor road. Popular with tourists for many years, the area has apartment buildings, bars and restaurants, and is popular with families. The pitches (70 sq.m) are partially shaded by trees which are growing well. Access to all the pitches is through one narrow central road which is busy with foot and vehicle traffic. An avenue of palms greets you on arrival here, and the pool with more tall palms and grassy areas, has two slides that delight children and adults alike.

Facilities

Two well located toilet blocks provide clean facilities with a new unit for disabled campers and well equipped baby rooms. Washing machines. Motorcaravan services. Supermarket. Restaurant. Snack bar. Swimming pools and pool bar. Play areas. Boules. Bicycle hire. Entertainment and activity programmes. ATM. Security boxes. Torches useful. Internet access. Off site: Resort town and beach outside the gate with usual attractions. Fishing. Bicycle hire 200 m. Riding 2 km. Golf 3 km.

Open: 3 April - 12 October.

Directions

From A7 or A16 take exits for El Vendrell. Then go east to Sant Salvador, and north on coast road towards Platja Calafell. Site is well signed on this road west of the town centre. GPS: N41:11.136 E01:33.324

Charges guide

Per person	€ 4,00 - € 8,50
child (3-11 yrs)	€ 2,00 - € 8,00
pitch incl. electricity	€ 12,00 - € 22,00

ES84100 Camping Playa Bará

Ctra N340 km 1183, E-43883 Roda de Bará (Tarragona)

Tel: 977 802 701. Email: info@barapark.es

www.alanrogers.com/ES84100

This is a most impressive, family owned site near the beach, which has been carefully designed and developed. On entry you find yourself in a beautifully sculptured, tree-lined drive with an accompanying aroma of pine and woodlands and the sound of waterfalls close by. Considering its size, with over 850 pitches, it is still a very green and relaxing site with an immense range of activities. It is well situated with a 50 m. walk to a long sandy beach via a tunnel under the railway (some noise) to a new promenade with palms and a quality beach bar and restaurant. Much care with planning and in the use of natural stone; palms, shrubs and flowering plants gives a most pleasing tropical appearance to all aspects of the site. The owners have excelled themselves in the design of the impressive terraced Roman-style pool complex, which is the central feature of the site. This complex is really amazing. Sunbathe on the pretty terraces or sip a drink whilst seated at the stools submerged in one of the pools or enjoy the panorama over the sea from the rooftop spa or the upper Roman galley bar. An extremely well equipped gym with an instructor and a massage service. A separate amphitheatre seats 2,000 people and is used to stage professional entertainment in season. Pitches vary in size and are being progressively enlarged; the older ones terraced and well shaded with pine trees, the newer ones more open, with a variety of trees and bushes between them. All have electricity (5A) and a sink with water. Arrive early to find space in peak weeks.

Facilities

Excellent, fully equipped toilet blocks include cabins and facilities for children and new block for disabled visitors. Private facilities to hire. Superb launderette. Motorcaravan service points. Supermarket and several other shops. Full restaurant. Large bar with simpler meals and takeaway. Three other bars and pleasant bar/restaurant on beach. Swimming pools. Jacuzzi/hydro-massage. Tennis (floodlit). Junior club. Sports area. Windsurfing school. Gym. Massage. Petanque. Minigolf. Fishing. Entertainment centre. Large games room. Cocktail bar/disco (23.00 to 04.00, weekends only in low season). Hairdresser. Internet room. Medical centre. Flights and excursions booked. WiFi. Off site: Bicycle hire 2 km. Riding 6 km. Golf 8 km.

Open: 7 March - October, with all amenities.

Directions

From the A7 take exit 31. Site entrance is at the 1183 km. marker on the main N340 just opposite the Arco de Bara Roman monument from which it takes its name. GPS: N41:10.200 E01:28.100

Charges guide

Per person	€ 3,00 - € 9,70
child (1-9 yrs)	€ 2,00 - € 6,80
pitch	€ 6,80 - € 19,70
electricity	€ 3,30

All plus 7% VAT. Low season reductions for pensioners and all sports charges reduced by 90%. No credit cards.

Subtropical exotica on Spain's Golden Coast

PARK PLAYA BARA

A botanical garden, a campers paradise.

Check real time availability and at-the-gate prices...

www.alanrogers.com

ES84810 Camping Cambrils Park

Avenida Mas Clariana s/n, E-43850 Cambrils (Tarragona)

Tel: 977 351 031. Email: mail@cambrilspark.es

www.alanrogers.com/ES84810

This is a superb site for a camping holiday providing for all family members, whatever their age. A drive lined with palm trees and flowers leads from a large, very smart round reception building at this impressive modern site. Sister site to no. ES84800, it is set 500 metres back from the excellent beach in a generally quiet setting with outstanding facilities. The 684 slightly sloping, grassy pitches of around 90 sq.m. are numbered and separated by trees. All have 10A electricity, 55 have water and waste water connections, some having more shade than others. The marvellous central lagoon pool complex with three pools and water slides is the main focus of the site with a raised wooden 'poop deck' sunbathing area with palm surrounds that doubles as an entertainment stage at night. There is a huge bar/terrace area for watching the magnificent floodlit spectacles, along with an excellent restaurant in the old farmhouse with an adjacent takeaway. By day there is a small bar at a lower level in the pool where you can enjoy a cool drink from submerged stools, plus a dryer version on the far side or just relax on the spacious grass sunbathing areas. A fabulous jungle theme children's pool is nearer the entrance – they love it, especially the elephants! An extra pool for adults has been added here, along with a snack bar. There are tour operator pitches and attractive thatched chalets.

Facilities

Four excellent sanitary buildings provide some washbasins in cabins, superb units for disabled visitors and immaculate baby sections. Huge serviced laundry. Motorcaravan services. Car wash. Restaurant. Takeaway. Huge supermarket, souvenir shop and 'panaderia' (freshly baked bread and croissants). Swimming pools. Minigolf. Tennis. Multisport court. Petanque. Animation and entertainment all season. Miniclub. Internet café. Medical centre. ATM. Gas supplies. Dogs are not accepted. Off site: Beach 500 m. Fishing, bicycle hire 400 m. Riding 3 km. Port Aventura theme park 4 km. Golf 7 km.

Open: 7 April - 8 October.

Directions

Site is about 1.5 km. west of Salou. From the A7 take exit 35 and at roundabout take signs for Cambrils. Follow new dual carriageway around the back of Salou and site is signed at last roundabout towards Cambrils. GPS: N41:04.584 E01:06.527

Charges guide

Per person	€ 6,00
child (4-12 yrs)	€ 4,00
pitch incl. electricity	€ 15,00 - € 49,00
incl. water and waste water	€ 15,00 - € 52,00

All plus 7% VAT. Special offers.
Camping Cheques accepted.

ES85060 Camping & Bungalow Park Serra de Prades

Sant Antoni s/n, E-43439 Vilanova de Prades (Tarragona)

Tel: 977 869 050. Email: info@serradeprades.com

www.alanrogers.com/ES85060

On the edge of the village of Vilanova, nestling in granite foothills with superb views from its elevation of 950 m, this is a welcoming and peaceful site. The 215 pitches are on terraces formed with natural stone and with good access. With 120 for touring units (all with 6A electricity), the remainder are occupied by seasonal units. The upper tent pitches have wonderful views although the sanitary facilities are on the lower level. Hedges and trees separate pitches providing a pleasant green environment and some shade, and 90% of the pitches have electricity. The site has won awards for its approach to ecology. Solar power is used to heat water for the showers and the pool. The swimming pool (supervised) is attractively set, with grass surrounds and a terrace for sunbathing overlooked by the lower bar. The strength of this site is the range of adventure and outdoor activities on offer. Professionally organized, climbing is a favourite followed by abseiling, paint ball, cycling, archery and a host of others. There is a horse riding area within the site and guided treks are offered in July/August. On site, less arduous activities are also organised for children and adults in season. From here it is possible to enjoy the wonderful Prades mountains or go to the beach an hour's drive away, returning to sleep well in the mild, sunny climate 900 m. above sea level.

Facilities

The modern, heated, well equipped toilet block has washbasins in cabins and is well maintained. Facilities for disabled visitors and babies. Laundry facilities. Motorcaravan service point. Shop. Bar and good quality restaurant. Swimming pool (open and heated 24/6-15/9). Gym. Internet points. Archery. Quad bike and 4x4 hire. Paint ball. Tennis. Riding with guided treks. Activities organised. Sports area. Entertainment in season. Safety deposit. Exchange facilities. Gas supplies. Torches required in some areas. Off site: Golf 12 km.

Open: All year.

Directions

From Tarragona on the AP2 take exit 9 (Montblanc) and continue towards Lleida on N240. At km. 48 just west of Vimbodi, turn left towards Vallclara and Vilanova de Prades. Site on right after roundabout at entrance to village. From Lleida leave the AP2 at exit 8 towards Tarragona on N240, then as above from km. 48 just before Vimbodi. GPS: N41:20.982 E00:57.511

Charges guide

Per person	€ 6,60
child (under 10 yrs)	€ 5,60
pitch incl. electricity (6A)	€ 12,20 - € 17,90

Plus 7% VAT.
Camping Cheques accepted.

ES84200 Kawan Village Stel

Ctra N340 km 1182, E-43883 Roda de Bará (Tarragona)
Tel: **977 802 002**. Email: **rodadebara@stel.es**

www.alanrogers.com/ES84200

Camping Stel is situated between the pre-Littoral mountains and the sea. The rectangular site is between the N340 road and the excellent beach, with the railway running close to the bottom of the site. Beach access is gained through a gate and under the railway – there is rail noise on the lower pitches. The pitches are generally in rows with hedges around the rows but at the lower end of the site the layout is less formal. Many pitches have individual sinks. There is a separate area where no radio or TV is allowed ensuring peace and quiet. The main facilities are grouped around the pools which are very pleasant with a large flume to an extension of the main pool (heated all season), an octagonal paddling pool and pleasant grass area carefully set out with palms. The central complex containing all the services is impressive with a large bar, terrace and snack area overlooking the pools. A small restaurant is behind the bar. Just outside the gate is the famous Roman Arc de Bara which sits astride the original road.

Facilities

Four clean, fully equipped, sanitary blocks. One offers excellent facilities for children and disabled campers and four high standard private cabins. Baby baths. Large launderette. Motorcaravan service area. Supermarket and tourist shop. Bar/restaurant and snack bar. Swimming pool, jacuzzi and paddling pool (4/4-28/9). Sport field. Bicycle hire. Minclub and activities for adults (high season). Internet room (10 units). Hairdresser. ATM. Dogs are not accepted. Torches useful. Off site: Fishing from beach. Golf and riding 4 km.

Open: 4 April - 30 September.

Directions

Site is at 1182 km. marker on the N340 near Arc de Bara, between Tarragona and Vilanova. GPS: N41:10.181 E1:27.881

Charges guide

Per person	€ 7,35 - € 7,75
child (3-10 yrs)	€ 5,75 - € 6,05
pitch incl. electricity	€ 23,15 - € 28,45
incl. water and drainage	€ 27,90 - € 37,70

All plus 7% VAT.
Camping Cheques accepted.

camping · bungalows · www.stel.es

Camping STEL - Roda de Barà
Ctra. N-340, Km. 1182
E-43883 Roda de Barà (Tarragona) · Spain
Tel. 977 80 20 02 · Fax 977 80 05 25
E-mail: rodadebara@stel.es · Skype: stel43883
GPS: N 41º 10.199' - E 001º 27.852'

1ª
★ ★ ★

roda
de barà
costa dorada

Check real time availability and at-the-gate prices...
www.**alanrogers**.com

ES84830 Camping Tamarit Park

N340 km 1172, Tamarit, E-43008 Tarragona (Tarragona)

Tel: **977 650 128**. Email: **tamaritpark@tamarit.com**   www.alanrogers.com/ES84830

This is a marvellous, beach-side site, attractively situated at the foot of Tamarit castle at one end of a superb one kilometre long beach of fine sand. Parts are landscaped with lush Mediterranean palms and shrubs; other areas have natural pine shade, all home to mischievous red squirrels. The 694 pitches, 50 of which are virtually on the beach, are marked out on hard sand and grass and some are attractively separated by green vegetation which provides good shade. There are about 120 tour operator pitches, a number of seasonal pitches and about 120 bungalows. All pitches have electricity (6A). Long electricity leads and metal awning pegs may be required in places but wide internal roads give good access for even the largest of units (American motorhomes accepted). Catering includes a beach-side waiter service restaurant with superb views and a terrace with tables just a few metres from the sea. A vast, attractively designed, lagoon-type swimming pool with bar and sun terrace has recently been added. The site is approached by a long access road, rather narrow but with passing places, reached across a bridge (6 m.) over the railway line (there is train noise on the site). Security is provided but the very low wall which is the site beach boundary must be viewed with caution. Tamarit would be a good choice for windsurfing enthusiasts or a family holiday by the sea. The early morning sun shining on the blue sea and the golden stone of Tamarit castle high above is a memorable sight! It is only 9 km. from Tarragona and 16 km. from Port Aventura.

Facilities

Sanitary blocks (one heated) are modern and tiled, providing good facilities. An unfortunate economy feature in the showers is push-button controlled hot water with tap controlled cold, leading to a confusing mix of temperatures. Private bathrooms to rent. Laundry facilities. Motorcaravan services. Gas supplies. Shop, bar/restaurant and takeaway. Swimming pool (15/5-15/10). Tennis. Petanque. Minigolf. Playground. Animation programme in season. Fishing. Internet access. Barbecues not permitted on pitches.
Off site: Riding 1 km. Bicycle hire 2 km. Golf 8 km.

Open: 30 March - 15 October.

Directions

From A7 take exit 32 towards Tarragona and continue for 4.5 km. At roundabout (km. 1172) turn back towards Atafulla and Tamarit and after 200 m. turn right to Tamarit (beside Caledonia Bungalow Park). Take care over railway bridge, then immediately sharp right. Site on left after 1 km.
GPS: N41:07.943 E01:21.652

Charges guide

Per person	€ 5,00
child (4-12 yrs)	free - € 4,00
pitch acc. to size and season	€ 18,00 - € 52,00
dog	€ 2,00 - € 4,00

All plus 7% VAT. Discounts for students, pensioners, large families and longer stays in low season.

ES84820 Camping La Pineda de Salou

Ctra Costa Tarragona - Salou km 5, E-43481 La Pineda (Tarragona)

Tel: **977 373 080**. Email: **info@campinglapineda.com**   www.alanrogers.com/ES84820

La Pineda is just outside Salou towards Tarragona and this site is just 300 m. from the Aquapark and 2.5 km. from Port Aventura, to which there is an hourly bus service from outside the site entrance. There is some noise from this road. The site has a fair-sized swimming pool adjoining a smaller, heated one, open from mid June, behind large hedges close to the entrance. A large terrace has sun loungers, and various entertainment aimed at young people is provided in season. The 366 flat pitches are mostly shaded and of about 70 sq.m. All have 5A electricity. The beach is about 400 m. The simple restaurant/bar is shaded and has a large cactus garden to the rear. This is a plain, friendly and convenient site, with reasonable rates, probably best used for visiting Tarragona and Port Aventura, or exploring the local area, rather than for extended stays. Note: the site is reasonably close to a large industrial centre.

Facilities

Sanitary facilities are mature but clean with baby bath, dishwashing and laundry sinks. Facilities for disabled visitors. Washing machines. The second building is opened in high season only. Gas supplies. Shop (1/7-31/8). Restaurant and snacks (1/7-31/8). Swimming pools (1/7-31/8). Bar (all season). Small TV room. Bicycle hire. Games room. Playground (3-12 yrs). Entertainment (1/7-30/8). Torches may be required. Off site: Beach and fishing 400 m. Golf 12 km.

Open: All year.

Directions

From A7 just southwest of Tarragona take exit 35 and follow signs to La Pineda and Port Aventura then campsite signs appear.
GPS: N41:05.310 E01:10.947

Charges guide

Per person	€ 5,00 - € 7,70
child (1-10 yrs)	€ 3,40 - € 5,80
pitch incl. car	€ 17,00 - € 36,60
electricity	€ 4,10 - € 4,40

All plus 7% VAT.

ES85350 Camping-Pension Cala d'Oques

Via Augusta s/n, E-43890 Hospitalet del Infante (Tarragona)

Tel: 977 823 254. Email: eroller@tinet.org

www.alanrogers.com/ES85350

This peaceful and delightful site has been developed with care and dedication by Elisa Roller over 30 years or so and she now runs it with the help of her daughter Kim. Part of its appeal lies in its situation beside the sea with a wide beach of sand and pebbles, its amazing mountain backdrop and the views across the bay to the town and part by the atmosphere created by Elisa, and staff – friendly, relaxed and comfortable. There are 255 pitches, mostly level and laid out beside the beach, with more behind on wide, informal terracing. Electricity is available although long leads may be needed in places. Odd pine and olive trees are an attractive feature and provide some shade. The restaurant with its homely touches has a super menu and a reputation extending well outside the site (the excellent cook has been there for many years) and the family type entertainment is in total contrast to that provided at the larger, brasher sites of the Costa Daurada. Gates provide access to the pleasant beach with useful cold showers to wash the sand away. Torches are needed at night. This is a pretty place to stay and Elisa gives a pleasant personal service but do not expect 'Costa' type entertainment. Ask how the nearby village of Hospitalet del Infante got its name – it's a royal riddle! The village itself is well worth exploring and if you are here in June watch for the fabulous fireworks of the celebration of St John. It is interesting to note that Cala d'Oques (Goose Bay) was where the migrant geese landed on return from wintering in South Africa, hence the geese featured on the site logo and the guard goose that watches the entrance.

Facilities

Toilet facilities are in the front part of the main building. Clean and neat, there is hot water to showers (hot water by token but free to campers – a device to guard against unauthorised visitors from the beach). New heated unit with toilets and washbasins for winter use. Additional small block with toilets and washbasins at the far end of the site. Motorcaravan service point. Restaurant/bar and shop (1/4-30/9). Play area. Kim's kids club. Fishing. Internet access and WiFi. Gas supplies. Torches required in some areas. Off site: Village facilities, incl. shop and restaurant 1.5 km. Bicycle hire or riding 2 km.

Open: All year.

Directions

Hospitalet del Infante is south of Tarragona, accessed from the A7 (exit 38) or from the N340. From the north take first exit to Hospitalet del Infante at 1128 km. Follow signs in the village, site is 2 km. south, by the sea. GPS: N40:58.666 E00:54.203

Charges guide

Per unit incl. 1 person	€ 13,65 - € 24,75
extra person	€ 4,55 - € 8,25
child (0-10 yrs)	free
electricity	€ 3,30 - € 3,90

Discounts for seniors and for longer stays.
No credit cards.

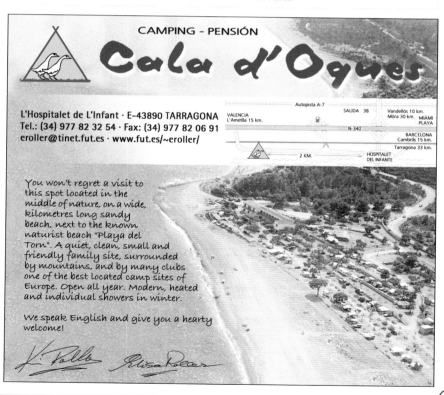

CAMPING - PENSIÓN

Cala d'Oques

L'Hospitalet de L'Infant · E-43890 TARRAGONA
Tel.: (34) 977 82 32 54 · Fax: (34) 977 82 06 91
eroller@tinet.fut.es · www.fut.es/~eroller/

You won't regret a visit to this spot located in the middle of nature, on a wide, kilometres long sandy beach, next to the known naturist beach "Playa del Torn". A quiet, clean, small and friendly family site, surrounded by mountains, and by many clubs one of the best located camp sites of Europe. Open all year. Modern, heated and individual showers in winter.

We speak English and give you a hearty welcome!

ES84850 Camping Las Palmeras

Ctra N340 km 1168, E-43080 Tarragona (Tarragona)

Tel: 977 208 081. Email: laspalmeras@laspalmeras.com

www.alanrogers.com/ES84850

Situated amongst pine, poplar and palm trees, running parallel to a fine, white sandy beach, Camping Las Palmeras has a wonderful location. Care must be taken on the final approach as you pass under the railway (some noise) and take a sharp turn into the parking area. Most of the 700 pitches are on grass with plenty of shade. All have access to 5A electricity, although long leads may be necessary in places. For its beachside location alone, Las Palmeras is worthy of a visit.

Facilities

Four large toilet blocks attractively tiled in a traditional style, are evenly located and kept to a high standard. Open style washbasins and good sized shower cubicles. Baby rooms. Laundry in each block. Shop. Bar and beach restaurant. Smaller bar and snack bar (high season only). Two swimming pools (June - Sept). Tennis. Two large play areas. Children's club in high season.

Open: 1 March - 15 October.

Directions

Las Palmeras is easily accessed from the N340 road (Barcelona - Tarragona) and is signed after the 1169 km. marker. Beware of the sharp bend at the entrance. GPS: N41:07.811 E1:18.702

Charges guide

Per person	€ 6,00 - € 10,50
pitch incl. electricity	€ 14,00 - € 29,00

Camping Cheques accepted.

ES85080 Camping Poboleda

Placa de les Casetes s/n, E-43376 Poboleda (Tarragona)

Tel: 977 827 197. Email: poboleda@campingsonline.com

www.alanrogers.com/ES85080

Time stands still at this unique site hidden away in a corner of the village, watched over by La Morera de Montsant, a peak of the Serra del Montsant. Situated among olive groves, yet almost in the heart of the lovely old village of Poboleda, it is an idyllic site for tents, small caravans and motorcaravans. Large units may have problems negotiating the narrow village streets. The 151 pitches of 80 sq.m. are set under olive and almond trees. Fairly level and 70 with 4A electricity, they provide a peaceful haven broken only by the peal of church bells or bird song.

Facilities

One small block, open all year, is fully equipped, as is a larger block open for high season. Shower for children. Facilities for disabled people (key). Laundry service. Breakfast can be ordered. Bar. Swimming pool (24/6-11/9). Tennis. Boules. Reception has tourist information, postcards and basic items. Off site: Beach and Port Aventura 30 km. Bicycle hire 10 km. Fishing 12 km.

Open: All year.

Directions

Bypass Reus (west of Tarragona) on N420. After Borges del Camp pick up C242, signed Alforja. Continue over Coll d'Alforja. Watch for left turn (T702) for Poboleda. Continue for 6 km. to village. Watch for tent signs and follow carefully through narrow village streets. Not recommended for large units. GPS: N41:14.000 E00:50.410

Charges guide

Per person	€ 5,67
pitch incl. car	€ 10,00 - € 15,00
electricity	€ 5,67

ES84860 Camping Torre de la Mora

Ctra N340 km 1171, E-43080 Tarragona (Tarragona)

Tel: 977 650 277. Email: campmora@tinet.fut.es

www.alanrogers.com/ES84860

Located on a promontory in a pleasant corner of the Costa Daurada with a village like atmosphere, Torre de la Mora takes advantage of its wonderful location, offering some pitches with beautiful views over the white sandy beaches and rocky promontories of the coastline. The hinterland is pine forest and there are areas where you can pitch a tent, access electricity (6A) and feel close to nature. The 200 touring pitches vary in just about every way, some are on the lower flat area, including a few with beach frontage, others are on steep terraces around the promontory.

Facilities

Two large and three small sanitary blocks are mature but clean. There is a mixture of washing facilities some of which have hot water, others not and most are dated. Facilities for disabled campers (careful selection of pitch is required). Washing machine. Motorcaravan services. Supermarket. Restaurant. Chicken bar (high season). Swimming pool and sports area (in need of renovation when we visited). Play area. Entertainment. Torches useful. Off site: Beach town outside the gate. Fishing. Bicycle hire 1 km. Golf 2 km. Riding 3 km. Boat launching 8 km.

Open: 18 March - 31 October.

Directions

From A7 (Barcelona - Tarragona) take exit 32, then N340 towards Tarragona. Turn off for Punta del la Mora and site is well signed approaching the village. The final approach is via some narrow streets so watch for one way signs and there is an unusual entry through a high wire fence alongside road. GPS: N41:07.680 E01:20.640

Charges guide

Per unit incl. 1 person and electricity	€ 19,15 - € 35,15
extra person	€ 4,30 - € 8,50

ES85300 Playa Montroig Camping Resort

Apdo 3, N340 km 1136, E-43300 Montroig (Tarragona)

Tel: **977 810 637**. Email: **info@playamontroig.com**

What a superb site! Playa Montroig is about 30 kilometres beyond Tarragona set in its own tropical gardens with direct access to a very long soft sand beach. The main part of the site lies between the sea, road and railway (as at other sites on this coast, there is some train noise) with a huge underpass. The site is divided into spacious, marked pitches with excellent shade provided by a variety of lush vegetation including very impressive palms set in wide avenues. There are 1,950 pitches, all with electricity and 330 with water and drainage. Some 48 pitches are directly alongside the beach. They are somewhat expensive and extremely popular. The site has many outstanding features: there is an excellent pool complex near the entrance with two pools (one heated for children). A high quality restaurant serves traditional Catalunian fare (seats 150) and overlooks an entertainment area where you may watch genuine Flamenco dancing and buffet food is served (catering for 1,000). A large terrace bar dispenses drinks or if you yearn for louder music there is a disco and smaller bar. If you prefer international food there is yet another eating option in a very smart restaurant (seats 500). Above this is the 'Pai-pai' Caribbean cocktail bar where softer music is provided in an intimate atmosphere. Activities for children are very ambitious – there is even a ceramics kiln. 'La Carpa', a spectacular open air theatre, is an ideal setting for keep fit sessions and the programme of professional entertainment. If you are 5-11 years old you can explore the 'Tam-Tam Eco Park', a 20,000 sq.m. forest zone where experts teach about the natural life of the area. You can even camp out for a night (supervised) to study wildlife (a once weekly activity). Adults are also allowed in to separate barbecues and other evening fun. Bathing, windsurfing, surfboarding two diving rafts and many beach sports are available on the beach. This is an excellent site and there is insufficient space here to describe all the activities. We recommend it for families with children of all ages and there is much emphasis on providing activities outside the high season. Member of Leading Campings Group.

Facilities

Fifteen sanitary buildings, some small, but of very good quality with toilets and washbasins, others really excellent, air conditioned larger buildings housing large showers, washbasins (many in private cabins) and separate WCs. Facilities for disabled campers and for babies. Several launderettes. Motorcaravan services. Good shopping centre. Restaurants and bars. The 'Eurocentre' equipped for entertainment (air conditioned). Fitness suite. Eco-park. TV lounges (3). Beach bar. Playground. Free kinder-garten with multilingual staff. Skate-boarding. Jogging track. Sports area. Tennis. Minigolf. Organised activities. Windsurfing and water skiing courses. Surfboard and pedalo hire. Boat mooring. Hairdressers. Bicycle hire. Internet café. Gas supplies. Dogs are not accepted. Off site: Riding and golf 3 km.

Open: 1 March - 31 October.

Directions

Site entrance is off main N340 nearly 30 km. southwest from Tarragona. From motorway take Cambrils exit and turn west on N340 at 1136 km. marker. GPS: N41:01.975 E00:58.153

Charges guide

Per unit incl. 2 persons	
and electricity	€ 16,00 - € 69,50
premium pitch	€ 29,00 - € 109,10
extra person	€ 5,80 - € 6,90
child (1-9 yrs)	free - € 5,30

All plus 7% VAT.
Discounts for longer stays and for pensioners.
See advertisement on the outside back cover.

ES85550 Camping Eucaliptus

Platja Eucaliptus s/n, E-43870 Amposta (Tarragona)

Tel: **977 479 046**. Email: **eucaliptus@campingeucaliptus.com**

Ideally situated in the Delta del Ebro national park, a unique area of wetland (320 square kilometre) and close to the golden sands of Platja Eucaliptus. Arriving at Camping Eucaliptus is like finding an oasis after the extraordinary drive through miles of flat marshland and rice fields. There are 264 small, level, shady grass pitches, 156 for touring, all with electricity. The site is well maintained and three modern buildings near the entrance house the reception, toilet block, shop, bar and restaurant. The terrace overlooks the pleasant pool area with lawned gardens for sunbathing and the campsite's own lagoon. There is access to the beach through a gate at the back of the site.

Facilities

The single toilet block is kept very clean and includes open style washbasins and good sized shower cubicles. Baby bath. Good facilities for disabled people. Laundry facilities. Dog shower. Well stocked shop. Gas supplies. Large bar with satellite TV. Good restaurant and snack bar with takeaway (all season). Play area. Swimming and paddling pools (1/6-15/9). Bicycle hire. Attractive barbecue area with covered seating. Off site: Fishing 300 m. Boat launching 8 km. Small town Sant Jaume.

Open: 27 March - 27 September.

Directions

From the A7 take exit 41, signed Amposta, N340. Immediately after crossing river Ebro leave N340 signed Els Muntells and Sant Jaume. On entering Sant Jaume turn right over canal, signed Els Muntells. At T-junction turn left. Site on right in 6 km. GPS: N40:39.395 E00:46.771

Charges guide

Per person	€ 4,40 - € 5,95
pitch incl. car	€ 10,10 - € 12,20
electricity (5A)	€ 4,05 - € 4,30

ES85330 Camping Els Prats – Marius

Ctra N340 km 1137, E-43892 Miami-Playa (Tarragona)

Tel: 977 810 027. Email: info@campingelsprats.com

www.alanrogers.com/ES85330

This Costa Daurada beach resort now combines two sites, Campings Els Prats and Marius. This is a very popular area, not far from Tarragona and the Port Adventura theme park. There are now almost 450 pitches, all with electricity. They are fairly close together, mostly flat and shaded, and a few have access to the pleasant narrow, white sand/shingle beach. There are bungalows to rent and an apartment block in one corner. A feature is the tropical style beach bar. Attractive tropical plants adorn the site including many banana trees. There is some road and rail noise on the western side of the site. The small irregularly shaped pool has two cascades which delight children, and a grassy area for sunbathing. A small pool bar serves drinks and ice creams. This is a family run site with the owner, his three sons and daughter in law, all working hard to make your holiday trouble free and give a more personalised service than some of the larger sites in the area. The site is popular with young people some of whom stay in a separate area and learn to windsurf. You also have a chance to try the 'hang loose' bar open until 03.00 hrs in high season!

Facilities

Two blocks, one for each sex, provide clean facilities. Separate unit for disabled campers. Children's bathroom. Washing machines. Motorcaravan services. Supermarket. Restaurant, takeaway and three bars. Swimming pool (3/4-17/10). Play area. Bicycle hire (organised trips). Windsurfing, canoeing and diving (free try dive Sat am). Animation programme and some evening entertainment in high season. Dogs are not accepted 1/7-31/8. Torches useful. Off site: Riding 3 km. Golf 5 km. Cambrils 7 km. Port Adventura 15 km.

Open: 6 March - 12 October.

Directions

Site is between Miami Playa and Cambrils on the N340. Take exit 37 from the A7 towards Cambrils, then 7 km. southwest of Cambrils at 1137 km. marker, take exit for Torre del Mar. Go under railway bridge and immediately right – site is 100 m. up this road. GPS: N41:02.167 E0:58.500

Charges 2009

Per person	€ 6,50 - € 7,00
child (under 10 yrs)	€ 1,00 - € 5,00
pitch incl. electricity (5A)	€ 11,00 - € 33,00

Camping Cheques accepted.

ES85370 Camping Naturista El Templo del Sol

E-43890 Hospitalet del Infante (Tarragona)

Tel: 977 823 434. Email: info@eltemplodelsol.com

www.alanrogers.com/ES85370

El Templo del Sol is a large, luxurious terraced naturist site with a distinctly Arabesque style and superb buildings in Moorish style. The owner has designed the magnificent main turreted building at the entrance with fountains and elaborate Moorish arches. The site has over 400 pitches of two different sizes, some with car parking alongside and 85 with full services. There is shade and the pitches are on terraces giving rewarding views over the sea. Attractive steps give ready access to the sandy beach. There is some daytime rail noise especially in the lower areas of the site where the larger pitches are located. Three large, tiered swimming pools are wonderful with water cascading from one to the other and are part of a supporting complex containing a huge luxurious jacuzzi with cracking views over the sea, a large bar with snacks, a games area, plus a sunbathing area on the roof. Also included is a 'Solar Park' where visitors may learn about how solar energy is used and applied. The main building contains an impressive reception area and has an elegant restaurant with a terrace and an elegant mosaic central, open area with a fountain and a luxury cinema. This grouping of services are said to be among the best in European naturist sites. Site lighting is provided from pleasing serpent shaped light assemblies. The site is under French management (the same as ES85400 Torre del Sol) and English is spoken.

Facilities

The sanitary blocks are amongst the best providing everything you could require. Extensive facilities for disabled campers. Washing machines. Well stocked supermarket. Health shop. Souvenir shop. Bars. Restaurant and snack bar (1/4-10/10). Swimming pools (20/3-15/10). Jacuzzi. Cinema. Games area. Boules. Separate round children's pool and play area. Miniclub. Library. Safety deposit boxes. Entertainment. Hairdresser. Bicycle hire. ATM. Dogs are not accepted. No jet skis. Off site: Fishing 100 m. Golf 2 km. (night time only). Bicycle hire and boat launching 3 km. Riding 7 km. Theme parks.

Open: 20 March - 20 October.

Directions

From N340 south of Tarragona, exit at km. 1126 towards L'Hopitalet Plaja and follow signs. I heading north, near km. 1124, turn right immediately after a modern railway bridge and site is just 400 m. on the right. GPS: N40:58.634 E00:54.056

Charges guide

Per unit incl. 2 persons and electricity	€ 18,70 - € 46,25
extra person	€ 3,30 - € 8,75
child (under 10 yrs)	free - € 6,25
small tent	€ 2,75 - € 5,10

Discounts for longer stays.

Apdo 240, Paraje Santes Creus, E-43860 Ametlla de Mar (Tarragona)

Tel: **977 267 784**. Email: **info@campingametlla.com**

www.alanrogers.com/ES85360

This site within a protected area has been well thought out and is startling in the quality of service provided, the finish and the materials used in construction. The 373 pitches are on a terraced hillside above colourful coves with shingle beaches and two small associated lagoons (with a protected fish species). The many bungalows here have been tastefully incorporated. There are great views, particularly from the friendly restaurant. There is some train noise. The site is used by tour operators (30 pitches). It is a very good site for families or for just relaxing. The site is environmentally correct and local planning regulations are extremely tight including the types of trees that may be planted. No transit traffic is allowed within the site in high season. Animation is organised for children in high season and there is a well equipped fitness room (free). There are good quality pools (with lifeguard) and a sub-aqua diving school operates on the site in high season and beginners may try a dive. This most attractive small site is in an idyllic situation near the picturesque fishing village of L'Ametlla de Mar, famous for its fish restaurants, and within the Ebro Delta nature reserve. It is about 20 minutes from Europe's second largest theme park, Port Aventura, but as there is no regular bus service your own transport is required (the owners arrange free buses to the local disco each Wednesday).

Facilities

Three really good toilet blocks. Some private cabins with WC and washbasin, plus others with WC, basin and shower. Motorcaravan services. Gas supplies. Supermarket (9/4-30/9; small shop incl. bread at other times). Good restaurant with snack menu and bar with TV (9/4-30/9). Swimming pool. Sub-aqua diving. Kayaking. Fishing. Children's club and play area. Fitness room. Bicycle hire. Entertainment (July/Aug). Barbecue area. Fishing. Off site: Boat launching 3 km. Golf 15 km. Riding 20 km. Theme parks.

Open: All year.

Directions

From A7/E15 (Barcelona - Valencia) take exit 39 for l'Ametlla de Mar. Follow numerous large white signs on reaching village and site is 2.5 km. south of the village. GPS: N40:51.870 E0:46.728

Charges 2009

Per person	€ 2,63 - € 6,27
child (under 10 yrs)	€ 2,15 - € 5,13
pitch incl. electricity	€ 10,64 - € 22,46

All plus 7% VAT.
Less for longer stays, especially in low season.

www.campingametlla.com · info@campingametlla.com

Open throughout the year

camping ametlla
VILLAGE PLATJA

WI-FI **20 min. from the theme park Port Aventura!**

At the sea, quiet situation in midst of nature. All facilities of a first class site, incl. swimming pools, diving centre, sports centre, medical service, etc. **New, fully furnished bungalows for hire, fitness centre.**

Tel.: +34 977 267 784 · Fax: +34 977 267 868 · Postadr.: Apartado 240
Paratge Santes Creus · E-43860 L'Ametlla de Mar (Tarragona) · A-7, exit 39

Barcelona is the capital of the Catalunya region of northeast of Spain on the Mediterranean coast, bordering France and Andorra in the north. It is an historic and vibrant city, boasting an array of superb museums, impressive architectural buildings, and numerous beaches – no-one should visit Spain without going to Barcelona!

Our advice on driving in Barcelona is quite simple – don't even think about it! Leave your car or motorcaravan somewhere outside the city and catch the train into the centre. The services are plentiful, usually run on time and fares are cheap by comparison with the UK. There are several stations in the centre of Barcelona, including the Placa de Catalunya.

Spend a few hours wandering around the maze of little streets that comprise the tree-lined Ramblas which leads down through the medieval heart of the city (the Barrio Gotico) towards the port area. Stop off at one of the many bistros and cafés that abound here; or maybe take in a visit to the Picasso Museum. A word of warning though, do stay alert for pick-pockets as it is also apparently a happy hunting ground for petty thieves.

Barelona's metro system is excellent and provides an easy way of getting around; a targeta (ticket strip) offers ten journeys at a discounted price. An alternative is to use the tourist buses which run from Catalonia Square. Complete with multi-lingual commentary, these offer unlimited travel on two different routes for an all-in price of around €12 for the day or €15 for two days. You will also receive a book of vouchers with your tickets giving discounts on entry fees to many of the city's main attractions and to some restaurants. The services operate half-hourly most of the year and you can get on and off as you please.

The buses pass numerous famous buildings, including those designed by Gaudi: the world-famous, but still unfinished Temple Expiatiori de la Sagrada Familia (Church of the Holy Family), his apartment block Casa Milã in the Passeig de Grãcia and the magnificent Palau Guell, the first modern building to be declared a World Heritage building by UNESCO. Also of interest en-route is the stadium, pool and sailing harbour used during the 1992 Olympic Games, the home of FC Barcelona, the old Bull Ring and the National Palace, now home to the Art Museum. The bus also stops by the funicular railway, which offers excellent views across the city.

If your time in Barcelona is limited, a day using the tourist buses, taking you from one point of interest to another, is time well spent and provides at least something of an insight into this fascinating city.

This Mediterranean region is famous for its magnificent orange groves and beautiful long, sandy beaches. Centuries of Moorish presence have resulted in a profound Hispano-Moorish heritage.

VALENCIANA IS MADE UP OF THE PROVINCES OF CASTELLON, VALENCIA AND ALICANTE

THE CAPITAL OF THE REGION IS VALENCIA

La Costa del Azahar (Orange-blossom Coast) stretches from Vinaros to Almanzora, with the great port of Valencia in the centre. Orange groves grow right down to the coast, particularly in the northern section. Good beaches can be found around Benicassim and Peñíscola. South of Valencia, the Costa Blanca derives its name from its 170 miles or so of silvery-white beaches – some of the best beaches are to be found on this coast, especially between Gandía and Benidorm. As a result, it is one of the most popular tourist areas in Spain. The capital city of Valencia boasts a great nightlife and plays host to numerous festivals held throughout the year, including the unique fiesta of Las Fallas de Saint Joseph, when enormous papiermâché sculptures are set ablaze. Throughout it all are bullfights, music and fireworks. Alicante, the capital of the province of the same name, is dominated by the great Moorish castle of Santa Barbara, which offers marvellous views of the entire city. It also has several beaches in and around the town.

Places of interest

Castellón de la Plana: Santa Maria cathedral.

El Puig: monastery, Museum of Print and Graphics (world's smallest book).

La Albufera: vast lagoon, home to 250 species of bird.

Morella: medieval fortress town, dinosaur museum.

Oropesa: 16th century Tower of the King.

Peñíscola: medieval castle.

Cuisine of the region

Rice is the dominant ingredient, grown locally in paddy fields; the most famous dish is the *Paella Valenciana*. Soups and stews known locally as *ollas* are popular and seafood is readily available. Tiger nut milk is a soft drink exclusive to this region, usually accompanied by *fartons* (local pastries).

Arnadí: dessert with pumpkin and sweet potato.

Arroz al horno: rice, baked with chickpeas.

Arroz con costra: meat-based paella topped with baked egg crust.

Arroz negro: rice cooked with squid.

Bajoques farcides: stuffed peppers.

Olla recapte: with potatoes and pork.

Turrón: made of nuts and honey, either soft and flaky or hard like nougat.

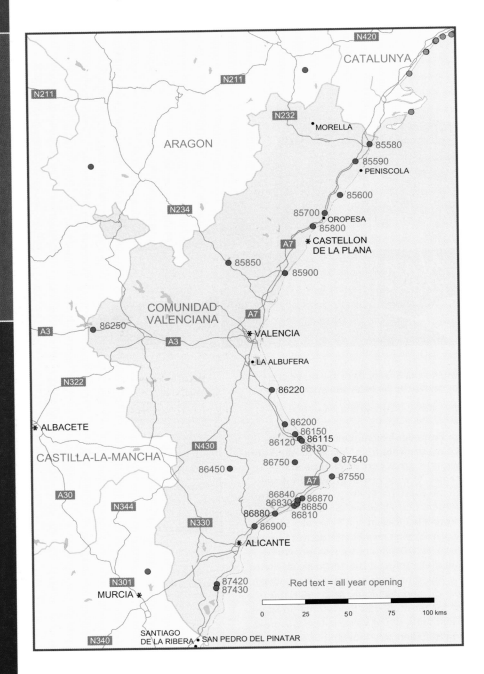

N420
CATALUNYA

N211

N211

N232

MORELLA

ARAGON

85580

85590
PENISCOLA

85600

N234

85700
OROPESA
85800

A7 ✳ CASTELLON
DE LA PLANA

85850

85900

COMUNIDAD
VALENCIANA

A7

A3 86250

A3 ✳ VALENCIA

N322 LA ALBUFERA

86220

✳ ALBACETE

86200
86150
86120 86115
86130
87540

CASTILLA-LA-MANCHA N430

86450 86750
87550

A30 A7

N344 86840 86870
86830 86850
86880 86810

N330 86900

✳ ALICANTE

N301 87420
87430
MURCIA ✳

Red text = all year opening

0   25   50   75   100 kms

N340 SANTIAGO
DE LA RIBERA SAN PEDRO DEL PINATAR

ES85580 Camping Vinaros

Ctra N340 km 1054, E-12500 Vinaros (Castelló)

Tel: 964 402 424. Email: info@campingvinaros.com

www.alanrogers.com/ES85580

Taking its name from the nearby seaside town with its fishing harbour and marina, this pleasant site has 258 flat numbered pitches of average size on flat ground. Mature trees provide shade and neat hedges separate the pitches, all of which have an individual sink. The site entrance is directly off the N340, with a restaurant outside the main boundary. There is a spacious entrance with lots of outside parking, but there is traffic noise. A swimming pool has a sunbathing area and a pleasant snack bar serves snacks all year. Large blocks of natural stone have been used for decoration around the site.

Facilities
Two exceptionally clean, fully equipped toilet blocks. Facilities for disabled campers. Laundry facilities. Motorcaravan services. Milk and bread delivered daily. Restaurant, snack bar and bar (all year). Play area. Swimming pool (1/4-30/10). Petanque. Musical and other entertainment in season. Large aviary and terrapin pool. Children's club (high season) and artistic activities for adults (all year). Off site: Beach and fishing 800 m. Bus service 500 m. Rail station. Vinaros 500 m. Golf 7 km.

Open: All year.

Directions
Take exit 43 (Ulldecona) from the A7 and head to Vinaros. At the junction with the N340, turn left and head towards Barcelona. Site is at 1054 km. marker directly off the N340, opposite a large garden centre. GPS: N40:29.586 E0:29.028

Charges guide
Per unit, all inclusive	€ 11,00 - € 16,00

All plus 7% VAT.

ES85590 Azahar Residencial Camping & Bungalow Park

Ptda Villarroyos s/n, E-12598 Peñiscola (Castelló)

Tel: 964 475 480. Email: info@campingazahar.com

www.alanrogers.com/ES85590

Set inland from the popular coastal resort of Peñiscola, Camping Azahar is set amongst the orange groves. This development of luxury residential and holiday park homes also provides 110 level touring pitches. All have electricity (6/10A), water and a drain, and are accessed by wide, gravel roads. Shade is provided by young palms, pines and plane trees. The pitches are not separated and large units can be accommodated. Recent developments at his new site include a spa with saunas, a steam room, sun beds, jacuzzi, hydrotherapy and massage. The sea and a 15 km. stretch of sandy beaches are within easy reach.

Facilities
Two modern toilet blocks include facilities for disabled visitors (all facilities and amenities are accessible). Washing machines and dryers. Shop. Bar/restaurant (all year). Swimming pool (Easter - Oct). Spa centre. Gym. Play area. Minigolf. Bicycle hire. Internet access. Activity programme. Dogs are not accepted July/Aug. Off site: Costa Azahar shopping and entertainment complex 1 km. Peñiscola 3 km. Fishing and golf 5 km. Beach 5 km.

Open: All year.

Directions
From A7 (Barcelona - Valencia) take exit 43 and N340 towards Peñiscola which will direct you onto the Cv141. Approaching outskirts of the town turn left signed Camping Azahar and follow signs. GPS: N40:24.120 E00:22.890

Charges guide
Per unit	€ 16,55 - € 24,15
extra person	€ 3,15 - € 4,00
child (3-10 yrs)	€ 2,88 - € 3,53

ES85900 Camping Monmar

Ctra Serratelles s/n, E-12593 Moncofa (Castelló)

Tel: 964 588 592. Email: campingmonmar@terra.es

www.alanrogers.com/ES85900

This purpose built, very neat site is in the small town of Moncofa, just 200 m. from the sea and right beside a water park with pools and slides. There are 170 gravel based pitches arranged in rows off tarmac access roads. The 100 touring pitches all have 6A electricity, water and a drain. Hedges have been planted to separate the pitches but these are still small so there is little shade (canopies can be rented in high season). The site's facilities and amenities are all very modern but small stone reminders of the area's Roman and Arab history are used to decorate corners of the site.

Facilities
Three modern toilet blocks are well placed and provide good, clean facilities. Free hot showers. Facilities and good access for disabled visitors. Laundry facilities. Shop (1/7-31/8). Bar and restaurant (weekends and high season). Swimming pool (all year). Good play area. Boules. Animals are not accepted. Off site: Beach 200 m. Water complex. Local amenities within walking distance.

Open: All year.

Directions
Turn off N340 Castellon - Valencia road on CV2250 signed Moncofa. Follow sign for tourist information office in town and then signs for site. GPS: N39:48.530 W0:07.686

Charges 2009
Per unit incl. 2 persons	€ 18,00 - € 26,00
extra person	€ 8,00

Discounts with this Guide.

BOOK THIS SITE

CALL 01580 214000

...we'll arrange everything

The Travel Service

Check real time availability and at-the-gate prices...

www.alanrogers.com

ES86115 Camping Azul

E-46780 Oliva (Valencia)

Tel: 962 854 106. Email: campingazul@ctv.es

www.alanrogers.com/ES86115

Camping Azul has an attractive location at Oliva Beach, north of Benidorm, and has direct access to a fine sandy beach with views of the mountains to the south. Pitches here vary in size, and are priced accordingly. They are mostly sandy with varying degrees of shade and most are equipped with electrical connections. A number of chalets are available for rent. This is a lively site in high season with a daily entertainment and activity programme, including a children's club and watersports. Sailing is possible at the nearby Oliva harbour. On-site amenities include a small bar and shop, as well as a cycle and car hire service. Oliva has traditionally been a popular resort with the Spanish but more recently foreign tourists have been attracted by the 10 km. of generally uncrowded beaches and excellent sports facilities. The Oliva Nova golf course and country club dominates much of the coastline and features a championship course, designed by Seve Ballesteros. Benidorm is a popular excursion destination with the large Terra Mitica theme park, Aqualandia water park and, of course, plenty of nightlife.

Facilities

Bar and snack bar. Shop. Children's play area. Activities and entertainment programme. Motorcaravan services. Tourist information. Direct beach access. Bicycle hire. Car hire service. Chalets for rent. Off site: Golf. Watersports. Fishing. Benidorm 40 km.

Open: 15 March - 31 December.

Directions

Leave the AP7 motorway at exit 61 (Oliva) and follow the N332 towards Oliva. Beyond Oliva follow signs for Platja d'Oliva. From here follow signs to the site which is well signed. GPS: N38:54.417 W00:04.117

Charges guide

Per unit incl. 2 persons and electricity	€ 24,35 - € 26,35
extra person	€ 4,30

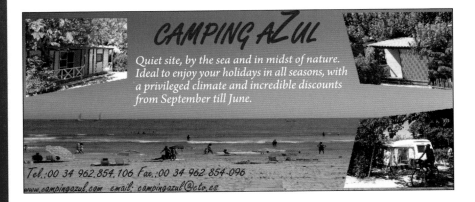

Quiet site, by the sea and in midst of nature. Ideal to enjoy your holidays in all seasons, with a privileged climate and incredible discounts from September till June.

Tel.:00 34 962.854.106 Fax.:00 34 962 854.096
www.campingazul.com email: campingazul@ctv.es

ES85700 Camping Torre La Sal 2

Cami l'Atall, E-12595 Ribera de Cabanes (Castelló)

Tel: 964 319 744. Email: camping@torrelasal2.com

www.alanrogers.com/ES85700

Torre La Sal 2 is a large site divided into two by a road, with a reception on each side with friendly, helpful staff. There are two pool complexes (one can be covered in cooler weather and is heated) which are both on the west side, whilst the beach (of shingle and sand) is on the east. Both sides have a restaurant – the restaurant on the beach side has two air conditioned wooden buildings and a terrace. On the western side are a children's play park, a large disco and sporting facilities including a sports centre, tennis, squash and two football pitches.

Facilities

Toilet facilities are of a good standard in both sections, four to the west and two to the east, with facilities for disabled campers in both. Baby rooms. Hot water to some sinks. Washing machines. Motorcaravan services. Shop, bars, restaurants and takeaway (all year). Swimming pools – one heated and covered. Jacuzzi and sauna (winter). Large play area. Games room. Sports facilities. Bullring. Hairdresser. Activities and entertainment. WiFi. Torches are required. Off site: Riding 10 km. Golf 20 km.

Open: All year.

Directions

From A7/E15 take exit 45 for Oropesa on N340. Move north to 1,000 km. marker and take road to the coast and town of Cami l'Atall. Site is well signed from here. GPS: N40:07.620 E00:09.480

Charges guide

Per person	€ 6,35
child (1-9 yrs)	€ 5,75
pitch incl. electricity	€ 15,25 - € 21,00
Plus 7% VAT.	

ES85600 Camping Playa Tropicana

Playa Tropicana, E-12579 Alcossebre (Castelló)

Tel: 964 412 463. Email: info@playatropicana.com

www.alanrogers.com/ES85600

Playa Tropicana is a unique site which will strike visitors immediately as being very different. It has been given a tropical theme with scores of 'Romanesque' white statues around the site including in the sanitary blocks. The site has 300 marked pitches separated by lines of flowering bushes under mature trees. The pitches vary in size (50-90 sq.m), most are shaded and there are electricity connections throughout (some need long leads). There are 50 pitches with shared water and drainage on their boundaries. The site has a delightful position away from the main hub of tourism, alongside a good sandy beach which shelves gently into the clean waters. To gain access to this it is necessary to cross a promenade in front of the site, which also has statues. It is in a quiet position and it is a drive rather than a walk to the centre of the village resort. The theme extends into an excellent restaurant where, in high season, you may dine on the upper terrace with uninterrupted sea views. A variety of entertainment is provided and there is also a children's club and social room with films and soft drinks bar in high season. The site has several large water features by the high quality restaurant (some are very cheeky!). Aviaries are housed in a corner of the site.

Facilities

Three sanitary blocks delightfully decorated, fully equipped and of excellent standard, include washbasins in private cabins. Baby baths and facilities for disabled people. Washing machine. Motorcaravan services. Gas supplies. Large supermarket. Superb restaurant, a little expensive. (Easter - late Sept). Swimming pool (18 x 11 m.) and children's pool. Playground. Bicycle hire. Children's club. Fishing. Torches necessary in some areas. No TVs allowed in July/Aug. Dogs are not accepted. Off site: Fishing and watersports on the beaches. Riding and boat launching 3 km. Golf 40 km.

Open: All year.

Directions

Alcoceber (or Alcossebre) is between Peñiscola and Oropesa. Turn off N340 at 1018 km. marker towards Alcossebre on CV142. Just before entering town proceed through two sets of traffic lights and turn right immediately after the second set, follow the road to the coast and site is 2.5 km. The entrance sliding gate faces the coast road and incorporates a pedestrian gate. Avoid alternative route given by GPS as that road is very narrow in places and very uneven. GPS: N40:13.320 E00:16.020

Charges guide

Per unit incl. 2 persons and electricity	€ 19,00 - € 63,00
extra person	€ 4,00 - € 8,00
child (1-10 yrs)	€ 3,00 - € 7,00

Camping Cheques accepted.

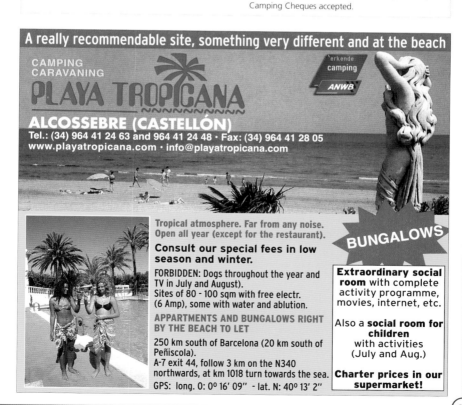

ES85850 Camping Altomira

Ctra Navajas - Pantano Regajo, E-12470 Navajas (Castelló)

Tel: **964 713 211**. Email: **info@campingaltomira.com**

www.alanrogers.com/ES85850

Camping Altomira is a terraced site in a rural, hillside setting, on the outskirts of a quiet village and offers superb views across the valleys and hills. There are 80 touring pitches situated on the higher levels of the site with some shade (artificial awnings are allowed). Due to the nature of this site we would not recommend it for people with mobility problems. Access roads to the gravel pitches are steep with some tight turns. All pitches, although not separated, have electricity and share water points with a neighbour. There are four toilet blocks, including a new one on the upper level. The two smaller ones accessed by stairways from the pitches.

Facilities

Four modern toilet blocks (see above) have showers in cubicles and open style washbasins. The larger block also housing laundry facilities is on the lowest level. Shop. Bar/restaurant with small terrace next to play area. TV room. Outdoor swimming pool. Communal barbecue area. Internet access. Bicycle hire. Off site: Village has a range of shops bars and restaurants. Lake fishing 2 km. Beach 13 km. Cycle route.

Open: All year.

Directions

From A23 (Sagunta - Teruel) road take Navajas exit (west of exit 31). Take CV216 through the town and follow CV213 to site which is 1 km. north of Navajas.

Charges guide

Per person	€ 5,95
child (1-10 yrs)	€ 4,65
pitch incl. car and electricity	€ 12,20 - € 13,60

Camping Cheques accepted.

ES86130 Camping Olé

Partida Aigua Morta s/n, E-46780 Oliva (Valencia)

Tel: **962 857 517**. Email: **campingole@hotmail.com**

www.alanrogers.com/ES86130

Olé is a large, well equipped seaside holiday site south of Valencia and close to the modern resort of Oliva. Its entrance is only 250 m. from the pleasant sandy beach. For those who do not want to share the busy beach, a large swimming pool is opened in July and August. There are 308 small pitches, 257 for touring (6/10A electricity), with the smallest ones for tents. Many pitches are separated with hedges with mature trees giving good shade to those away from the beach. The site has a large number of simple huts without their own sanitation. Access is difficult for large units.

Facilities

Three bright and clean sanitary blocks provide very reasonable facilities. The central one serves most of the touring pitches. Supermarket. Various vending machines. Bar with TV. Good quality restaurant. Takeaway. Swimming pool. Playground. Fishing off the beach. Off site: Many shops, restaurants and bars near. Golf club is close. Bicycle hire.

Open: All year.

Directions

From AP7 (Alicante - Valencia) take exit 61 onto N332 to Oliva. Exit at km. 312 or km. 310 and follow signs to site. GPS: N38:53.658 W0:03.216

Charges guide

Per unit incl. 2 persons and electricity	€ 29,00 - € 34,00
extra person	€ 5,38
child (3-10 yrs)	€ 4,06

Low season discounts.

ES86120 Euro Camping

Playa de Oliva, E-46780 Oliva (Valencia)

Tel: **962 854 098**. Email: **info@eurocamping-es.com**

www.alanrogers.com/ES86120

This English owned site with an intimate and friendly atmosphere is located beside the Playa de Oliva's golden sands. To reach it, you travel through the famous Valencia orange orchards. However be warned the final approach road to the site is very narrow and large units will find it necessary to drive through overhanging foliage. The rectangular site has tarmac and gravel roads. The 315 gravel pitches, all with electricity, are on the small side but are well maintained and eucalyptus trees provide shade for many. The reception staff are helpful and speak excellent English.

Facilities

Two mature sanitary blocks and a third newly built are well maintained. British style WCs, preset hot water in showers. Push-button lighting in toilet blocks – torch required. Toilet facilities for disabled campers. Washing machines and dryer. Motorcaravan services. Well stocked supermarket. Restaurant/bar. Play area. Petanque. Animation in high season. Fridge hire. WiFi. Electronic games. Off site: Golf and riding 1 km. Bicycle hire 5 km.

Open: All year.

Directions

From Alicante - Valencia autopista A7 take exit 61 onto N332 to Oliva. Exit at km. 213 or 210 and follow campsite signs. GPS: N38:54.300 W00:03.960

Charges guide

Per person	€ 4,70
child (2-10 yrs)	€ 3,26
pitch incl. electricity	€ 22,15 - € 36,75

Camping Cheques accepted.

ES85800 Bonterra Park

Avenida de Barcelona 47, E-12560 Benicasim (Castelló)

Tel: **964 300 007**. Email: **info@bonterrapark.com**   www.alanrogers.com/ES85800

If you are looking for a town site which is not too crowded and has very good facilities, this one may be for you. It is a 300 m. walk to a good beach – and parking is not too difficult. The site has 320 pitches (70-90 sq.m), all with electricity (6/10A) and a variety of bungalows, some attractively built in brick. There are dedicated 'green' pitches for tents. Bonterra has a clean, neat appearance with tarmac roads, gravel covered pitches, palms, grass and a number of trees which give good shade. Overhead sunshades are provided for the more open pitches in summer. There is a little road and rail noise. The site has an attractive pool complex including a covered pool for the winter months. The beach is good for scuba diving or snorkelling – hire facilities are available at Benicasim. This is a well run, Mediterranean style site with English spoken by reception staff. It is usefully located for visiting attractions such as the Carmelite monastery at Desierto de las Palmas, 6 km. distant or the historic town of Castellon.

Facilities

Four attractive, well maintained sanitary blocks provide some private cabins, washbasins with hot water, others with cold. Baby and dog showers. Facilities for disabled campers. Laundry. Motorcaravan services. Restaurant/bar. Shop. Swimming and paddling pools. Covered, heated pool (all year). Playground (some concrete bases). Tennis. Multisport court. Gym. Disco. Bicycle hire. Miniclub. Satellite TV. Internet access (WiFi). Off site: Town facilities. Sandy beach and fishing 500 m. Riding 3 km. Boat launching 5 km. Golf 10 km. Nature Park.

Open: All year.

Directions

Site is on the quiet old main road running through Benicasim. From either direction leave the N340 at km. 987. At roundabout turn left and travel for about 1.5 km. to site on the left (white painted walls)t. Look for two supermarkets, one 200 m. before site and a second directly opposite.Site is well signed. GPS: N40:03.416 E00:04.464

Charges guide

Per person	€ 3,75 - € 5,51
child (0-9 yrs)	€ 3,21 - € 4,49
pitch acc. to type and season	€ 8,72 - € 38,31
electricity	€ 3,75 - € 6,21

All plus 7% VAT. Less in low season and special long stay rates excl. July/Aug.

Check real time availability and at-the-gate prices...

www.**alanrogers**.com

ES86200 Camping L'Alqueria

E-46730 Gandia (Valencia)

Tel: **962 840 470**. Email: **info@campinggandia.es**

www.alanrogers.com/ES86200

Camping L'Aqueria is situated on the main Gandia to Gau road and, although in an urban location, it is near (2 km.) the beaches of Gandia. The 137 touring pitches are of a good size and on level ground, all with 6/10A electricity and easy access to one of many water points. Some are separated by dividing hedges and there is plenty of shade from mature trees. An orchard area to the rear of the site is designated for casual camping and is adjacent to the football pitch. There is a large swimming pool (caps required) with a sliding cover and a small paddling pool, adjacent but outside. Below the pools are a steam room, hydro-bath, sauna and jacuzzi. When we visited a temporary structure provide a small bar and snack bar whilst a new building at the entrance is being completed. A wooden cabin houses a small shop that is reasonably well stocked.

Facilities

Four toilet blocks, three with British style toilets, placed evenly around the site. Mostly combined shower and washbasin cubicles. Laundry facilities (key from reception). Motorcaravan service point. Shop (all year) and snack bar (1/4-15/10). Covered swimming pool (1/10-31/5) and outdoor paddling pool (1/6-15/10). Steam room and spa facilities. Fridge hire. Off site: Fishing, golf, bicycle hire, riding and boat launching 1 km. Beach 2 km. Shops, restaurant etc. within 1 km.

Open: All year.

Directions

From A7 (Valencia - Alicante) take exit 60 and follow signs to Gandia on the N332. Through the town follow signs for Gau and Platja de Gandia. Site is northwest of Gandia. GPS: N38:59.176 W0:09.819

Charges 2009

Per person	€ 3,48 - € 5,33
child	€ 2,86 - € 4,23
pitch incl. electricity	€ 15,26 - € 28,13

ES86250 Kiko Park Rural

Ctra Embalse Contreras km 3, E-46317 Villargordo del Cabriel (Valencia)

Tel: **962 139 082**. Email: **kikoparkrural@kikopark.com**

www.alanrogers.com/ES86250

Approaching Kiko Park Rural, you will see a small hilltop village appearing in a landscape of mountains, vines and a jewel-like lake. Kiko was a small village and farm and the village now forms the campsite and accommodation. Amenities are contained within the architecturally authentic buildings, some old and some new. The 76 pitches (with 6A electricity and water) all have stunning views, as do the swimming and paddling pools. Generous hedge plantings have been made which already afford some privacy. Hundreds of trees planted in 2003 are yet to provide shade due to their size, although this will soon remedy itself. The new Valencia - Madrid rail link will cut through the valley, due for 2009.

Facilities

Three toilet blocks are very well equipped, including excellent facilities for disabled people. Motorcaravan services. Gas. Well stocked shop. Excellent restaurant. Pleasant bar. Swimming and paddling pools. Very good playground. Bicycle hire. Animation in high season. Many adventurous activities can be arranged, including white water rafting, gorging, orienteering, trekking, bungee and riding. Large families and groups catered for. Off site: Fishing, canoeing and windsurfing on the lake. Village 3 km.

Open: All year.

Directions

From autopista A7/E15 on Valencia ring road (near the airport) take A3 to west. Villargordo del Cabriel is 80 km. towards Motilla. Take the village exit and follow signs through village and over a hill – spot the village on a hill 2 km. away. That is the campsite! GPS: N39:31.800 W01:26.400

Charges guide

Per person	€ 4,75 - € 5,95
child (up to 10 yrs)	€ 3,60 - € 4,10
pitch	€ 4,75 - € 13,45

ES86150 Kiko Park Oliva

E-46780 Oliva (Valencia)

Tel: **962 850 905**. Email: **kikopark@kikopark.com**

www.alanrogers.com/ES86150

Kiko Park is a smart site nestled behind protective sand dunes alongside a 'blue flag' beach. There are sets of attractively tiled steps over the dunes or a long boardwalk near the beach bar (good for prams and wheelchairs) to take you to the fine white sandy beach and the sea. The 180 large pitches all have electricity and the aim is to progressively upgrade all these to serviced 'super' pitches. There are plenty of flowers, hedging and trees adding shade, privacy and colour. A pool complex provides a spa, whirlpool, solarium, gym and a pool bar. An award winning restaurant with architecture that reminds one of a ship is near the tropical style beach-bar, both overlooking the marina, beautiful beach and sea. This is an excellent site for watersport enthusiasts, as it is beside a marina for boat launching. A wide variety of entertainment is provided all year.

Facilities

Four modern sanitary blocks are very clean with large showers, washbasins (a few in cabins), British style WCs and excellent facilities for disabled visitors (who will find a large part of this site flat and convenient). Laundry facilities. Motorcaravan services. Gas supplies. Supermarket (all year, excl. Sundays). Restaurant. Bar with TV. Beach-side bar and restaurant (all year). Swimming pools and gym. Playground. Watersports facilities. Diving school in high season (from mid June). Entertainment for children from mid June. Petanque. Bicycle hire. Off site: The footpath to the marina leads into the town, about 10 minutes walk. Indoor pool 1 km. Golf 5 km. Riding 7 km.

Open: All year.

Directions

From A7 north of Benidorm take exit 61 to the town and then the beach; site is at the northwest end. GPS: N38:55.896 W0:05.808

Charges guide

Per person	€ 3,21 - € 6,53
child (under 10 yrs)	€ 2,68 - € 5,78
pitch acc. to services	€ 10,60 - € 32,40
dog	€ 0,80 - € 2,68
electricity (per kWh)	€ 3,75

ES86450 Camping Mariola

Ctra Bocairent - Alcoi km 9, E-46880 Bocairent (Valencia)

Tel: **962 135 160**. Email: **info@campingmariola.com**

www.alanrogers.com/ES86450

Situated high in the Sierra Mariola National Park, in a beautiful rural setting but only 12 km. from the old town of Bocairent, this is a real taste of Spain with hilltop views all around. Used mainly by the Spanish, the site is an undiscovered jewel with 170 slightly sloping pitches. These are well spaced and have shade from a mixture of young and mature trees. An orchard area well away from the main site (with no amenities close by) is used for more casual camping. A traditional, stone built restaurant is slightly elevated with views over the site. Accessed by a few steps, this attractive building is covered in roses.

Facilities

Six identical small toilet blocks offer adequate facilities with British style WCs and showers with shared changing area. Open style washbasins. No facilities for disabled persons. Washing machine. Motorcaravan services. Small shop (weekends only). Bar/restaurant (weekends only in low season). Satellite TV. Outdoor pool with separate paddling pool (June - Sept). Two multisport pitches. Play area. Communal barbecue area. Children's club and entertainment (August only). Off site: Riding and golf 12 km.

Open: All year.

Directions

From the CV40 take exit for Ontinyent and follow the CV81. Pass town of Bocairent heading west and in 2 km. look for camping sign. Turn south on VV2031 to Alcoy. Turn right at first roundabout and straight on at next through small industrial estate. Onwards and upwards for about 10 km. and site is a turn to left. GPS: N38:45.16 W00:32.53

Charges guide

Per person	€ 4,45
pitch incl. electricity	€ 8,65- € 10,20

Camping Cheques accepted.

ES86220 Camping Santa Marta

Ctra de Faro km. 2, E-46400 Cullera (Alacant)

Tel: **961 721 440**. Email: **info@santamartacamping.com**   www.alanrogers.com/ES86220

Santa Marta is beautifully located on the slopes of a mountain and shaded by old Mediterranean umbrella pine trees. Originally a municipal site, it was recently purchased by a group of four campsites and is being fully renovated and modernised. There are 250 small, terraced pitches, 235 for touring with 16A electricity. Access can be difficult due to the many trees. An olive grove has been bought to make 18 motorcaravan pitches. During the winter of 2007/2008 the whole site was to be redeveloped. This includes better fire protection, new water points and better access to the pitches.

Facilities

Four toilet blocks are well equipped. Facilities for campers with disabilities. Separate baby room. Small shop. Bar with terrace serving snacks (all season). Swimming and paddling pools (23/6-16/9). Multisports field. Hiking trails. Barbeuces are not permitted. Off site: Town of Cullera. Beach 100 m. Shop facing the site.

Open: All year, excl. 16 December - 14 January.

Directions

From A7/N-332 (Valencia - Alicante) take exit for Cullera. Follow signs into Cullera and then for Faro or Far, through the town. From the centre follow signs to site. GPS: N39:10.617 W00:14.600

Charges guide

Per unit incl. 2 persons

Plus VAT.

ES86750 Camping Vall de Laguar

Ctra Sant Antonio 24, la Vall de Laguar, E-03791 Campell (Alacant)

Tel: **965 577 490**. Email: **info@campinglaguar.com**   www.alanrogers.com/ES86750

Near the pretty mountain-top village of Campell, this new site is perched high on the side of a mountain with breathtaking views of hilltop villages, the surrounding hills and distant sea. With a wholehearted welcome from the owners, the well maintained site promises a real taste of Spain. The pitches, pool, terrace and restaurant all share the views. The 68 average size gravel pitches are on terraces and all have electricity and water. Trees and hedges have been planted and give ample shade. This is a great place to get away from the coastal hustle, bustle and high rise of the beaches.

Facilities

Two new sanitary blocks have excellent clean facilities including some for disabled campers. Washing machines and dryers. WiFi. Restaurant with pretty terrace. Bar and pool bar. Swimming pool and small pool bar. Small entertainment programme in high season. Barbecue area with sinks. Torches useful. Off site: Attractive town close by. Golf and beach 18 km.

Open: All year.

Directions

Site is 20 km. west of Xabia/Javea. From the A7/E15 exit 62 head towards Ondara and Valencia on the N332 and at the roundabout on the Ondara by-pass head to Benidoleig/Orba At Orba turn right after the lights and follow the site signs GPS: N38:46.596 W0:06.300

Charges 2009

Per unit incl. 2 persons and electricity	€ 21,50 - € 24,00
extra person	€ 5,00

ES86810 Camping Villasol

Avenida Bernat de Sarria, E-03503 Benidorm (Alacant)

Tel: **965 850 422**. Email: **camping-villasol@dragonet.es**   www.alanrogers.com/ES86810

Benidorm is increasingly popular for winter stays and Villasol is a genuinely good, purpose built modern site. Many of the 309 well separated pitches are arranged on wide terraces which afford views of the mountains surrounding Benidorm. All pitches (80-85 sq.m.) have electricity and satellite TV connections, with 160 with full services for seasonal use. Shade is mainly artificial. Reservations are only accepted for winter stays of over three months (from 1 Oct). There is a small indoor pool, heated for winter use, and a very attractive, large outdoor pool complex (summer only) overlooked by the bar/restaurant and restaurant terrace.

Facilities

Modern toilet blocks provide free, controllable hot water to showers and washbasins and British WCs. Good facilities for disabled campers. Laundry facilities. Good value restaurant. Bar. Shop. Swimming pools, outdoor and indoor. Playground. Evening entertainment programme. Dogs are not accepted. Off site: Fishing and bicycle hire 1.3 km. Golf 8 km.

Open: All year.

Directions

From autopista exit 65 (Benidorm) and turn left at second set of traffic lights. After 1 km. at another set of lights turn right, then right again at next lights. Site is 400 m. GPS: N38:32.280 W00:07.140

Charges guide

Per person	€ 5,30 - € 6,90
pitch incl. electricity	€ 14,80 - € 22,50

All plus 7% VAT.
Good discounts for longer stays in winter.

ES86830 Camping Benisol

Avenida de la Comunidad Valenciana s/n, E-03500 Benidorm (Alacant)

Tel: **965 851 673**. Email: **campingbenisol@yahoo.es**   www.alanrogers.com/ES86830

Camping Benisol is a well developed and peaceful site with lush, green vegetation and a mountain background. Mature hedges and trees afford privacy to each pitch and some artificial shade is provided where necessary. There are 298 pitches of which around 115 are for touring units (60-80 sq.m). All have electrical hook-ups (4/6A) and 75 have drainage. Some daytime road noise should be expected. The site has an excellent restaurant serving traditional Spanish food at great prices, with a pretty, shaded terrace overlooking the pool with its palms and thatched pool bar.

Facilities

Modern sanitary facilities, heated in winter and kept very clean, have free, solar heated hot water to washbasins, showers and sinks. Laundry facilities. Gas supplies. Restaurant with terrace and bar (all year, closed 1 day a week). Shop. Swimming pool (Easter - Nov). Small, old style play area. Minigolf. Jogging track. Tennis. Golf driving range. ATM. Off site: Riding 1 km. Bicycle hire 3 km. Fishing (sea) 3 km. Golf 14 km. Bus route.

Open: All year.

Directions

Site is northeast of Benidorm. Exit N332 at 152 km. marker and take turn signed Playa Levant. Site is 100 m. on left off the main road, well signed. GPS: N38:33.540 W00:05.820

Charges guide

Per person	€ 4,95 - € 5,25
pitch incl. electricity	€ 16,05 - € 20,90

All plus 7% VAT. Less 15-60% in low seasons. No credit cards.

ES86850 Camping Caravaning El Raco

Avenida Doctor Severo Ochoa 19, E-03503 Benidorm (Alacant)

Tel: **965 868 552**. Email: **info@campingraco.com**   www.alanrogers.com/ES86850

This purpose built site with good facilities and very competitive prices provides about 425 pitches (90 for touring units). There is wide access from the Rincon de Loix road. The site is quietly situated 1.5 km. from the town, Levante beach and promenade. It has wide tarmac roads and pitches of 80 sq.m. or more, separated by low cypress hedging and some trees which provide some shade. Satellite TV connections are provided and there are 94 with all services including electricity. The restaurant, bar and elegant pools are all at the entrance, some distance from the touring pitches.

Facilities

Four large toilet blocks are well equipped. Facilities for disabled people. Dishwashing sinks. Laundry facilities. Gas supplies. Motorcaravan services. Restaurant. Bar. Well stocked shop. Busy bar with TV also open to public and good value restaurant. Outdoor swimming pool, no slides or diving board (1/4-31/10). Indoor heated pool (1/11-31/3). Playground. ATM. Off site: Beach 1 km. Bicycle hire 2 km. Golf 6 km. Theme parks.

Open: All year.

Directions

From autopista exit 65 (Benidorm, Levante) at second set of traffic lights turn left on N332 (Altea, Valencia). After 1.5 km. turn right (Levante Playa), then straight on at next lights for 300 m. to site on right. GPS: N38:32.922 W0:05.946

Charges guide

Per person	€ 5,20 - € 6,60
pitch incl. electricity	€ 16,50 - € 23,10

Discounts for longer stays. No credit cards.

ES86880 Camping Playa Paraiso

Ctra Valencia - Alicante, km. 136, Partida Paraiso, 66, E-03570 Villajoyosa (Alacant)

Tel: **966 851 838**. Email: **jacinto@playaparaiso.com**   www.alanrogers.com/ES86880

This site has been reopened by new owners who lost one of their other sites to housing developers. Major works are underway to provide modern facilities. When we visited in 2008 work was being done on the upper levels of the site to provide serviced pitches and a fully refurbished toilet block. On the lower level, the main site road is of tarmac and the gravel pitches are on shallow terraces as the site slopes gently down to the sea which provides one of the boundaries. The views are pleasant and trees provide a degree of shade for some pitches, with overhead sunshades on others. Electricity is available (16A). Since the opening of a new bypass, the site has become very quiet with only local traffic passing the gate, so pitches nearer the sea will hear no traffic noise at all. Access to the shingle beach is fenced with a key available from reception to open large gates to facilitate boat launching.

Facilities

Two toilet blocks are old but are well maintained and very clean. Spacious showers. Facilities for disabled visitors. Separate wooden building with facilities for babies. Washing machines and dryer. Bar and restaurant with limited menu. Indoor games and TV. Swimming pool (Easter - Oct). Off site: Beach. Bus stop 100 m. Riding and bicycle hire 15 km. Benidorm.

Open: 2 February - 31 December.

Directions

From the N332 take exit at km. 136 to Villajoysa Playa and site is 100 m. on the right. GPS: N38:30.003 W00:14.943

Charges guide

Per unit incl. 2 persons	€ 27,00 - € 43,00

Discounts of up to 50% in low season.

Check real time availability and at-the-gate prices...

www.**alanrogers**.com

ES86840 Camping Almafrá

Passeig de la Mitja Llegua, s/n, E-03503 Benidorm (Alacant)

Tel: 965 889 075. Email: info@campingalmafra.es

www.alanrogers.com/ES86840

Camping Almafrá is a good quality site, open all year and close to Benidorm. There are a good range of amenities here, most of which are open to the general public. These include a spa and wellness centre, a well equipped gym and tennis courts. There is a large outdoor pool and separate covered pool complex which also includes a steam bath and massage room. The site restaurant is large with a terrace overlooking the pool and surrounding gardens. Various grades of pitch are available, all including electricity (10A), and some with water, drainage and satellite TV and WiFi connections. Pitch sizes vary from 94-164 sq.m. A nursery service is available, as well as introductory swimming classes for babies. A children's club (for 5-12 year olds) operates in the peak season. Various family activities and entertainment are organized throughout the high season. Almafrá is located on the edge of Benidorm, close to the little town of Alfaz del Pi and to the beaches of Levante and Albir.

Facilities

Bar. Restaurant. Shop. Outdoor swimming pool. Covered swimming pool. Wellness centre. Gym. Tennis. Minigolf. Play area. Games room. Activity and entertainment programme. Children's club. Mobile homes and equipped tents for rent. Dogs are not accepted. Off site: Railway station/tram stop 200 m. Benidorm centre 5 km. Fishing. Golf. Cycle tracks.

Open: All year.

Directions

Leave the AP7 at exit 65 (Playa de Levante) and take the N332 towards Altea. After 4 km. turn left towards Alfaz del Pi and site entrance is to the left after a further 500 m.
GPS: N38:34.086 W00:05.678

Charges 2009

Per unit incl. 2 persons and electricity	€ 28,21 - € 48,20
extra person	€ 6,00 - € 9,48
child	€ 4,69 - € 7,08
dog	€ 2,14

Camping Cheques accepted.

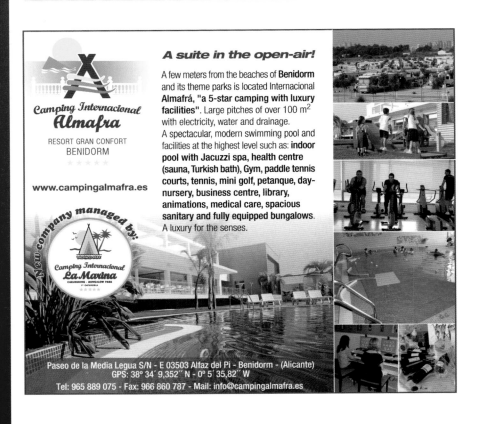

ES87430 Camping Marjal

Ctra N332 km 73,4, E-03140 Guardamar del Segura (Alacant)

Tel: 966 727 070. Email: camping@marjal.com   www.alanrogers.com/ES87430

Marjal is located beside the estuary of the Segura river, alongside the pine and eucalyptus forests of the Dunas de Guardamar natural park. The fine sandy beach can be reached through the forest (800 m). This is a new site with a huge lagoon-style pool and a superb sports complex. There are 212 pitches on this award winning site, all with water, electricity, drainage and satellite TV points, the ground covered with crushed marble, making the pitches clean and pleasant. There is some shade and the site has an open feel with lots of room for manoeuvring. Reception is housed in a delicately coloured building complete with a towering Mirador, topped by a weather-vane depicting the 'Garza Real' (heron) bird which frequents the local area and forms part of the site logo. The large leased restaurant overlooks the pools and the river that leads to the sea in the near distance. This situation is shared with the taperia (high season) and bar with large terraces fringed by trees, palms and pomegranates. The impressive pool/lagoon complex (1,100 sq.m) has a water cascade, an island bar plus bridge, one part sectioned as a pool for children and a jacuzzi. The extensive sports area is also impressive with qualified instructors who will customise your fitness programme whilst consulting the doctor. No effort has been spared here, the quality heated indoor pool, light-exercise room, sauna, solarium, beauty salon, fully equipped gym, including facilities for disabled visitors, are of the highest quality. Aerobics and physiotherapy are also on offer. All activities are discounted for campers. A programme of entertainment is provided for in season by a professional animation team.

Facilities

Three excellent heated toilet blocks have free hot water, elegant separators between sinks, spacious showers and some cabins. Each block has high quality facilities for babies and disabled campers, modern laundry and dishwashing rooms. Car wash. Well stocked supermarket. Restaurants. Bar. Large outdoor pool complex (1/6-31/10). Heated indoor pool (low season). Fitness suite. Jacuzzi. Sauna. Solarium. Aerobics and aquarobics. Play room. Minigolf. Floodlit tennis and soccer pitch. Bicycle hire. Games room. TV room. ATM. Business centre. Internet access. Off site: Beach 800 m. Riding or golf 4 km.

Open: All year.

Directions

On N332 40 km. south of Alicante, site is on the sea side between 73 and 74 km. markers.
GPS: N38:06.560 W00:39.280

Charges guide

Per person	€ 3,00 - € 8,50
child (4-12 yrs)	free - € 5,50
dog	€ 2,20 - € 3,20

MARJAL
Camping · Bungalows
GRUPOMARJAL

Ctra. N-332, Km.73,4
03140 Guardamar del Segura (Alicante) · Spain
Telf. 96 672 70 70 / 96 672 50 22
Fax : 96 672 66 95
camping@marjal.com
www.campingmarjal.com

MARJAL Natura
Camping · Caravaning
www.marjalnatura.com

Next opening

ES86870 Camping Cap Blanch

Playa de Cap Blanch 25, E-03590 Altea (Alacant)

Tel: **965 845 946**. Email: **capblanch@ctv.es**   www.alanrogers.com/ES86870

This well run, small site has plenty of character. It is open all year and is very popular for winter stays. Alongside the beach road, it has direct access to the pebble beach and is within a few hundred yards of all Albir's shops and restaurants. The 250 pitches on flat, hard gravel are of a good size and well maintained with 5A electricity. The site tends to be full in winter and is very popular with several nationalities, especially the Dutch. For winter stays, it would pay to get there before Christmas as January and February are the peak months. Although it is on the coast, the site is well sheltered and something of a sun-trap.

Facilities

The refurbished sanitary block can be heated and provides good facilities including some washbasins in cabins, baby facilities and a room for disabled visitors (both these accessed by key). Motorcaravan services. Gas supplies. Laundry. Bar and restaurant. Takeaway. Playground. Tennis. Boules. Fitness centre. Organised entertainment and courses. ATM. Off site: Restaurants, shops and commercial centre close. Golf 500 m. Bicycle hire 1 km. Riding 5 km.

Open: All year.

Directions

Site is on the Albir - Altea coast road and can be reached from either end. From N332, north or south, watch for sign Playa del Albir and proceed through Albir to the coast road. Site is on north side of Albir, well signed. GPS: N38:34.646 W0:03.871

Charges guide

Per person	€ 3,90 - € 6,00
child (3-12 yrs)	€ 3,25 - € 5,00
pitch incl. car	€ 8,45 - € 13,00
electricity	€ 3,25 - € 5,00

VAT included. Less 10-35% for low season stays 7-30 days, special rates for long stays.

ES87540 Camping Jávea

Ctra Cabo de la Nao km 1, Apdo 83, E-03730 Jávea (Alacant)

Tel: **965 791 070**. Email: **info@camping-javea.com**   www.alanrogers.com/ES87540

The 200 metre long access road to this site is a little unkempt as it passes some factories, but all changes on the final approach with palms, orange and pine trees, the latter playing host to a colony of parakeets. English is spoken at reception. The boxed hedges and palms surrounding this area with a backdrop of hills dotted with villas presents an attractive setting. Three hectares provides space for 214 numbered pitches with 183 for touring units. Flat, level and rectangular in shape, the pitches vary in size 60-80 sq.m. (not advised for caravans or motorhomes with an overall length exceeding 7 m). All have a granite chip surface and 8A electricity. Being a typical Spanish site, the pitches are not separated so units may be close to each other. Some pitches have artificial shade, although for most the pruned eucalyptus and pepper trees will suffice. The area has a large number of British residents so a degree of English is spoken by many shopkeepers and many restaurants provide multi language menus. Besides being popular for a summer holiday, Camping Jávea is open all year and could be of interest to those that wish to 'winter' in an excellent climate. Discounts can make an extended stay extremely viable.

Facilities

Two very clean, fully equipped, sanitary blocks include two children's toilets plus a baby bath. Two washing machines. Fridge hire. Small bar and restaurant where in high season you purchase bread and milk. Large swimming pool with lifeguard and sunbathing lawns. Play area. Boules. Electronic barriers (deposit for card). Caravan storage. WiFi. Tennis. Off site: Sandy beach 3 km. Old and New Jávea within easy walking distance with supermarkets and shops catering for all needs.

Open: All year.

Directions

Exit N332 for Jávea on A134, continue in direction of Port (road number changes to CV 734). At roundabout (Lidl supermarket) turn right signed Arenal Platges and Cabo de la Nao. Straight on at next roundabout to camping sign and slip road in 100 m. If you miss slip road go back from next roundabout. GPS: N38:47.000 E00:10.190

Charges guide

Per person	€ 5,22 - € 5,80
child	€ 4,50 - € 5,00
pitch	€ 12,42 - € 16,00
electricity	€ 3,50
dog	€ 1,50 - € 2,00

ES87420 Camping Internacional La Marina

Ctra N332 km 76, E-03194 La Marina (Alacant)

Tel: **965 419 200**. Email: **info@campinglamarina.com**   www.alanrogers.com/ES87420

Efficiently run by a friendly Belgian family, La Marina has 381 pitches of seven different types and size ranging from about 50 sq.m. for tents to 100 sq.m. with electricity (10/16A), TV, water and drainage. Artificial shade is provided and the pitches are extremely well maintained on level, well drained ground with a special area allocated for tents in a small orchard. The lagoon swimming pool complex is absolutely fabulous and has something for everyone (with lifeguards). William Le Metayer, the owner, is passionate about La Marina and it shows in his search for perfection. A magnificent new, modern building houses some superb extra amenities. These include a relaxed business centre with internet access, a tapas bar decorated with amazing ceramics (handmade by the owner's mother) and a quality restaurant with a water fountain feature and great views of the lagoon. There is also a conference centre and an extensive library, with the whole of the lower ground floor dedicated to children with a play area and a 'cyber zone' for teenagers. With a further bar and a soundproofed disco, the building is of an exceptional, eco-friendly standard. A fine fitness centre and covered, heated pool (14 x 7 m) are close by. A pedestrian gate at the rear of the site gives access to the long sandy beach through the coastal pine forest that is a feature of the area. We recommend this site very highly whatever type of holidaying camper you may be. Member of Leading Campings Group.

Facilities

The elegant sanitary blocks offer the very best of modern facilities. Heated in winter, they include private cabins and facilities for disabled visitors. Laundry facilities. Motorcaravan services. Gas. Supermarket. Bars. Restaurant (all year). Swimming pools (1/4-15/10). Indoor pool. Fitness centre. Sauna. Play rooms. Extensive activity and entertainment programme. Sports area. Tennis. Huge playground. Hairdresser. Bicycle hire. Off site: Fishing 500 m. Boat launching 5 km. Golf 7 km. Riding 15 km. Hourly bus service from outside the gate. Theme parks.

Open: All year.

Directions

Site is 2 km. west of La Marina. Leave N332 Guardamara de Segura - Santa Pola road at 75 km. marker if travelling north, or 78 km. marker if travelling south. Site is well signed. GPS: N38:07.779 W00:38.974

Charges 2009

Per person	€ 5,35 - € 8,00
child (under 10 yrs)	€ 3,75 - € 5,50
pitch incl. electricity, acc. to type and season	€ 22,58 - € 46,61
dog	free - € 2,14

Seven grades of pitch. Good discounts for longer stays 16/9-14/6, excluding Easter.

Do as the sun does, spend your holidays at...

RECOMENDED BY THE BEST EUROPEAN GUIDES

Welcome

VACANCE-PARK

Camping Internacional La Marina
CARAVANING - BUNGALOW PARK
1ᵃ CATEGORIA

www.campinglamarina.com

The Leading Campings & Caravaning Parks of Europe

Located at the Elche coastline, in the middle of nature, close to a beautiful beach of fine sand, distinguished with the ECC blue flag for optimal water quality. We offer luxurious installations: 3.000 m² thematic swimming complex, heated swimming-pool, fitness center, very high quality sanitary, entertainment to the highest level for children, young and adults. All free of charge for our clients. Prices in accordance with season and duration of the stays. Open all year.

COMUNITAT VALENCIANA   Costa Blanca

Information and reservations
Ctra. N-332a Km.76 - E-03194 LA MARINA (Alicante) SPAIN
Telf.: (34) 96 541 92 00 - Fax: (34) 96 541 91 10 • info@campinglamarina.com

Check real time availability and at-the-gate prices...

www.**alanrogers**.com

ES86900 Camping Costa Blanca

Calle Convento 143, N332 km 120,5, E-03560 El Campello (Alacant)

Tel: **965 630 670**. Email: **info@campingcostablanca.com**   www.alanrogers.com/ES86900

This small site has 80 pitches with 60 for tourers, some with views of the distant hills. Bungalows line three sides of the white walled rectangular site with a railway (not too busy) on the final side. Reception is efficient with keen staff members speaking several languages. The flat pitches are on gravel and all have 6A electricity. Some are small (40, 60 or 80 sq.m) and will be a challenge for large units. There is natural shade from trees and some artificial shade. A pleasant pool is the centre-piece with a bright poolside bar and a restaurant with a patio. The pool is open to the restaurant and bar area. The bar and restaurant are open all year offering a pleasant menu and a takeaway service. The beach is 500 metres away and there is a key at reception for the rear gate short cut. Lots of thought has gone into trying to provide facilities for visitors and the owner is keen that you enjoy your stay. If you are over 18 you can use the small weight training room or otherwise relax in the reading room.

Facilities

Four clean refurbished sanitary units offer a variety of facilities including cabins with toilet and basin, toilet and bidet, washbasins with hot water, others with cold. Two baby baths in cabins. Facilities for disabled campers. Washing machines and dryer. Motorcaravan services at entrance (€ 4 per token). Restaurant/bar (all year). Shop (1/7-1/10). Swimming pool. Basic play area (supervision required). Limited live entertainment in season. WiFi. Communal barbecue. Off site: Town facilities. Fishing, sailing and watersports 500 m. Riding 8 km. Golf 8 km. Boat launching 500 m. ATM 1 km.

Open: All year.

Directions

From the N332 take exit for El Campello Costa. Go through traffic lights onto the roundabout and take the first exit right. Site is visible from the roundabout although the name is behind the sliding gate! GPS: N38:26.167 W0:23.284

Charges guide

Per person	€ 3,50 - € 5,00
child (1-10 yrs)	€ 2,80 - € 4,00
pitch	€ 9,25 - € 23,35
electricity	€ 4,00

ES87550 Camping Caravanning Moraira

Camino Paellero 50, E-03724 Moraira-Teulada (Alacant)

Tel: **965 745 249**. Email: **campingmoraira@campingmoraira.com**   www.alanrogers.com/ES87550

This small hillside site with some views over the town and marina is quietly situated in an urban area amongst old pine trees and just 400 metres from a sheltered bay. Terracing provides shaded pitches of varying size, some really quite small (access to some of the upper pitches may be difficult for larger units). Some pitches have water and drainage and a few have sea views. There are electricity connections. An attractive irregularly shaped pool with paved sunbathing terrace is below the small bar/restaurant and terrace. The pool has observation windows where you can watch the swimmers, and is used for sub-aqua instruction. The site runs a professional diving school for all levels (the diving here is good and the water warm, even in winter). A sandy beach is 1.5 km. A large, painted water tower stands at the top of the site. The reception building is being extended to provide a range of new facilities.

Facilities

The high quality toilet block, with polished granite floors and marble fittings, is built to a unique and ultra-modern design with extra large free hot showers (hot water may be variable during the winter). Washing machine and dryer. Motorcaravan services. Bar/restaurant and shop (1/7-30/9). Small swimming pool (not all year). Sub-aqua with instruction. Tennis. Torches may be required. Off site: Shops, bars and restaurants within walking distance. Beach 1.5 km. Fishing 400 m. Bicycle hire 1 km. Golf 8 km.

Open: All year.

Directions

Best approach is from Teulada. From A7 exit 63 take N332 and in 3.5 km. turn right (Teulada and Moraira). In Teulada fork right to Moraira. At junction at town entrance turn right signed Calpe and in 1 km. turn right into road to site on bend immediately after Res. Don Julio. Do not take the first right, as the signs seem to indicate, otherwise you will go round in a loop. GPS: N38:41.520 E00:08.400

Charges guide

Per person	€ 6,42
child (4-9 yrs)	€ 4,82
pitch incl. car	€ 16,60
electricity	€ 3,85
All plus 7% VAT. Less 15-60% in low season.	

In the province of Murcia you'll find sandy beaches, dunes and unspoilt coves along the coast; inland hills and valleys plus the regional parks of Sierra de Carche, Sierra de la Pila, Sierra de Espuña, and Carrascoy and El Valle.

Alan Rogers

THE CAPITAL OF THE REGION IS THE CITY OF MURCIA

Murcia, the capital of the region, was founded in the ninth century by the Moors on the banks of the Río Segura. The square of Cardinal Belluga houses two of the town's architectural gems, the Episcopal Palace and the Cathedral, and there is a range of museums and exhibitions to visit. With narrow medieval streets, the characterful town of Cartagena has lots of bars and restaurants plus two nautical museums: the National Museum of Maritime Archaeology and the Naval Museum. Also on a nautical theme, the International Nautical Week is celebrated here in June. Along the coast there are numerous beaches offering a wide range of water sports: sailing, windsurfing, canoeing, water skiing and diving. And the area between the coastal towns of Águilas and Mazarrón is a breeding ground for tortoises and eagles. Inland are the historic towns of Lorca and Caravaca de le Cruz. The former is known as the 'baroque city' with its examples of baroque architecture, seen in the parish churches, convents, and houses; the latter too is home to beautiful churches, including El Santuario de Vera Cruz.

Places of interest

Águilas: seaside town with good beaches.

Moratalla: pretty village, castle offering stunning views of the surrounding countryside and forests.

Puerto de Mazarrón: Enchanted City of Bolnuevo - a small area of eroded rocks, nature reserve and lagoon at La Rambla de Moreras.

San Pedro del Pinatar: seaside resort, La Pagan beach is renowned for its therapeutic mud, which reputedly relieves rheumatism and is good for the skin.

Santiago de la Ribera: upmarket resort with sailing club.

Cuisine of the region

Vegetables are important and found in nearly every dish. Fish is also popular, cooked in a salt crust or *a la espalda* (lightly fried and baked), and usually accompanied by rice. Fig bread is a speciality of the region.

Bizcochos borrachos: sponge soaked in wine and syrup.

Cabello de Ángel: pumpkin strands in syrup.

Caldero: made of rice, fish and the hot ñora pepper.

Caldo con pelotas: stew made of turkey with meatballs.

Chuletas de cordero al ajo cabañil: suckling lamb chops served with a dressing of garlic and vinegar.

Tocino de cielo: dessert made with egg yolks and syrup.

Yemas de Caravaca: cake made with egg yolks.

ES87520 Camping Naturista El Portus

El Portus, E-30394 Cartagena (Murcia)

Tel: **968 553 052**. Email: **elportus@elportus.com**

www.alanrogers.com/ES87520

Set in a secluded south facing bay fringed by mountains, El Portus is a fairly large naturist site enjoying magnificent views and with direct access to a small sand and pebble beach. This part of Spain enjoys almost all year round sunshine. There are some 400 pitches, 300 for tourers, ranging from 60-100 sq.m, all but a few having electricity (6A). They are mostly on fairly level, if somewhat stony and barren ground. El Portus has a reasonable amount of shade from established trees and nearly every pitch has a view. Residential units are situated on the hillside above the site.

Facilities

Five acceptable toilet blocks, all unisex, are of varying styles and fully equipped. Opened as required, they are clean and bright. Showers all with hot water. Unit for disabled visitors, key from reception. Washing machines. Motorcaravan services. Well stocked shop. Bar with TV and library. Restaurants. The beach restaurant is closed in low season. Swimming pools (June - Sept). Wellness centre. Play area. Tennis. Petanque. Yoga. Scuba-diving club (high season). Windsurfing. Spanish lessons. Small boat moorings. Entertainment programme all season. Off site: Fishing from beach. Golf 28 km. Riding 40 km.

Open: All year.

Directions

Site is on the coast, 10 km. west of Cartagena. Follow signs to Mazarron then take E22 to Canteras. Site is well signed for 4 km. If approaching through Cartagena, exit the town on N332 following signs for Canteras. Site signed on joining the N332. GPS: N37:35.100 W01:04.030

Charges guide

Per person	€ 7,00
child (3-9 yrs)	€ 5,00
pitch	€ 16,30
pitch incl. 6A electricity	€ 22,20
dog	€ 4,70

Plus 7% VAT.
Special discounts for longer stays and in low season. Camping Cheques accepted.

Check real time availability and at-the-gate prices...

www.**alanrogers**.com

ES87530 Caravaning La Manga

Autovia Cartagena - La Manga Salida 11, E-30386 La Manga del Mar Menor (Murcia)
Tel: 902 021 352. Email: lamanga@caravaning.es

This is a very large well equipped 'holiday style' site with its own beach and both indoor and outdoor pools. With a good number of typical Spanish long stay units, the length of the site is impressive (1 km) and a bicycle is very helpful for getting about. The 1,000 regularly laid out, gravel touring pitches (100 or 110 sq. m) are generally separated by hedges which also provide a degree of shade. Each has 10A electricity supply, water and the possibility of satellite TV reception. This site's excellent facilities are ideally suited for holidays in the winter when the weather is very pleasantly warm. If you are suffering from aches and pains try the famous local mud treatment. Reception will assist with bookings. November daytime temperatures usually exceed 20°C. La Manga is a 22 km. long narrow strip of land, bordered by the Mediterranean on one side and by the Mar Menor on the other. There are sandy bathing beaches on both sides and considerable development in terms of hotels, apartments, restaurants, night clubs, etc. in between – a little reminiscent of Miami Beach! The very end of the southern part is great for 'getting away from it all' (take a picnic for the beach and be sure to go over the little bridge for privacy). The campsite is situated on the approach to 'the strip' enjoying the benefit of its own semi-private beach with impressive tall palm trees alongside the Mar Menor which provides shallow warm waters, ideal for families with children. Here you will find a sailing, canoeing and windsurfing school, and an excellent restaurant/bar serving traditional Spanish tapas and meals. In winter, when British occupancy exceeds 60%, typical British meals are available including Sunday roast and full breakfasts.

Facilities

Nine clean toilet blocks of standard design, well spaced around the site, include washbasins (all with hot water). Laundry. Gas supplies. Large well stocked supermarket. Restaurant. Bar. Snack bar. Swimming pool complex (April - Sept). Indoor pool, gymnasium (April - Oct), sauna, jacuzzi and massage service. New outdoor fitness course for adults. Open air family cinema (July/Aug). Tennis. Petanque. Minigolf. Play area. Watersports school. Internet café (also WiFi). Winter activities including Spanish classes. Pet washing area. Off site: Buses to Cartagena and Murcia from outside site. Golf, bicycle hire and riding 5 km.

Open: All year.

Directions

Use exit 11 from MU312 dual carriageway towards Cabo de Palos, signed Playa Honda (site signed also). Cross road bridge and double back on yourself. The site entrance is clearly visible beside dual carriageway with many flags flying. GPS: N37:37.467 W00:44.665

Charges guide

Per pitch incl. 2 persons	€ 18,85 - € 33,00
extra person	€ 3,85 - € 4,80
child	€ 3,30 - € 3,85
dog	€ 1,25

All plus 7% VAT. Discounts and special prices for low season and long winter stays. Camping Cheques accepted.

ES87440 Camping La Puerta

Ctra de La Puerta s/n, E-30440 Moratalla (Murcia)

Tel: 968 730 008. Email: info@campinglapuerta.com

www.alanrogers.com/ES87440

Camping La Puerta is part of the Camping La Manga group. It is a typical Spanish weekend and holiday site and advance booking is essential for high season and most weekends. Set in the secluded hills above Moratalla, it provides a rural base from which to explore the surrounding countryside. It is a place where you can relax and forget about the hustle and bustle of city life whilst relaxing around the magnificent pool complex. Most of the 159 touring pitches are rather small and large units could have difficulty in manoeuvring due to randomly growing trees. Limited English is spoken.

Facilities

Three fully fitted sanitary blocks provide toilets, washbasins and shower cubicles. Facilities for disabled visitors. Washing machines. Shop. Bar and terrace. Cafeteria and restaurant serving a variety of local dishes. Play area. Tennis. Fishing. Barbecues are not permitted. Off site: Riding 5 km.

Open: All year.

Directions

From the A7 (Murcia - Lorca) exit at 651 km onto the C415 in the direction of Mula and Caravaca. Follow signs to Moratalla and then on to site which is well signed. GPS: N38:12.333 W01:55.185

Charges guide

Per person	€ 3,35 - € 4,35
pitch incl. electricity	€ 10,80 - € 14,05

Camping Cheques accepted.

ES87450 Camping La Fuente

Camino de La Bocamina, E-30626 Banos de Fortuna (Murcia)

Tel: 968 685 125. Email: info@campingfuente.com

www.alanrogers.com/ES87450

Located in an area known for its thermal waters since Roman and Moorish times and with just 87 pitches and 6 bungalows, La Fuente is a gem. Unusually winter is high season here. The main attraction here is the huge hydrotherapy centre where the water is constant at 36°C all year. The pool can be covered in inclement weather. The site is in two sections, one where pitches are in standard rows and the other where they are in circles around blocks. The hard, flat pitches are on shingle (rock pegs advised), have 10A electricity and 53 have their own mini-sanitary unit.

Facilities

All pitches have their own facilities including a unit for disabled campers. Washing machines and dryers. High quality restaurant shared with accommodation guests. Snack bar by pool. Supermarket. Bicycle hire. Communal barbecues. Jacuzzi. Off site: Spa town, massage therapies, hot pools 500 m. Fortuna, shops, bars, restaurants 3 km. Golf and riding 20 km.

Open: All year.

Directions

From A7/E15 Alicante - Murcia road take C3223 to Fortuna then follow signs to Banos de Fortuna. The site with its bright yellow walls can be easily seen from the road and is very well signed in the town. GPS: N38:12.409 W01:06.439

Charges guide

Per person	€ 3,25
child (3-12 yrs)	€ 1,25
pitch incl. electricity	€ 9,50 - € 11,50

ES87480 Camping Los Madriles

Ctra de la Azohia km 4.5, E-30868 Isla Plana (Murcia)

Tel: 968 152 151. Email: camplosmadriles@terra.es

www.alanrogers.com/ES87480

An exceptional site with super facilities, Los Madriles is run by a hard working team, with continual improvements being made. Twenty kilometres west of Cartegena, the approach to the site and the surrounding area is fairly unremarkable, but the site is not. A fairly steep access road leads to 313 flat, good to large size terraced pitches, each having electricity, water and a waste point. Most have shade from large trees with many benefiting from panoramic views of the sea or behind to the mountains. The site has huge rectangular and lagoon style pools with water sprays and jacuzzis.

Facilities

Four sanitary blocks and one small toilet block provide excellent facilities, including services in one block for disabled campers. Private wash cabins. Washing machines and dryers. Motorcaravan services. Car wash. Supermarket, restaurant/snack bar and bar (all open all season but hours are limited). Swimming pools with jacuzzi. Boules. Play areas. Animals are not accepted. Off site: Town close by. Beach 800 m and fishing 800 m. (Licence required, purchase in Puerto Mazarron). Boat launching 3 km. Riding 6 km. Golf 20 km.

Open: All year.

Directions

From E15/A7 take exit 845 and follow RM3 in direction of Cartagena, Fuente Alamo and Mazarron (do not turn into Mazarron). Continue towards Puerto Mazarron and take N332 (Cartagena). On reaching coast continue with N332 (Cartagena and Alicante). At roundabout turn right towards Isla Plana and La Azohia. Site is well signed and on the left in 5 km. GPS: N37:34.410 W01:11.470

Charges guide

Per person	€ 4,50 - € 5,50
child (1-7 yrs)	€ 4,50 - € 5,50
pitch incl. electricity	€ 17,00 - € 20,00

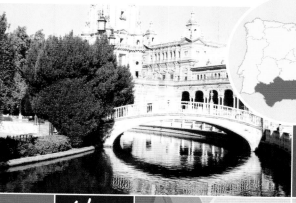

Famous for its sun, its beautiful traditions, its poets, original folklore, age-old history and magnificent heritage left behind by the Moors, Andalucía is one of the most attractive regions in Spain.

Alan Rogers

THIS COMPRISES EIGHT PROVINCES: ALMERIA, CADIZ, CORDOBA, GRANADA, HUELVA, MALAGA, JAEN AND SEVILLE

THE REGIONAL CAPITAL IS SEVILLE

With the River Guadalquivir running through it, the charming city of Seville is one of the most visited places in the region. The old city, with its great monuments; the Giralda tower, Cathedral and the Alcázar, plus the narrow, winding streets of Santa Cruz, is particularly popular. Also on the Guadalquivir, Cordoba is located northeast of Seville. It too has a picturesque Jewish Quarter along with a rich Moorish heritage. Indeed, the Mezquita is one of the grandest mosques ever built by the Moors in Spain. Located further east on the foothills of the Sierra Nevada mountain range, Granada is home to the impressive Alhambra, a group of distinct buildings including a Royal Palace, splendid gardens, and the fortress of Alcazaba. The Sierra Nevada, Spain's highest range, offers good skiing and trekking. Further south, you'll find the fine beaches and tourist areas of the Costa Tropical and the Costa del Sol, including the developed resort of Malaga. There are more beaches on the west coast plus one of the oldest settlements in Spain, the bustling port of Cádiz.

Places of interest

Almeria: preserved Moorish heritage with greatest purity. Located on a beautiful bay.

Casa-Museo Pablo Ruiz Picasso: art museum including collection of originals by Pablo Picasso.

Jaen: medieval fortress, Renaissance cathedral, 11th century Moorish baths, Santa Catalina castle.

Jerez de la Frontera: birthplace of sherry and Spanish brandy, site of renowned equestrian school.

Mijas: enchanting village, with narrow streets bordered by brilliantly white-washed houses.

Parque Natural de las Sierras de Cazorla y Segura: largest park in Spain with mountains, river gorges, forests and wildlife.

Ronda: beautiful town on the edge of an abrupt rocky precipice.

Cuisine of the region

Andalucía has more tapas bars than anywhere else in Spain. Sea food in abundance, fresh vegetables and fruit: oranges from Cordoba; persimmons, pomegranates, figs, strawberries from Alpujarra; avocados, mangos, guavas, papayas from the coast of Granada and Malaga. Locally produced wine and sherry.

Alboronía: vegetable stew.

Alfajors: almond and nut pastry.

Gazpacho ajoblanco: cold soup with garlic and almond.

Gazpacho salmorejo: much thicker and made with tomatoes only.

Pestiños: honey coated pastries.

Tocinillo de cielo: pudding made with egg yolks and syrup.

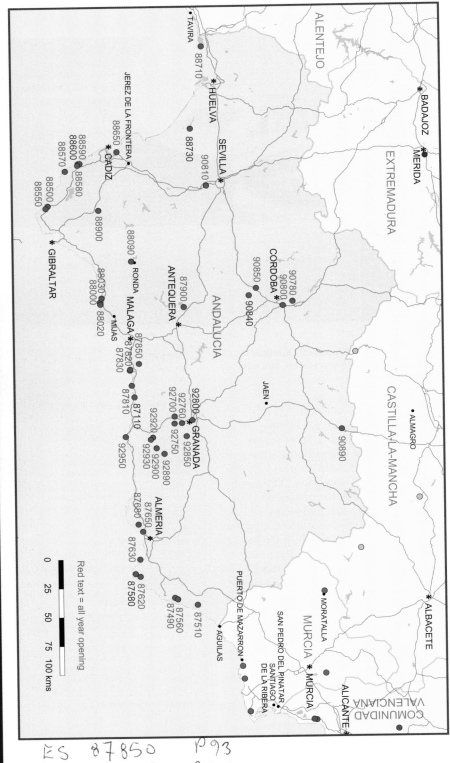

ES 87850   P93
87810   P95
92950 - P92

Check real time availability and at-the-gate prices...

www.**alanrogers**.com

ES90890 Camping Despenaperros

Ctra Infanta Elena, E-23213 Santa Elena (Jaén)

Tel: **953 664 192**. Email: **info@campingdespenaperros.com**   www.alanrogers.com/ES90890

This site is on the edge of Santa Elena in a natural park with shade from mature pine trees. This is a good place to stay en-route from Madrid to the Costa del Sol or to just explore the surrounding countryside. The 116 pitches are fully serviced including a satellite TV/internet link. All rubbish must be taken to large bins outside the site gates (a long walk from the other end of the site). The site is run in a very friendly manner where nothing is too much trouble. Reception has a monitor link with tourist information and access to the region's sites of interest.

Facilities

Two traditional, central sanitary blocks have Turkish style WCs and well equipped showers. One washing machine (launderette in town). Shop. Excellent bar (all year) and charming restaurant (12/3-20/10). Swimming pools (15/6-15/9). Tennis. Caravan storage. Night security. Off site: Walking, riding and mountain sports nearby. The main road gives good access to Jaén and Valdepeñas.

Open: All year.

Directions

Travelling north towards Madrid on A4 (E5) take exit 259 (Santa Elena). Drive through town and site is on right up steep slope (alternative entrance for tall vehicles. Travelling south towards Bailén take exit 257 and as above. GPS: N38:20.584 W03:32.117

Charges guide

Per person	€ 3,90 - € 4,40
pitch incl. electricity	€ 12,15 - € 12,50

ES87490 Camping Sopalmo

Apdo 761, Sopalmo, E-04638 Mojacar (Almería)

Tel: **950 478 413**. Email: **info@campingsopalmoelcortijillo.com**   www.alanrogers.com/ES87490

This is a tiny, homely site run by the cheerful Simon and his charming wife Macu (both speaking some English) who are determined that you will enjoy your stay. The site is on three levels (with a slightly steep gravel track to the gates) with space for 32 tents, caravans or medium sized motorcaravans. All the pitches are marked, level and on gravel with electricity (6A). The site is unspoilt and has much rustic charm with the family house providing the focal point. Attractive trees and shrubs around the site include olives, figs, mimosa and cacti.

Facilities

The small sanitary block is very clean and fully equipped. Hot showers assisted by solar power. Facilities for disabled campers. Basic laundry and dishwashing facilities. Bar. Breakfast available in summer and the baker calls at 10.30 daily. Torch useful. Internet access. Poor to nil mobile phone reception. Off site: Bus to Mojecar from site. Beach 2 km. Nearest serious shops 5 km. Riding 6 km. Golf 10 km.

Open: All year.

Directions

Exit from main coast road (N340) at junction 520 (northeast of Almeria). Take the AL152 (formerly A150) to Mojacar Playa and continue south towards Carboneras. Site is 6 km. south of Mojacar Playa, signed off the road GPS: N37:03.920 W01:52.129

Charges 2009

Per person	€ 3,65 - € 4,30
pitch incl. electricity	€ 9,70 - € 12,30

Reductions for low season. No credit cards.

ES87510 Camping Cuevas Mar

Cuevas del Almanzora, E-04618 Palomares (Almería)

Tel: **950 467 382**. Email: **cuevasmar@arrakis.es**   www.alanrogers.com/ES87510

The popularity of this well-established, neat and tidy campsite during the warm winter months has demanded an extension to the site with the number of pitches now 180. The 'new' area already has a mature appearance with shrubs and trees planted to provide pitch dividers and shade. Some of these places are quite close to the road although a little nearer the beach at 200 m. All the pitches are flat and are of an acceptable 80-100 sq.m. with a stone chip surface and 6/10A electricity supply. During the hot summer months overhead shade canopies are erected on several pitches.

Facilities

The well designed sanitary blocks provide sufficient showers and toilets for all. Washing machines and dryer. Water to the taps is to European standard, however a single tap provides high quality water from a nearby mountain spring source (175 m. from some pitches). Daily fresh bread, emergency provisions and gas from reception. Open air unheated swimming pool and jacuzzi (May - Sept). Off site: Many restaurants in the near vicinity. Fishing 200 m. Bicycle hire 3 km. Golf 4 km. Riding 12 km. Beach 600 m.

Open: All year.

Directions

From E15/A7 take exit 537, pass under autovia and follow signs for Cuevas Del Almanzora. At T-junction turn right toward Palomares. In 1 km. on right hand bend turn left towards Palomares. Continue to roundabout, take first exit and site is on left in 2 km. GPS: N37:14.220 W01:47.880

Charges guide

Per unit incl. 1 or 2 persons	€ 8,60 - € 17,90
extra person	€ 4,20
electricity (6A)	€ 3,00

Generous discounts for longer winter stays. No credit cards.

ES87560 Camping Cueva Negra

Camino Lotaza 2, Frenta - Playa Macenas, E-04638 Mojacar (Almería)
Tel: 950 475 855. Email: info@campingcuevanegra.es

www.alanrogers.com/ES87560

This tiny jewel of a site, just 9 km. south of Mojacar is approached by a short, steep and winding road with passing places. There are only 15 pitches but they are all 100 sq.m. and have electricity, water and a drain, with artificial shade provided in summer. The elevated site is attractively laid out with views to the nearby sea. The superb covered swimming pool has four jacuzzis and a large, partly covered terrace with an open air shower for disabled people. There are facilities for tennis and petanque and a play area for children.

Facilities

Modern toilet block with facilities for disabled visitors. Laundry with washing machine and dryer. Well stocked shop and small bar (all year). Takeaway (high season). Covered swimming pool (all year). Tennis. Petanque. Play area. Apartment and bungalow for rent. Off site: Beach 400 m. Five golf courses nearby. The towns of Mojacar, Aguilas Nijar and Almeria within easy reach.

Open: All year.

Directions

Site is 9 km. south of Mojacar on the Mojacar - Carboneras road, on the right when travelling south. GPS: N37:05.205 W01:51.238

Charges guide

Per person	€ 3,41 - € 5.57
pitch	€ 9.28 - € 15.47

Credit cards accepted but 3% discount for cash.
Special prices for long stays in low season.

ES87580 Camping Tau de San José

Calle de Cala Higuera s/n, E-04118 San José (Almería)
Tel: 950 380 166. Email: tau@parquenatural.com

www.alanrogers.com/ES87580

This attractive and quiet site was originally part of an old farm, typical of this region. It is well shaded and is particularly suitable for tents and low units. There is limited space for caravans and campers and phoning ahead is strongly advised. Electricity hook-ups are provided (6/16A) but long leads may be required. A level site, it is set in a nature park and is about 300 m. from the beach and the unspoilt village of San José. There is a new toilet block and the small bar/restaurant has a Spanish atmosphere with a large shady terrace outside, ideal for that relaxing drink.

Facilities

Large modern toilet block with extra unisex showers. Facilities for disabled visitors. Laundry. Small, well stocked shop. Covered barbecue area. A further covered area has pool and electronic games. Play area. Dogs are not accepted. Off site: Village of San José where fish restaurants are a speciality, beach and harbour 300 m. Almeria, and the white villages of Nijar and Mojacar are close by.

Open: Easter - 1 October.

Directions

From E15 exit 471 or 479 follow signs for San José. Site is north of the village on left hand side (keep the white buildings to your right). Follow made up road to site.

Charges guide

Per person	€ 4,75
pitch incl. car	€ 9,50 - € 13,00
electricity	€ 3,50 - € 5,50

Credit cards accepted for a minimum €100.

ES87620 Camping Los Escullos

Paraje de los Escullos s/n, E-04118 San Jose-Nijar (Almería)
Tel: 950 389 811. Email: info@losescullossanjose.com

www.alanrogers.com/ES87620

This gradually sloping, well maintained, medium sized site has many bungalows and permanent caravans. Visiting touring units have 100 pitches (60-70 sq.m) divided by hedges and trees and each with a 16A electric supply. Specific taps about the grounds provide drinking water. The months of May and June are very quiet, whilst the site is near full through the winter months with many British visitors enjoying the warm climate. Food at the restaurant is good including typical Spanish 'menu del dia' at very low prices. The salinas on the approach to Cabo de Gata are famous for bird life (including flocks of pink flamingo).

Facilities

The main sanitary block is large, clean and fully equipped including facilities for disabled campers. Second small block close to reception. Shop. Bar/restaurant (full board available). Takeaway (15/6-15/9). Large outdoor pool. Jacuzzi. Hairdresser. Massage. Gym. Internet access. Scuba diving. TV room. Bicycle hire. Only gas or electric barbecues permitted. Off site: No public transport (a vehicle is required here). Fishing 1 km. Riding 7 km. Golf 25 km. Walking track to nearest beach (stony) 1 km.

Open: All year.

Directions

From A7/E15 autovia exit at either exit 479 or 471 in direction of San Jose. On approach to San Jose left turn toward Los Escullos. Site is signed. GPS: N36:48.173 W2:04.654

Charges guide

Per person	€ 5,00 - € 6,50
child (2-14 yrs)	€ 4,00 - € 5,50
pitch incl. electricity	€ 15,00 - € 18,75

ES87630 Camping Cabo de Gata

Ctra Cabo de Gata s/n, Cortijo Ferrón, E-04150 Cabo de Gata (Almería)

Tel: 950 160 443. Email: info@campingcabodegata.com   www.alanrogers.com/ES87630

Since this medium sized site opened in 1993, it has strived continually to make improvements and today can be regarded as a very pleasant, all year campsite offering facilities to a good standard. Very popular with British visitors through the winter, it is located within the Cabo de Gata-Nijar natural park and set in open farmland, yet is only a 1 km. walk from a fine sandy beach. The 250 gravel pitches are level and of a reasonable size, with 6/16A electricity and limited shade from maturing trees or canopies. There are specific areas for very large units and 7 chalets for rent.

Facilities

Two, well maintained, clean toilet blocks provide all the necessary sanitary facilities. including British type WCs, washbasins and free hot showers. Facilities for disabled campers. Restaurant, bar and shop (all year). Swimming pool. Tennis. Small playground. Library. Bicycle hire. English spoken. Entertainment programme. Off site: Nearest beach 1 km. Bus 1 km. Fishing 1 km. Golf 10 km. Riding 15 km.

Open: All year.

Directions

From A7-E15 take exit 460 or 467 and follow signs for Retamar via N344 and for Cabo de Gata. Site is on the right before village of Cabo de Gata. The final stretch of road is in a poor state of repair due to restrictions imposed within the natural park. GPS: N36:48.113 W2:14.683

Charges guide

Per person	€ 5,50
pitch incl. electricity	€ 16,20 - € 16,80

Special offers outside July/August.
Camping Cheques accepted.

ES87650 Camping La Garrofa

Ctra N340 km 435,4, direccion a Aguadulce via Litoral, E-04002 Almería (Almería)

Tel: 950 235 770. Email: info@lagarrofa.com   www.alanrogers.com/ES87650

One of the earliest sites in Spain (dating back to 1957), La Garrofa nestles in a cove with a virtually private beach accessed only by sea or through the campsite. It is rather dramatic with the tall mountain cliffs behind. Many of the rather small 100 flat and sloping sandy pitches are shaded, with some very close to the beach and sea. An old fortress looks down on the campsite – you can walk to it via a valley at the back of the site and across an old Roman bridge. Other walks directly from the site include a Roman road providing fine coastal views.

Facilities

Sanitary facilities are mature but clean. Facilities for disabled campers. Restaurant/snack bar. Shop. Play area. Torches useful. Fishing. Off site: Town close by. Walks. Sub-aqua diving. Bicycle hire 2 km. Golf 8 km. Excursions – tickets to attractions sold. Bus stop nearby to Almería or Aguadulce.

Open: All year.

Directions

Site is west of Almería. Take 438 exit from the N340 and follow the camping signs. Site is below the minor road on the beach side. GPS: N36:49.542 W2:30.966

Charges 2009

Per person	€ 5,00
pitch incl. car	€ 7,80 - € 10,50
electricity	€ 4,50 - € 4,90

ES87680 Camping Roquetas

Ctra Los Parrales s/n, E-04740 Roquetas de Mar (Almería)

Tel: 950 343 809. Email: info@campingroquetas.com   www.alanrogers.com/ES87680

This level, very well maintained site is conveniently situated 9 km. from the A7 motorway within easy reach of Roquetas de Mar and 400 m. from a stony beach. It is a family run site and English is spoken. There are excellent facilities including two swimming pools and the site is within easy reach of the popular resort of Almeria and the Cabo de Gata nature park. There are 731 quite small pitches (60 sq.m), although during the winter months two pitches are allocated for the price of one. There are 18 pitches for longer units with water, electricity and waste connections.

Facilities

Five well equipped toilet blocks spread throughout the site. Two units for disabled people are close to the pools, as well as a baby room. Spanish restaurant with excellent menu and reasonable prices. Shop. Two swimming pools, one with paddling pool. Tennis. Petanque. Off site: Towns of Roquetas de Mar and Almeria nearby. Mojacar, Nijar, 'Mini Hollywood' and the Tabernas desert are within easy reach.

Open: All year.

Directions

From A7/E15 exit 429 head towards Roquetas de Mar. Site is well signed and is about 9 km. from the motorway. GPS: N36:47.51 W02:35.27

Charges guide

Per person	€ 4,25
child (under 12 yrs)	€ 4,00
pitch incl. electricity	€ 11,85 - € 15,20

Discounts in low season (20-58%), larger if paying by cash (up to 60%).

ES90800 Camping Municipal El Brillante

Avenida del Brillante 50, E-14012 Córdoba (Córdoba)

Tel: **957 403 836**. Email: elbrillante@campings.net

www.alanrogers.com/ES90800

Córdoba is one of the hottest places in Europe and the superb pool here is more than welcome. If you really want to stay in the city, then this large site is a good choice. It has 120 neat pitches of gravel and sand, the upper pitches covered by artificial and natural shade but the lower, newer area with little. The site becomes very crowded in high season. The entrance is narrow and may be congested so care must be exercised – there is a lay-by just outside and it is easier to walk in initially. The newer area has 32 fully serviced pitches and an area for a few large motorhomes. The site is on the north side of the river with a canal running through the centre (well fenced) and pleasant terraced gardens where you can sunbathe. The bar/restaurant (open in high season) is close to reception and there is a pleasant terrace which overlooks the pool gardens. Cordoba is a fascinating town and the Mosque/Cathedral is one of the great buildings of Europe and it is worth allowing two days here to investigate the area. Buses go from outside the site to town.

Facilities

The toilet blocks include facilities for babies and disabled people. Motorcaravan services. Gas supplies. Shop (all year). Bar and restaurant (1/7-30/9). Swimming pool (15/6-15/9). Play area. Off site: Bus service to city centre from outside site. Commercial centre 300 m. (left out of site, right at traffic lights).

Open: All year.

Directions

Site is north of the river. From the NIV/E25 road from Madrid, take exit km. 403 (the middle of three exits for Cordoba) and follow signs for Mosque/Cathedral into city centre. Pass it (on right) and turn right onto the main avenue. Continue and take right fork where the road splits, and follow signs for site and/or green signs for district of El Brillante. Site is on right on this avenue. GPS: N37:53.000 W4:45.998

Charges 2009

Per unit incl. 2 persons and electricity	€ 26,00
extra person (over 10 yrs)	€ 5,80
child (0-10 yrs)	€ 3,50
No credit cards.	

ES90780 Camping Los Villares

Parque Periurbano, avenida de l Fuen Santa 8, E-14071 Córdoba (Córdoba)

Tel: **957 330 145**

www.alanrogers.com/ES90780

This is a site with a difference. Unusually it is in one of Spain's natural parks and the environmental rules must be strictly followed. For peaceful, simple camping with no frills, there is an area with electricity for 30 units about five minutes walk from a toilet block, restaurant and reception. The 170 tent pitches are delightfully informal. Bountiful pine, olives, gums and other trees provide shade and the setting is absolutely natural. Thoughtfully some natural stone tables and benches are scattered around. The natty little bar and restaurant provide a simple menu and drinks – practise your Spanish here! You will most certainly need torches as you find your way home through the strange noises emanating from the densely wooded area beyond the site. The friendly warden will assist as necessary. This is a great site with reasonable prices for those who have their own transport for visiting the amazing city of Cordoba, or it will suit those who do not need the entertainment of bigger sites and just wish to relax at one with nature.

Facilities

The single toilet facility is centrally located, provides free hot water and is of good quality. Washing machines. Shop. Restaurant/bar. Off site: Natural Park (protected) with walks and wildlife.

Open: All year.

Directions

Site is 7 km. north of Córdoba, north of the river which bisects the city. It is simpler to go to the centre to find the small access road to Parque and site. Follow signs for Parador or Parque Periurbano (small camping sign inside green edged signs). Also follow signs for municipal camping which help. All these bring you past the municipal camping – then look for a major right turn and follow clear signs out of city. GPS: N37:57.443 W04:48.620

Charges guide

Per person	€ 3,75
pitch incl, car	€ 7,00 - € 8,00
No credit cards.	

ES90840 Camping La Campiña

Ctra A-379, km 46,2 La Guijarrosa, E-14547 Santaella (Córdoba)

Tel: **957 315 303**. Email: **info@campinglacampina.com**

www.alanrogers.com/ES90840

A charming site amongst the olive trees and set high on a hill to catch cool summer breezes. Matilde, the daughter of the Martin-Rodriguez family, runs this site with enthusiasm and hard work, making a visit here a delightful experience. Everything is immaculately kept and we rarely see sites of this size with such excellent amenities and standards. The 35 pitches are level and most have shade, the surface is gravel and there are views over the olive fields to the surrounding hills. There is a large pool in a garden setting and the restaurant, with its traditional rustic charm, has a delightful menu of home made food. Breakfast is included in pitch prices.

Facilities

Two small traditional sanitary blocks have clean services including facilities for disabled campers (key at reception). Washing machines. Restaurant. Snack bar. Shop. Outdoor swimming pool (April - October). Bicycle hire. Yoga lessons. Torches useful. Walks and excursions arranged. Off site: Bus from gate to Cordoba. Town 2 km. Riding 15 km. Golf 40 km.

Open: All year.

Directions

From the NIV/E5 (Sevilla - Cordoba) take exit 441 or 443 (La Rambla - Montilla). Continue past Santaella towards La Victoria. La Campiña is tucked off this road behind high hedging. From the A45 Malaga - Cordoba road, take exit 27 (La Ramba) and on towards Santaella. GPS: N37:37.380 W4:51.522

Charges guide

Per person	€ 5,00
pitch incl. electricity	€ 13,85 - € 14,05

ES90850 Camping Carlos III

Ctra Madrid - Cadiz km 430, E-14100 La Carlota (Córdoba)

Tel: **957 300 338**. Email: **camping@campingcarlosiii.com**

www.alanrogers.com/ES90850

This rural site lies 25 km. south of Córdoba, just off the main Córdoba - Sevilla road and may be a good alternative to staying in the city. A very large, busy site especially at weekends, it has many supporting facilities including a good swimming pool and a pool, play area and animal corner for children. With the catering areas open all year, the site has a more open feel than the bustling municipal site in Córdoba. The touring areas are canopied by trees which offer considerable shade for 300 pitches. On sandy, gently sloping ground, two-thirds have 5/10A electricity.Permanent units, mobile homes and bungalows are in a separate area, where there are further sporting facilities. There may be some slight road noise.

Facilities

Modern toilet blocks provide a mix of British and Turkish WCs, with hot showers in the block near reception. Laundry service. Motorcaravan services. Bar/restaurant, shop (all year). Swimming pools (1/6-15/9). Aviary. Boules. Minigolf, Play area. Hairdressers. Off site: Bus service outside site. Riding 500 m. Village 2 km.

Open: All year.

Directions

From NIV Cordoba-Seville motorway take La Carlota exit (at km. 429 point northbound or exit 432 southbound). Site is 500 m. and well signed. GPS: N37:40.598 W4:55.997

Charges 2009

Per unit incl. 2 persons and electricity	€ 21,30 - € 24,20
extra person	€ 5,20
child (3-12 yrs)	€ 3,00 - € 9,00

ES92700 Camping Suspiro del Moro

Ctra Bailén - Motril km 144, Puerto Suspiro del Moro, E-18630 Granada (Granada)

Tel: **958 555 411**. Email: **campingsuspirodelmoro@yahoo.es**

www.alanrogers.com/ES92700

Suspiro Del Moro is eleven kilometres south of Granada just off the Motril road and can also be approached on the scenic mountain road from Almunecar. Based high in the Sierra Nevada mountain range, the area offers spectacular views from just outside the site. The site is small and rectangular with a cool and peaceful atmosphere (there may be road noise from the A44). Family run, it is well kept with gravel paths leading to the flat pitches which benefit from the shade of the mature trees.

Facilities

Clean and tidy, small toilet blocks are situated around the camping area with British style WCs and free hot showers. Laundry and dishwashing facilities. Small basic shop. Small simple restaurant/bar (high season). Small play area on gravel. Off site: Swimming pool and restaurant adjacent. Sierra Nevada and Granada within reasonable distance to explore.

Open: All year.

Directions

Leave Granada to Motril road (E902/A44) at exit 144 (from south) or 139 (from north) and follow un-named campsite signs. At roundabout go towards Suspiro, then left (signed after turn). Site is about 600 m. on right on A4050 beside large restaurant. GPS: N37:04.092 W03:39.118

Charges guide

Per person	€ 3,60 - € 4,80
pitch incl. electricity	€ 10,50 - € 12,80

ES92750 Camping Los Avellanos de Sierra Nevada

Ctra de la Fábrica s/n, E-18152 Dilar (Granada)

Tel: 958 596 016. Email: Avellano@Teleline.es

www.alanrogers.com/ES92750

This is a fascinating tiny business with a philosophy of peace and tranquillity, a world apart from other sites in southern Spain. This has been achieved by Pilar and her brother Idvier. The site is also called Camping Cortijo, which loosely translates from the Spanish as a 'big house in grounds with animals, birds and produce where people work towards people'. There is a fabulous old house and 20 beautifully terraced pitches (mainly for tents) with amazing views enjoying the sound of water tinkling through the ancient irrigation channels on its way to the crops (cars are parked separately).

Facilities

Toilet facilities are modern and clean. Pretty bar/restaurant serves typical local fare and sells basic supplies (very limited in low season). Kitchen for hire. Restaurant/bar. Swimming pool (high season only). Bicycle hire. Riding. Fishing in river Dilar. Details of walks from reception. Torches essential. Excellent rooms to let. Off site: Tours of Granada (20 minutes away), especially the Alhambra, organised. Site also useful for skiing in Sierra Nevada in season.

Open: All year.

Directions

Heading south from Granada on (E902) A44 exit 139 (Otura). Heading north exit 144. Head towards Otura on GR 5025. Proceed through town and right at roundabout (Dilar/Rio Dilar) on through village. In 2 km. site on right, very steep climb. Not suitable for American RVs. GPS: N37:04.080 W03:34.860

Charges guide

Per person	€ 3,16
pitch	€ 5,71 - € 6,62

Electricity and larger units - price on application. All plus 7% VAT. No credit cards.

ES92890 Camping Trevélez

Ctra Trevélez-Orgiva, km 1, E-18417 Trevélez (Granada)

Tel: 958 858 735. Email: info@campingtrevelez.net

www.alanrogers.com/ES92890

Set high up in the Alpujarras region of the Sierra Nevada, Camping Trevelez is a super site that was bought in 2005 by the resident owners, Richard and Alexandra Sitges. Since taking over they have worked tirelessly to improve the site and each year have made significant progress. The site, which is open all year, is reached via a narrow, winding road and is ideally suited to tents and smaller motorcaravans which are sited on terraced plots, each with spectacular mountain views. Sit outside at night and wonder at the stars above but make sure you have a torch. It gets very dark at night.

Facilities

One sanitary block, recently redecorated, provides toilets, washbasins and shower cubicles. Facilities for disabled visitors. Washing machine and dryer. Shop. Bar and restaurant. Play area. Swimming pool (1/6-15/9). Barbecues only allowed in designated areas and not at all 15/6-15/10. Fishing. Riding.

Open: All year.

Directions

From A44 (E902) Granada - Motril road, exit at 164 km. onto A348. At Orgiva take A4132 for 32 km. to Trevelez. Road is winding and very narrow in places and is not suitable for large units. GPS: N36:59.509 W03:16.652

Charges guide

Per person	€ 4,50
pitch incl. electricity	€ 10,50 - € 12,00

ES92800 Camping Sierra Nevada

Avenida Madrid 107, E-18014 Granada (Granada)

Tel: 958 150 062. Email: campingmotel@terra.es

www.alanrogers.com/ES92800

This is a good site either for a night stop or for a stay of a few days while visiting Granada and for a city site it is surprisingly pleasant. Quite large, it has an open feeling and, to encourage you to stay a little longer, an irregular shape pool with a smaller children's pool open in high season. There is some traffic noise around the pool as it is on the road boundary. With 148 pitches for touring units (10/20A electricity), the site is in two parts with more mature trees and facilities to the northern end.

Facilities

Two very modern sanitary blocks, with excellent facilities, including cabins, very good facilities for disabled people and babies. Washing machines. Motorcaravan services. Gas supplies. Shop (15/3-15/10). Swimming pools with lifeguards and charge of € 1.50 (15/6-15/9). Bar/restaurant by pool. Tennis. Petanque. Large playground. Doctor lives on site. Off site: Fishing 10 km. Golf 12 km. Bus station 50 m. from site gate.

Open: 1 March - 31 October.

Directions

Site is just outside the city to north, on road to Jaén and Madrid. From autopista, take Granada North - Almanjayar exit 123 (close to central bus station). Follow road back towards Granada and site is on the right, well signed. From other roads join the motorway to access the correct exit. GPS: N37:12.241 W03:37.022

Charges guide

Per person	€ 5,70
child (3-10 yrs)	€ 4,85
pitch incl. electricity (10A)	€ 17,00

ES92850 Camping Las Lomas

Ctra de Sierra Nevada, E-18160 Güejar-Sierra (Granada)

Tel: **958 484 742**. Email: **laslomas@campings.net**

www.alanrogers.com/ES92850

This site is high in the Güéjar–Sierra and looks down on the Patano de Canales reservoir. After a wonderful drive to Güéjar-Sierra, you are rewarded with a site boasting excellent facilities. It is set on a slope but the pitches have been levelled and are quite private, with high separating hedges and many mature trees giving good shade (some pitches are fully serviced, with sinks and most have electricity). The large bar/restaurant complex and pools have wonderful views over the lake and a grassed sunbathing area runs down to the fence (safe) looking over the long drop below.

Facilities

Pretty sanitary blocks (heated in winter) provide clean facilities. First class facilities for disabled campers and well equipped baby room (key at reception). Spa for hire. Motorcaravan services. Good supermarket. Restaurant/bar. Swimming pool. Play area. Minigolf. Many other activities including parascending. Barbecue. Internet access. Torches useful. Off site: Buses to village and Granada (15 km). Tours of the Alhambra organised. Useful site for winter skiing.

Open: All year.

Directions

Heading south towards Granada on A44 (E902 Jaén - Motril) take exit 132 onto A395 (Alhamba - Sierra Nevada). After 4 km. marker, exit 5B (Sierra Nevada). At 7 km. marker, exit right onto slip road. At junction turn left (Cenes de la Vega - Güéjar-Sierra). In 200 m. turn right on A4026. In 1.6 km. turn left (Güéjar-Sierra). Drive uphill, past dam and site is on right in 2.8 km. GPS: N37:09.644 W3:27.233

Charges guide

Per person	€ 4,00 - € 6,00
pitch	€ 12,00 - € 14,00

ES92900 Camping El Balcon de Pitres

Ctra Orgiva - Ugijar km 51, E-18414 Pitres (Granada)

Tel: **958 766 111**. Email: **info@balcondepitres.com**

www.alanrogers.com/ES92900

A simple country site perched high in the mountains of the Alpujarras, on the south side of the Sierra Nevada, El Balcon de Pitres has its own rustic charm. Many thousands of trees planted around the site provide shade. There are stunning views from some of the 175 level grassy pitches (large units may find pitch access difficult). The garden is kept green by spring waters, which you can hear and sometimes see, tinkling away in places. The Lopez family, have built this site from barren mountain top to cool oasis in the mountains in just fifteen years. It is a wonderful relaxing place to cool down, away from the heat of the coast.

Facilities

Two toilet blocks provide adequate facilities but the steeply sloping site is unsuitable for disabled campers and thus there are no facilities for them. Snack bar. Bar. Shop (closed Tuesdays). Swimming pools (extra charge). Bicycle hire. Torches useful. Off site: Fishing. Canyoning. Trekking. Parascending. Quad bikes.

Open: All year.

Directions

Site is about 30 km. northeast of Motril. Heading south on A44 (E902) exit 164 (Lanjaron) onto E348 towards Orgiva. Fork left at sign (A4132) Pampaneira 8 km. Continue to Pitres (7 km). Site is signed. (Steep and winding roads). GPS: N36:55.911 W03:19.961

Charges guide

Per person	€ 5,00
pitch incl. electricity	€ 12,50 - € 14,50

ES92760 Camping Reina Isabel

Ctra Granada - La Zubia, km. 4, E-18140 La Zubia (Granada)

Tel: **958 590 041**. Email: **info@reinaisabelcamping.com**

www.alanrogers.com/ES92760

Reina Isabel can be found just 3 km. from the centre of Granada and just 1 km. from the entrance to the spectacular Sierra Nevada National Park. The site is open for an extended season and is well located for winter sports holidays in the Sierra Nevada. There are 51 shady touring pitches here (each around 70 sq.m), all with electrical connections. A number of chalets and apartments are also available for rent. A regular bus service operates to the city centre and to other places of interest, notably the Alhambra palace. On-site facilities include a swimming pool and a bar/restaurant.

Facilities

Bar/restaurant. Shop. Swimming pool. Play area. Chalets and apartments for rent. Off site: Bus stop with regular service to the city centre (20 minutes). Sierra Nevada ski resort 29 km.

Open: All year.

Directions

Site is south of Granada. Leave A44 motorway at exit 132 and head east on A395. Follow signs to La Zubia, joining the southbound Calle de Laurel de la Reina. Site is clearly signed from here. GPS: N37:07.474 W03:35.175

Charges guide

Per unit incl. 2 persons	€ 18,95 - € 23,00
extra person	€ 4,60

ES92920 Camping Puerta de La Alpujarra

Ctra Lanjarón - Orgiva (Las Barreras), E-18400 Orgiva (Granada)

Tel: 958 784 450. Email: puertadelapujarra@campings.net

www.alanrogers.com/ES92920

You will receive a warm welcome from the family who run this site and nothing is too much trouble. The site overlooks the Sierra Nevada with lovely panoramic views. There are 77 pitches, terraced and with plenty of shade (43 with electricity connections). This is an area that is becoming more popular with tourists and is an ideal spot from which to explore the mountain villages. Orgiva, steeped in history, is just 1.5 km. from the site and there are many interesting walks from here.

Facilities
Three central sanitary blocks are clean and provide open washbasins and roomy shower cubicles. Toilet for disabled visitors (no shower). Laundry facilities. Shop (baker delivers daily). Bar, restaurant and takeaway (all season, closed Wednesdays). Outdoor swimming and paddling pools (mid June - mid Oct). Play area. Torches useful. Off site: Orgiva 1.5 km. Pampaneria, Bubion and Capileira (steep and winding with many bends so time and care should be taken).

Open: All year.

Directions
Head south from Granada on A44 (E902) and exit 164 signed Lanjaron onto A348. Alpujarra is signed with Orgiva. Site is on right on outskirts of Orgiva (signed). GPS: N36:54.225 W3:26.335

Charges guide
Per person	€ 4,00 - € 5,00
child	€ 2,50 - € 4,00
pitch	€ 8,00 - € 10,00
electricity	€ 3,00 - € 4,00

ES92930 Camping Orgiva

Ctra A348, km. 18,9, E-18400 Orgiva (Granada)

Tel: 958 784 307. Email: campingorgiva@descubrelaalpujarra.com

www.alanrogers.com/ES92930

Set in the high slopes of the Sierra Nevada and only 2 km. from Orgiva, this is a small and well managed site that offers the opportunity to escape into rural Spain. It is open all year and is an ideal place to relax. For those who feel more energetic, there are facilities for climbing, horse riding and canoeing, all within close proximity of the site. The 40 touring pitches are well defined and separated by shrubs and small trees and all have views of the surrounding countryside. Access to the site is good but being high in the mountains it is not suitable for large units. Information on places to visit and a selection of local walks is available on site and from the tourist office in Orgiva. The site has a traditional style restaurant offering regional dishes, together with a well stocked bar.

Facilities
One centrally placed sanitary block provides toilets, washbasins and shower cubicles. Facilities for disabled visitors. Washing machine and dryer. Very good swimming pool with adjacent small pool for children (June - Sept). Shop. Terrace bar. No barbecues allowed on site. Off site: Fishing 10 km. Golf 35 km.

Open: All year.

Directions
From A44-E902 Granada - Motril road, exit at 164 km. and take A348 east to Lanjaron and Orgiva. Continue past Orgiva and the site is well signed on left. GPS: N36:53.225 W03:25.052

Charges guide
Per person	€ 4,74
pitch incl. car	€ 8,45
electricity	€ 3,64

ES92950 Camping Don Cactus

Ctra N340 km 343, Playa de Carchuna, E-18730 Carchuna-Motril (Granada)

Tel: 958 623 109. Email: camping@doncactus.com

www.alanrogers.com/ES92950

Situated between the main N340 and the beach, this family run campsite is pleasantly surprising with clever planning and ongoing improvements. It is a comfortable site of 320 pitches (280 for touring). The flat pitches vary in size with electricity, some also with water and satellite TV connections, and are arranged along avenues with eucalyptus trees (which keep the mosquitoes away apparently) for shade. This quieter section of the coast is beautiful with coves and access to larger towns if wished. The friendly reception staff are very helpful with tourist advice and can arrange trips if needed.

Facilities
The large toilet block is dated but clean and provides British style WCs, showers and plenty of washbasins. Laundry facilities. Beach showers. Well stocked shop. Bar, restaurant and takeaway (all year). Swimming pool (in high season € 1.50 per day). Tennis. Play area. Summer activities for children. Outdoor fitness centre for adults. Pets corner. ATM. Internet point. Dogs are not accepted in July/Aug. Barbecues only in special area. Caravan storage. Off site: Bus service 500 m.

Open: All year.

Directions
From Motril - Carchuna road (N340/E15) turn towards the sea at km. 343. (site signed, but look at roof level for large green tent on the top of the building!). Travel about 600 m. then turn east to site on left. GPS: N36:41.743 W03:26.609

Charges guide
Per person	€ 6,00
pitch incl. electricity (5A)	€ 18,30

Low season discounts for longer stays.
Camping Cheques accepted.

ES87110 Nerja Camping

Ctra N340 km 297, E-29787 Maro (Málaga)

Tel: **952 529 714**. Email: **info@nerjacamping.com**

www.alanrogers.com/ES87110

This site is set on the lower slopes of the Sierra Laminar, some five kilometres from Nerja and two kilometres from the excellent beaches. Nerja Camping is a small site of 55 pitches with impressive views of the surrounding mountains and the sea. There are 25 touring pitches (15A electricity) and 4 new mobile homes to rent. The pitches are on the small side and set on slopes with some terracing along with some artificial shade. The roads, although sloping, should present few problems for siting units. A new motorway will be close, but extensive sound barriers are being installed. The small hut-style restaurant doubles as a bar and has a small terace where you can order snacks.

Facilities

The single sanitary block has been refurbished and tiled; all washbasins and showers have hot water. Laundry facilities. Small restaurant/bar (March - Sept). Essentials from the bar. Small swimming pool (March - Sept). Off site: Beach 2 km. Nerja limestone caves 1 km. Fishing 3 km. Bicycle hire or riding 5 km. Sub-aqua diving, parascending and watersports. Day trips to Granada or Gibraltar. Sierra Nevada 100 km. (1.5 hours in winter).

Open: All year excl. October.

Directions

Site signed from main N340 coast road about 5 km. east of Nerja after 296 km. marker. If coming from Nerja, go 500 m. past site entrance (opposite radio masts) to cross very busy main road. GPS: N36:45.630 W03:50.085

Charges 2009

Per person	€ 5,50
pitch incl. electricity	€ 14,00 - € 17,5
No credit cards.	

ES87850 Camping Rural Iznate

Ctra Iznate - Benamocarra s/n, E-29792 Iznate (Málaga)

Tel: **952 535 613**. Email: **info@campingiznate.com**

www.alanrogers.com/ES87850

This brand new site is situated amid beautiful scenery 1 km. away from the picturesque village of Iznate. It is surrounded by avocado and olive trees and is on the wine route – the region is the centre of Spain's Muscadet production. The site is well thought out and immaculately maintained. The large swimming pool is an ideal spot for cooling off after a walk and the next door restaurant serves excellent food at very reasonable prices. This is a small new site and we would recommend booking during high season. There are wonderful views all round the site and eagles, wild boar and black squirrels can be seen in the surrounding countryside.

Facilities

The modern toilet block has hot showers and facilities for disabled visitors. Laundry facilities under a covered area. Small shop. Bar/restaurant with terrace adjoining the site. Swimming pool and jacuzzi. Summer entertainment. Petanque. Play area. Off site: Beach 20 minutes drive. Towns of Sayalonga and Frigeliana nearby.

Open: All year.

Directions

From A7/E15 take exit 265 and head towards Cajiz and Iznate. Site is on left 1 km. past Iznate. GPS: N36:47.532 W04:10.279

Charges guide

Per person	€ 4,20
pitch incl. electricity	€ 10,60 - € 11,90

Discounts in low season (15/9-15/6) depending on length of stay.

ES88000 Camping Marbella Playa

Ctra N340 km 192,8, E-29600 Marbella (Málaga)

Tel: **952 833 998**. Email: **recepcion@campingmarbella.com**

www.alanrogers.com/ES88000

This large site is 12 kilometres east of the internationally famous resort of Marbella with public transport available to the town centre and local attractions. A sandy beach is about 150 metres away with direct access. There are 430 individual pitches of up to 70 sq.m. with natural shade (additional artificial shade is provided to some), and electricity (10/20A) available throughout. Long leads may be required for some pitches. The site is busy throughout the high season but the high staff/customer ratio and the friendly staff approach ensures a comfortable stay. A large swimming pool complex with a restaurant/bar provides a very attractive feature.

Facilities

Four sanitary blocks of mixed ages, are fully equipped and well maintained. Three modern units for disabled visitors. Laundry service. Large supermarket. Bar, restaurant and café (all open all year). Supervised swimming pool (free: April - Sept). Playground. Children's activities. Torches advised. Off site: Bus service 150 m. Fishing 100 m. Golf and bicycle hire 5 km. Riding 10 km. Beach 200 m.

Open: All year.

Directions

Site is 12 km. east of Marbella. Access is close to the 193 km. point on the main N340. Signed Elviria, then camping signs. GPS: N36:29.476 W04:45.795

Charges guide

Per person	€ 3,42 - € 5,67
pitch incl. electricity	€ 7,57 - € 20,67

All plus 7% VAT. Reductions (up to 50%) for long stays and senior citizens outside 1/6-16/9.

ES87820 Camping Caravaning Laguna Playa

Prolongacion Paseo Maritimo, E-29740 Torre del Mar (Málaga)

Tel: 952 540 631. Email: info@lagunaplaya.com

www.alanrogers.com/ES87820

Laguna Playa is a pleasant and peaceful site run by a father and son team (the son speaks excellent English) and they give a personal service, alongside one of the Costa del Sol beaches. Trips are organised to the famous Alhambra Mosque in Granada on a weekly basis and the site is well placed for visits to Malaga and Nerja. The pitches are flat, of average size and with good artificial shade supplementing that provided by the many established trees on site. All pitches have electricity (10A). The busy restaurant with a terrace offers good value for money and many locals use it.

Facilities

Two well equipped, modern, sanitary blocks include baby baths and good facilities for disabled campers. Laundry facilities. Supermarket. Bar and busy restaurant also used by locals (closed for two weeks in May and October). Swimming pools (high season). Play area. Children's entertainment. Off site: Beach 200 m. Bicycle hire 500 m. Regular bus service 700 m. outside site. Golf 1.5 km.

Open: All year.

Directions

Site is on the sea front west of the town of Torre del Mar. Go to the end of the 'paseo' on the west side of the town. Site is on the right.
GPS: N36:43.460 W04:06.080

Charges guide

Per person	€ 4,80
pitch	€ 4,80 - € 19,00
electricity	€ 3,70

ES87830 Camping Naturista Almanat

Carril de la Torre Alta s/n, E-29749 Almayate (Málaga)

Tel: 952 556 462. Email: info@almanat.de

www.alanrogers.com/ES87830

With direct access to a one kilometre grey sand and shingle naturist beach, this established all year naturist site, set amongst agricultural land with mountain backdrop, is proving a firm favourite with many British seeking winter sun. The facilities on site are to a very high standard. The entire 2-hectare site is flat with a fine shingle surface. A large number of mature trees provide much needed shade in the summer months. The 194 touring pitches with 16A electricity, vary in size and shape with the majority demanding physical manoeuvring of a touring caravan.

Facilities

The large, unisex toilet block is fully equipped, regularly cleaned and all under cover. Good facilities for disabled campers near reception. Small shop. Bar/restaurant with terrace. Large unheated swimming pool. New indoor pool with jacuzzi (closed 15/6-15/9). Sauna and gym. Cinema (56 seats). Social room. Play area. Minigolf. Weather permitting, one is expected to be nude which is obligatory in the pool area and bar during the day. Off site: Torre del Mar is 2 km. Regular bus service 1 km. Fishing, riding nearby.

Open: All year.

Directions

Approaching from the east (Torre del Mar) it is necessary to turn left to access the 600 m. single track access to the site. It is illegal to make that left turn. From east or west on N340 autovia take exit 265 signed Cajiz Iznate and Costa 340a. Follow Costa direction and on reaching the coast turn left on 340a toward Torre del Mar. Site well signed in 5 km. on right. GPS: N36:43.607 W04:06.796

Charges guide

Per person	€ 4,80
pitch incl. electricity (16A)	€ 8,50 - € 22,70

All plus 7% VAT. Camping Cheques accepted.

ES87900 Espacios Rurales Fuente de Piedra

Ctra La Rábita s/n, E-29520 Fuente de Piedra (Málaga)

Tel: 952 735 294. Email: info@camping-rural.com

www.alanrogers.com/ES87900

In a remote area of Andalucia, this tiny campsite with just 30 touring pitches looks over the salty lakes and marshes of the Laguna de Fuente. The average size pitches are on a sloping, terraced hillside, with some having a view of the lake. With a gravel surface and good shade, many pitches slope so chocks would be useful. There is a separate grassy area for tents near the pool and bungalows (cars are not permitted here). Unusually for a site of this size there is a pool and an excellent bar, snack bar and huge restaurant which serves Spanish food. Try the excellent, inexpensive 'menu del dia'.

Facilities

Sanitary facilities are in one block and are looking a little tired. Facilities for disabled campers. Washing machines. Shop. Restaurant. Bar with TV. Snack bar. Swimming pool. Pool bar. Electronic games. Bicycle hire. Off site: Lake with flamingos. Bicycle hire 1 km. Fishing 5 km. Riding 10 km. Golf 40 km. Excursions organised in July and August.

Open: All year.

Directions

Site is 20 km. northwest of Antequera. From Antequera take A92 and exit at 132 km. point and follow road to the town. Site is well signed from the town but the signs are small.
GPS: N37:07.752 W4:44.004

Charges guide

Per person	€ 5,40 - € 6,00
pitch incl. electricity	€ 8,60 - € 13,00

ES87810 Camping El Pino

Ctra Nacional 340 Km 285, E-29793 Torrox-Costa (Málaga)
Tel: **952 532 578**. Email: **info@campingelpino.com**

www.alanrogers.com/ES87810

El Pino is located in the Axarquia region of the Costa del Sol, east of Malaga and is surrounded by avocado groves. The site enjoys some fine views of the surrounding countryside. There are 470 pitches here, mostly well shaded, and a further 47 mobile homes and chalets for rent. Most pitches have electrical connections and vary in size from 60-100 sq.m. The site is open all year and has some impressive facilities including a swimming pool, supermarket and bar/restaurant. The nearest beach is 800 m. distant – a bus service runs there from the site. The site can be found close to Torrox Costa, an area claiming to have the best climate in Europe. The old village of Torrox, like many in the area, has traces of its Arabic origins, with narrow winding streets and white washed houses. Torrox Costa is quite different and has been extensively but attractively developed with a lighthouse at one end and a fine sandy beach, the Playa Ferrara.

Facilities

Bar. Restaurant. Shop. Swimming pool. Play area. Games room. Children's club. Mobile homes and chalets for rent. Off site: Nearest beach 800 m. Malaga 45 km. Fishing. Golf.

Open: All year.

Directions

Leave the A7 Autovia del Mediterraneo at exit 285 (Torrox) and follow signs to Torrox Park. The site is well signed from here.
GPS: N36:44.365 W03:56.973

Charges guide

Per unit incl. 2 persons and electricity	€ 16,00 - € 21,50
extra person	€ 3,00 - € 4,25
child (under 10 yrs)	€ 2,00 - € 3,00
dog	€ 1,50 - € 2,50

UrbanizationTorrox Park s/n
29793 Torrox Costa · Malaga (Spain)
Tel.: (00 34) 95 253 25 78 · Fax: (00 34) 95 253 00 06

GPS: N 36° 44' 22" · W 3° 56' 56"

Camping El Pino gives you the opportunity to enjoy the most of your holiday on the Costa del Sol. Located in a tropical tree planting the campsite is known for its tranquillity and friendly atmosphere. It is a second category campsite and has 470 pitches and 47 bungalows and accommodations, we have a bar, restaurant, supermarket, swimming pool, laundry, etc... is open all year.

ES88020 Kawan Village Cabopino

Ctra N340 km 194,7, E-29604 Marbella (Málaga)
Tel: **952 834 373**. Email: **info@campingcabopino.com**

www.alanrogers.com/ES88020

This large, mature site is alongside the main N340 Costa del Sol coast road, 12 km. east of Marbella and 15 km. from Fuengirola. The Costa del Sol is also known as the Costa del Golf and fittingly there is a major golf course alongside the site. The site is set amongst tall pine trees which provide shade for the sandy pitches (there are some huge areas for large units). The 300 touring pitches, a mix of level and sloping (chocks advisable), all have electricity (10A), but long leads may be required for some. There is a separate area on the western side for groups of younger guests.

Facilities

Five mature but very clean sanitary blocks provide hot water throughout (may be under pressure at peak times). Washing machines. Bar/restaurant and takeaway (all year). Shop. Outdoor pool (1/5-15/9) and indoor pool (all year). Play area. Some evening entertainment. ATM. Charcoal barbecues are not permitted. Off site: Beach and golf 200 m. Fishing, bicycle hire and riding within 1 km.

Open: All year.

Directions

Site is 12 km. from Marbella. Approaching Marbella from the east, leave the N340 at the 194 km. marker (signed Cabopino). Site is off the roundabout at the top of the slip road. GPS: N36:29.610 W04:44.630

Charges guide

Per unit incl. 2 persons and electricity	€ 20,95 - € 33,00

Discounts outside high season and for over 7 days. Camping Cheques accepted.

ES88030 Camping La Buganvilla

Ctra N340 km 188,8, E-29600 Marbella (Málaga)

Tel: 952 831 973. Email: info@campingbuganvilla.com

www.alanrogers.com/ES88030

This site has a total of 500 pitches, of which 250 are for touring units. They are mostly on terraces so there are some views across to the mountains and hinterland of this coastal area. La Buganvilla is a large, uncomplicated site with mature trees providing shade to some pitches. The terrain is a little rugged in places and the buildings are older in style but all were clean when we visited. A pool complex near the bar and restaurant is ideal for cooling off after a day's sightseeing.

Facilities

Three painted sanitary blocks are clean and adequate. Laundry facilities (not all sinks have hot water). Bar/restaurant with basic food. Well stocked small supermarket. Play area. Tennis (high season). Dogs are not accepted in July/Aug. Off site: Bus service close to site entrance. Fishing and watersports 400 m. Bicycle and scooter hire 1 km. Golf 5 km. Resort type entertainment.

Open: All year.

Directions

Site is between Marbella and Fuengirola off the N340. Access at 188.8 km. marker is only possible when travelling west, i.e. from Fuengirola. From the other direction, continue to the 'cambio de sentido' signed Elviria and back over the dual-carriageway. Site is signed. GPS: N36:30.123 W4:48.281

Charges guide

Per person	€ 5,50 - € 7,50
pitch incl. electricity	€ 10,32 - € 13,82

All plus 7% VAT. Discounts in low season.

ES88090 Camping El Sur

Ctra Ronda - Algeciras km 1,5, Apdo 127, E-29400 Ronda (Málaga)

Tel: 952 875 939. Email: info@campingelsur.com

www.alanrogers.com/ES88090

The delightfully decorated entrance with generous manoeuvring area at this site are a promise of something different which is fulfilled in all respects. The very friendly family who run the site have worked hard for many years combining innovative thinking with excellent service. The 125 terraced pitches have electricity (6/10A) and water, and are partially shaded by olive and almond trees. Levels vary so chocks are recommended. Most have relaxing views of the surrounding mountains but at an elevation of 850 m. the upper pitches (the very top 45 pitches are for tents only) allow a clear view of the fascinating town of Ronda.

Facilities

The immaculate sanitary block is fully equipped. Laundry facilities in a separate block. Gas supplies. Bar and very large, high quality restaurant (1/2-31/10). Kidney shaped pool (1/6-30/9). Playground and adventure play area. Separate camping area for groups. Minigolf. Off road bicycle hire. Internet terminal. Off site: Riding 1.5 km. Bicycle hire 2.5 km. The famous town of Ronda with all its attractions. The coast is about an hour's drive (50 km).

Open: All year.

Directions

Site is on the A369 Ronda - Algerciras road at the 3 km. point south of Ronda (which now has a ring road so one does not have to go through the town). GPS: N36:43.276 W05:10.319

Charges guide

Per person	€ 4,80
pitch incl. electricity	€ 8,60 - € 18,15

Plus 7% VAT. Discounts in low season depending on length of stay. No credit cards (except in restaurant).

ES88550 Camping Tarifa

Ctra N340 km 78,87, E-11380 Tarifa (Cádiz)

Tel: 956 684 778. Email: camping-tarifa@camping-tarifa.com

www.alanrogers.com/ES88550

The long, golden, sandy beach adjacent to this site is a good feature being ideal for windsurfing and also clean and safe for swimming. The site has a pleasant, open feel and is reasonably sheltered from road noise. It has been thoughtfully landscaped and planted out with an amazing variety of shrubs and flowers and is clean. The 265 level pitches are of varying sizes and are surrounded by pine trees which provide ample shade. All have electricity (5/10A) and there are adequate water points. There is a smart, modern reception area with an attractive water feature close by.

Facilities

Two modern, fully equipped sanitary blocks include facilities for campers with disabilities and baby room. All spotless when seen. Motorcaravan services. Gas supplies. Supermarket and excellent bar/restaurant – fast food only, all open all year with patio. Swimming pool complex with bar. Large play area. Dogs are not accepted. Off site: Fishing 100 m. Riding 300 m. Bicycle hire 5 km. Excursions.

Open: All year.

Directions

Site is on main N340 Cadiz road at 78.87 km. marker, 7.5 km. northwest of Tarifa. Large modern signs well ahead of the site with a deceleration lane if approaching from the Tarifa direction. GPS: N36:03.678 W5:40.152

Charges guide

Per person	€ 4,17 - € 6,95
pitch incl. electricity	€ 4,48 - € 10,70

Camping Cheques accepted.

ES88570 Camping Pinar San José

Carretera de Vejer-Caños de Meca. km 10,2, Los Caños de Meca, E-11159 Barbate (Cádiz)
Tel: 956 437 030
www.alanrogers.com/ES88570

Pinar San José is a new site, first opened in 2008. The site is located in the La Breña natural park and has been developed to reflect the natural beauty that surrounds it. The nearest beaches on the Costa de la Luz are around 1 km distant. On site amenities are modern and well designed and include two swimming pools, tennis and a sports court. Pitches are grassy and all have electrical connections. There is a good provision of water points and many pitches also have drainage and internet connections. A number of brick built chalets are available for rent. Cabo de Trafalgar (Cape Trafalgar) is very close and, of course, gave its name to the famous battle several kilometres to the west. The nearest village to the site is Zahora and the great cities of Cádiz and Jerez, as well as Gibraltar are all accessible in less than an hour. La Breña natural park was formerly a massive sand dune and is now a large, forested area, criss-crossed with cycle tracks and footpaths. Riding is also possible in the park.

Facilities

Bar. Restaurant. Shop. Two swimming pools. Tennis. Sports court. Play area. Games room. Chalets for rent. Off site: Nearest beach 1 km. Cádiz 50 km. Fishing. Golf. Watersports.

Open: All year.

Directions

Heading south from Cádiz on the A48 motorway at the Vejer de la Frontera exit and head west on the A2230 and then south on A2233 to Zahora. The site is well signed from here.
GPS: N36:11.999 W06:02.078

Charges guide

Per unit incl. 2 persons and electricity	€ 22,95 - € 44,30
extra person	€ 4,00 - € 5,20
child (2-11 yrs)	€ 3,00 - € 3,80

CAMPING
Pinar SanJosé

*Our modern campsite is located in an extend pine forest, near to the beautiful beaches of the Costa de la Luz.
Extremely well-equipped bungalows, all amenities of a first class site, large swimming pool, satellite TV, Internet connection, etc.
We are open throughout the year.*

**Carretera de Vejer-Caños de Meca Km 10,2 (Cádiz)
Telf.: 0034 956 43 70 30
www.campingpinarsanjose.com**

ES88500 Camping Paloma

Ctra Cadiz - Malaga km 70, E-11380 Tarifa (Cádiz)
Tel: 956 684 203
www.alanrogers.com/ES88500

This spacious, neat and tidy, family orientated site is popular with Spanish families and young people of all nations in high season. Paloma is well established and the many tall palms around the site remind one of how close Africa and the romance of Tangier is. The site has 337 pitches on mostly flat ground, although the westerly pitches are sloping. They are of average size with some places for extra large units, some are separated by hedges and most are shaded by mature trees; around 150 pitches have electrical connections (10A). A large, smart restaurant serves excellent Spanish fare and the bar with a large courtyard buzzes with activity. Snacks are served here. There is a small pool with a paved and grassed sunbathing area and an attractive thatched, stone bar. Paloma is 700 m. from a fabulous beach with white sands and enormous dunes.

Facilities

Two sanitary blocks, one of a good size, although a long walk from the southern end of the site. The other block is smaller and open plan. British style WCs with some Turkish, washbasins have cold water. Facilities for disabled visitors in the smaller block. Washing machine. Gas supplies. Shop. Busy bar and good restaurant. Swimming pool. Play area. Off site: Beach 700 m. Bicycle hire 5 km. Riding 10 km. Tarifa 12 km. Golf 25 km.

Open: All year.

Directions

Site is signed off N340 Cadiz road at Punta Paloma, about 10 km. northwest of Tarifa, just west of km. 74 marker. Watch carefully for the site sign (no advance notice). Be sure to use the slip road to turn left if coming from Tarifa. Follow signs down the road for 300 m. GPS: N36:04.566 W5:41.622

Charges guide

Per person	€ 3,30 - € 5,50
pitch incl. electricity	€ 8,00 - € 13,00

ES90810 Camping Villsom

Ctra Sevilla - Cadiz km 554,8, E-41700 Sevilla (Sevilla)

Tel: **954 720 828**   www.alanrogers.com/ES90810

This city site was one of the first to open in Spain and it is still owned by the same pleasant family. The administrative building consists of a peaceful and attractive bar with patio and satellite TV (where breakfast is served) and there is a pleasant, small reception area. It is a good site for visiting Seville with a frequent bus service to the centre. Camping Villsom has around 180 pitches which are level and shaded. A huge variety of trees and palms are to be seen around the site and in summer the bright colours of the flowers are very pleasing. There are no static caravans here, although there is an area for groups. The site has a most inviting, palm-surrounded pool which is quite secluded.

Facilities

Sanitary facilities require modernisation in some areas. Some washbasins have cold water only. Laundry facilities. Small shop selling basic provisions. Bar with satellite TV (open July/Aug). Swimming pool (June - Sept). Putting. Drinks machine. Off site: Bus stop close. Most town facilities including restaurant, supermarket, cinema and theatre.

Open: All year.

Directions

On main Seville - Cadiz NIV road travelling from Seville take exit at km. 553 signed Dos Hermanos - Isla Menor. Go under road bridge and turn immediately right (Isla Mentor) to site 80 m. on right. GPS: N37:16.641 W05:56.210

Charges guide

Per person	€ 4,45
pitch incl. electricity	€ 12,45 - € 14,55

ES88580 Camping La Rosaleda

Ctra del Pradillo km 1,3, E-11140 Conil de la Frontera (Cádiz)

Tel: **956 443 327**. Email: **info@campinglarosaleda.com**   www.alanrogers.com/ES88580

This excellent site in Andalucia was opened in 1999. Its owner has many years of experience and has listened to what campers want and has then delivered. Much money has been spent and will continue to be spent to make this an even better site. Great care has been taken with the planning to ensure campers have an enjoyable holiday, with many top class facilities and a first class service. There are 335 well kept pitches of three different sizes, the smallest just for tents, the largest with electricity and water. This is an ideal place to experience the sunshine and culture of Spain.

Facilities

Four modern, fully equipped sanitary blocks include facilities for campers with disabilities and were spotless when seen. Motorcaravan services. Gas supplies. Excellent supermarket (all year). Bar/restaurant (all year). Swimming pool complex (large with stunning views). Large play area. Massage, sauna, gym, yoga room, hairdressing. Dogs are not accepted in high season. Wooden bungalows with good facilities with own gardens. Off site: Water based activities at beach 1.5 km. Conil town with bars, restaurants and shops. Excursions.

Open: All year.

Directions

Follow signs to Conil from N340, then signs to site around several roundabouts. Site is 1 km. from centre on Ctra del Pradillo, on the side of this road with a car park in front and a large campsite sign high in the air. GPS: N36:17.590 W06:05.728

Charges 2009

Per person	€ 4,72 - € 8,00
child (3-10 yrs)	€ 3,24 - € 5,50
pitch incl. electricity	€ 11,80 - € 21,00

ES88590 Camping Roche

N340 km 19,5, Carril de Pilahito, E-11140 Conil de la Frontera (Cádiz)

Tel: **956 442 216**. Email: **info@campingroche.com**   www.alanrogers.com/ES88590

Camping Roche is situated in a pine forest near white sandy beaches in the lovely region of Andalucia. It is a clean and tidy, welcoming site. Little English is spoken but try your Spanish, German or French as the staff are very helpful. A family site, it offers a variety of facilities including a sports area and swimming pools. The restaurant has good food and a pleasant outlook over the pool. Games are organised for children. A recently built extension provides further pitches, a new toilet block and a tennis court. There are now 240 pitches which include 104 bungalows to rent.

Facilities

Three toilet blocks are traditional in style and provide simple, clean facilities. Washbasins have cold water only. Washing machine. Supermarket. Bar and restaurant. Swimming and paddling pools. Sports area. Tennis. Play area. Off site: Bus stops 3 times daily outside gates.

Open: All year.

Directions

From the N340 (Cádiz - Algeciras) turn off to site at km. 19,5 point. From Conil, take El Pradillo road. Keep following signs to site. From CA3208 road turn at km 1 and site is 1.5 km. down this road on the right. GPS: N36:18.653 W6:06.761

Charges guide

Per person	€ 6,00
pitch incl. electricity	€ 19,00

ES88600 Camping Fuente del Gallo

Apdo 48, E-11149 Conil de la Frontera (Cádiz)

Tel: 956 440 137. Email: camping@campingfuentedelgallo.com   www.alanrogers.com/ES88600

Fuente del Gallo is a well maintained site with 221 pitches allocated to touring units. Each pitch has 10A electricity and a number of trees create shade to some pitches. Although the actual pitch areas are generally a good size, the majority are long and narrow. This could, in some cases, prevent the erection of an awning and your neighbour may feel close. In low season it is generally accepted to make additional use of an adjoining pitch. The attractive pool, restaurant and bar complex with its large, shaded terrace, are very welcoming in the height of summer. Good beaches are 300 m.

Facilities

Two modernised and very clean sanitary blocks include excellent services for babies and disabled visitors and hot water at all facilities. Laundry room. Motorcaravan services. Gas supplies. Shop. Attractive bar and restaurant (breakfast served). Swimming pool (all season, lifeguard in high season with small charge). Play area. TV and games rooms. Excursions. Torches useful. Off site: Watersports on beach. Fishing 300 m. Riding 1 km. Golf 5 km.

Open: 27 March - 30 September.

Directions

From the N340 (Cadiz - Algeciras) at km. 23, follow signs to Conil de la Frontera town centre, then shortly right to Fuente del Gallo and 'playas', following signs. GPS: N36:17.776 W06:06.611

Charges 2009

Per person	€ 6,00
pitch incl. electricity	€ 15,00

Less 11-30% for longer stays (except Jul/Aug).

ES88650 Camping Playa Las Dunas

Paseo Maritimo, Playa de la Puntilla s/n, E-11500 El Puerto de Santa Maria (Cádiz)

Tel: 956 872 210. Email: info@lasdunascamping.com   www.alanrogers.com/ES88650

This site lies within the Parque Natural Bahia de Les Dunes and is adjacent to the long and gently sloping golden sands of Puntilla beach. This is a pleasant and peaceful site (though very busy in August) with some 539 separate marked pitches, 260 for tourers, with much natural shade and ample electrical connections (10A). Motorcaravans park in an area called the Oasis which is very pretty. The tent and caravan pitches, under mature trees, are terraced and separated by low walls. This is a spacious site with a tranquil setting and is popular with people who wish to 'winter over' in peace.

Facilities

Immaculate modern sanitary facilities with separate facilities for disabled campers and a baby room. Laundry facilities are excellent. Gas supplies. Bar/restaurant (all year). Supermarket (high season). Very large swimming pool and paddling pool (1/7-31/8). Play areas. Night security all year. Barbecues not permitted 15/5-15/10. Off site: Beach 100 m. Fishing 500 m. Bicycle hire, riding and golf 2 km. Municipal sports centre. Local buses for town and cities visits and a ferry to Cadiz.

Open: All year.

Directions

Site is 5 km. north of Cadiz off the N443. Take road to Puerto Santa Maria, site is very well signed throughout the town (small yellow signs high on posts). From south, turn left into town just after large bridge. Keeping sea inlet on your left, follow road for about 1 km. Site on right opposite beach. GPS: N36:35.340 W6:14.304

Charges guide

Per person	€ 4,03 - € 4,47
pitch incl. electricity (5A)	€ 9,13 - € 11,53

ES88900 Camping Los Gazules

Ctra de Patrite km 4, E-11180 Alcala de los Gazules (Cádiz)

Tel: 956 420 486. Email: losgazules@hotmail.com   www.alanrogers.com/ES88900

The first impression of this site is that it looks a little sad with the pitches having a rather unkempt appearance. However, the main building complex, consisting of the shop and restaurant has been newly painted outside and improved and the well furnished restaurant/bar is a pleasant place to eat. The sanitary facilities have also been improved and there is an inviting swimming pool, open from the end of June. The site is set in the beautiful surroundings of the Los Alcornocales natural park and has 135 touring pitches with 10A electricity. Although basic, this would make an ideal site for a quiet, relaxing holiday in the countryside.

Facilities

A circular sanitary block offers clean facilities, including facilities for disabled campers. Washing machine in supervised room. Bar/restaurant. Shop in bar sells basic supplies. Swimming pool (June - Sept). Playground. Off site: Site is well placed for exploring the local area and excursions to Cadiz.

Open: All year.

Directions

From A381 Algecieras - Jerez road take exit to Alcalá de los Gazules onto A375 (C440). Continue around village on A375 to Ubrique and proceed to 42 km. marker. Then turn onto the road to Patrite, the site is on the right at the 4 km. marker. GPS: N36:27.780 W05:39.840

Charges 2009

Per unit incl. 2 persons and electricity	€ 18,00 - € 20,50

ES88710 Camping Giralda

Ctra Provincial 4117, E-21410 Isla Cristina (Huelva)

Tel: 959 343 318. Email: campinggiralda@infonegocio.com

www.alanrogers.com/ES88710

The fountains at the entrance and the circular 'thatched' reception building set the tone for this very large site. The 587 pitches are quite spacious on sand, most benefiting from the attractive mature trees which abound on the site. Most pitches have electricity (142 are for tents). Access to the excellent beach is gained by a short stroll, crossing the minor road alongside the site and passing through attractive pine trees. This is a quiet site out of the main tourist areas, with good leisure and adventure facilities. The many additional activities are listed below. There is a separate area within this huge site where organised groups come to enjoy the activities offered within a dedicated adventure area (low season only).

Facilities

Four large, modern, semi-circular 'thatched' sanitary blocks are clean and fully equipped. Laundry. Shop and bar (all year). Restaurant and snacks (June - Sept). Swimming pools. Archery. Petanque. Mountain biking. Beach games. Watersports school. Play area. Organised activity area for groups low season. Excursions booked. Off site: Beach and fishing 200 m. Bicycle hire 1.5 km. Golf 4 km. Riding 7 km.

Open: All year.

Directions

Leave E1/A49 at exit 113 signed Lepe on the N444. Turn right on N431, use Lepe bypass, then left to Le Antilla and then on to Isla Cristina. Site is on right (signed) just as you reach Isla Christina (this route avoids Pozo del Camino and many speed bumps). GPS: N37:11.999 W07:18.052

Charges guide

Per person	€ 5,80
child (2-10 yrs)	€ 4,20
pitch	€ 9,00 - € 10,95
electricity	€ 5,25

Plus 7% VAT. Winter discounts.

ES88730 Camping La Aldea

El Rocio, E-21750 Almonte (Huelva)

Tel: 959 442 677. Email: info@campinglaaldea.com

www.alanrogers.com/ES88730

This impressive site lies just on the edge of the Parque Nacional de Donana, southwest of Sevilla on the outskirts of El Rocio. The town hosts a fiesta at the end of May with over one million people attending the local shrine. They travel for days in processions with cow drawn or motorized vehicles to attend. If you want to stay this weekend book well in advance! The well planned, modern site is well set out and the 246 pitches have natural shade from trees or artificial shade and 10A electricity. There are 52 serviced pitches with water and sewage connections. There are also pitches for tents and bungalows for rent. The facilities are new, large and very clean. A waiter service restaurant (where the Spanish eat) provides lovely local food. The staff are welcoming and helpful. Expeditions on horseback or by 4 x 4 vehicle can be arranged in the national park.

Facilities

Two sanitary blocks provide excellent facilities including provision for disabled visitors. Motorcaravan service point. Swimming pool (May - Oct). Restaurant and bar in separate new complex. Shop. Internet connection. Playground. Off site: Bus stop 5 minutes walk. Huelva and Sevilla are about an hour's drive. Beach 15 km.

Open: 6 January - 25 December.

Directions

From main Huelva - Sevilla road E1/A49 take exit 48 and drive south through Almonte to outskirts of El Rocio. Site is on left just past 25 km. marker. Go down to the roundabout and back up to be on the right side of the road to turn in. GPS: N37:08.495 W6:29.463

Charges guide

Per person	€ 5,00 - € 6,50
child	€ 4,00 - € 5,00
pitch incl. car	€ 8,00 - € 12,00
electricity	€ 5,00

Less 10-15% for low season stays over 3 days.

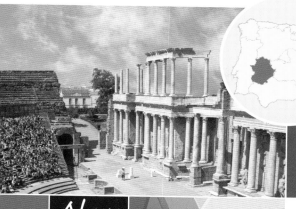

This is one of the most beautiful, and perhaps least known, regions of inland Spain. Its beautiful cities, first Roman and Moorish, then medieval and aristocratic, gave birth to many of the conquistadors - conquerors of the New World.

Alan Rogers

EXTREMADURA HAS TWO PROVINCES: BADAJOZ AND CÁCERES

Extremadura is a large and sparsely populated region in the west of Spain, bordering central Portugal and consisting of two provinces, both of which bear the name of their main town. Cáceres, to the north, has a fascinating old quarter, ringed by old Moorish walls and superb watchtowers. Nearby Plasencia is home to a splendid Gothic cathedral, old medieval walls and beautiful Baroque and Renaissance palaces. And the attractive town of Trujillo, birthplace of Pizzaro, the conqueror of Peru, has palaces, churches and a bustling town square. To the south is Badajoz, the second province and the largest in Spain. With its fortified main town and Alcazaba (citadel), the city of Badajoz is located on the Vía de la Plata (Silver Route), an old pilgrimage route to Santiago de Compostela used during the Middle Ages. Located on this route, Mérida is one of the best preserved archaeological sites in Spain. Indeed, the city boasts more Roman remains than any other city, including a Roman theatre and amphitheatre, a Roman bridge spanning over 800 metres long, with 60 arches, Roman villas and a Museum of Roman Art.

Places of interest

Alcántara: six-arched Roman bridge, castle, mansions.

Corio: quiet old town enclosed by 4th century Roman walls, cathedral.

Cuacos de Yuste: town with 15th century Jeronimos Monastery.

Guadalupe: old pilgrimage centre, church and monastery.

Jerez de los Caballeros: birthplace of various conquistadores.

Olivenza: town with strong Portuguese influence, castle, ethnographic museum, 17th century church.

Pedroso de Acim: Convento del Palancar – said to be the smallest monastery in the world.

Cuisine of the region

Local cuisine includes the Iberian cured ham and a variety of cheeses; *Torta del Casar, La Serena, Ibores, Gata* and *Cabra del Tietar*. Game abounds in this region (partridge, pigeon, turtledove, rabbit, hare, wild boar, deer) served with wild mushrooms, truffles or wild asparagus. Honey, thyme, heather, rosemary, lavender, lime and eucalyptus are used to prepare a great variety of desserts.

Alfeñiques: caramel dessert.

Nuégados: egg yolk and orange buns.

Perrunillas: small round cakes.

Rosquillas: ring-shaped biscuits.

Técula-mécula: cinnamon, almond and tea.

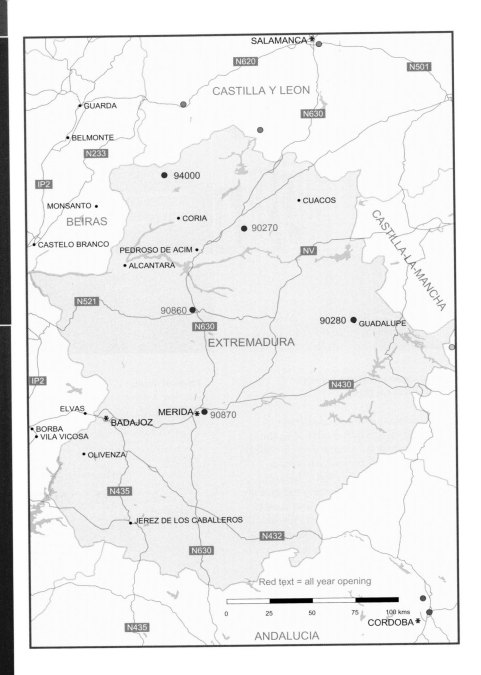

SALAMANCA ✱

N620

N501

CASTILLA Y LEON

GUARDA

N630

BELMONTE

N233

IP2

● 94000

MONSANTO ●

● CUACOS

BEIRAS

● CORIA

● 90270

● CASTELO BRANCO

PEDROSO DE ACIM ●

NV

● ALCANTARA

CASTILLA-LA-MANCHA

N521

90860 ●

90280 ● GUADALUPE

N630

EXTREMADURA

IP2

N430

ELVAS

MERIDA ✱ ● 90870

✱ BADAJOZ

● BORBA
● VILA VICOSA

● OLIVENZA

N435

JEREZ DE LOS CABALLEROS

N432

N630

Red text = all year opening

0   25   50   75   100 kms

N435

CORDOBA ✱

ANDALUCIA

ES90870 Camping Mérida

Ctra NV Madrid - Portugal km 336,6, E-06800 Mérida (Badajoz)

Tel: **924 303 453**. Email: **proexcam@jet.es**

www.alanrogers.com/ES90870

Camping Mérida is situated alongside the main N-V road to Madrid, the restaurant, café and pool complex separating the camping site area from the road where there is considerable noise. The site has 80 good sized pitches, with some shade and on sloping ground, with ample electricity connections (long leads may be needed) and hedges with imaginative topiary. No English is spoken, but try out your Spanish. Reception is open until midnight. Camping Mérida is ideally located to serve both as a base to tour the local area or as an overnight stop en-route when travelling either north/south or east/west. Mérida was the tenth city of the Roman Empire and it is purported that it contains the most Roman remains in all of Spain. The 60-arched Roman bridge, the amphitheatre and the National museum of Roman art are just some of the attractions that can be enjoyed here. In July and August the theatre festival stages classical Greek plays and Roman tragedies.

Facilities

The central sanitary facility includes hot and cold showers, British style WCs. Gas supplies. Small shop for essentials. Busy restaurant/cafeteria and bar, also open to the public. Medium sized swimming and paddling pools (May - Sept). Bicycle hire. Play area (unfenced and near road). Caravan storage. Torches useful. Off site: Town 5 km.

Open: All year.

Directions

Site is alongside NV road (Madrid - Lisbon), 5 km. east of Mérida, at km. 336.6. From east take exit 334 and follow camping signs (doubling back). Site is actually on the 630 road that runs alongside the new motorway. GPS: N38:56.143 W06:18.306

Charges guide

Per person	€ 4,06
child	€ 3,42
pitch incl. car	€ 19,50
electricity	€ 3,24
All plus VAT.	

ES90270 Camping Parque Natural de Monfrague

Ctra Plasencia - Trujillo km 10, E-10680 Malpartida de Plasencia (Cáceres)

Tel: **927 459 233**. Email: **contacto@campingmonfrague.com**

www.alanrogers.com/ES90270

Situated on the edge of the Monfrague National Park, this well managed site owned by the Barrado family, has fine views to the Sierra de Mirabel and delightful surrounding countryside. Many of the 130 good-sized grass pitches are on slightly sloping, terraced ground. Scattered trees offer a degree of shade, there are numerous water points and 10A electricity. It would prove difficult to find a more suitable location for those that savour tranquility. On rare occasions a goods train travels along the nearby railway line. Created as a National Park in 1979, Monfrague is now recognised as one of the best locations in Europe for anyone interested in birdwatching. During our visit we saw Spanish imperial eagles, eagle owl, griffon, black and Egyptian vultures, black and red kites, azure-winged magpies, purple gallinule, purple heron, black-eared wheatear, bee-eater, blue rock thrush and the more rare black stork to name but a few. Nearby Plasencia has a medieval aqueduct, fine cathedral (14th century) and the town's original twin ring of walls containing 68 towers. To the south, are the classic historical towns of Merida, Caceres and Trujillo.

Facilities

Large modern toilet blocks, fully equipped, are very clean. Facilities for disabled campers and baby baths. Laundry. Motorcaravan service point. Supermarket/shop. Restaurant, bar and coffee shop. TV room with recreational facilities. WiFi. Swimming and paddling pools (June - Sept). Play area. Tennis. Bicycle hire. Riding. Animation for children in season. Barbecue areas. Guided safaris into the Park for birdwatching. Off site: Large supermarket at Plasencia.

Open: All year.

Directions

From the north on the N630 take the EX-208 road (previously C524) Plasencia - Trujillo; site on left in 6 km. From the south turn right just south of Plasencia on EX-108 (previously C511) in direction of Malpartida de Plasencia. Right at main junction onto EX-208 to site. GPS: N39:56.370 W06:05.040

Charges guide

Per person	€ 4,00
child (3-12 yrs)	€ 3,50
pitch	€ 7,00 - € 7,50
VAT included.	
Camping Cheques accepted.	

ES90280 Camping Las Villuercas

Ctra Villanueva, E-10140 Guadalupe (Cáceres)

Tel: 927 367 139

www.alanrogers.com/ES90280

This rural site nestles in an attractive valley northwest of Guadalupe. The 50 pitches (25 with 10A electricity) are level and of a reasonable size; although large units may experience difficulty in getting into the more central pitches. With an abundance of mature trees most pitches offer some degree of shade. A river runs alongside the site and the ground can be muddy in very wet periods. The site is co-located with hostel accommodation. The restaurant provides excellent food at low prices and leads to a pretty patio with overhead vines and potted plants allowing elevated views of the pools. There is a separate patio across the village street which is pleasant for sitting out with drinks whilst the management provide a barbecue and more casual food. An ideal location for visiting the Monastery of Guadalupe, and the town of Guadalupe in the Sierra de Guadalupe, an attractive historic tourist town with plenty of bars and restaurants.

Facilities

The single toilet block is older in but very clean, one area for women and one for men, providing British type WCs, washbasins and showers (hot water is from a 40 litre immersion heater which could be overwhelmed in busy periods). Facilities for disabled visitors. Laundry facilities. Restaurant. Bar. Swimming pools. Shop. Tennis. Small playground. Barbecue area. No English spoken. Off site: Riding 2 km. Fishing 3 km.

Open: 1 March - 30 November.

Directions

From NV/E90 Madrid - Mérida exit at Navelmoral de la Mata. Follow south to Guadalupe on CC713 (83 km). Site is 2 km. from Guadalupe (near Monastery). From further southwest take exit 102 off main E90/NV (northeast of Merida). Follow signs (Guadalupe). Go through a few villages and near 72 km. marker turn left to site, 100 m. on right. GPS: N39:27.600 W05:19.320

Charges guide

Per person	€ 3,21
child (2-12 yrs)	€ 2,67
pitch	€ 4,28 - € 5,88
electricity	€ 2,67
No credit cards.	

ES94000 Camping Sierra de Gata

Ctra Ex109 a Gata km 4,100, E-10860 Gata (Cáceres)

Tel: 927 672 168. Email: sierradegata@campingsonline.com

www.alanrogers.com/ES94000

For a taste of the real, rural Spain this very Spanish site (no English was spoken when we visited) is situated just before the tiny village of Sierra de Gata, south of Ciudad Rodrigo and northwest of Plasencia. Situated in beautiful countryside with a small stream alongside the site, the pitches are on grass with plenty of shade from trees. This site is undergoing refurbishment with the addition of 12 beautiful new bungalows to sleep 4-6 people. A special area with huts for groups of children to stay is positioned in one corner of the site. We suspect that it is a popular site with Spanish people which would give the opportunity to practice the language and get an insight into the Spanish way of life. The village of Gata is small with only a few houses and if you continue along the road you will climb into the mountains and natural park, good for walks and picnics. The other side of the hill leads down into another town but this has very small streets and is probably best not driven through with a motorcaravan!

Facilities

Two toilet blocks with British style toilets also include child size toilets, a laundry room and dishwashing facilities. Medium sized shop for necessities in summer. Smart restaurant/bar complex provides good food. Two swimming pools. Tennis. Play area. Fishing. Riding. Bicycle hire. Off site: Restaurant near site entrance.

Open: 18 March - 3 November.

Directions

Approach ONLY from the southwest from the 109 Ciudad Rodrico - Coria road. Where the 205 meets the 109 take turn 20-30 m. north signed Gata 10. Travel along this road until km. 4. Turn left (near restaurant and small bridge) and site is ahead through gate. GPS: N40:12.728 W06:38.526

Charges guide

Per person	€ 3,75 - € 4,25
child (3-12 yrs)	€ 3,25 - € 3,75
pitch	€ 4,50 - € 8,00
electricity	€ 3,75 - € 4,25

Check real time availability and at-the-gate prices...

www.alanrogers.com

ES90860 Cáceres Camping

Ctra N630 km 549,5, E-10005 Cáceres (Cáceres)

Tel: **927 233 100**. Email: **info@campingcaceres.com**   www.alanrogers.com/ES90860

Recommended by our agent in Spain, we plan to conduct a full inspection of this all-year site in 2008. Cáceres Camping is quite a small site, located to the west of the interesting city of Cáceres, a World Heritage site. There are 130 pitches here, and, unusually, each has a chalet providing a shower, washbasin and toilet. The pitches are of a reasonable size (80 sq.m.) and are well shaded. A range of leisure facilities is provided, including a swimming pool and a separate children's pool. Cáceres is a city with much interest, and a fascinating history. Cave paintings on the city outskirts date back 30,000 years! The city is capital of High Extremadura and close by, the Montanchez mountain range offers many opportunities for walking and cycling.

Facilities

Individual toilet blocks. Bar, restaurant, cafeteria and takeaway meals. Supermarket. Swimming pool.
Off site: City centre 2 km. Golf, walking and cycling opportunities.

Open: All year.

Directions

From the east (E90 motorway) take the N521 to Cáceres. Continue on this road to the west of the city. At the large roundabout sign for 'Campo de Futbol Principe Felipe' is the entrance to the site. GPS: N39:29.340 W06:24.768

Charges guide

Per person	€ 4,00
child	€ 3,00
pitch	€ 12,00
electricity	€ 3,20

Cáceres camping

Ctra. N-630, km. 549,5
E-10005 CÁCERES
Tel/Fax: 927 233 100

www.campingcaceres.com
info@campingcaceres.com

Fantastic site in the town of Caceres, open throughout the year and with installations of the first category. Private individual sanitary install. on each site - equipped wooden bungalows – studio's for 2 p. - Wi-Fi service in install. –social room w. TV - launderette – supermarket – cafeteria and restaurant with terrace – 2 swimming pools and large green areas with children's playground and sports zone.

Offer Sept. 08/June 09 except Easter week: 1 week 99 €; 15 days 175 €; 1 month 275 € including private bathroom on site, electr., hot water, 1 car and 2 adults.

Widely regarded as the 'Bible' by site owners and readers alike, there is no better guide when it comes to forming an independent view of a campsite's quality. When you need to be confident in your choice of campsite, you need the Alan Rogers Guide.

☑ **Sites only included on merit**

☑ **Sites cannot pay to be included**

☑ **Independently inspected, rigorously assessed**

☑ **Impartial reviews**

☑ **Over 40 years of expertise**

This region is located south of Madrid and occupies what was the southern part of the ancient kingdom of Castille, including the area known as La Mancha, universally famous as the setting for Miguel de Cervantes great novel 'Don Quijote de la Mancha'.

CASTILLA-LA MANCHA HAS FIVE PROVINCES: ALBACETE, CIUDAD REAL, CUENCA, GUADALAJARA AND TOLEDO

THE CAPITAL OF THE REGION IS TOLEDO

The terrain can be divided into two distinct parts: the plateau, an extensive, flat land with very few mountains, and the mountainous areas, which encircle the plateau around the region's borders, including the foothills along the massifs of the Central mountain range, the Iberian mountain range and the Sierra Morena. Toledo is crammed with monuments and nearly all the different stages of Spanish art are represented with Moorish-Mudejar-Jewish buildings; Gothic structures, such as the splendid cathedral; and Renaissance buildings. Toledo was also home to El Greco and many of his paintings are displayed in the Museum of El Greco. The region of Cuenca is surrounded by mountainous, craggy countryside, with the city itself home to extraordinary houses which hang over the cliff tops of the deep gorges. One of these has been converted into the Museum of Abstract Art. In the heartland of La Mancha, through the region of Ciudad Real, you can follow the Ruta de Don Quixote and see the famous windmills at Campo de Criptana.

Places of interest

Almagro: home of international theatre festival.

Albacete: renowned for its knife-making industry, 16th century cathedral.

Guadalajara: preserved Moorish walls, 10th century bridge, Santa Maria la Mayor, 15th century Duque del Infantado Palace.

Cuisine of the region

Local produce features heavily: aubergines, garlic, peppers, tomatoes, olive oil, meat, including both game and farm animals. Wine from La Mancha, Valdepeñas, Méntrida, Almansa, Dominio de Valdepusa and Finca de Elez.

Alajú: an almond and nut pastry.

Bizcochás de Alcázar: a tart soaked in milk with sugar, vanilla and cinnamon.

Caldereta manchega: lamb stew.

Morteruelo: paté made of pork and game birds.

Pisto manchego: a type of ratatouille with tomatoes, red and green peppers, courgettes, served either hot or cold.

Tiznao: filleted cod which is flame-grilled in an earthenware dish with pepper, tomatoes, onions and garlic.

Red text = all year opening

0   25   50   75   100 kms

ES90900 Camping El Greco

Ctra CM4000 km 0,7, Puebla de Montalban, E-45004 Toledo (Toledo)

Tel: **925 220 090**. Email: **campingelgreco@telefonica.net**   www.alanrogers.com/ES90900

Toledo was the home of the Grecian painter and the site that bears his name boasts a beautiful view of the ancient city from the restaurant, bar and superb pool. The friendly, family owners make you welcome and are proud of their site which is the only one in Toledo (it can get crowded). The 150 pitches are of 80 sq.m. with electrical connections and shade from strategically planted trees. Most have separating hedges that give privacy, with others in herring bone layouts that make for interesting parking in some areas. The river Tagus stretches alongside the site which is fenced for safety. There is an attractive, tree-lined approach to the site. Ivy clad pergolas run down each side of the swimming pool (also fenced for safety) and a large shaded terrace offers shelter from the sun which can be very hot here. This site makes a relaxing base to return to after a hard day visiting the amazing sights of the old city of Toledo.

Facilities

Two sanitary blocks, both modernised include facilities for disabled campers and everything is of the highest standard and kept very clean. Laundry. Motorcaravan services. Swimming pool (15/6-15/9, charged). Restaurant/bar (1/4-30/9) with good menu and fair prices. Small shop in reception. Playgrounds. Ice machine. Off site: Fishing in river. Golf 10 km. Riding 15 km. An hourly air-conditioned bus service runs from the gates to the city centre, touring the outside of the walls first.

Open: All year.

Directions

Site is on C4000 road on the edge of the town, signed towards Puebla de Montelban; site signs also in city centre. From Madrid on N401, turn off right towards Toledo city centre but turn right again at the roundabout at the gates to the old city. Site is signed from the next right turn.
GPS: N39:51.900 W04:02.820

Charges 2009

Per person	€ 6,10
child (3-10 yrs)	€ 5,25
pitch incl. electricity	€ 15,55 - € 15,85

ES90960 Camping El Mirador de Cabaneros

Canada Real Segoviana s/n, E-13110 Horcajo de Los Montes (Ciudad Real)

Tel: 926 775 439
www.alanrogers.com/ES90960

With panoramic views all around of the Sierra de Valdefuertes mountains, Camping El Mirador is set in the Cabaneros National Park. This is a well cared for, landscaped site with 80 terraced pitches on gravel and all with electricity. Although level once sited, the approach is via a steep slope which may cause difficulties for larger units. Run by a very helpful and friendly family, this site is in a peaceful location where you can just sit and relax or visit the many attractions that the National Park has to offer. It is an ideal base for walking and birdwatching.

Facilities

One spotlessly clean central toilet block with solar heating includes open washbasins and cubicled showers. Facilities for disabled visitors and babies. Laundry facilities. Motorcaravan services. No shop but bread and gas from reception. Bar and restaurant (15/6-15/9, weekends in low season). Outdoor swimming pool. Games room. Basic (unfenced) play area. Off site: Village of Horcajo de los Montes 200 m.

Open: All year.

Directions

From north head towards Toledo (southwest from Madrid). At Toledo, take CM4013 to Cuerva and pick up CM403 to El Molinillo. Turn right onto CM4017 to Horcajo de los Montes. Through village onto CM4016 towards Alcoba de los Montes, past garage and up hill for 2 km. Site is on left (narrow approach). GPS: N39:19.372 W4:39.106

Charges guide

Per person	€ 3,60 - € 4,00
pitch incl. electricity	€ 6,50 - € 8,50

ES90880 Camping de Fuencaliente

Ctra N420 km 105,8, E-13130 Fuencaliente (Ciudad Real)

Tel: 926 698 170
www.alanrogers.com/ES90880

This quiet site nestles in an attractive valley between the Sierra Modrona and the Sierra Morena. It is a site for getting away from it all and sampling the peaceful mountain beauty. It could be a useful stopover if crossing Spain coast to coast or if you wish to visit the fascinating historic town of Cordoba. With very few other desirable sites in this region of Castilla - La Mancha, this one is spacious with 91 generously sized pitches (over 100 sq.m) all with electricity (6A) and water. There is natural shade from pine trees and the beautiful, restful views.

Facilities

The large, modern toilet block has reasonable facilities. Laundry sinks. Washing machine. Swimming pool (1/6-15/9; free). Restaurant/bar. Supermarket. Playground. Barbecue area with table and benches overlooking the countryside Off site: Fuencaliente 5 km.

Open: Easter - 30 September.

Directions

From the N420 road (Cuidad Real - Cordoba) turn by 105 km. marker (about 5 km. north of Fuencaliente) onto unmade road signed Camping San Isidro to site. GPS: N38:26.520 W04:19.200

Charges guide

Per person	€ 4,00 - € 4,50
pitch incl. electricity	€ 7,50 - € 11,00
Plus 7% VAT.	

ES90980 Camping Rio Mundo

Ctra Comarcal 412 km 205, Mesones, E-02449 Molinicos (Albacete)

Tel: 967 433 230. Email: riomundo@campingriomundo.com
www.alanrogers.com/ES90980

This typically Spanish site is situated in the Sierra de Alcaraz (south of Albacete), just off the scenic route 412 between Elche de la Sierra and Valdepenas. The drive to this site is through beautiful scenery (well worth the drive) and although from the west the main road is winding in some places, it should cause no problems if driven carefully. Shade is provided either by trees or by artificial means for the 100 pitches and electricity is supplied to the centre ones. It is a beautiful setting with majestic mountains and wonderful countryside which begs to be explored.

Facilities

One toilet block has been upgraded and provides clean modern facilities. Basic toilet facilities for disabled people. Washing machine. Small shop for basics. Outside bar serving snacks with covered seating area. Takeaway. Another bar by the swimming pool. Playground. Petanque. Barbecue area. Off site: Riding 7 km.

Open: 18 March - 12 October.

Directions

Site is just off the 412 road which runs west to east between the A30 and 322 roads south of Albacete. Turn at km. 205 on the 412, 5 km. east of village of Riopar and west of Elche de la Sierra. From here follow signs to site. The road narrows to one lane for a few hundred yards but keep straight on for 1-2 km. to site. GPS: N38:29.347 W02:20.781

Charges guide

Per person	€ 3,80 - € 5,00
pitch incl. electricity	€ 11,40 - € 17,45

ES90970 Camping Los Batanes

Ctra Lagunas de Ruidera km 8, E-02611 Ossa de Montiel (Albacete)

Tel: 926 699 076. Email: camping@losbatanes.com   www.alanrogers.com/ES90970

This large campsite is in a lovely setting at the side of one of the many lakes in this area. The route to get here is beautiful and it is well worth the trip, but careful driving was necessary in parts with our large motorhome. A smaller, older part of the campsite houses reception, a small shop and a bar/restaurant. Here are medium sized pitches, shaded by pine trees with a small river running through. Over a wooden bridge is the main newer, part of the site with over 200 level, gravel and sand pitches of mixed size, shaded again by pine trees. There is a new toilet block (cleaner and more modern than the one the other side) plus two barbecue areas. Another small stream runs towards the lake which can be seen from a few of the pitches. Towards one end of this new site is the swimming pool complex with two pools surrounded by hedges and grass for sunbathing, more toilets and places to eat, drink and have fun. In summer children's club activities are run from here and this is definitely the part of the campsite with a lot going on. The site is increasingly popular with Spanish campers who come to relax and enjoy watersport activities in a beautiful area. Because of its popularity it is being extended and should develop into a good large place to stay.

Facilities

One old toilet block and a newer, more spacious one. If cleaning is maintained they should cope in high season. Small shop. Simple restaurant, snacks and bar. Swimming pools (16/6-9/9). Play area. Children's activities. Off site: Beautiful walks and many lakes to explore. Watersports in summer. Tourist information either at reception or 9 km. at nearest village. Bus stop in village.

Open: All year.

Directions

On E5/NIV Cordoba - Madrid road (south of Madrid) take 430 road towards Albacete. Coming into Ruidera turn right (just after lake on the right) signed Lagunas de Ruideria. Drive 8 km. along this country road to site on right. GPS: N38:56.230 W2:50.846

Charges guide

Per person	€ 4,60 - € 5,60
child (1-13 yrs)	€ 3,80 - € 4,70
pitch	€ 18,50 - € 27,00
electricity (5A)	€ 3,40 - € 3,50
Discounts for longer stays.	

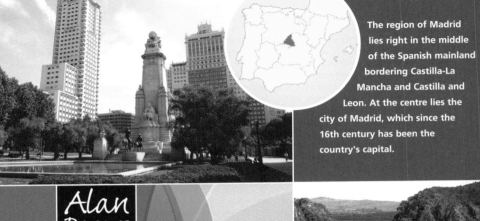

The region of Madrid lies right in the middle of the Spanish mainland bordering Castilla-La Mancha and Castilla and Leon. At the centre lies the city of Madrid, which since the 16th century has been the country's capital.

THE REGION OF MADRID IS A ONE PROVINCE AUTONOMY, ALSO CALLED MADRID

The mountainous region of Madrid can be divided into two areas: the Sierra, in the north and west of the region, which includes part of Somosierra and Guadarrama; and the central and southern parts, where the area is flatter and forms part of the plateau of La Mancha and La Alcarria. Founded by the Moors in the 9th Century, Madrid is now a modern, vibrant city offering innumerable attractions to the visitor. Its architectural heritage is immense. Some of the oldest parts of Madrid lie around the Puerta del Sol; a good starting place for exploring the city. Full of outdoor restaurants and bars, Plaza Mayor is considered to be one of the finest in Spain, and in summer becomes an outdoor theatre and music stage. The city also has a large number of parks and gardens, among them el Retiro, the Botanical Gardens, the Parque del Oeste and the Casa de Campo; and numerous museums and art galleries. Outside the capital, the Sierra de Madrid is ideal for winter sports and the beautiful town of Aranjuez, home to the Royal Palace and glorious gardens, is a popular retreat from the city.

Places of interest

Alcala de Henares: university town, birthplace of Cervantes, author of Don Quixote, Cervantes House Museum, Archepiscopal Palace Cathedral.

Chinchón: 15th century castle, beautiful medieval square, 19th century church with painting by Goya, home of Alchoholera de Chinchón – aniseed liqueur!

Parque Natural de la Cumbre: mountain park, the highest mountains in the Madrid region.

San Lorenzo de El Escorial: town in heart of Guadarrama Mountains, Monastery of El Escorial, Royal Pantheon.

Cuisine of the region

Tapas is popular with typical dishes including seafood: steamed mussels, anchovies in vinegar and pickled bonito plus croquettes and mini-casseroles. Sea bream and cod is used a lot. Local produce includes beef from the Guadarrama Mountains, olives from Campo Real, aniseed from Chinchón and asparagus from Aranjuez. Madrid is also a good place to experience every regional style of Spanish cooking.

Buñuelos: a type of fritter which is filled with custard, chocolate and cream.

Cocido: meat, potato and chickpea stew.

Con gabardina: prawns cooked in beer.

Torrijas: bread pudding.

Red text = all year opening

| 0 | 25 | 50 | 75 | 100 kms |

ES92100 Camping Pico de la Miel

Ctra NI Madrid - France km 58, E-28751 La Cabrera (Madrid)

Tel: **918 688 082**. Email: **pico-miel@picodelamiel.com**   www.alanrogers.com/ES92100

Pico de la Miel is a very large site 60 km north of Madrid. Mainly a long-stay site for Madrid, there is a huge number of very well established, fairly old statics. There is a small separate area with its own toilet block for touring units. The pitches are on rather poor, sandy grass, some with artificial shade. Others, not so level, are under sparse pine trees and there are yet more pitches for tents (the ground could be hard for pegs). The noise level from the many Spanish customers is high and you will have a chance to practise your Spanish! Electricity connections are available. Tall hedges abound and with the trees, make it resemble a giant maze. No internal signs are provided and the long walk to the pool can be a challenge. The site is well signed and easy to find, two or three kilometres southwest off the main N1 road, with an amazing mountain backdrop.

Facilities

Dated but clean tiled toilet block, with some washbasins in cabins. It can be heated. En-suite unit with ramp for disabled visitors. Motorcaravan services. Gas supplies. Shop. Bar/restaurant and takeaway (1/6-30/9). Excellent swimming pool complex (15/6-15/9). Tennis. Playground. Off site: Bicycle hire and riding 200 m. Fishing 8 km.

Open: All year.

Directions

Site is well signed from the N1. Going south or north use exit 57 and follow site signs. When at T-junction, facing a hotel, turn left. (Exit 57 is closer to site than exit 60). GPS: N40:51.547 W03:37.034

Charges guide

Per person	€ 5,80
child (3-9 yrs)	€ 5,00
pitch	€ 5,80 - € 14,00
car	€ 5,80
electricity	€ 4,20

All plus 7% VAT. Less 10-25% for longer stays.

ES92120 Camping Monte Holiday

Finca el Fercio Novo, E-28739 Gargantilla de Lozoya (Madrid)

Tel: **918 695 065**. Email: **monteholiday@monteholiday.com**   www.alanrogers.com/ES92120

The Somosierra offers spectacular scenery and is very popular with Spanish skiers. This site is situated in an open, sunny lower valley, in the Madrid area's only beech forest near a large nature reserve. The area is ideal for anglers and walkers and also offers many opportunities for outdoor sports enthusiasts. The site is on terraces and has 308 small pitches with 100 for touring (7-5A electricity; long leads required in some areas). These pitches are mainly flat with grass or gravel surfaces and shade from mature trees but unfortunately are very uneven. The upper area is taken by permanent units. The site has an attractive swimming pool with sunbathing areas. The bar/restaurant offers a limited choice of meals including some regional dishes. The strength of this site is the range of adventure and outdoor activities in the nearby mountains. There is horse riding in the area within the site and skiing on the nearby slopes in winter. On site, less arduous activities are also organised for children (high season). From here it is possible to enjoy the wonderful Somosierra mountains or even to make a shoirt trip to Spain's exciting capital, Madrid.

Facilities

The modern, heated and well equipped toilet block is well maintained. Facilities for disabled visitors and babies. Laundry facilities. Motorcaravan services. Shop. Bar and fair quality restaurant (15/6-15/9 and weekends). Swimming pool (1/7-7/9). Multisports court. Tennis. Play area. Gas supplies. Barbecues are not permitted in summer. Off site: Mountain trips, guided climbs. Skiing 20 minutes. Bicycle hire 2 km. Riding 8 km. Fishing 1 km.

Open: All year.

Directions

From A1 motorway (Burgos - Madrid) take exit 69 towards Rascafria. Turn right after passing under a railway tunnel and site is on left after 800 m. GPS: N40:56.982 W3:43.757

Charges guide

Per person	€ 6,00
child (4-11 yrs)	€ 5,60
pitch incl. car	€ 11,65 - € 12,00
electricity	€ 4,00

ES92000 Caravanning El Escorial

Apdo 8, Ctra M600, km 3,5, E-28280 El Escorial (Madrid)

Tel: **918 902 412**. Email: **info@campingelescorial.com**   www.alanrogers.com/ES92000

There is a shortage of good sites in the central regions of Spain, but this is one (albeit rather expensive). El Escorial is very large, there are 1,358 individual pitches of which about 600 are for touring, with the remainder used for permanent or seasonal units, but situated to one side of the site. The pitches are shaded (ask for a pitch without a low tree canopy if you have a 3 m. high motorcaravan). There are another 250 pseudo 'wild' spaces for tourists on open fields, with good shade from mature trees (long cables may be necessary for electricity). The general amenities are good and include three swimming pools (unheated), plus a paddling pool in a central area with a bar/restaurant with terrace and plenty of grassy sitting out areas. At weekends in high season the site can be noisy. It is well situated for sightseeing visits especially to the magnificent El Escorial monastery (5 km). Also, the enormous civil war monument of the Valle de los Caidos is very close plus Madrid and Segovia both at 50 km.

Facilities

One large toilet block for the touring pitches, plus two smart, small blocks for the 'wild' camping area, are all fully equipped with some washbasins in cabins. Baby baths. Facilities for disabled campers. The blocks can be heated. Large supermarket (1/3-31/10). Restaurant/bar and snack bar (all year; w/ends only in low season). Disco-bar. Swimming pools (15/5-15/9). Three tennis courts. Two well equipped playgrounds on sand. ATM. Off site: Town 3 km. Riding or golf 7 km.

Open: All year.

Directions

From the south go through town of El Escorial, and follow M600 Guadarrama road. Site is between the 2 and 3 km. markers north of the town on the right. From the north use A6 autopista and exit 47 to M600 towards El Escorial town. Site is on the left. GPS: N40:37.440 W04:05.940

Charges guide

Per person	€ 3,25
child (3-10 yrs)	€ 6,15
pitch	€ 18,75
electricity	€ 4,15
VAT included. No credit cards.	

ES90910 Camping Internacional Aranjuez

Soto del Rebollo, s/n antigua NIV km 46,8, E-28300 Aranjuez (Madrid)

Tel: **918 911 395** Email: **info@campingaranjuez.com**   www.alanrogers.com/ES90910

Aranjuez, supposedly Spain's version of Versailles, is worthy of a visit with its beautiful palaces, leafy squares, avenues and gardens. This useful, popular and unusually well equipped site is therefore excellent for enjoying the unusual attractions or for an en-route stop. It is 47 km. south of Madrid and 46 km. from Toledo. The site is alongside the River Tajo in a park-like situation with mature trees. There are 178 touring pitches, all with electricity (10A), set on flat grass amid tall trees. The site has recently been acquired by the owners of La Marina (ES87420) who are working hard to improve the pitches and the site. Two little tourist road trains run from the site to the palaces daily. You can visit the huge, but slightly decaying Royal Palace or the Casa del Labrador (translates as farmer's cottage) which is a small neo-classical palace in unusual and differing styles. It has superb gardens commissioned by Charles II. Canoes may be hired from behind the supermarket and there is a lockable moat gate to allow access to the river. There is good security backed up with CCTV around the river perimeter.

Facilities

The largest of three modern, good quality sanitary blocks is heated in winter and well equipped with some washbasins in cabins. Laundry facilities. Gas supplies. Small shop, bar and restaurant (all year) with attractive riverside patio (also open to the public). Takeaway. TV room. Swimming and paddling pools (15/6-15/9). Play area. Bicycle hire. Canoe hire. Torch useful. Off site: Within easy walking distance of palace, gardens and museums. Riding 5 km. Golf 20 km.

Open: All year.

Directions

From the M305 (Madrid - Aranjuez) look for 8 km. marker on the outskirts of town. Then follow campsite signs – these lead back onto the M305 (going north now) and the site is signed off right at 300 m. on the first left bend. Follow signs down the narrow road for 400 m. If coming from the south ensure that you have the M305 to Madrid (other roads are signed to Madrid). If in doubt ask as it is very confusing if the M305 road is missed. GPS: N40:02.556 W3:5.970

Charges guide

Per person	€ 4,28 - € 5,88
child (3-10 yrs)	€ 3,21 - € 4,81
pitch incl. electricity	€ 14,44 - € 19,84

Plus 7% VAT. Discounts for groups or long stays. Camping Cheques accepted.

Life in this single province region that occupies the geographical centre of the Iberian peninsula revolves around the city of Madrid, which since the 16th century has been the country's capital.

Alan Rogers

Founded by the Moors in the 9th Century, Madrid today is something of an enigma. On one hand it is a modern, active city, whilst in the centre the streets are crowded with ancient buildings which reveal much about the development of the city over many centuries. The medieval village has been preserved around the Plaza de la Paja, and the quarter known as 'Madrid of the Austrian' (it was the Habsburg capital in the 16th century) near the traditional city centre, Puerta del Sol, was built in the Golden Age. Located in this area is the Plaza de la Villa, with its beautiful city hall building, and the Plaza Mayor, which is colonaded and considered to be one of the finest in Spain; both are Baroque in style and date from the 17th century.

Another popular attraction is the Royal Palace, a magnificent example of 18th century palatial art, which is surrounded by gardens that are now partially open to the public. Elsewhere, the city also has many interesting treasures from the 19th and 20th centuries and a large number of parks and gardens. Among these are El Retiro, the botanical gardens crafted by royal decree in the 17th Century, the Parque del Oeste and the Casa de Campo.

The city suffered major damage during the Civil War but in the 25 years since Franco's death, thanks to the late mayor, Tierno Galvin, much has been restored. Very much part of the city's modern day life are its two football clubs, Real Madrid and Madrid Atletico.

The Madrid of the 21st century is a vibrant, lively city offering a wide range of events and cultural performances. There are more than thirty theatres, one hundred cinemas, fifty live-music venues, and dozens of galleries and exhibition halls throughout the city. A permanent season of classical music, opera and zarzuela (Spanish operetta) is held in the Auditorio Nacional, the Teatro Real and the Teatro de la Zarzuela. Among Madrid's many museums and art galleries is the Prado Museum, housing one of the oldest collections of art in the world; the archaeological museum, with collections representing practically all the different cultures that have flourished in Spain; and the Reina Sofia Art Centre, which proudly displays Picasso's greatest picture, 'Guernica'.

The large region of Castilla y León is located inland, bordering Portugal to the west. It has a rich legacy dating back to the Romans, with an extraordinary wealth of castles, cathedrals and mansions, historic cities and towns.

THE REGION IS MADE UP OF THE FOLLOWING PROVINCES: AVILA, BURGOS, LEON, PALENCIA, SALAMANCA, VALLADOLID, ZAMORA, SEGOVIA AND SORIA

Steeped in history and architectural sights, the major towns and cities of the provinces all have something to offer. In the south, the town of Ávila is set on a high plain, surrounded by 11th century walls; and the graceful city of Salamanca was once home to one of the most prestigious universities in the world. Its grand Plaza Mayor is the finest in Spain. In the east, Segovia is well known for its magnificent Roman aqueduct, with 163 arches and 29 metres at its highest point; the cathedral; and the fairy-tale Alcázar, complete with turrets and narrow towers. And the attractive city of Soria still retains a Romanesque legacy in its network of medieval streets. Burgos in the north, is the birthplace of El Cid and has a Gothic cathedral of exceptional quality. The lively university city of Leon boasts a Royal Pantheon, decorated by Romanesque wall paintings, and also an impressive Gothic cathedral. There too is a Gothic cathedral in Palencia plus an archaeology museum. South of Leon, the old walled quarters of Zamora have a retained medieval appearance, with a dozen Romanesque churches. And in the centre of the region, Valladolid is famous for its extravagant and solemn processions during the Holy Week celebrations.

Places of interest

Astorga: city of Roman origin, chocolate museum, cathedral.

Ciudad Rodrigo: Renaissance mansions, cathedral, 12th century walls.

Coca: impressive Mudejar castle, birthplace of the famous Roman emperor Theodosius the Great.

Pantano de Burgomillodo: reservoir, great for bird-watchers.

Parque Natural del Cañón del Río Lobos: park created around the canyon of the River Lobos with rock formations, cave and good walking tracks.

Parque Natural del Lago de Sanabria y alrededores: mountainous area with deep valleys and glacier lagoons, variety of flora and fauna including 76 types of birds and 17 large mammals.

Cuisine of the region

The region is best known for its roast pork and lamb which has earned it the nickname *España del Asado* (Spain of the Roast). Other local products include trout from Leon and Zamora, and a variety of pulses: white, red and black beans, Castilian and *Pedrosillano* chickpeas, and various types of lentils. Soups feature a lot in winter: trout soup, typical of Órbigo de Leon; garlic soup; Zamora soup, a garlic soup with ripe tomatoes and hot chilli peppers.

Bizcochos de San Lorenzo: sponge cakes.

Farinatos: sausages made from breadcrumbs, pork fat and spices.

Hornazos: sausage and egg tarts.

Judias del barco con chorizo: haricot beans with sausage.

Yemas: a sweet made with egg yolks and sugar.

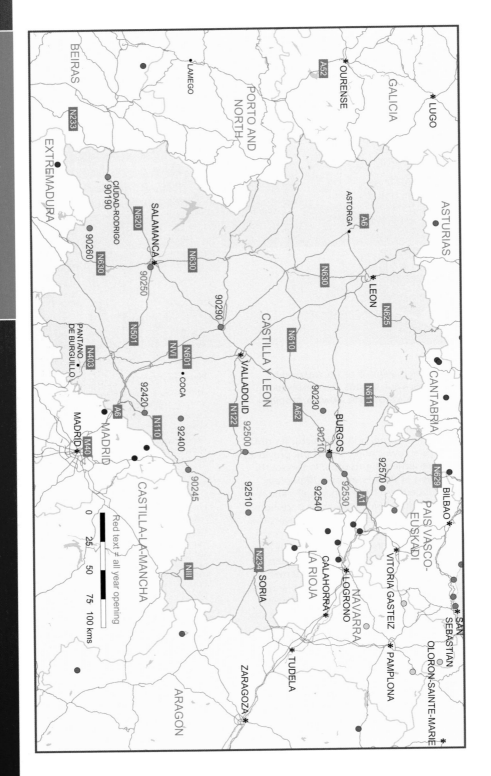

ES92500 Camping Costajan

Ctra NI E-5 km 164-165, E-09400 Aranda de Duero (Burgos)

Tel: **947 502 070**. Email: **costajan@circulopyme.com**   www.alanrogers.com/ES92500

This site is well placed as an en-route stop for the ferries, being 80 km. south of Burgos. This is the capital of the Ribera del Duero wine region that produces many fine wines competing with the great Riojas. With 225 unmarked pitches, all with electricity available, there are around 100 for all types of tourer. Large units may find access to the 225 unmarked, variably sized pitches a bit tricky among dense olive and pine trees and on the slightly undulating sandy ground but the trees provide good shade. There are 115 electricity connections. The welcome from Juan Carlos is warm and friendly (in any one of seven languages).

Facilities

Good, heated, modern sanitary facilities have hot and cold water. Facilities for disabled people. Washing machine. Gas supplies. Shop with essentials (all year). Bar serving simple meals (all year). Free access to adjacent large swimming pool (June - Sept). Tennis. Minigolf. Torch useful. If reception is unmanned, choose a pitch and book in later). Off site: Riding 2 km. River beach 3 km.

Open: All year.

Directions

From A1/E5 take exit at 164,5 km. and turn south on N1 towards Aranda de Duero. The site is on the right at the 162 km. mark. GPS: N41:42.120 W03:41.282

Charges guide

Per person	€ 5,15 - € 5,35
child	€ 4,90 - € 5,10
pitch	€ 4,90 - € 9,10
electricity	€ 4,85

ES92530 Camping Picon del Conde

Ctra NI km 263, E-09292 Monasterio de Rodilla (Burgos)

Tel: **947 594 355**   www.alanrogers.com/ES92530

This all year site is unusual, in that it has been amazingly decorated by the owner, Pedro Fasseler Sagredo who is lively and friendly, as are his family. The experience begins as you drive under an art nouveau style entry arch. The 65 level, grass pitches, all with electricity (6A), are of a reasonable size with separating hedges giving some privacy and trees offering shade. Long cables may be needed on some pitches. There is some traffic noise from the busy N1 road alongside and from the nearby motorway. This site is a good stopover if heading for the ferry or for exploring the area.

Facilities

Modern, tiled toilet block with controllable showers but cold water to basins. Dishwashing is up 12 steps and toilets and showers a further 12! Good facilities at ground level for disabled campers. Motorcaravan services. Shop. Restaurant and friendly bar. Attractive pool (July/Aug). Play area. Tennis. Off site: Fishing 2 km. Riding and golf 18 km. Burgos 25 km. Skiing 40 km.

Open: All year.

Directions

Monasterio de Rodilla is 25 km. northeast of Burgos. From A1 (Burgos - Vitoria) motorway, join N1 at exit 2 (heading northeast) or exit 3 (southwest) Site is on the N1 at the 263 km. marker (behind motel). GPS: N42:27.625 W03:27.488

Charges guide

Per person	€ 3,70
pitch incl. electricity	€ 7,65 - € 9,25

ES92570 Camping Frias

E-09211 Ciudad de Frias (Burgos)

Tel: **947 357 198**. Email: **info@campingfrias.com**   www.alanrogers.com/ES92570

Located in a natural park northeast of Burgos, on the edge of the old, small Spanish town of Frias, much of this site is taken up with static units. However, an area at the end is reserved for touring caravans and motorcaravans. A beautiful river runs alongside, about 20 feet below the campsite but with access for fishing, and the level, numbered pitches (30 for touring) have views across the really beautiful scenery surrounding the campsite. A little shade is provided from a few trees. This is a very Spanish site (no English was spoken when we visited). It may be noisy in summer with lively Spanish visitors but it was quiet when we visited in June.

Facilities

One toilet block provides basic facilities with British style WCs, washbasins with cold water only and coin operated showers. Washing machine and dryer. Shop with good range of produce (from 1/6). Bar and restaurant (from 1/6). Two swimming pools (22/6-15/9) and paddling pool. Off site: Transport would be needed to visit any interesting places.

Open: 1 April - 30 September.

Directions

Site is on the north side of Frias – approach only from this side. From A1 exit 5 onto A2122 (Quintana Martin Galindez), with a few tunnels but spectacular scenery (turn right on 625 then left to Quintana). After 16 km. turn left signed Frias. Site is 3 km. on right. GPS: N42:44.908 W03:18.382

Charges guide

Per person	€ 4,00
pitch incl. electricity	€ 11,00

Less 10% in low season. Plus 7% VAT.

ES92540 Camping Puerta de la Demanda

Ctra de Pineda km 2, E-09199 Villasur de Herreros (Burgos)

Tel: 983 796 819

www.alanrogers.com/ES92540

This recently built site is being improved and shows great promise. On flat ground, it is overlooked on three sides by the hills and mountains of the Sierra de la Demanda which give the site its name. There is little shade over 50 well marked large pitches all of which have electricity (5A) and drainage. The modern buildings are of local stone and wood in sympathy with the quiet surroundings, yet providing an excellent set of facilities.

Facilities

Attractive new sanitary building with British WCs and free hot showers. Washing machine. Facilities for disabled campers. Bar serving meals and selling basics (all season). Torches useful. Off site: River fishing 1 km. Sailing on nearby reservoir. Shop, restaurants and bars in attractive village 1 km. Superb walking area.

Open: 1 February - 30 November.

Directions

From the N120 (Burgos - Logroño), turn east at Ibeas de Juarros (about 13 km. east of Burgos) on Bu-P8101/Bu820 through Arlanzon to Villasur de Herreros. Site is beyond the village. GPS: N42:18.360 W03:22.500

Charges guide

Per person	€ 3,11
pitch incl. electricity	€ 7,70 - € 8,48

Plus 7% VAT.

ES90210 Camping Municipal Fuentes Blancas

Ctra Cartuja - Miraflores km 3,5, E-09193 Burgos (Burgos)

Tel: 947 486 016. Email: info@campingburgos.com

www.alanrogers.com/ES90210

Fuentes Blancas is a comfortable municipal site on the edge of the historical town of Burgos and within easy reach of the Santander ferries. There are around 350 marked pitches of 70 sq.m. on flat ground, 250 with electrical connections (6A) and there is good shade in parts. A small shop caters for most needs, the typically Spanish bar serves snacks and in the evening a restaurant is open offering basic, inexpensive meals. The site has a fair amount of transit trade and reservations are not possible for August, so arrive early. Burgos is an attractive city, ideally placed for overnight stop.

Facilities

Clean, modern, fully equipped sanitary facilities in five blocks with controllable showers and hot and cold water to sinks (not all are always open). Facilities for babies. Washing machine. Fresh water hoses for motorcaravans. Small shop (all season). Bar/snack bar and restaurant (all season). Swimming pool (1/7-30/8). Playground. English is spoken. Off site: Fishing and river beach 200 m. Bus service to city or a fairly shaded walk. Golf 30 km.

Open: All year.

Directions

From the north (Santander) continue on the N623 through city. Follow signs for E5/A1 Madrid. Cross river and take slip road for N120/A231 Leon but then turn left towards Fuentes Blancas and Cartuja de Miraflores for 3 km. Site is well signed on left. GPS: N42:20.453 W03:39.469

Charges guide

Per person	€ 2,90 - € 4,50
pitch incl. electricity	€ 10,00 - € 12,70

ES90230 Camping Camino de Santiago

Avenida Virgen del Manzano s/n, E-09110 Castrojeriz (Burgos)

Tel: 947 377 255. Email: info@campingcamino.com

www.alanrogers.com/ES90230

This tranquil site lies to the west of Burgos on the outskirts of Castrojeriz, a small unspoilt Spanish rural town. In a superb location, almost in the shadow of the ruined castle high on the hillside. The 50 marked pitches are level, grassy and divided by hedges, with electricity (5A) and drainage available to all. There are new mobile homes and bungalows to rent and some permanent pitches. Mature trees provide shade and there is a pretty orchard in one corner of the site. English is spoken here. The site has a shop and a bar/restaurant serving meals for pilgrims, campers and everybody who wants to taste the traditional cuisine.

Facilities

Adequate sanitary facilities with showers, British and Turkish style WCs, and washbasins with cold water only. These facilities are in older style, but are well maintained and clean. Washing machine. Bar/restaurant and takeaway. Swimming pool. Bicycle hire. Small library. Internet access and WiFi. Games room. Tennis. Play area. Bicycle hire. Barbecue area. Off site: Fishing and riding 17 km.

Open: 1 March - 30 November.

Directions

Castrojeriz is 45 km. west of Burgos. From the N120/A231 (Leon - Burgos), turn on BU404 (Villasandino, Castrojeriz). Turn left at crossroads on southwest side of town, then left at site sign. From A62 (Burgos - Valladolid) turn north at Vallaquirán on Bu400/401 to Castrojeriz. Turn sharp right at filling station and as above. GPS: N42:17.484 W04:07.899

Charges guide

Per person	€ 4,50
pitch incl. electricity	€ 11,00 - € 12,00

Check real time availability and at-the-gate prices...

www.alanrogers.com

ES90190 Camping La Pesquera

Ctra de Caceres - Arrabal, E-37500 Ciudad Rodrigo (Salamanca)
Tel: 923 481 348

www.alanrogers.com/ES90190

This modest site has just 54 pitches and is located near the Rio Agueda looking up to the magnificent fortress ramparts of Ciudad Rodrigo. Entry to the site is through a municipal park with a large play area. Whilst the site is small it can take even the largest units, the centrally located facilities have all been refurbished to a high standard, the pitches are flat and grassy and the roads are well maintained gravel. The pitches are shaded by trees by day and there is site lighting at night although you may find torches useful due to the tree canopy. The reception and a small bar which serves snacks in summer is near the front of the site.

Facilities

Attractive ochre stone sanitary building with British style WCs and free hot showers. Facilities for disabled campers. Washing machine. Basics sold from bar in high season. Bar/snacks (April - Sept). Playground and barbecue area outside gates. Torches useful. Off site: River fishing 1 km. Riding 5 km. Superb walking area.

Open: 25 April - 30 September.

Directions

Site is southwest of Salamancar close to Ciudad Rodrigo. From the E80 N260, any direction, take the 526 to Coria. Site is alongside river directly off the road and well signed. GPS: N40:35.940 W6:31.980

Charges guide

Per person	€ 3,20
child (up to 12 yrs)	€ 3,00
pitch incl. electricity	€ 6,60 - € 9,40

ES90245 Camping Riaza

Ctra de la Estacion s/n, E-40500 Riaza (Segovia)
Tel: 921 550 580. Email: info@campingriaza.com

www.alanrogers.com/ES90245

We visited this beautiful site shortly after its inauguration in 2007. It is situated in the province of Segovia, a hundred or so kilometres north of Madrid, making an ideal spot for a few days rest en-route north or south. Of the 350 spacious pitches 213 are for touring, all with 8A electricity, water, drainage and sewage. The pitches are divided by hedges and oak trees giving some shade. The buildings on the site are sympathetically built of local stone housing a large clubroom, a bar and welcoming restaurant lit by chandeliers, a good place to relax and enjoy the excellent menu.

Facilities

Two excellent, centrally located toilet blocks with underfloor heating. Shop. Bar, restaurant and clubroom (all year). Swimming pool (1/6-31/8). Two natural pools in the river bordering site. Large modern play area. Wellness centre with all year heated indoor pool, gym, massage room, jacuzzi and sauna. Minigolf. New sports area. Tennis. Archery. Children's club (summer only). Off site: Village of Riaza 2 km. with restaurant and some shopping. Riding 2 km. Golf 9 km.

Open: All year.

Directions

From the A1 (Burgos - Madrid) take exit 104 and the N110 towards Soria. Leave the N110 signed Riaza and follow camping signs. At roundabout follow signs for 'Estacion' and site is 50 m. on left. GPS: N41:16.167 W03:29.850

Charges guide

Per person	€ 5,80
child (1-10 yrs)	€ 5,00
pitch	€ 5,60 - € 9,10
electricity (10A)	€ 4,20

ES92400 Camping El Cantosal

Ctra de Santiuste km 2, E-40480 Coca (Segovia)
Tel: 627 445 906. Email: info@asecal.net

www.alanrogers.com/ES92400

On the 'Ruta de Mudejar' (Mudejar castles and buildings), near the nature reserve 'Hoces del Duraton' is this tiny campsite of 46 pitches, all with 5A electricity. The setting has a fairy tale air about it – the magnificent 15th century Castillo de Coca can be seen from most of the site. The grass and sand pitches are flat and partly shaded by tall trees in the daytime, and lit by pretty post lights at night. Designed in sympathy with the surroundings, the recently built stone buildings and all the facilities are of the highest quality. The bar serves snacks and excellent coffee.

Facilities

The huge, modern toilet block has British style WCs and free showers. Washing machine, dishwashing (H&C) and laundry sinks under cover. Facilities for disabled campers. Bar. Large playground just outside the site. Off site: Village with shops bars and restaurants. Swimming pool (discount). Fishing 2 km. Golf 20 km. Village of Coca with superb castle with attractive flowered gardens and bull ring 2 km.

Open: 15 June - 15 September.

Directions

Coca is 65 km. SSE of Valladoid. From N601 (Madrid - Valladoid) at Olmedo turn southeast on Vp1105 to Coca. At T-junction marked Coca 2 km, Santiuste 7 km, turn into site road through stone pillars on the left and signed Zona De Picnic El Catalos. GPS: N41:12.447 W04:02.097

Charges guide

Per person	€ 3,48
pitch incl. electricity	€ 7,06 - € 8,88

ES90250 Camping Regio

Ctra de Madrid km 4, E-37900 Santa Marta de Tormes (Salamanca)

Tel: **923 138 888**. Email: recepcion@campingregio.com   www.alanrogers.com/ES90250

Salamanca is one of Europe's oldest university cities, and this beautiful old sandstone city has to be visited. This is also a useful staging post en-route to the south of Spain or central Portugal. The site is 7 km. outside the city on the old road to Madrid, behind the Hôtel Regio where campers can take advantage of the hotel facilities. The 129 pitches (with a large area for tents) are clearly marked on slightly sloping ground, with some shade in parts and plentiful electricity points (10A). Access to those pitches not on the wide central road can be difficult for caravans. The hotel facilities include a quality restaurant, a somewhat cheaper cafeteria (discounts for campers), and an excellent swimming pool and children's pool (small charge). There is a pool bar and a shaded patio. The site itself has a small bar and restaurant. Visit the city and find the famous frog which is hidden in the fabulous University facade and discover what unusual Spanish fortune will be granted you! Or just enjoy the wonderfully accessible Salamantine architecture and myriad bars around the Plaza Mayor.

Facilities

Very large, fully equipped sanitary block is very clean. Good facilities for disabled campers. Washing machines. Gas supplies. Motorcaravan services. Bar. Supermarket (1/6-30/9). The hotel restaurant, café and swimming pool may be used by campers (discounts at the café and restaurant). Play area. Tennis. Internet and WiFi (both within hotel area). English is spoken. Off site: Bus to town terminates at hotel carpark. Fishing 2 km. Bicycle hire 4 km. Town centre 7 km. Golf 14 km.

Open: All year.

Directions

Take the main N501 route from Salamanca towards Avila, then to St Marta de Tormes 7 km. east of the city. Hôtel Regio is on the right just outside the town at the 90 km. marker. There are yellow hotel and camping signs through the city and on the roads to the east. GPS: N40:56.860 W05:36.870

Charges guide

Per person	€ 3,00 - € 3,70
child	€ 2,70 - € 3,30
pitch incl. electricity	€ 15,30 - € 17,70

ES90260 Camping El Burro Blanco

Camino de las Norias s/n, E-37660 Miranda del Castañar (Salamanca)

Tel: **923 161 100**. Email: el.burro.blanco@hotmail.com   www.alanrogers.com/ES90260

Set on a hill side, within the Sierra Peña de Francia and with views of the romantic walled village of Miranda del Castañar and its charming, crumbling castle, this site has been developed by a Dutch team; husband and wife Jeff and Yvonne and their friend Paul. You are welcomed at the gate and are walked around the facilities. There are a total of 31 level touring pitches, all between 80 and 120 sq.m. and 25 have electricity. The pitches are beautifully set in 3.5 hectares of the most attractive natural woodland. Owners of large caravans and motorhomes should contact the site first due to the restricted number of suitable pitches. There are rough tables and chairs made from local stone, unusual statues, a fountain fed by a well and a small stream which traces a route though the site. The owners keep an exhaustive list of all the birds and other wildlife spotted around the campsite, and in one area (wet in winter, but dry in summer), there are beautiful luminous green tree frogs and other aquatic reptiles (you will hear their 'barking' at night in the mating season – May). A copy of the site regulations is provided on arrival to all campers, along with your own rubbish bin. If you wish to explore some of the unique villages in the area you may wish to avoid La Alberca which has been spoiled by over exploitation. Try instead Cepeda or Casas del Conde.

Facilities

One central modern sanitary facility, fully equipped includes a baby bath. Two washbasins have hot water. Out of season part of the unit is closed and therefore facilities are unisex. Launderette. Gas supplies. Library with book swap and small bar. Off site: Restaurants, bars, shops and ATM in village 600 m. Municipal swimming pool nearby. River swimming and fishing 1.5 km. Riding 15 km.

Open: 1 April - 1 October.

Directions

From north - south direction take Salamanca - Coria road southwest for about 70 km. through Vecinos, Linares de Rio Frio towards Coria (numbers change but keep on this main road, the easiest route). From east - west direction take Bejar - Ciudad Rodrigo road turning south towards Cepeda/Coria. The road to Miranda del Castañar is 7 km. northeast of the village of Cepeda. Turn off main road signed Miranda. After 1.2 km. going downhill towards town look for left turn onto a concrete road. Follow road for 1.1 km. (a short stretch unmade) and site is on right. GPS: N40:28.488 W05:59.931

Charges guide

Per person	€ 4,80
child (0-5 yrs)	€ 3,00
pitch	€ 8,00
electricity (2-10A)	€ 1,50 - € 4,80

Plus 7% VAT. Discounts after 7 days of 10% increasing to 15% after 14 days. No credit cards.

ES92420 Camping El Acueducto

Avenida D Juan de Borbón 49, E-40004 Segovia (Segovia)

Tel: **921 425 000**. Email: **informacion@campingacueducto.com**

www.alanrogers.com/ES92420

Located right on the edge of the interesting city of Segovia with lovely views across the open plain with mountains in the background, this is a family run, typically Spanish site. The grass pitches are mostly of medium size, although a few pitches near the gate would have room for larger units. Reception is small but the owner is helpful and speaks good English. El Acueducto is well positioned for discovering Segovia. About 5 km. Segovia is deeply and haughtily Castilian, with plenty of squares and mansions from its days of Golden Age grandeur, when it was a royal resort.

Facilities

Two traditional style toilet blocks provide basic facilities and are kept clean. Laundry room. Small shop for basics. Bar. Two swimming pools. Large play area. Off site: Large restaurant nearby. Bus service into city centre. Madrid is within driving distance.

Open: 1 April - 30 September.

Directions

From the north on N1 (Burgos - Madrid) take exit 99 on N110 towards Segovia. On outskirts of city take third exit onto N603 signed Madrid. Pass one exit to Segovia and take second signed Segovia and La Granja. At roundabout turn right and site is 500 m. on the right. GPS: N40:55.875 W4:05.546

Charges guide

Per person	€ 5,00 - € 5,40
pitch incl. electricity (5A)	€ 19,50 - € 20,40

ES92510 Camping Cañon del Rio Lobos

Ctra Burgos de Osma - San Leonardo, E-42317 Ucero (Soria)

Tel: **975 363 565**

www.alanrogers.com/ES92510

This is a delightful site with vast amounts of flowers, set among attractive limestone cliffs of the Burgos canyons. The site is pricey but facilities are excellent and there are few others in the area. Reception is purpose built and control of the security barrier is from within – everything here is very organised. The campsite logo depicts a bird of prey and many of these wheel above the site. The very attractive swimming pool is within a secure walled area, which again has many flowers and shrubs and is private from the road that runs alongside the site (some traffic noise).

Facilities

Two fully equipped toilet blocks (only one opened when site is quiet). Bar serving a 'menu del d'a' and smart restaurant. Basic shopping from bar. Swimming pool (charge). Two excellent tennis courts (charge). Play area. Bicycle hire. Fishing. Torch useful. Dogs are not accepted. Off site: Local bus service 1 km. on Wed./Sat. for town. Walking, climbing, caving, fishing in nearby 'Parque Natural'. Riding 10 km. Golf 35 km.

Open: Easter - 30 September.

Directions

From N234 (Burgos - Soria) turn south in San Leonado de Yagüe on SO690. Turn left after village on SO920 (El Burgo). Site is on left in 18 km. just before Ucero. From N122/A11 (Valladolid - Soria) turn north in El Burgo on SO920 (San Leonardo), 16 km. to Ucero. GPS: N41:43.750 W3:02.884

Charges guide

Per person	€ 5,00
pitch incl. electricity	€ 17,10 - € 18,60
All plus 7% VAT.	

ES90290 Kawan Village El Astral

Camino de Pollos 8, E-47100 Tordesillas (Valladolid)

Tel: **983 770 953**. Email: **info@campingelastral.es**

www.alanrogers.com/ES90290

The site is in a prime position alongside the wide River Duero (safely fenced). It is homely and run by a charming man, Eduardo Gutierrez, who has excellent English and is ably assisted by brother Gustavo and sister Lola. The site is generally flat with 154 pitches separated by thin hedges. They vary in size from 60-200 sq.m. with mature trees providing shade. There is an electricity pylon tucked in one corner of the site but this is hardly noticeable. This is a friendly site ideal for exploring the area.

Facilities

One attractive sanitary block including two cabins with WC, bidet and washbasin. Some facilities for disabled campers, including ramps. Baby room in ladies' area. Washing machines. Motorcaravan services. Supermarket. Bar. Restaurant. Swimming and paddling pools (1/6-15/9). Playground. Tennis (high season). Minigolf. Internet point and WiFi. English speaking staff. Local bus service. Animation daily in high season. Torches are useful. Off site: River fishing 100 m. Golf 10 km. Riding 20 km.

Open: 1 March - 31 October.

Directions

Tordesillas is 28 km. southwest of Valladolid. From all directions, leave the main road towards Tordesillas and follow signs to campsite or 'Parador' (a hotel opposite the site). GPS: N41:29.779 W05:00.312

Charges 2009

Per person	€ 4,30 - € 6,60
pitch incl. electricity	€ 11,10 - € 18,50
Plus 7% VAT.	
Discounts in low season and for longer stays.	
Camping Cheques accepted.	

With a coastline of inlets and wide, rocky estuaries, sheltering traditional old fishing villages and fine beaches, Galicia is perhaps best known for Santiago de Compostela, the place where the famous pilgrim's route comes to an end.

THIS REGION IS MADE UP OF FOUR PROVINCES: OURENSE, LUGO, A CORUÑA AND PONTEVEDRA

The obvious highlight in the region has to be the beautiful medieval city of Santiago de Compostela, capital of Galicia and world famous centre of the old European pilgrimage. Now a World Heritage Site, the city boasts an impressive Romanesque cathedral with more churches, convents and monasteries dotted around. One of the best times to go to Santiago de Compostela is during the Festival of St James on 25 July, which has also been designated Galicia Day. Following the route into the city, are the towns of Portomarín and Samos. Near Samos, the Lóuzara valley and the Sierra do Oribio are ideal for those interested in hiking and wildlife. The Galician coastline is characterized by high cliffs and estuaries collectively known as the Rías Atlas and Rías Baixas with the Costa da Morte or Coast of Death separating them; so called because of the hundreds of shipwrecks that litter the cliffs and rocks. It was also once considered by the pilgrimages to be the 'end of the world'. Along the coast are medieval towns and villages including Noia, Muros, A Coruña and Finisterre. Corcubión, Camariñas and Corme-Laxe are other rias with fishing villages and home to some of the best barnacles in the region.

Places of interest

A Coruña: medieval quarters, Romanesque churches, Roman lighthouse.

Baiona: one of the region's best resorts.

Camariñas: town on the 'end of the world', good barnacle hunting ground, lacemaking traditions.

Lugo: town completely enclosed within preserved Roman walls, along which are 85 towers.

Malpica: seaside harbour, jumping off point for nearby islands.

Pontevedra: picturesque old town with lively atmosphere.

Vigo: fishing port, beaches.

Viveiro: beaches, old town surrounded by Renaissance walls.

Cuisine of the region

Local cuisine features heavily in fiestas and throughout the region are numerous markets. Good quality seafood is found in abundance; *percebes* (barnacles) are a favourite. *Pulpo* (octopus) is also popular and special *pulperias* will cook it in the traditional way. Vegetable dishes include the Galician broth, made with green beans, cabbage, parsnip, potatoes and haricot beans. *Aguardiente gallego*, a regional liqueur, is used to make the traditional mulled drink known as *queimada*, where fruit, sugar and coffee grains are added and then set alight.

Caldeirada: fish soup.

Caldo gallego: thick stew of potato cabbage.

Empanada: light-crusted pastries often filled with pork, beef, tuna or cod.

Lacon con grelos: ham boiled with turnip greens.

Red text = all year opening

0   25   50   75   100 kms

VIVERO

A CORUÑA 89420
MALPICA
CAMARINAS
N634
A9
ASTURIAS
N634
LUGO
90240
SANTIAGO
89300
A6
GALICIA
N540
N541
89380 PONTEVEDRA
N120
OURENSE
VIGO
BAYONA
89360
A52
CASTILLA Y LEON
N101
PONTE
DE LIMA
VIANA DO
CASTELO
PORTO AND
NORTH
BRAGANCA

ES89300 Camping San Francisco

Camino do Convento 21, Louro, E-15291 Muros (A Coruña)
Tel: **981 826 148**. Email: **ofmlouro@yahoo.es**

www.alanrogers.com/ES89300

Situated 400 m. from the coast, this small and attractive touring site with 104 small pitches occupies a clearing on a hillside that is undoubtedly a magnet for Spanish holidaymakers. Advance booking is recommended. The neatly laid out and numbered pitches are on level grass, divided by trees but with little shade. All have 10A electricity and 74 pitches are fully serviced. The surrounding countryside is scenic and unspoilt by development and the superb white sandy beaches and rocky coves provide endless hours of fun or relaxation for the whole family. Bars and restaurants, together with a few small shops are all within 300 m. of the site but for everything else, the small town of Muros is only 3.5 km.

Facilities

One modern spotlessly clean toilet block is centrally positioned with all necessary facilities. A family shower room with facilities for disabled visitors is provided in both male and female areas. Washing machines, dryers and a first aid point are housed in separate rooms. Well stocked shop. Café/bar. Restaurant with terrace. Play area. Tennis and multisport court. Off site: Sandy beach, fishing 400 m. Bicycle hire 500 m. Boat launching, sailing 3.5 km.

Open: 21 June - 7 September.

Directions

From Santiago de Compostela take AC543 to Noia. Just before Noia turn right onto road signed Muros and continue on AC550. Site well signed 3.5 km. past Muros on right, up a narrow road.
GPS: N42:45.75 W09:04.42

Charges guide

Per person	€ 5,50
child	€ 4,00
pitch incl. car	€ 10,75 - € 11,25
electricity	€ 3,90

ES89380 Camping Paxarinas

Ctra San Xenxo - O'Grove km., E-36979 Portonovo (A Coruña)

Tel: 986 723 055. Email: info@campingpaxarinas.com

www.alanrogers.com/ES89380

Paxarinas is a family owned and managed coastal site open all year, set on a gently sloping area of hillside overlooking Ria de Pontevedra. Of the 260 very small pitches only 60 are for touring, in the centre of the site. All pitches are numbered and have 3A electricity, there is very little shade. It gets very busy in high season and advance booking is advised. Care is needed with larger units at busy times. The site is in an attractive area of Galicia and, with access to two excellent beaches, it makes a good stop whilst visiting the area. Although open all year, facilities are very limited in low season.

Facilities

Two well maintained modern sanitary blocks. Private cabins. Facilities for visitors with disabilities. Washing machine and dryer. Play area. Shop, bar and snacks (20/6-5/9). Separate restaurant in adjacent hotel. Off site: Two beaches adjacent. Riding 4 km. Golf 8 km.

Open: All year.

Directions

Exit AP9, junction 129 Pontevedra. Follow signs to Sanxenxo. Follow coast road PO308 for 22 km. Site poorly signed on left hand side, behind hotel, 3 km. past Sanxenxo and just before a bend. GPS: N42:23.54 W08:50.69

Charges guide

Per person	€ 5,30
pitch incl. electricity	€ 17,00

ES89420 Camping Los Manzanos

Avenida de Emilia Pardo Bazan, E-15179 Santa Cruz (A Coruña)

Tel: 981 614 825. Email: info@camping-losmanzanos.com

www.alanrogers.com/ES89420

Los Manzanos has a steep access drive down to the site, which is divided by a stream into two sections linked by a bridge. Pitches for larger units are marked and numbered, 85 with electricity (12A) and, in one section, there is a fairly large, unmarked field for tents. Some aircraft noise should be expected as the site is under the flight path to La Coruña (but no aircraft at night). The site impressed us as being very clean, even when full, which it tends to be in high season. Some interesting huge stone sculptures create focal points and conversation pieces.

Facilities

One good toilet block provides modern facilities including free hot showers. Small shop with fresh produce daily (limited outside June - Sept). High quality restaurant/bar (July/Aug). Swimming pool with lifeguard, free to campers (15/6-30/9). Playground. Barbecue area. Bungalows for rent. Off site: Bus service at end of entrance drive. Beach and fishing 800 m. Bicycle hire 2 km. Golf and riding 8 km.

Open: Easter - 30 September.

Directions

From AP9 take exit 7, signed O Burgo and carry on through town. At roundabout (signed airport to left), go straight ahead. Continue and immediately at entry to underpass take slip road and turn right into NV1. Take next left (Santa Cristina/Santa Cruz) and follow AC173. In Santa Cruz turn right and follow sign to site for 0.8 km. Site on left. GPS: N43:20.945 W08:20.140

Charges guide

Per person	€ 5,90
pitch incl. electricity	€ 15,10 - € 17,10
All plus 7% VAT.	

ES89360 Camping Bayona Playa

Ctra Vigo - Bayona km 19, E-36393 Bayona (Pontevedra)

Tel: 986 350 035. Email: campingbayona@campingbayona.com

www.alanrogers.com/ES89360

Situated on a narrow peninsula with the sea and river estuary all around it, this large and well maintained campsite is great for a relaxing break. The 450 pitches, 358 for touring, benefit from the shade of mature trees whilst still maintaining a very open feel. All have 5A electricity and 50 are fully serviced. It is busy here in high season so advance booking is recommended. Sabaris is a short walk away and Bayona is a 20 minute walk along the coast, where you can find a variety of shops, supermarkets, banks, bars and eating places. Maximum unit length is 7.5 m.

Facilities

Three well maintained modern toilet blocks (one open low season), washbasins and shower cubicles. Service wash. Facilities for visitors with disabilities. Large well stocked supermarket and gift shop (June - Sept). Terrace bar, cafeteria, restaurant. Excellent pool complex with slide. Play area. Activities July/Aug. Off site: Fishing 100 m. Bicycle hire 5 km. Riding 8 km. Golf 20 km.

Open: All year.

Directions

From Vigo leave AG57, exit 5 Bayona North. Follow signs to site at Sabaris, 2 km. east of Bayona. GPS: N42:06.84 W08:49.55

Charges guide

Per person	€ 6,30
child (3-12 yrs)	€ 3,95
pitch	€ 3,95 - € 13,05
electricity	€ 3,95

ES90240 Camping As Cancelas

Rue do 25 de Xullo 35, E-15704 Santiago de Compostela (A Coruña)

Tel: 981 580 476. Email: info@campingascancelas.com

www.alanrogers.com/ES90240

The beautiful city of Santiago has been the destination for European Christian pilgrims for centuries and they now follow ancient routes to this unique city, the whole of which is a national monument. The As Cancelas campsite is excellent for sharing the experiences of these pilgrims in the city and around the magnificent cathedral. It has 125 marked pitches (60-90 sq.m), arranged in terraces and divided by trees and shrubs. On a hillside overlooking the city, the views are very pleasant, but the site has a steep approach road and access to most of the pitches can be a challenge for large units. Electrical hook-ups (5A) are available, the site is lit at night and a security guard patrols. There are many legendary festivals and processions here, the main one being on July 25th, especially in holy years (when the Saint's birthday falls on a Sunday). Examine for yourself the credibility of the fascinating story of the arrival of the bones of Saint James at Compostela (Compostela translates as 'field of stars'), and also discover why the pilgrims dutifully carry a scallop shell on their long journey. There are many pilgrims' routes, including one commencing from Fowey in Cornwall.

Facilities

Two modern toilet blocks are fully equipped, with ramped access for disabled campers. The quality and cleanliness of the fittings and tiling is good. Laundry with service wash for a small fee. Small shop. Restaurant. Bar with TV. Well kept, unsupervised swimming pool and children's pool. Small playground. Internet access. Off site: Regular bus service runs into the city from near football ground 200 m. from site. Huge commercial centre (open late and handy for off season use) 20 minutes walk downhill (uphill on the return!).

Open: All year.

Directions

From motorway AP9-E1 take exit 67 and follow signs for 'Casco Historico' and 'Centro Ciudad' then follow site signs. GPS: N42:53.360 W08:31.450

Charges guide

Per person	€ 4,50 - € 5,90
child (up to 12 yrs)	€ 2,70 - € 4,50
pitch	€ 4,50 - € 19,00
electricity	€ 4,10
All plus VAT.	

Like its neighbouring province, Cantabria, Asturias also has a beautiful coastline, albeit more rugged and wild, with the Picos range separating them. In the south the Cantabrian mountains form a natural border between Asturias and Castilla-León.

THIS IS A ONE PROVINCE REGION

THE CAPITAL IS OVIEDO

Situated between the foothills of the Picos mountains and the coast is the seaside town of Llanes, in the east. It has several good beaches, beautiful coves and given its location, is a good base for exploring the Picos del Europa. Along the coast towards Gijón are more seaside resorts including Ribadesella, with its fishing harbour and fine beach. The cities of Gijón and, in particular, Avilés are renowned for their Carnival festivities, a national event which takes place in late February. This week-long party involves dancing, live music, fireworks and locals who dress up in elaborate fancy-dress costumes. South of here towards the centre of the province is the capital, Oviedo. The city boasts a pedestrian old quarter with numerous squares and narrow streets, a cathedral, palaces, a Fine Arts Museum, Archaeological Museum plus various remarkable churches that date from the 9th century. There are also plenty of sidrerías (cider houses).The west coast of Asturias is more rugged. One of the most attractive towns along here is Luarca, built around a cove surrounded by sheer cliffs. With a fishing harbour and an array of good restaurants and bars, the town's traditional character is reflected in its chigres – old Asturian taverns – where visitors can learn the art of drinking cider.

Places of interest

Avilés: 14th and 15th century churches and palaces.

Cudillero: small, charming fishing port.

Gijón: 18th century palace, beaches, museums.

Villahormes: seaside town with excellent swimming coves.

Villaviciosa: atmospheric old town, 13th church, cider factory.

Cuisine of the region

Local specialities include *fabada*, a type of stew made with haricot beans called *fabes*, *potes* (soups) and of course cider, which can be drunk in *sidrerías*. The customary way to serve cider is to pour it from a great height, a practice know as *escanciar*, into a wide-mouthed glass only just covering the *culin* or bottom. Rice pudding is the traditional dessert and *frixuelos* (crepe), *huesos de santo* (made from marzipan) and *tocinillo de cielo* (syrup pudding) are eaten during festivals.

Brazo de gitano: a type of Swiss roll.

Carne gobernada: beef in white wine with bacon, eggs, peppers and olives.

Fabada asturiana: haricot beans, chorizo, cabbage, cured pork shoulder and potatoes.

Pastel carbayón: almond pastry.

ES89400 Camping Los Cantiles

Ctra N634 km 502,7, E-33700 Luarca (Asturias)

Tel: **985 640 938**. Email: **cantiles@campingloscantiles.com**   www.alanrogers.com/ES89400

Luarca is a picturesque little place with a pretty inner harbour and two sandy beaches, and Los Cantiles is two kilometres to the east of town on a cliff top that juts out into the sea, giving excellent views from some pitches and the sound of the waves to soothe you to sleep. The site is well maintained and is a pleasant place to stop along this under-developed coastline. The 150 pitches, 105 with electricity, are mostly on level grass, divided by huge hedges of hydrangeas and bushes. Some pitches have gravel surfaces. There is a separate area for late arrivals in high season. The owners speak excellent English and Hubert, who is Dutch, and Cornelia, who is German, are charming and eager that you enjoy your stay here. You can take the car to the Luarca beaches and the small town is within walking distance downhill (the return is steep!) – or you can usually park the car by the roadside at the top of the descent and find your way down the steps to the harbour. This is a pleasant site as a base for exploring the area or as a transit site if moving to or from Portugal.

Facilities

Two modern, fully equipped sanitary blocks (one in low season which is heated in winter) are kept very clean. Facilities for disabled people and babies. Laundry. Freezer service. Gas supplies. Small shop (open all year for basics). Bar with hot snacks (1/7-15/9). Day room for backpackers with tables, chairs and cooking facilities (own gas). Off site: Indoor swimming pool, sauna and fitness centre, plus a bar/restaurant and shop 300 m. Luarca 2 km. Beach and fishing 700 m. Riding 4 km.

Open: All year.

Directions

Luarca is 85 km. west of Gijon. From A8 Oviedo - La Coruña exit at 467 onto N634 for Luarca. After km. 502 east of Luarca, turn right at petrol station and follow signs to site for 2.5 km. Last 150 m. is narrow. GPS: N43:32.953 W06:31.459

Charges guide

Per person	€ 4,20
pitch	€ 8,10 - € 9,70
electricity (3/6A)	€ 2,00 - € 2,50

Plus 7% VAT. No credit cards.

ES89440 Camping La Cascada

Arbón Villayón, E-33718 Arbón (Asturias)

Tel: 985 625 081. Email: campinglacascada@hotmail.com

www.alanrogers.com/ES89440

Located in a clearing of the attractive Arbon Valley this friendly, family run site offers the chance to experience the delights of rural Spain. There are 74 very small pitches (60 for touring units), all sited on gently sloping grass with electricity 4A, long leads are required. The beaches and small villages of the Costa Verde are only 12 km. away and the site has information about this spectacular region. Access to the site is not difficult but a 3500 kg. weight restriction on the small bridge at the site entrance makes it unsuitable for larger units. The focal point of this small and well maintained site is its traditional style restaurant. It is open during July and August and serves a variety of home cooked, locally grown produce. The unheated, fenced swimming pool is open all season.

Facilities

Well maintained and modern toilet block. No specific facilities for visitors with disabilities. No washing machine. Shop, bar and snacks (all season). Restaurant (July/Aug). Swimming pool with sun terrace (all season). Play area. Fishing. Off site: Bicycle hire 500 m. Beaches 12 km.

Open: Easter - September.

Directions

From A8 (direction of La Coruna), exit, Navia onto N634. Turn left, AS25 (direction of Arbon). Site is 10 km. on right, well signed. Note: sign at site entrance refers to it as Camping Arbon. GPS: N43:28.796 W06:42.157

Charges guide

Per person	€ 3,21
pitch incl. electricity	€ 16,18

ES89480 Camping l'Amuravela

El Pito, E-33150 Cudillero (Asturias)

Tel: 985 590 995

www.alanrogers.com/ES89480

This very well maintained, family run site, is close to the quaint old town of Cudillero and it is an ideal stop over when visiting 'Green Spain'. Nearby is some of the most attractive mountain scenery in the region and if you stay here for one night it can easily extend to a much longer visit. There are 70 good sized touring pitches on level or gently sloping grass with easy access. Some pitches can accommodate large units. Mature trees give some shade and all pitches have 5A electricity. The excellent swimming pool and separate children's pool provide an area for relaxation. This is a relatively quiet site but can be busy and noisy at week ends. The spectacular Costa Verde has many places to explore and the towns of Gigon and Oviedo are places that have to be visited.

Facilities

One modern and very well maintained toilet block is close to all pitches and includes washbasins and shower cubicles. There are no specific facilities for visitors with disabilities. Washing machines and dryers. Well stocked shop. Café/bar and restaurant area (20/6-10/9). Swimming pool (June - Sept). Play area. Very little English is spoken. Off site: Fishing, beach 2 km. Golf 28 km.

Open: June - September.

Directions

From A8 take N632 towards Cudillero. After 120 km. marker turn right onto CU2 signed El Pito. Site is well signed on right in 2 km. On no account take caravans into Cudillero. GPS: N43:33.29 W06:08.66

Charges guide

Per person	€ 4,21 - € 4,60
child	€ 3,85 - € 3,95
pitch incl. electricity	€ 10,76 - € 12,40

ES89500 Camping Costa Verde

Playa de la Griega, E-33320 Colunga (Asturias)

Tel: 985 856 373

www.alanrogers.com/ES89500

This coastal site with a marked Spanish flavour is just 1.5 km. from the town of Colunga. Although little English is spoken, the cheerful owner and his helpful staff will make sure you get a warm welcome. The great advantage for many is that, 200 m. from the gate, is a spacious beach with a low tide lagoon, ideal for younger children. Some of the 200 pitches are occupied on a seasonal basis, but there are 155 for tourers. These are flat but with little shade and electricity (6A) is available (long leads needed in places). The site gets very busy in high season.

Facilities

The single toilet block is of a high standard with a mixture of British and Turkish style toilets (all British for ladies), large showers and free hot water throughout. Laundry. Well stocked shop. Bar/restaurant is traditional and friendly. Play area. Torches needed. Off site: Nearby towns of Ribadesella, Gijón and Oviedo. Excellent beaches. Fishing in river alongside site. Bicycle hire 2 km. Sailing 4 km. Golf and riding 18 km.

Open: Easter - 1 October.

Directions

Colunga is 45 km. east of Gijón. Leave the A8 Santander - Oviedo motorway at km. 345 exit and take N632 towards Colunga. In village, turn right on As257 towards Lastres; site is on right after 1 km. marker. GPS: N43:29.797 W05:15.868

Charges guide

Per person	€ 4,70
pitch incl. electricity	€ 8,20 - € 12,40
VAT included.	

ES89450 Camping Lagos de Somiedo

Valle de Lago, E-33840 Somiedo (Asturias)

Tel: 985 763 776

www.alanrogers.com/ES89450

This is a most unusual site in the Parque Natural de Somiedo. Winding narrow roads with challenging rock overhangs, hairpin bends and breathtaking views (for 8 km.) finally bring you to the lake and campsite at an elevation of 1,200 m. This is a site for 4x4s, powerful small campervans and cars – not for medium or large motorhomes, and caravans are not accepted. It is not an approach for the faint hearted! The friendly Lana family make you welcome at their unique site, which is tailored for those who wish to explore the natural and cultural values of the Park without the 'normal' campsite amenities. There are 210 pitches (just 4 with electric hook-up), undefined in two open meadows. In this extraordinary glacial valley you can leave reality behind in the exploration of the marvels of nature including bears, wolves, capercailles and a unique wild goat which frequent these mountains. A building, in keeping with the area, provides the amenities and contains many items of natural interest. A small bar/restaurant set tight into the vertical rock face offers traditional Asturian food, but watch out for the local's stilted wooden clogs scattered in the entrance hall. There is a cool wind here most of the time and a torch is essential at night. Cars are parked away from the pitches.

Facilities

There are British style toilets and free hot water to clean hot showers and washbasin. Facilities for babies and children. Washing machine. Combined reception, small restaurant, bar and reference section. Shop for bread, milk and other essentials, plus local produce and crafts. Horses for hire, trekking. Lectures on flora, fauna, history and culture. Fishing (licence required). Barbecue area. Small play area. Gas supplies. No caravans accepted. Off site: The very small village is 500 m. and it maintains the Spanish customs and traditions of this area.

Open: 1 April - 30 September.

Directions

From N634 via Oviedo turn left at 442 km. marker on AS-15 signed Parque Natural de Somiedo. At 9 km. marker past village of Longoria, turn left on AS-227. At 38 km. marker, turn left into Pol de Somiedo, signed Centro Urbano. Follow signs for Valle de Lago and El Valle; 8 km. of hairpin bends from Pola, passing Urria on the left, brings you to the valley. Site is signed on the right.
GPS: N43:06.320 W06:10.110

Charges guide

Per person	€ 5,35
child	€ 4,28
pitch incl. car	€ 11,23
motorcaravan incl. electricity	€ 11,77
dog	€ 3,21

All plus 7% VAT.
No credit cards.

ES89550 Camping Caravaning Arenal de Moris

A8 Salida 337, E-33344 Caravia Alta (Asturias)

Tel: 985 853 097. Email: camoris@teleline.es

www.alanrogers.com/ES89550

This smart, well run site is close to three fine sandy beaches so gets very busy at peak times. It has a backdrop of the mountains in the nature reserve known as the Sueve which is important for a breed of short Asturian horses, the 'Asturcone'. The site has 330 grass pitches (269 for touring units) of 40-70 sq.m. and with 200 electricity connections available (5A). With little shade, some pitches are terraced with others on an open, slightly sloping field with views of the sea. The restaurant with a terrace serves local dishes and overlooks the pool with hills and woods beyond. The mountains of 'Picos de Europa' are only 35 km. away, Covadonga and its lakes are near and Ribadesella is 12 km. It is an ideal area forsea and mountain sports, horse riding, walking, birdwatching and cycling. In the middle distance a new motorway viaduct curves its way across the valley. There was little noise when we visited but this must be considered a possibility when the site is busy.

Facilities

Three sanitary blocks provide comfortable, controllable showers (no dividers) and vanity style washbasins, laundry facilities and external dishwashing (cold water). Supermarket. Bar/restaurant. Swimming pool. Tennis. Play area in lemon orchard. English is spoken. Off site: Fishing 200 m. Golf 5 km. Riding, bicycle hire and sailing 10 km. Bar and restaurants in village 2 km. Beach 200 m.

Open: 1 June - 17 September.

Directions

Caravia Alta is 50 km. east of Gijón, Leave the A8 Santander - Oviedo motorway at km. 337 exit, turn left on N632 towards Colunga and site is signed to right in village, near 16 km. marker.
GPS: N43:28.349 W05:10.999

Charges guide

Per person	€ 5,20 - € 5,40
child	€ 4,20 - € 4,60
pitch incl. car	€ 13,05 - € 13,70
electricity	€ 4,00 - € 4,40

Check real time availability and at-the-gate prices...
www.alanrogers.com
129

ES89600 Camping La Paz

Ctra N634 Irun - Coruña km 292, E-33597 Vidiago-Llanes (Asturias)

Tel: **985 411 235**. Email: **delfin@campinglapaz.com**

www.alanrogers.com/ES89600

This site occupies a spectacular location. The reception building is opposite a solid rock face and many hundred feet below the site and the climb to the upper part of the site is quite daunting but staff will place your caravan for you, although motorcaravan drivers will have an exciting drive to the top, especially to the loftier pitches. Once there, the views are absolutely outstanding, both along the coast and inland to the Picos de Europa mountains. There is also a lower section in a shaded valley to which access is easier, if rather tight in places. The upper area is arranged on numerous terraces, many of which require you to park your car by the roadside and climb the hill to your tent. The way down to the attractive beach is quite steep; from the lower area there is an easy walk to a smaller beach. There are 434 pitches, 350 with electricity. The cliff-top restaurant and bar has commanding views over the ocean and beach. The site is very popular in high season so it does get crowded.

Facilities

Four good, modern toilet blocks are well equipped and include controllable hot showers. They are kept very clean even at peak times. Baby bath. Full laundry facilities. Motorcaravan services. Restaurant and bar/snack bar with small shop (all season). Watersports. Games room. Fishing. Torches useful in some areas. English spoken. Off site: Shop, bar and restaurant in nearby village. Golf, riding, sailing and boat launching all 8 km.

Open: Easter - 30 September.

Directions

Vidiago is 85 km. west of Santander. Site is signed from A8/N634 Santander - Oviedo/Gijón road near km. 292 marker (on non-motorway section). GPS: N43:23.974 W04:39.089

Charges guide

Per person	€ 5,73
child	€ 5,30
pitch	€ 12,00 - € 14,14
electricity	€ 4,00

All plus 7% VAT.

ES89650 Camping Picos de Europa

E-33556 Avin-Onis (Asturias)

Tel: **985 844 070**. Email: **info@picos-europa.com**

www.alanrogers.com/ES89650

This delightful site is, as its name suggests, an ideal spot from which to explore these dramatic limestone mountains on foot, by bicycle or on horseback. The site itself is newly developed and the dynamic owner, José or his nephew who helps out when he is away are both very pleasant and nothing is too much trouble. The site is in a valley beside a pleasant, fast flowing river. The 140 marked pitches are of varying sizes and have been developed in three avenues, on level grass backing on to hedging and with 6A electricity to all. An area for tents is over a bridge past the pleasant, fairly small, round swimming pool. Local stone has been used for the L-shaped building at the main entrance which houses reception and a very good bar/restaurant which has an unusual circular window and a fireplace for when it is cold. The site specialises in caving activities and has information about the Bulnes funicular railway, the Cares gorge and the many energetic ways of exploring the area, including by canoe and quad-bike!

Facilities

Toilet facilities include a new fully equipped block. Facilities for disabled visitors and babies. Room with tables and chairs for poor weather. Washing machine and dryer. Shop (July - Sept). Swimming pool (Feb - Sept). Bar and cafeteria style restaurant (all year) serves a good value 'menu del dia' and snacks. WiFi in restaurant area. Play area. Fishing. Torches necessary. Off site: Riding 12 km. Bicycle hire 15 km. Golf 25 km. Coast at Llanes 25 km.

Open: All year.

Directions

Av'n is 15 km. east of Cangas de On's on AS114 road to Panes and is probably best approached from this direction especially if towing. From A8 (Santander - Oviedo) use km. 326 exit and N634 northwest to Arriondas. Turn southeast on N625 to Cangas and join AS114 (Covodonga/Panes) by-passing Cangas. Site is just beyond Av'n after 16 km. marker. GPS: N43:20.178 W04:56.699

Charges guide

Per person	€ 5,02
child (under 14 yrs)	€ 4,01
pitch incl. car	€ 8,57 - € 9,64
electricity	€ 3,48

All plus 7% VAT.

The region of Cantabria in the north of Spain offers the best of both worlds. On the one hand there is the glorious coastline with beautiful beaches and pretty fishing villages; while inland there are a number of national parks including the mountainous, Picos de Europa.

CANTABRIA IS A ONE PROVINCE REGION

THE CAPITAL IS SANTANDER

The capital, Santander, is an elegant city which extends over a wide bay with views of the Cantabrian Sea. Its historic quarter is situated against a backdrop of sea and mountains, although the town is best known for its beaches; the Playa de la Magdalena, which has a summer windsurfing school, and the popular El Sardinero beach. There is also a Maritime Museum and Museum of Prehistory and Archaeology, plus a small zoo housed in the gardens of the old royal palace. A short distance from the city is the pretty medieval village of Santillana del Mar and the prehistoric caves of Altamira. Despite being closed indefinitely for restoration work, the adjacent Altamira Museum houses a replica of these caves and their impressive prehistoric drawings. Also on the outskirts of the capital is the Cabárceno Nature Park with more protected areas scattered around the region, including those at Oyambre, Peña Cabarga and Saja-Besaya. The largest is the mountain range of Picos de Europa, a national park which shares its territory with Asturias and Castilla-León. With river gorges, valleys, woodlands and an abundance of wildlife, it is popular with walkers, trekkers and climbers.

Places of interest

Castro Urdiales: beaches, Gothic church, Roman bridge, old quarter.

Comillas: rural town, beaches, Gaudí-designed villa.

Laredo: lively seaside resort, 13th church, 5 km. long sandy beach.

Lienganes: 17th and 18th architecture, spa.

Potes: on east side of Picos de Europa, mountain bike hire, paragliding available.

San Vicente de la Barquera: picturesque fishing port.

Cuisine of the region

Seafood is used a lot, including fresh shellfish, sardines, *rabas* (fried squid), *bocartes rebozados* (breaded whitebait). Cheese is produced throughout the region; *queso de nata* (cream cheese), *picón* from Treviso Bejes, and smoked cheeses from Áliva or Pido. A typical dish of the region is the Cantabrian stew, which contains haricot beans, cabbage, rice and sausage. Desserts include the traditional cheesecakes of the Pas Valley and pastries. The local tipple is *orujo*, a strong liquor.

Maganos encebollados: squid with onion.

Quesada: cheesecake.

Sobaos pasiegos: sponge cakes.

Sorropotún: type of fish stew.

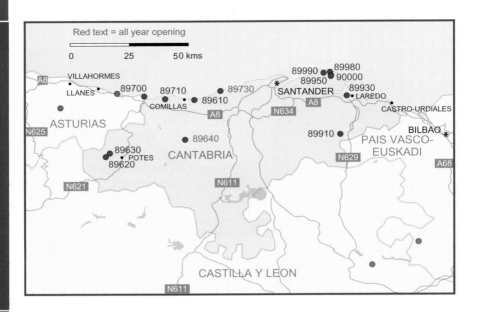

ES89610 Camping El Helguero

Ctra Santillana - Comillas, E-39527 Ruiloba (Cantabria)

Tel: **942 722 124**. Email: **reservas@campingelhelguero.com**   www.alanrogers.com/ES89610

This site, in a peaceful location surrounded by tall trees and impressive towering rock formations, caters for 240 units (of which 100 are seasonal) on slightly sloping ground. There are many marked pitches on different levels, all with access to electricity (6A), but with varying amounts of shade. There are also attractive tent and small camper sections set close in to the rocks and some site owned chalets. The site gets very crowded in high season, so it is best to arrive early if you haven't booked. The reasonably sized swimming pool and children's pool have access lifts for disabled campers. This is generally a good site for disabled visitors, although the ramps to one of the toilet blocks are steep. The site is used by tour operators and there are some site owned chalets. There is a large Spanish presence at weekends, especially in high season, so if you wish to share the boisterous atmosphere, see if you can get one of the pitches near the restaurant area. Comillas fiesta is in mid-July and the site gets very crowded.

Facilities

Three well placed toilet blocks, although old, are clean and all include controllable showers and hot and cold water to all basins. Facilities for children and disabled visitors. Washing machines and dryers. Motorcaravan services. Small supermarket (July/Aug). Bar/snack bar plus separate more formal restaurant. Swimming pool (caps compulsory). Playground. Activities and entertainment (high season). ATM. Torches useful in some places. Off site: Bus service 500 m. Bar/restaurants in village (walking distance). Beach, fishing, sailing, golf and riding, all 3 km. Santillana del Mar 12 km.

Open: 1 April - 30 September.

Directions

Site is 45 km. west of Santander. From the A8 (Santander - Oviedo) take km. 249 exit (Cabezón and Comillas) and turn north on CA135 towards Comillas, At km. 7 turn right on CA359 to Ruilobuca and Barrio la Iglesia. After village turn right up hill on CA358 to site on right (note: signs refer to 'Camping Ruiloba'). GPS: N43:22.973 W04:14.880

Charges 2009

Per person	€ 4,50 - € 5,35
child (4-10 yrs)	€ 3,95 - € 4,00
pitch incl. electricity	€ 8,55 - € 15,30

Camping Cheques accepted.

ES89620 Camping La Isla Picos de Europa

Picos de Europa, E-39570 Potes-Turieno (Cantabria)

Tel: 942 730 896. Email: campicoseuropa@terra.es

www.alanrogers.com/ES89620

La Isla is beside the road from Potes to Fuente Dé, with many mature trees giving good shade and glimpses of the mountains above. Established for over 25 years, a warm welcome awaits you from the owners (who speak good English) and a most relaxed and peaceful atmosphere exists in the site. The 121 unmarked pitches are arranged around an oval gravel track under a variety of fruit and ornamental trees. Electricity (6A) is available to all pitches, although some need long leads. A small bar and restaurant are located under dense trees by the small river which runs through the site.

Facilities

Single, clean and smart sanitary block retains the style of the site. Washbasins with cold water. Washing machine. Gas supplies. Freezer service. Small shop and restaurant/bar (all season). Small swimming pool (caps compulsory; 1/5-30/9). Play area. Barbecue area. Fishing. Bicycle hire. Riding. Off site: Shops, bars and restaurants plus Monday morning market in Potes 4 km. Fuente Dé and its spectacular cable car ride 18 km.

Open: 1 April - 30 October.

Directions

From A8/N634 (Santander - Oviedo) take exit at km. 272t for Unquera (end of motorway section). Take N621 south to Panes and up spectacular gorge (care needed if towing) to Potes. Take CA165 to Funte De and site is on the right, 3 km.beyond Potes. GPS: N43:08.999 W04:41.998

Charges guide

Per person	€ 3,75 - € 4,05
pitch incl. electricity	€ 6.15 - € 13,80

All plus VAT. Low season reductions.

ES89630 Camping La Viorna

Ctra Santa Toribio, E-39570 Potes (Cantabria)

Tel: 942 732 021. Email: campinglaviorna@hotmail.com

www.alanrogers.com/ES89630

The wonderful views of the valley below from the open terraces, with its spectacular backdrop of mountains, make this site an attractive base from which to tour this region or to relax by the excellent swimming pool. It is popular with both families and couples. There are beds of flowers and the trees are maturing, providing shade on many pitches. Access is good for all sizes of unit to the 115 pitches of around 70 sq.m, all of which have electricity (3/6A). In high season, however, tents may be placed on less accessible, steeply sloping areas.

Facilities

Single, neat sanitary block of high standard, clean and modern. Washbasins have cold water only. Facilities for disabled visitors (key). Laundry. Shop. Restaurant/bar (all season). Swimming pool (23 x 13 m) and paddling pool (15/5-30/9; caps compulsory). Play area. Games room. Many sporting activities arranged such as parascending, mountain biking, rafting and canoeing. Off site: Potes 1.5 km. Bicycle hire 1 km. Fishing and riding 1.5 km. Fuente Dé and its spectacular cable car ride 20 km.

Open: Easter/1 April - 30 October.

Directions

From A8/N634 (Santander - Oviedo) take km. 272 exit for Unquera (end of motorway). Take N621 south to Panes and up spectacular gorge (care needed if towing) to Potes. After town fork left signed Toribio de Liébana and site is on right after 800 m. GPS: N43:09.261 W04:38.609

Charges 2009

Per person	€ 3,90 - € 4,40
pitch incl. electricity (3/6A)	€ 13,00 - € 14,70

ES89640 Camping El Molino de Cabuerniga

Sopeña de Cabuérniga, Ctra C625, km 42, E-39510 Cabuérniga (Cantabria)

Tel: 942 706 259. Email: cmcabuerniga@campingcabuerniga.com

www.alanrogers.com/ES89640

Located in a peaceful valley with magnificent views of the mountains, beside the Saja river and only a short walk from the picturesque and unspoiled village of Sopeña, this gem of a site is on an open, level, grassy meadow with trees. Wonderful stone buildings and artefacts are a feature of this unique site. There are 102 marked pitches, all with electricity, although long leads may be needed in places. This site is very good value and ideal for a few nights whilst you explore the Cabuérniga Valley.

Facilities

A single, modern sanitary block provides spacious, controllable showers and hot and cold water to washbasins. Washing machines and free ironing. Unit for disabled campers. Baby and toddler room. Bar serving breakfasts and 'bocadillos' (sandwiches) includes small shop. Wonderful playground in rustic setting (supervision needed). Fishing. Bicycle hire. Off site: Bus service 500 m. Restaurant in village 1 km. Riding and bicycle hire 3 km. Golf 20 km. Beach 20 km. Skiing 50 km.

Open: All year.

Directions

From the A8 (Santander - Oviedo) take km. 249 exit and join N634 to Cabezón de la Sal. Turn southwest on CA180 towards Reinosa for 11 km. to Sopeña (site signed to left). Turn into village (watch for low eaves/gutters on buildings), continually bearing right following site signs. GPS: N43:13.556 W4:17.420

Charges guide

Per person	€ 4,35
pitch incl. electricity	€ 12,50

All plus VAT.

Check real time availability and at-the-gate prices...
www.alanrogers.com
133

ES89700 Camping Las Arenas-Pechón

Ctra Pechón - Unquera km 2, E-39594 Pechón (Cantabria)

Tel: **942 717 188**. Email: **lasarenas@ctv.es**

This site is in a very quiet, but rather spectacular location bordering the sea and the Tina Mayor estuary, with views to the mountains and access to an attractive little beach. Otherwise, enjoy the pleasant kidney shaped pool that also shares the views. Taking 350 units, half the site has grassy pitches (60 sq.m) in bays or on terraces with stunning sea and mountain views, with 5A electricity. There are some quite steep slopes to tackle – reception is at the top, as are the bar and restaurant.

Facilities

Clean, well tiled sanitary facilities are in the older, simple style. Various blocks include showers (no divider; add hot water to the cold by pushing a switch). Washing machines. Well stocked supermarket. Restaurant/bar and snack bar (all season). Small playground. Fishing. Riding arranged (collected from site). Torches helpful. English is spoken. Off site: Shops, bars and restaurants in Pechón, plus a disco/bar 1 km. Golf 28 km.

Open: 1 June - 30 September.

Directions

On A8 from Santander, take km. 272 exit for Unquera (N621) at end of motorway. Take first exit CA380 signed Pechón and site which is 2 km. on left. From Oviedo/Gijón on A8/N634 at km. 272 take N621 slip-road for Unquera (do not join motorway), then as above. GPS: N43:23.491 W04:30.635

Charges guide

Per person	€ 6,10
pitch incl. electricity	€ 9,60 - € 14,20
All plus 7% VAT.	

ES89710 Camping Caravaning Playa de Oyambre

Finca Peña Guerra, E-39547 San Vicente de la Barquera (Cantabria)

Tel: **942 711 461**. Email: **camping@oyambre.com**

This exceptionally well managed site is ideally positioned to use as a base to visit the spectacular Picos de Europa or one of the many sandy beaches along this northern coast. Despite its name, it is in fact a kilometre from the beach on foot, further if you go by car. The 100 touring pitches all have 10A electricity (long leads needed in places). The fairly flat central area is allocated to tents while caravans are mainly sited on wide terraces (access to some could be a little tight for larger units) and there is some shade. There may be some traffic noise on the lower terraces.

Facilities

Good, clean sanitary facilities are in one, well kept block. Showers are spacious but have a frustrating mixture of push-button hot and ordinary cold controls. Facilities for babies and disabled visitors. Washing machines. Motorcaravan services. Well stocked supermarket (15/6-15/9). Restaurant. Bar and takeaway. Swimming pools with lifeguard (1/6-15/9). Playground. Off site: Bus service at site entrance. Fishing and superb beach 1 km. Golf 2 km. Riding 5 km. San Vicente de la Barquera 5 km.

Open: Easter/1 April - 30 September.

Directions

From A8 (Santander - Oviedo) take exit for Caviedes at km. 258 and join N634. Turn towards San Vicente. Site is signed at junction to Comillas, at km. 265 on the E70, 5 km. east of San Vicente de la Barquera. The entrance is quite steep. Another 'Camping La Playa' at Oyambre within 500 m. is not so good. GPS: N43:22.999 W4:23.999

Charges guide

Per person	€ 4,50
pitch incl. electricity	€ 13,00
All plus VAT.	

ES89730 Camping Santillana

Ctra de Comilias s/n, E-39330 Santillana del Mar (Cantabria)

Tel: **942 818 250**. Email: **complejosantillana@cantabria.com**

This is an attractive site on a hill above the charming mediaeval village of Santillana del Mar and five to ten kilometres from some of Costa Verde's good beaches. There are 400 pitches, all with access to electricity (5A), some mainly for tents informally arranged on a slope, with others for caravans and motorcaravans on the lower part of the site. Where the pitches are numbered but unmarked some overcrowding may occur in high season and those alongside the road will experience some noise.

Facilities

Toilet blocks are well placed (only one open in low season), fully equipped and with facilities for disabled campers. Washing machines and irons. Supermarket and souvenir shop (1/6-30/9). Bar/restaurant and self-service café (all year). Swimming and paddling pools (1/5-30/9). Play areas. Minigolf. Tennis. Bicycle hire. Entertainment in high season. Off site: A short, if rather steep, walk leads to the centre of the charming village with shops, bars and restaurants. Riding 300 m. Fishing 5 km. Golf 20 km.

Open: All year.

Directions

Santillana is 30 km. west of Santander. From A8 (Santander - Oviedo) take km. 234 exit west of Torrelavega and follow CA133 north to Santillana. Turn left at T-junction (busy) towards Comillas and site is on right in 300 m. GPS: N43:25.572 W04:06.789

Charges guide

Per person	€ 5,00 - € 5,61
pitch	€ 4,86 - € 6,82
No credit cards. Camping Cheques accepted.	

Check real time availability and at-the-gate prices...

www.alanrogers.com

ES89910 Camping La Barguilla

E-39800 Ramales de la Victoria (Cantabria)

Tel: 942 646 586

www.alanrogers.com/ES89910

Located in a rural setting on the outskirts of the small Spanish town of Ramales de la Victoria, this small site provides an opportunity to sample traditional Spanish life. Access to the town is via an easy 1 km. walk. There are 79 small pitches with 50 for touring, all with 3/6A electricity. Some pitches have shade, whilst others enjoy views of the nearby Sierra del Hornijo mountains. Facilities are minimal but the site is well maintained and you are sure of a comfortable stay. Booking in high season is recommended. Be sure to sample the on site Periguena restaurant which serves a variety of cuisine.

Facilities

One heated toilet block provides WCs, washbasins and shower cubicles. No facilities for visitors with disabilities. Washing machines. Shop. Terrace bar, cafeteria, restaurant (all season). Fenced play area. Games room. Barbecues are not permitted. Off site: Fishing 200 m. Riding 10 km. Golf 20 km. Beaches in Larado.

Open: All year (except November).

Directions

From A8, take exit 173 and N629 to Ramales de la Victoria. At entry to town, turn right, CA261 signed Arredondo. In 1.6 km. turn left over bridge into Parque Publico. Site is on right behind Restaurant Perigena. Sharp incline to site so care is needed. GPS: N43:15.57 W03:28.99

Charges guide

Per person	€ 4,82
pitch incl. electricity	€ 7,50 - € 11,78

ES89930 Camping Playa del Regaton

El Regaton 8, E-39770 Laredo (Cantabria)

Tel: 942 606 995. Email: campingregaton@wanadoo.es

www.alanrogers.com/ES89930

Situated a short distance from the bustling seaside town of Laredo and easily accessible from Santander and Bilbao, Camping del Regaton is an ideal stop-over for those en route to the ferries. The site has direct access to the beach and the estuary of the Ria del Ason and is an important marsh area for migrating birds. Of the 128 small pitches, 100 are for touring and have 5A electricity and a sink. All are on level grass, with mature trees providing separation and a degree of shade. The site is popular with Spanish holidaymakers. The owners and their staff are keen to ensure you enjoy your stay. Only limited English is spoken outside high season.

Facilities

One modern, heated toilet block. Baby bath. Facilities for visitors with disabilities. Washing machine and dryer. Small shop (28/3-27/9) sells most essentials. Café/bar (28/3-27/9) with snacks (1/7-31/8). Play area. Children's club in high season. Games room. Dogs are not accepted. Off site: Fishing 200 m. Riding 500 m. Boat launching 3 km. Golf 20 km. Beaches in Larado.

Open: 28 March - 27 September.

Directions

From the A8 (Santander - Bilbao) take exit 172 to Laredo. Straight on at roundabout signed Hospital and beaches. Do not go into Laredo. At traffic lights turn left, site is well signed on left, 500 m. past Hospital. GPS: N43:24.67 W03:27.17

Charges guide

Per person	€ 3,00 - € 3,75
pitch incl. electricity (10A)	€ 7,50 - € 13,90

ES89950 Camping Los Molinos

Ctra La Ris s/n, E-39180 Noja (Cantabria)

Tel: 942 630 426. Email: losmolinos@ceoecant.es

www.alanrogers.com/ES89950

Camping Los Molinos is close to the village of Noja, a seaside resort that gets very busy in high season. It is on the coast of Cantabria, a ten minute walk from the Playa del Ris beach which has fine sand and clear water. The site is divided into two main areas, both with a large number of permanent units, some of which look a little run down. There are 100 (60 sq.m) touring pitches for caravans or motorcaravans on level ground, but with little shade; 42 have 3A electricity. A separate large area without electricity is used for tents.

Facilities

Six fully equipped toilet blocks, two new and two recently refurbished, are kept clean. Facilities for disabled campers. Washing machines. Supermarkets and butcher. Restaurant (July/Aug). Bars and café bar serving tapas and pizzas. Swimming and paddling pools with lifeguard (20/6-7/9). Play area. ATM. Torch useful. Off site: Beach and fishing 400 m. Indoor pool and bicycle hire 1 km. Golf 9 holes 1 km, 18 holes 20 km. Boat launching 7 km. Riding 10 km. Free bus to the beach and town in high season.

Open: 1 June - 30 September.

Directions

From A8 (Bilbao - Santander) take exit at km. 185 and join N634 towards Beranga and almost immediately turn right on CA147 to Noja. In 10 km. turn left and go down through town. At beach roundabout turn left and then left again just before Camping Playa Joyel at large sign for site. GPS: N43:29.155 W03:32.281

Charges guide

Per person	€ 4,50 - € 6,00
pitch incl. electricity	€ 11,50 - € 115,00
No credit cards.	

ES89980 Camping Playa de Isla

Ctra Arnadal no. 1, E-39195 Isla (Cantabria)

Tel: **942 679 361**. Email: **bernac@teleonica.net**

www.alanrogers.com/ES89980

This well maintained site is set on a headland, overlooking the sea on one side and the village of Isla on the other. The 200 well defined small pitches (100 for touring) with little shade are on two levels. All have 6A electricity and some have sea views. Large units may experience difficult access to some pitches. There is direct access via a short flight of steps to the superb beach with its golden sand and rocky pools. The site has an illuminated 500 m. footpath to the village of Isla, where there are restaurants, shops and bars. Since its opening in 1979 this site has undergone continuous improvement and the owners are justifiably proud of the results. The lower level consists mainly of seasonal pitches, with the upper level currently used to accommodate most of the touring units and tents.

Facilities

One modern spotless toilet block is centrally positioned. Family shower room. Washing machines and dryers. Well stocked shop (Easter - Sept). Café/bar (July - Sept), with terrace overlooking the sea. Play area. Fishing from adjacent beach. Dogs are not accepted. Off site: Boat launching 500 m. Golf, bicycle hire 5 km. Riding 6 km.

Open: Easter - 30 September.

Directions

From A8 (Santander - Bilbao) take exit at 185 km. marker onto N634 towards Beranga. Almost immediately turn right, CA147 (Noja). At roundabout turn left, CA141, towards Somo, Santander. Turn right, CA449 signed Isla. Site is 5 km. through village. GPS: N43:30.14 W03:32.54

Charges guide

Per person	€ 5,13 - € 5,35
child	€ 4,60 - € 4,92
pitch	€ 11,55 - € 12,30
electricity	€ 4,28

ES89990 Camping Punta Marina

Playa de la Arena s/n, E-39195 Isla (Cantabria)

Tel: **942 679 349**. Email: **puntamarina@ceoecant.es**

www.alanrogers.com/ES89990

This well maintained site is open from Easter to the end of September. It has 98 pitches with only 28 for touring, on grass with little shade and all with 3A electricity, water and drainage. Most have sea views. The site comes alive at weekends and in the high season, when it can become very busy. Advanced booking is advisable. The small holiday village of Isla, with its many shops, restaurants and bars is only 1 km. away, and here there is also an excellent beach, rocky coves and a boat launching slipway. Care is needed with large units when approaching the site. The swimming pool with its own sunbathing area becomes the focal point of the site and you can relax there all day if you choose.

Facilities

One modern, very clean toilet block with family shower room and good facilities for visitors with disabilities. Washing machine and dryers. Well stocked shop (July/Aug). Separate restaurant, bar and takeaway (June - Sept). Swimming pools (July/Aug). Play area. Children's club (July/Aug). Tennis. Bicycle hire. Games room. TV room. Dogs are not accepted. Off site: Fishing, boat launching 1 km. Golf 5 km. Riding 6 km.

Open: Easter - 30 September.

Directions

Exit A8 at 185 km. marker and take N634 towards Beranga. Turn right, CA147, in towards Noja. At roundabout turn left, CA141 (Somo/Santander). Turn right, CA449 to Isla. Turn left CA448 to Playa la Arena. In 1.6 km. turn right to site. GPS: N43:29.89 W03:34.56

Charges guide

Per person	€ 4,00 - € 4,30
child	€ 3,40 - € 3,70
pitch incl. car	€ 13,40 - € 14,50
electricity	€ 2,70 - € 3,00

ES90000 Camping Playa Joyel

Playa de Ris, E-39180 Noja (Cantabria)

Tel: 942 630 081. Email: playajoyel@telefonica.net

www.alanrogers.com/ES90000

This very attractive holiday and touring site is some 40 kilometres from Santander and 80 kilometres from Bilbao. It is a busy, high quality, comprehensively equipped site by a superb beach providing 1,000 well shaded, marked and numbered pitches with 3A electricity available. These include 80 large pitches of 100 sq.m. Some 250 pitches are occupied by tour operators or seasonal units. This well managed site has a lot to offer for family holidays with much going on in high season when it gets crowded. The swimming pool complex with lifeguard is free to campers and the superb beaches are cleaned daily 15/6-20/9. One of the beach exits leads to the main beach, or if you turn left out of the other you will find a safe, placid estuary with water at rising tide. An unusual feature is the natural park within the site boundary which has a great selection of animals to see. It overlooks a protected area of marsh where European birds spend the winter. There are security patrols at night.

Facilities

Six excellent, spacious and fully equipped toilet blocks include baby baths. Large laundry. Motorcaravan services. Gas supplies. Freezer service. Supermarket (all season). General shop. Kiosk. Restaurant and takeaway (1/7-31/8). Bar and snacks (all season). Swimming pools, bathing caps compulsory (20/5-15/9). Entertainment organised with a soundproof pub/disco (July/Aug). Gympark. Tennis. Playground. Riding. Fishing. Natural animal park. Hairdresser (July/Aug). Medical centre. Torches necessary in some areas. Animals are not accepted. Off site: Bicycle hire and large sports complex with multiple facilities including an indoor pool 1 km. Sailing and boat launching 10 km. Riding and golf 20 km.

Open: Easter - 27 September.

Directions

From A8 (Bilbao - Santander) take km. 185 exit and N634 towards Beranga. Almost immediately turn right on CA147 to Noja. In 10 km. turn left at multiple campsite signs and go through town. At beach roundabout turn left and continue to site at end of road. GPS: N43:29.369 W03:32.220

Charges 2009

Per person	€ 4,20 - € 6,40
child (3-9 yrs)	€ 3,00 - € 4,80
pitch	€ 15,00 - € 27,30
electricity	€ 3,60 - € 4,70

No credit cards.
Camping Cheques accepted.

Check real time availability and at-the-gate prices...

www.alanrogers.com

Located in northern Spain, this is a region steeped in Basque traditions, which is reflected in the architecture, native language, local sports and cuisine.

**THERE ARE THREE PROVINCES:
ALAVA, GIPUZKOA AND BIZKAIA**

THE REGIONAL CAPITAL IS VITORIA

The province of Gipuzkoa adjoins France in the east. Its capital, San Sebastian, is a bustling, picturesque seaside town with a strong Basque identity. Overlooking La Concha Bay and enclosed by rolling low hills, this popular resort boasts four good beaches, including the celebrated La Concha Beach. As cider production is one of oldest traditions in Basque country there are also plenty of sidrerías (cider houses) to visit. Heading along the rocky fringe of Costa Vasca towards Bilbao in Bizkaia are more excellent beaches and pretty fishing villages including Orio, Zarautz and Getaria. The biggest attraction in Bilbao is the famous Guggenheim Museum. Opened in 1997 this spectacular building is completely covered with titanium sheets and houses a collection of modern and contemporary art from around the world. The city also boasts a beautiful old quarter with a Gothic cathedral, the Plaza Nueva and a museum. Further inland in Alava is Vitoria, the region's capital. Its medieval streets intermingle with Renaissance Palaces and fine churches and are lined with lively bars and tavernas. In the summer the city plays host to a jazz festival. Elsewhere in the province are several nature reserves.

Places of interest

Encartanciones: one of the world's largest cave chambers Torca del Carlista, wildlife sanctuary

Hondarribia: fishing port, beaches, charming walled old town

Laguardia: old walled town with cobbled streets, historic buildings, in wine-growing district of Rioja Alavesa

Oñati: Baroque architecture, old university

Tolosa: impressive old town square, carnival in February

Zarautz: seaside town, famous for production of *txakoli*

Zumaia: beaches, good coastal walks, July fiesta with Basque sports, dancing and bull racing

Cuisine of the region

Basque cuisine is considered to be the finest in Spain. Tapas or *pintxos* is readily available in bars, served with the local white wine *txakoli*. Fish is popular, especially *bacalao* (cod) and seafood is often used to make casseroles and sauces. Lots of milk based desserts. Founded in the 19th century, the tradition of dining clubs or *txokos* are unique to the Basque country

Alubias pochas: white haricot bean stew

Chipirones en su tinta: squid cooked in its ink

Goxua: sponge cake with whipped cream and caramel

Intxaursalsa: milk pudding with cinnamon and walnuts

Marmitaco: fish and potato stew

Pantxineta: custard slice

ES90450 Camping Angosto

Ctra Villanañe - Angosto no. 2, E-01425 Villanañe (Araba)

Tel: **945 353 271**. Email: **info@camping-angosto.com**   www.alanrogers.com/ES90450

This is a smart eco-friendly site with good facilities surrounded by wooded hills near the Valderejo National Park. Opened in 1999, the facilities are improving every year and a keen young team run things efficiently, gearing the site towards families. Most of the pitches are seasonal and in high season it is bustling and very Spanish! The limited number of touring pitches are flat and of average size. There is a large area for tents. Young trees have been planted around the site and are beginning to provide a little shade. The attractive new, heated pool has a sliding roof for inclement weather. A phone call before arriving is essential to establish availabilty. Attractive walks start just outside the site perimeter and deer can often be spotted. The area has one of the largest colonies of vultures in Northern Spain. As the site is one hour from Bilbao we see it as a most pleasant stopover or a chance to sample the rustic simplicity of the area.

Facilities

Fully equipped and well maintained toilet block with facilities for disabled campers. Washing machine. Good shop (1/3-30/9). Stylish bar with takeaway and separate restaurant (June to Sept; weekends only at other times). Small fenced play area close to entrance and grass toddler play area. Activities for children (high season). Mountain bike hire. Fishing. Ice machine. Off site: Many outdoor activities arranged locally. Riding 30 km. Sailing 40 km. Golf 45 km. Sea 60 km.

Open: 15 February - 12 December.

Directions

Villanañe is 25 km. northwest of Miranda de Ebro. From Miranda de Ebro, take A1 towards Burgos, leave at exit 5 and take A2122 to Puentelarrá and on to Espejo. From N1 Burgos - Victoria road, turn north on A2625 (west of Ameyugo) to Sta Gadea and Espejo. Site is just after village, clearly signed. GPS: N42:50.548 W03:04.119

Charges guide

Per person	€ 4,65
child	€ 4,30
pitch	€ 5,15 - € 6,25
electricity	€ 4,30
All plus 7% VAT.	

ES90340 Camping Leagi

Calle Barrio Leagi s/n, E-48289 Mendexa (Bizkaia)

Tel: **946 842 352**. Email: **leagi@campingleagi.com**   www.alanrogers.com/ES90340

This site is perched high above Lekeitio and has commanding views of the town, sea and surrounding areas. A steep road leads up to the site, but upon arriving at the car park and reception, the area becomes flat. There are 111 touring pitches on open, level grass with good mountain views. All have electricity (5A). There is little shade and the pitches are not defined. This is a quiet site, suitable for couples and families with small children and for those wishing to explore the attractive local towns or the many rural walks in the area. Transport is essential.

Facilities
Two modern, clean sanitary blocks are well equipped and there are separate facilities for those with disabilities. Excellent laundry. Motorcaravan services. Shop (1/7-10/9). Restaurant, bar and takeaway (all year, closed Tues/Wed). Dog washing area. Small toddlers' play area in car park. Off site: Fishing, sailing and beach 1.5 km.

Open: All year.

Directions
From Lekeito cross bridge heading east. Turn right on BI4449 to Mendexa. Continue up hill for 800 m. Site is signed on bend. Turn sharp right and access via a steep, narrow road. GPS: N43:21.098 W02:29.522

Charges 2009
Per person	€ 4,60 - € 5,50
pitch incl. electricity	€ 14,50 - € 17,50

ES90350 Camping Portuondo

Ctra Gernika - Bermeo, E-48360 Mundaka (Bizkaia)

Tel: **946 877 701**. Email: **recepcion@campingportuondo.com**   www.alanrogers.com/ES90350

This well kept site has a lovely reaturant, bar and terrace taking full advantage of the wonderful views across the ocean and estuary. Set amongst gardens, the pitches are mainly for tents and smaller vans, but there are 8 large pitches at the lower levels for caravans and motorhomes. The access to these is a little difficult as the road is steep and there is no turning space. In high season (July/Aug) it is essential to ring to book a space. With its mostly small pitches, in high season the site is popular with surfers and young people without children. English is spoken and the friendly owner Imanol and his staff are keen to help.

Facilities
Two fully equipped toilet blocks can be heated and include mostly British WCs and a smart baby room. Washing machines and dryers. Shop (15/6-15/9). Bar and two restaurants, all open to public (28/1-14/12). Takeaway (15/6-15/9). Swimming pools (15/6-15/9). Barbecue area. Torches may be useful. Off site: Fishing 100 m. Beaches 500 m. bracing walk. Surfing on Mundaka beach 500 m. Boat launching 1 km. Shops, bars and restaurants 2 km. Riding 8 km. Bicycle hire 10 km. Golf 40 km. Buses to Bilbao and Gernika (every 30 mins) 300 m.

Open: 28 January - 16 December.

Directions
From the A8 (San Sebastián - Bilbao) take exit 18 and follow signs for Gernika on BI635. Continue on the BI2235 towards Bermeo. Site is on right approaching Mundaka. Care is needed as a wide approach may be necessary as this is a sharp right turn with a steep access. Road signs do not permit turning left to site. GPS: N43:23.951 W02:41.766

Charges guide
Per person	€ 5,10 - € 5,70
pitch incl. electricity	€ 14,40 - € 15,20
From mid June to end August	
one week minimum reservation is required.	

ES90380 Camping Itxaspe

Ctra Nacional 634 km 38, E-20829 Itziar-Deba (Bizkaia)

Tel: **943 199 377**   www.alanrogers.com/ES90380

Set on a hill, surrounded by farmland and with views of the mountains, this site is ideal for a stopover or a couple of days rest. A fifteen minute walk through the woods leads to a rocky beach and the sea. Pitches are of medium size, flat and on grass, with plenty of water and electrical connections (5A). comfortable bar, restaurant and swimming pool open in July and August. Offering plenty of rural walks, this site will appeal to those wanting peace and quiet but with little entertainment and some unfenced areas, children will need supervision.

Facilities
The single traditional style sanitary block is basic but clean. In need of refurbishment, some new showers were being installed and more modernisation is ongoing. Facilities for disabled visitors. Washing machine. Shop. Restaurant and bar. Swimming pool (1/7-31/8 only). WiFi. Play area (unfenced). Off site: Fishing 1 km. Golf 15 km. Riding and bicycle hire 7 km. Beach 7 km.

Open: 1 April - 30 September.

Directions
From the A8 take exit 13 and follow signs for Itziar. At junction turn left. In 150 m. take right slip road for immediate turn left onto GI3291 (i.e. to cross main road). Site is signed and at end of road. GPS: N43:17.639 W02:19.787

Charges guide
Per person	€ 4,75
pitch incl. electricity	€ 13,40

ES90300 Camping Igueldo

Paseo Padre Orkolaga no. 69, Barrio de Igueldo, E-20008 San Sebastian (Gipuzkoa)

Tel: 943 214 502. Email: info@campingigueldo.com

www.alanrogers.com/ES90300

A five kilometre drive from the city takes you to this terraced campsite, high above San Sebastian, between the mountains and the sea. It offers mostly level, shaded, small (max. 70 sq.m.) grass pitches with electricity and drainage. The restaurant and bar are open all year and a sun terrace looks toward the mountains. An excellent bus service to and from San Sebastian runs every 30 minutes (all year). There are 25 attractive chalets to rent at the entrance to the site. With few sporting facilities, this site is for those wishing to mix quiet surroundings with city life. English is spoken in reception.

Facilities

Three traditional toilet blocks are clean and light. Facilities for disabled people and babies (accessed by key). Adequate covered dishwashing and laundry facilities. Motorcaravan service point. Shop for basics (20/6-15/9). Bar/restaurant (all year, Wed-Sun in early/late season, every day in summer). Play area. Off site: The town of Igueldo is within walking distance with shops, restaurants and bars. Bicycle hire and fishing 5 km. Beach 5 km. Golf 9 km.

Open: All year.

Directions

From A8 take exit 8 for San Sebastian West (oeste). Head for Ondarreta. At Playa de Ondarreta, follow beach road on Avda de Satrustegui. At T-junction turn left. Keep right on Pase O De Igueldo. Continue up hill for 5 km. to site on left. GPS: N43:18.276 W02:02.763

Charges 2009

Per unit incl. 2 persons	€ 16,20 - € 30,50
extra person	€ 3,70 - € 4,80
child (3-10 yrs)	€ 2,60 - € 3,40
electricity	€ 4,00

Special winter prices available.

ES90390 Gran Camping Zarautz

Monte Talai-Mendi, Ctra N634 San Sebastian - Bilbao, E-20800 Zarautz (Gipuzkoa)

Tel: 943 831 238. Email: info@grancampingzarautz.com

www.alanrogers.com/ES90390

This friendly site sits high in the hills to the east of the Basque town of Zarautz and has commanding views over the bay and the island of Getaria. Of the 400 pitches, 300 are for touring units, with 5A electricity; 10 also have water and drainage. The remaining pitches are for tents and seasonal caravans. The grass pitches are of average size, shaded by mature trees and are reasonably level; those on the perimeter have superb sea views. Between the site and the sea is a protected public area where flora and fauna flourish and you can enjoy watching the birds and wildlife. The ruins of a once busy iron ore works on the shore and the adjacent small island of Mollarri are to be explored. A 'bodega' adjacent to the site produces the local white wine, Txakoli (pronounced Char-coal-lee). The town of Zarautz offers a cultural programme in summer and the pedestrian promenade with modern sculptures is a good vantage point to enjoy the beach and watch the surfers.

Facilities

Three well-equipped toilet blocks. Facilities for disabled campers. Washing machines. Bar/snack-bar with TV plus terrace. Play area. Restaurant with 'menu del dia' and 'à la carte' meals. Well stocked shop (all facilities open all year). Off site: Beach, fishing and golf (9 holes) 1 km. Bicycle hire 2 km. Boat launching 4 km. Shops, bars, restaurants, bars, bus/train services in Zarautz 2 km.

Open: All year.

Directions

Zarautz is 20 km. west of San Sebastián. From A8 (San Sebastián - Bilbao) take exit 11 for Zarautz and turn east on N634 towards Orio. Entrance road to site is on left in 200 m. If using the N634 coast road, site is signed near km. 17 marker. GPS: N43:17.399 W02:08.787

Charges guide

Per unit incl. 2 persons and electricity	€ 19,70
extra person	€ 4,80
child (under 12 yrs)	€ 3,50

VAT included.
Camping Cheques accepted.

This small region located in the north eastern part of the country is the most outstanding wine-growing area in Spain. Its production, Rioja wine, figures among the finest wines in the world.

THIS IS A ONE PROVINCE REGION

THE CAPITAL IS LOGROÑO

The capital of the region, Logroño, did not gain importance till the 11th century, when the rise in popularity of the Pilgrims' Route to Santiago de Compostela attracted people. Indeed the 12th century Codex Calixtinus, the first guide to the route, mentions the city. And throughout the region, every town along the way has a church dedicated to the saint. Pilgrimages aside, La Rioja is best known for its wine. At the centre of the region's wine production is Haro, a stately town northwest of Logroño, and obviously a good place to stock up on a bottle or two! For those interested in the wine processes the Museum of Wine is worth a visit; admission includes cheese and wine tasting. During the last week of June the town comes alive with festivities. With free outdoor concerts, costumed characters on giant stilts, wine tastings and bargain buys, the climax of these fiestas is the Battle of the Wine, where thousands of people happily gather to be drenched in wine.

Places of interest

Calahorra: main town in Lower Rioja, Cathedral Museum.

Ezcaray: in the Sierra de la Demanda mountains, the surrounding area is made up of streams, forests and peaks over 2,000 metres high.

Nájera: monastery of Santa María la Real, built in 1032, History and Archaeological Museum.

San Millán de la Cogolla: traditional town, Monasteries of Suso and Yuso where the first texts written in Spanish are preserved.

Santo Domingo de la Calzada: last great staging post of the Pilgrim's Route in La Rioja, Cathedral of San Salvador.

Cuisines of the region

Asparagus, beans, peppers, garlic, artichokes and other vegetables and pulses are the basic ingredients of a long list of dishes such as vegetable stew, potatoes a la riojana, lamb cutlets with vine shoots or stuffed peppers. Traditional desserts include pears in wine, almond pastries from Arnedo or marzipan from Soto.

Camerano Cheese: cheese made from goat's milk, typical of La Rioja, usually eaten as a dessert with honey.

Fardelejo: pastry cake filled with marzipan.

Riojan-style potatoes: prepared with chorizo, peppers, garlic and lamp chops (optional).

ES90400 **Camping de Haro**

Avenida Miranda 1, E-26200 Haro (La Rioja)

Tel: 941 312 737. Email: campingdeharo@fer.es

www.alanrogers.com/ES90400

This quiet riverside site is on the outskirts of Haro, the commercial centre for the renowned Rioja wines. It is a family run site with excellent pools. Staff in the modern reception are helpful and you may well get a cheery welcome from Carlos, the owner's son, who speaks excellent English. All of the 236 pitches are on level ground and of reasonable size. Approximately 50% are occupied on a seasonal basis. Many of the touring pitches have some shade, a few have a great deal. Electricity connections (3/5A) are provided, although long leads may be required on some pitches. The river Tirón running alongside the site can provide fishing, and there is secure fencing. Reception provides information on the jewel of a town, and on tastings at the 'Bodegas' close by – CUNE and Muga are just two of those within easy walking distance. The famous Paternina is a few minutes drive away.

Facilities

Two toilet blocks, one heated in winter, the other with facilities for disabled campers. Laundry. Bar/snack bar with small counter selling basic provisions and adjacent swimming pool (15/6-15/9). Play area and animation for children in season. WiFi. Fishing. Torch useful. Off site: Large municipal pool complex nearby. Shops, bars, restaurants within walking distance. Bicycle hire 1 km. Riding 3 km. Boat launching 6 km. Golf 25 km.

Open: All year, excl. 9 December - 11 January.

Directions

Haro is between Miranda de Ebro and Logroño. From AP68 (Bilbao - Logroño) take exit 9 to Haro. Keep to LR-111 (Victoria) bearing left, crossing lights and over river where site is signed to left. From N124 (Victoria - Logroño) leave at exit north of Haro onto LR-111 towards town and turn right before bridge (site signed). Avoid other turnings into town centre! GPS: N42:34.736 W02:51.094

Charges 2009

Per unit with 2 persons and electricity	€ 18,55 - € 23,65
extra person	€ 3,95 - € 4,95
child (3-10 yrs)	€ 3,15 - € 3,95

Camping Cheques accepted.

ES92250 Camping de La Rioja

Ctra de Haro - St Domingo de la Calzada, E-26240 Castanares de Rioja (La Rioja)

Tel: **941 300 174**. Email: **info@campingdelarioja.com**   www.alanrogers.com/ES92250

This site is situated just beyond the town of Castanares de Rioja. This is a busy site during the peak season with many sporting activities taking place. In low season it becomes rather more quiet with limited facilities available. There are 30 level, grass touring pitches, out of a total of 250, and these are separated by hedges and trees allowing privacy. Each has their own water, drainage and electricity connection. To the rear of the site is the Oja River which is ideal for fishing and there are views of the Obarenes mountains in the distance. Some noise from the main road is possible.

Facilities

The central sanitary facilities are old and traditional in style but clean. Open style washbasins and controllable showers. Laundry facilities. Shop, bar, restaurant and takeaway (on request) all 20/6-20/9. Swimming pool (20/6-20/9 supervised). Multisport court. Tennis. River fishing. Riding. Play area. No individual barbecues. Off site: Town 1.5 km. The Guggenheim Museum in Bilbao. City of San Sebastian with beaches and aquarium.

Open: 1 January - 9 December.

Directions

Head west on N120. Turn right onto LR111 signed Castanares de Rioja. Continue through town towards Haro. Site is on left, 800 m. after leaving town speed restriction. GPS: N42:31.747 W2:55.346

Charges guide

Per person	€ 4,60 - € 5,75
child	€ 4,00 - € 5,00
pitch	€ 10,00 - € 12,50
electricity	€ 3,60

ES92260 Camping Los Cameros

Ctra de la Virgen de Lomos de Orios km 3, E-26125 Villoslada de Cameros (La Rioja)

Tel: **941 747 021**. Email: **info@camping-loscameros.com**   www.alanrogers.com/ES92260

Situated 3 km. from the small town of Villoslada de Cameros, this site is in a quiet location, in a valley surrounded by tree covered mountains. The area provides the opportunity for plenty of hill walking and a footpath from the site takes you into the town. Of the 150 pitches, 40 are available for touring. They are open with some shade and have 5A electricity. This is a simple site with limited facilities available but it is well kept and has character; ideal for relaxation.

Facilities

One heated sanitary block provides WCs, washbasins with cold water only (one with hot water) and cubicled showers. No facilities for disabled visitors. Cold water only for washing machine and dishwashing. No shop but bread and gas available. Bar with games. Restaurant with comprehensive menu and takeaway to order. Playing field and play area. Bicycle hire. Picnic area. Off site: Town 3 km. with shops, bars and restaurants and swimming pool.

Open: All year.

Directions

From Logroño (AP68) turn left onto N111 heading south towards Soria and Madrid. At sign for Villoslada de Cameros turn right, pass the centre and turn left by camping sign (LR448). Site on left in 3 km. Road uneven, drive with care and watch for animals on road. GPS: N42:04.841 W2:40.634

Charges guide

Per person	€ 4,85 - € 4,96
pitch	€ 4,00 - € 8,50
electricity	€ 4,30

ES92270 Camping Navarrete

Ctra de Entrena km 1, E-26370 Navarrete (La Rioja)

Tel: **941 440 169**. Email: **campingnavarrete@fer.es**   www.alanrogers.com/ES92270

Camping Navarrete is a spotlessly clean site in which the owners take great pride. Ideal as a base for exploring the surrounding countryside and sampling wonderful wines as it is located in the heart of La Rioja. Many of the 180 pitches are taken up by static caravans but a designated grassy area has been set aside for 40 unmarked, spacious touring pitches with 5A electricity. Some have shade and there are good views of the Rioja valley. Facilities on site are limited until the height of the season but the area is surrounded by many villages and places of artistic and historical importance. Noise is possible from the main road.

Facilities

One modern central sanitary block is clean and provides communal washbasins and separate shower cubicles. Facilities for disabled visitors, one unisex cabin. Laundry facilities. Shop (15/6-15/9). Bar and takeaway. Restaurant. Motorcaravan services. Outdoor swimming and paddling pools (15/6-15/9). Games machines. Tennis. Bicycle hire. Unfenced play area. Barbecues are allowed in special area of the campsite. Off site: Large town of Logroño 10 km.

Open: All year.

Directions

From Logroño proceed west along AP68. Exit at junction 11 signed Navarrete. At town centre turn left onto LR137 signed Entrena. Site on right in 800 m. GPS: N42:24.968 W2:33.103

Charges guide

Per person	€ 4,25 - € 4,95
child (under 10 yrs)	€ 3,95 - € 4,50
pitch	€ 4,25 - € 9,20
electricity	€ 3,75

ES92280 Camping Berceo

Ctra de Nájera - Sto. Domingo dir. San Millán, E-26227 Berceo (La Rioja)

Tel: 941 373 227   www.alanrogers.com/ES92280

Camping Berceo would ideally suit those looking for a quiet break at a site with limited facilities. It sits low in the San Millan valley in the heart of the Sierra de la Demanda and a steep walk of about 20 minutes will take you into the village. Here you will find several bars and restaurants, but little English is spoken. The 30 touring pitches are varied in size and separated by hedges. Some have shade and there are views of the green valley and mountains. Apart from the swimming pool which is open in peak season, there are few activities provided.

Facilities

One main toilet block providing sufficient facilities, but none for disabled visitors. Laundry area. Shop for basic supplies. Bar/restaurant. Takeaway on request. TV in bar and games area. Swimming and paddling pools. Play area. Off site: Berceo village 20 minute uphill walk. San Millan monasteries.

Open: All year.

Directions

From A68 head west until N120 exit. Turn left onto N120 signed Najera. Turn left onto LR113 (Bobadilla). Within 5 km. turn right onto 205 (Cárdenas) until Berceo village. In village centre follow site arrow down steep hill. Site is on left within 500 m. GPS: N42:20.098 W2:51.197

Charges guide

Per person	€ 4,28 - € 4,81
child	€ 3,75 - € 4,30
pitch	€ 3,00 - € 9,50
electricity	€ 4,17

ES92290 Camping El Ruedo

Paseo San Julián 24, E-26300 Najera (La Rioja)

Tel: 941 360 102   www.alanrogers.com/ES92290

Camping El Ruedo is situated 500 m. from the town of Najera and the river Rio Najerilla runs close by. There are numerous walks possible and seating provided along the riverbank. This is a small site with a total of 20 touring pitches on level ground, unmarked and with no separation. You can pitch at your own discretion. The traditional style sanitary block is kept clean and tidy with ample provision for the small amount of visitors. Extremely quiet and with very basic facilities, this site would suit those looking for peace and tranquillity. The site is not suitable for large units. No English is spoken.

Facilities

One immaculate toilet block with washbasins and showers. No facilities for disabled visitors. Washing machines (rather old). No shop, but provisions in town. Swings. No site lighting so torches useful. Off site: Town 500 m. (10 minutes walk).

Open: 1 April - 10 September.

Directions

From Logroño head west on AP68 until sign for N120 Najera. Turn left onto LR113 signed Najera. At traffic lights turn sharp left immediately before cobbled bridge. Site on left within 500 m. It is poorly signed after the A12. GPS: N42:24.641 W02:43.970

Charges guide

Per person	€ 5,00
child (under 10 yrs)	€ 4,80
pitch	€ 5,00 - € 13,00
electricity	€ 3,00

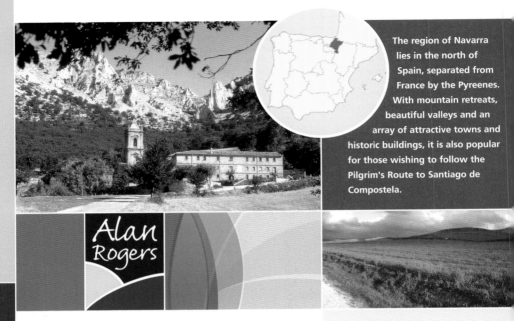

The region of Navarra lies in the north of Spain, separated from France by the Pyreenes. With mountain retreats, beautiful valleys and an array of attractive towns and historic buildings, it is also popular for those wishing to follow the Pilgrim's Route to Santiago de Compostela.

THERE IS ONLY ONE PROVINCE ALSO KNOWN AS NAVARRA

THE CAPITAL IS PAMPLONA

Founded by the Roman general Pompey in 75 BC, the region's capital Pamplona is perhaps best known for the Fiestas de San Fernmín (July), when the encierro takes place – a tradition which involves people running through the streets in front of bulls. The city also boasts its fair share of sights including the old town, with its ancient churches and elegant buildings. Outside the city is the Sierra de Aralar, with well-marked paths of all grades. A wander through here will take you past waterfalls and caves and in Excelsis you'll come across Navarra's oldest church, the Sanctuario de San Miguel, a popular pilgrimage destination. In the south, the historic medieval town of Olite is home to an outstanding 15th century castle, with turrets galore, and a Romanesque and Gothic church. To the west is the Urbasa and Andía Nature Reserve. Further north and in the east, the villages and valleys of the Pyrenees provide some of the most beautiful landscapes in the province and offer the perfect place to relax. Of particular note are the Valle de Baztán and the Valle de Salazar. For the more active, the Valle de Roncal is a good place to explore the mountains as is the Pirenaico National Park.

Places of interest

Andía Nature Reserve: forests, ponds, wildlife including the golden eagle, wild boar and wildcat.

Camino de Santiago: ancient Pilgrim's route. There are variants but the most popular point of entry into Spain was the pass of Roncesvalles, in the Pyrenees. It then continues south through Navarra via Sangüesa, Puente La Reina and Estella, then west through the provinces of La Rioja and Castilla-León till it reaches Santiago in the Galicia province.

Orreaga-Roncesvalles: a town established as a sanctuary and hospital in 1132 and first staging post for pilgrims, museum with exhibition on Pilgrim's Route.

Sangüesa: small town, 14th century churches, medieval hospital.

Ujué: medieval defensive village, Romanesqe church.

Cuisine of the region

Typical products found in abundance in this area include asparagus grown on the river banks, small red peppers and artichokes from Tudela, pork from Estella, cherries from Ciriza, cheese made in the Roncal Valley and *chorizo* from Pamplona.

Ajoarriero: cod cooked with garlic, potato, 'choricero' peppers and tomatoes.

Canutillos de Sumbilla: sweet pastry made with aniseed, filled with lemon flavouring.

Chorizo: shaped like a candle, stuffed in thick tripe with pork and beef, seasoned with salt, paprika, garlic and sugars.

Cordero al chilindrón: lamb stew.

Cuajada: made from sheep's milk and natural curd, sweetened by honey or sugar.

Pacharán: traditional aniseed liquor.

ES90480 Camping Urrobi

Ctra Pamplona - Valcarlos km 42 N135, E-31694 Espinal (Navarra)

Tel: **948 760 200**. Email: **info@campingurrobi.com**   www.alanrogers.com/ES90480

This large site is in a beautiful location with mountain views. At the entrance is a lively bar, a reasonably priced restaurant and a well stocked shop. The site is popular with Spanish families and there are many mobile homes, so it can be busy at holiday times and weekends. However, there is plenty of room on the 150 unmarked grass pitches. All have electricity points (6A) and there are plenty of water taps. Water activities of all types are catered for with both a swimming pool and an area of the river sectioned off for safe bathing and paddling. This is a suitable site for families. With many walks and bicycle tracks, there is plenty of scope for discovering this delightful area.

Facilities

Clean sanitary blocks include facilities for disabled visitors (key from reception). Laundry facilities. Motorcaravan service point. Shop, bar and restaurant (all season). Swimming pool. Games room with TV (Spanish). Internet access. Minigolf. Tennis. Playing field. Play area. Off site: Village 1 km. with shops, restaurant and bars. Forest of Irati 15 mins. Bicycle hire 15 km. Golf and riding 40 km. Beach 70 km. One bus per day to and from Pamplona.

Open: 1 April - 31 October.

Directions

From Pamplona take N135 northeast for 42 km. After village of Auritzberri turn right onto NA172. The site is on the left.
GPS: N42:58.389 W01:21.109

Charges guide

Per person	€ 4,50
child (2-12 yrs)	€ 3,60
pitch	€ 4,50 - € 8,10
electricity	€ 4,50

ES90420 Camping Etxarri

Paraje Dambolintxulo s/n, E-31820 Etxarri-Aranatz (Navarra)

Tel: **948 460 537**. Email: **info@campingetxarri.com**

www.alanrogers.com/ES90420

Situated in the Valle de la Burundi the site is a peaceful oasis with superb views of the 1,300 m. high San-Donator Mountains. The approach to the constantly improving site is via a road lined by huge 300 year old oak trees, which are a feature of the site. Reception is a purpose built chalet with a touring reference library (mostly in Spanish). There are 100 pitches of average size on flat ground (50 for tourers) with 6A electricity to all and water to 25. The site is well placed for fascinating walks in unspoilt countryside and is close to three recognised nature walks. There are two new swimming pools and animation is organised in August for children. The site gets very crowded during the Fiestas de San Fermín (bull-running) in Pamplona early in July. It is essential to make a reservation if you wish to stay. A visit to Pamplona is recommended. Parking is difficult – try to the west of the bullring, then wander down to Plaza de Toros (renamed Plaza Hemingway), to savour the atmosphere. It is common to use dual-naming of places and roads (one in the Spanish language, the other in Basque and it can be confusing) – ask for advice if in doubt.

Facilities

Toilet facilities are good and include a baby bath and facilities for disabled visitors. Laundry. Gas supplies. Essential supplies kept in high season. Bar (1/4-30/9). Restaurant and takeaway (1/6-15/9). Large new swimming and paddling pools (15/6-15/9) also open to the public and can get crowded. Bicycle hire. Minigolf. Play area. Off site: Bus and trains nearby. Bars, restaurants and shops 2 km. Golf, fishing, riding all 20 km. Pamplona 40 km.

Open: 1 April - 1 October.

Directions

Etxarri-Aranatz is 40 km. northwest of Pamplona. From A8 (San Sebastian - Bilbao) take A15 towards Pamplona, then 20 km. northwest of Pamplona, take A10 west towards Vitoria/Gasteix. At km. 19 take NA120 to and through town following site signs. Turn left after crossing railway to site at end of road. GPS: N42:54.780 W02:04.800

Charges 2009

Per person	€ 4,80
pitch incl. electricity	€ 12,45 - € 15,26

Situated amidst a leafy oakwood in the centre of the Sakana Valley.

Its magnificent setting makes it a perfect base for visiting two outstandingly beautiful areas: the mountains of Urbasa and Aralar.

These are lands of shepherds inhabited since the paleolithic times, and they still boast many prehistoric remains.

Due to varying altitudes, they are accessible to all ages.

Camping ETXARRI . E-31820 ETXARRI ARANATZ (Navarra) . Tel./fax: (34) 948 46 05 37
info@campingetxarri.com . www.campingetxarri.com

ES90490 Camping Baztan

Ctra Francia s/n, E-31714 Erratzu (Navarra)

Tel: **948 453 133**. Email: **campingbaztan@campingbaztan.com**

www.alanrogers.com/ES90490

When driving through the small town of Erratzu extreme caution is required due to the narrowness of the streets and it is not advised at all for large units. This site's rural setting and the mountain views make this a retreat for those who enjoy camping in quiet surroundings. It consists of a main building housing reception, a shop, bar and a small restaurant and above, 14 tidy apartments. There are also ten timber cottages for rent. Tarmac roads lead to the grass touring pitches which are supplied with water and electricity (10A). Shady and of a good size, most of the pitches are level.

Facilities

The single sanitary block is clean and has facilities for disabled visitors. Shop, bar and restaurant (weekends only outside 1/6-20/9). Swimming pool (1/6-20/9). In April, May and 20/9-1/11 the site is only open at weekends. If you wish to stay on week days, entry can be obtained by dialling a number displayed at reception (sanitary block will be open). Off site: Activity centre (riding, kayaking, rafting) 15 km. Village (5 mins).

Open: 1 June - 20 September (other times see above).

Directions

From Hendaye head south on the N121A. Turn east on N121B. Continue north to the junction with NA2600. Turn right to Erratzu. Proceed through village, bear left at sign 'Francia NA2600' and site is on the right. GPS: N43:10.840 W1:27.083

Charges guide

Per person	€ 5,90 - € 6,95
child (2-10 yrs)	€ 3,20 - € 4,00
pitch incl. electricity	€ 15,50 - € 18,20

Check real time availability and at-the-gate prices...

www.**alanrogers**.com

ES90430 Camping Caravanning Errota el Molino

E-31150 Mendigorria (Navarra)

Tel: **948 340 604**. Email: **info@campingelmolino.com**

www.alanrogers.com/ES90430

This is an extensive site set by an attractive weir near the town of Mendigorria, alongside the river Arga. It takes its name from an old disused water mill (molino) close by. The site is split into separate permanent and touring sections. The touring area is a new development with good-sized flat pitches with electricity and water for tourers, and a separate area for tents. Many trees have been planted around the site but there is still only minimal shade. The friendly owner Anna Beriain will give you a warm welcome. Reception is housed in the lower part of a long building along with the bar/snack bar which has a cool shaded terrace, a separate restaurant and a supermarket. The upper floor of this building is dormitory accommodation for backpackers. The site has a sophisticated dock and boat launching facility and an ambitious watersport competition programme in season with a safety boat present at all times. There are pedaloes and canoes for hire. The site is very busy during the festival of San Fermín (bull running) in July in Pamplona (28 km). Tours of the local bodegas (groups of ten) to sample the fantastic Navarra wines can be organised by reception.

Facilities

The well equipped toilet block is very clean and well maintained, with cold water to washbasins. Facilities for disabled campers. Washing machine. Large restaurant, pleasant bar. Supermarket. Superb new swimming pools for adults and children (1/6-15/9). Bicycle hire. Riverside bar. Weekly animation programme (July/Aug) and many sporting activities. Squash courts. Internet access. River walk. Torches useful. Off site: Bus to Pamplona 500 m. Riding 15 km. Golf 35 km.

Open: All year (excl. 23 December - 4 January).

Directions

Mendigorria is 30 km. southwest of Pamplona. From A15 San Sebastian - Zaragoza motorway, leave Pamplona bypass on A12 towards Logon. Leave at km. 23 on NA601 to hill top town of Mendigorria. At crossroads turn right towards Larraga and down hill to site. GPS: N42:37.497 W01:50.533

Charges guide

Per person	€ 4,70 - € 5,00
child	€ 3,95 - € 4,22
pitch incl. car and electricity	€ 12,90 - € 13,80

Plus 7% VAT. Discounts outside high season. Camping Cheques accepted.

ARAGÓN IS MADE UP OF THREE PROVINCES: HUESCA, ZARAGOZA AND TERUEL

THE CAPITAL OF THE REGION IS ZARAGOZA

The region can be separated into three different areas: the central area consisting of the Ebro basin, a vast flat lowland, the northern Pyrenees, and the area made up of the Iberian mountain range in the northwest and southeast of the region. The northern-most province of Huesca is located in the foothills of the Pyrenees Mountains, a beautiful area with plenty of picturesque towns and villages to visit. It is also good walking country with numerous trails offering anything from short day-walks in the valleys to long-distance treks in the mountains. Skiing is popular too. Bordering Huesca, the province of Zaragoza is home to the region's capital, also of the same name. Zaragoza is a lively town with plenty of bars and restaurants, plus numerous museums and architectural treasures. Outside the capital you'll find more villages, countryside, and vineyards where the best of the region's wine is produced; the mapped out Ruta del Vino will take you through the area. The third province of Teruel is largely comprised of the Iberian mountain range, with attractive towns, medieval sights and more dramatic scenery to admire.

Places of interest

Aljafería Palace: spectacular Moorish monument.

Basílica de Nuestra Señora del Pilar: Baroque temple from the 17th and 18th centuries.

Benasque: attractive alpine town, gateway to Pyrenees.

Casa-Museo de Goya: art museum, including engravings by Goya.

Jaca: home of the country's oldest Romanesque cathedral.

Monasterio de San Juan de la Peña: 17th century Baroque monastery and 10th century Old monastery in Romanesque style.

Parque Nacional de Ordesa y Monte Perdido: alpine national park.

Cuisine of the region

Specialities include lamb, locally-produced ham and sausages; fruit is also used a lot in desserts.

Chilindrones: sauces of tomato and pepper.

Frutas de Aragón: sugar-candied fruits covered in chocolate.

Pollo al chilindrón: chicken (or lamb) stew with onions, tomatoes and red peppers.

Salmorrejos: cold soups.

Suspiros de amante: dessert with cheese and egg.

Ternasco: roast lamb.

Tortas de alma: made with pumpkin, honey and sugar.

Trenza de Almudévar: with nuts and raisins soaked in liqueur.

Red text = all year opening

RONCESVALLES

PAMPLONA

NAVARRA

N240

NIII

SANGUESA

UJUE

A15

CALAHORRA

LA RIOJA

TUDELA

PARQUE NACIONAL DE ORDESA

90640

JACA

90700

BENASQUE

N260

90620 90600 90580

90610

91250

HUESCA

N330

N240

LLEIDA/
LERIDA

ZARAGOZA

91040

A2

N11

ARAGON

N330

91050

N420

CATALUNYA

91100

N211

N211

N232

MORELLA

90950

COMUNIDAD
VALENCIANA

PENISCOLA

N234

OROPESA

CASTELLON
DE LA PLANA

A7

CASTILLA-LA-MANCHA

ES90580 Camping Baliera

Ctra N260 km 355,5, E-22486 Bonansa (Huesca)

Tel: 974 554 016. Email: info@baliera.com

www.alanrogers.com/ES90580

With its wonderful location in a quiet river valley with views of the surrounding mountains all around, Camping Baliera is an excellent site for enjoying this beautiful area. Combining camping with timber chalets and apartments, the site has 190 well kept grass touring pitches (80-120 sq.m) all with electricity (5/10A). The pitches are mostly located close to the attractive, stone built reception building which also houses a comfortable bar and shop. The approach to this site is by narrow and winding mountain roads and it is 5 km. from the nearest village. However, for all but the largest units, the trip is well worth making. An outdoor swimming pool is open in high season.

Facilities

Two toilet blocks, one part of the apartment block near the entrance, the other in the reception building (this closed in low season). Heated, they are good with well equipped showers, vanity style washbasins. Laundry room and drying room. Motorcaravan services. Shop (1/7-31/8). Bar (all season). Takeaway (1/7-31/8). Swimming pool (15/7-15/9). Fitness equipment. Play area. Entertainment in high season. Off site: National parks and outdoor activities. Nearest village 5 km.

Open: All year, excl. November.

Directions

On N230, 34 km. south of Vielha, turn on N260 for 2-3 km, then onto A1605 signed Graus for 100 m. to site on left. Reception is 200 m. through the site. Approach roads are narrow and winding, but navigable. GPS: N42:26.211 E00:41.539

Charges 2009

Per unit incl. 2 persons and electricity	€ 25,78 - € 30,10
extra person	€ 4,64 - € 5,00

Camping Cheques accepted.

ES90610 Camping Ligüerre de Cinca

Ctra A-138 km 28 de Barbastro a Ainsa, E-22393 Ligüerre de Cinca (Huesca)

Tel: 974 500 800. Email: info@liguerredecinca.com

www.alanrogers.com/ES90610

Linguerre de Cinca, a medieval village abandoned when the El Grado reservoir was constructed, is now being regenerated for tourism. It is situated near the Ordesa National Park in a beautiful region of the Pyrenees mountains and has the advantage of being open all year. The swimming and paddling pools are surrounded by grass sunbathing areas with wonderful mountain views. There are 150 small, terraced, level pitches marked out and shaded by tall trees. These include 110 for touring units, all with 10A electricity. Access is easy for large outfits.

Facilities

Adequate central toilet block, heated in winter, with smaller one on periphery. No facilities for campers with disabilities. Shop (July/Aug). Bar, restaurant, takeaway (all year). Swimming pool (July/Aug). Miniclub (July/Aug). Tennis. Boules. Playground. Fishing and watersports, boat storage. Organised watersports including courses. Internet access. ATM. Barbecues are not allowed. Off site: Bus to Huesca. Riding 18 km. Rafting, canyoning, climbing.

Open: All year.

Directions

Site is between El Grado and Ainsa on the N138. From the Tunnel de Bielsa at the French/Spanish border, go south on N138, through Ainsa. Site is on left in about 20 km. GPS: N42:16.867 E00:11.783

Charges guide

Per person	€ 4,85
child (2-10 yrs)	€ 4,25
pitch	€ 5,75 - € 7,05

Low season and long stay discounts.

ES90640 Camping Gavín

Ctra N260 km 503, E-22639 Gavín (Huesca)

Tel: 974 485 090. Email: info@campinggavin.com

www.alanrogers.com/ES90640

Camping Gavín is set on a terraced, wooded hillside and you will find a friendly welcome. The site offers 150 pitches of 90 sq m. in size and with electricity available to all (6A). In some areas the terracing means that some pitches are quite small. The main site buildings are built of natural stone. There are also 24 mobile homes, 13 new bungalows and 11 superb, balconied apartments. At about 900 m. the site is surrounded by towering peaks at the portal of the Tena Valley. One can enjoy the natural beauty of the Pyrenees and venture near or far along the great Pyrenean footpaths.

Facilities

Excellent shower and toilet facilities in three main buildings include facilities for babies and disabled people. Laundry facilities. Bar and snacks. Well stocked supermarket. Swimming and paddling pools (15/6-15/9). Tennis. Playground. Barbecues are not permitted at some times of the year. Off site: Windsurfing, rafting, fishing, walking and climbing in the vicinity. Bicycle hire 2 km. Riding 6 km. Golf 15 km.

Open: All year.

Directions

Site is off the N260, 2 km. from Biescas at the km. 503 point. GPS: N42:37.164 W00:18.245

Charges 2009

Per person	€ 4,60 - € 6,30
pitch	€ 12,50 - € 16,90
incl. electricity	€ 18,50 - € 22,00

Camping Cheques accepted.

ES90700 Centro de Vacaciones Pirineos

Ctra N240 km 300, E-22791 Santa Cilia de Jaca (Huesca)

Tel: 974 377 351. Email: pirineos@pirinet.com

www.alanrogers.com/ES90700

This pretty site which is open most of the year, is directly on the pilgrimage route to Santiago. The area has a mild climate, being near the River Aragon, not too high and it is convenient for touring the Pyrenees. This is a friendly site which is useful for transit stops and off-season camping on the large, mostly level wooded area which can accommodate 250 units (no marked pitches), with electric points throughout. The trees provide good shade and the attractive swimming pool is being rebuilt and updated. There is some road noise along the south side of the site.

Facilities

One heated sanitary block is open all year, providing a quite satisfactory supply. A second, more modern block is open April - Sept. only. Launderette. Supermarket (15/6-15/9, otherwise essentials kept in bar). Restaurant. Bar. Swimming pools (15/6-15/9). Tennis. Playground. Games room. Petanque. Bicycle hire. Torches required in some areas. Off site: Fishing and bathing in river 200 m.

Open: All year excl. 3 November - 3 December.

Directions

Site is 15 km. west of Jaca on N240 at km. 300 (65 km. northwest of Huesca). GPS: N42:33.040 W00:45.660

Charges guide

Per person	€ 4,89 - € 6,08
child (2-9 yrs)	€ 4,55 - € 5,69
pitch	€ 4,89 - € 10,80

All plus 7% VAT. 20% discount in low season.

ES90600 Camping Peña Montañesa

Ctra Ainsa - Francia km 2, E-22360 Labuerda (Huesca)

Tel: 974 500 032. Email: info@penamontanesa.com

www.alanrogers.com/ES90600

A large site situated quite high up in the Pyrenees near the Ordesa National Park, Peña Montañesa is easily accessible from Ainsa or from France via the Bielsa Tunnel (steep sections on the French side). The site is essentially divided into three sections opening progressively throughout the season and all have shade. The 288 pitches on fairly level grass are of about 75 sq.m. and 10A electricity is available on virtually all. Grouped near the entrance are the facilities that make the site so attractive, including a fair sized outdoor pool and a glass-covered indoor pool with jacuzzi and sauna. Here too is an attractive bar/restaurant (with an open fire) and a terrace with a supermarket and takeaway opposite. There is an entertainment programme for children (21/6-15/9 and Easter weekend) and twice weekly for adults (July/Aug). This is quite a large site which has grown very quickly and as such, it may at times be a little hard pressed, although it is very well run. The site is ideally situated for exploring the beautiful Pyrenees. The complete town of Ainsa is listed as a national monument of Spain and should be explored while you are here, along with the national park.

Facilities

A newer toilet block, heated when necessary, has free hot showers but cold water to open plan washbasins. Facilities for disabled visitors. Small baby room. Washing machine and dryer. Bar. Restaurant. Takeaway. Supermarket. Outdoor swimming pool (1/4-31/10). Indoor pool (all year). Playground. Boules. Bicycle hire. Riding. Rafting. Only gas barbecues are permitted. Torches required in some areas. Off site: Fishing 100 m. Skiing in season.

Open: 1 March - 10 December.

Directions

Site is 2 km. from Ainsa, on the road from Ainsa to France. GPS: N42:26.112 E00:08.171

Charges guide

Per person	€ 3,60 - € 6,80
child (1-9 yrs)	€ 3,10 - € 5,70
pitch	€ 13,00 - € 21,60
electricity	€ 5,15

All plus 7% VAT.

Check real time availability and at-the-gate prices...

www.alanrogers.com

153

ES90620 Kawan Village Boltaña

Ctra N260 km 442, E-22340 Boltaña (Huesca)

Tel: **974 502 347**. Email: **info@campingboltana.com**   www.alanrogers.com/ES90620

Nestled in the Rio Ara valley, surrounded by the Pyrenees mountains and below a tiny but enchanting, historic, hill top village, is the very pretty, thoughtfully planned Camping Boltaña. Generously sized, grassy pitches have good shade from a variety of trees and a stream meanders through the campsite. The landscaping includes ten charming rocky water gardens and a covered pergola doubles as an eating and play area. A stone building houses the site's reception, social room and supermarket. Angel Moreno, the owner of the site, is a charming host and has tried to think of everything to make his guests comfortable.

Facilities

Two modern sanitary blocks include facilities for disabled visitors and laundry facilities. Supermarket. Bar (1/7-31/8). Swimming pools (1/6-15/9). Playground. Barbecues. Animation for children (high season). Petanque. Guided tours, plus hiking, canyoning, rafting, climbing, mountain biking and caving. Torches useful in some parts. Off site: Local bus service.

Open: 15 January - 15 December.

Directions

Site is about 50 km. from Jaca near Ainsa. From Ainsa travel northwest on N260 toward Boltaña (near 443 km. marker) and 1 km. from Boltaña turn south toward Margudgued. Site is well signed and is 1 km. along this road. GPS: N42:25.811 E00:04.729

Charges 2009

Per person	€ 6,50
pitch incl. electricity	€ 22,00
Camping Cheques accepted.	

ES91250 Kawan Village Lago Barasona

Ctra N123a km 25, E-22435 La Puebla de Castro (Huesca)

Tel: **974 545 148**. Email: **info@lagobarasona.com**   www.alanrogers.com/ES91250

This site, alongside its associated ten room hotel, is beautifully positioned on terraces across a road from the shores of the Lago de Barasona (a large reservoir), with views of hills and the distant Pyrenees. The very friendly, English speaking owner is keen to please and has applied very high standards throughout the site. The grassy, fairly level pitches are generally around 100 sq.m. with 35 high quality pitches of 110 sq.m. for larger units. All have electricity (6/10A), many are well shaded and some have great views of the lake and/or hills. Water skiing and other watersports are available in July and August. You may swim and fish in the lake which has a shallow area.

Facilities

Two toilet blocks in modern buildings have high standards and hot water throughout including cabins (3 for ladies, 1 for men). Bar/snack bar and two excellent restaurants (all season). Shop (1/4-30/9). Swimming pools (1/6-30/9). Tennis. Mountain bike hire. Canoe, windsurfing motor boat and pedalo hire. Miniclub (high season). New wellness centre (open all year). Lake swimming, fishing, canoeing, etc. Walking (maps provided). Money exchange. Mini-disco. Off site: Riding 4 km.

Open: All year.

Directions

Site is on the west bank of the lake, close to the km. 25 point on the N123A, 6 km. south of Graus (about 80 km. north of Lleida/Lerida). Travelling from the south, the site is on the left from a roundabout and slip road. GPS: N42:08.498 E00:18.915

Charges 2009

Per unit incl. 2 persons and electricity	€ 23,00 - € 35,00
extra person	€ 4.50 - € 6.50
Camping Cheques accepted.	

ES90950 Camping Ciudad de Albarracin

Junto al Polideportivo, Camino de gea, E-44100 Albarracin (Teruel)

Tel: **978 710 197**   www.alanrogers.com/ES90950

Albarracin, in southern Aragon is set in the 'Reserva Nacional de los Montes Universales' and is much frequented, fascinating town with a Moorish castle. The old city walls towering above date from its days when it attempted to become a separate country within Spain. This neat and clean family site is set on three levels on a hillside behind the town, with a walk of 1 km. to the centre. It is very modern and has high quality facilities including a superb building for barbecuing (all materials provided). There are 140 pitches (70 for touring units), all with electricity and separated by trees.

Facilities

The two spotless, modern sanitary buildings provide British style WCs, quite large showers and hot water throughout. Baby bath. Washing machines. Bar/restaurant (all season). Essentials from bar. Special room for barbecues with fire and wood provided. Play area. Torches required in some areas. Off site: Municipal pool 100 m. (high season). Town 500 m. Fishing 1 km.

Open: 1 March - 3 November.

Directions

From Teruel north on the N330 for about 8 km. then west onto A1512 for 30 km. From the A23 use exit 124 then the A1512, from the N235 take exit for Albarracin and the A1512. Site is well signed in the town. GPS: N40:24.993 W1:25.999

Charges 2009

Per person	€ 3,80
pitch incl. electricity	€ 11,00 - € 11,25

ES91100 Camping La Fresneda

Partida Vall del Pi, E-44596 La Fresneda (Teruel)

Tel: 978 854 085. Email: info@campinglafresneda.com
www.alanrogers.com/ES91100

La Fresneda is a great little campsite, situated on three terraces at the foot of a wooded escarpment and overlooking the huge valley of the natural reserve of 'Los Puertos de Beceite'. Everything is in line with the natural beauty of the area and the very clean, very well equipped, toilet block is partly underground. The cosy bar is in rustic style with a terrace to enjoy your afternoon drink whilst enjoying a view of the valley. There are 28 pitches with grass and gravel surfaces. All used for touring, 26 have 4A electricity. The site is quite new and the enthusiastic Dutch owners, Jet Knijn and her partner Joost Leeuwenberg, built the site from scratch.

Facilities

New toilet block with hot water throughout. Washing machine. Bar with terrace where tapas and a menu are served a few times a week. Fresh bread daily. Information on walking and cycling routes. Barbecues are only permitted in communal areas. Dogs are not accepted. Off site: Baker, grocery and butcher in the village. Supermarkets at Alcañiz 30 minutes drive. Riding and bicycle hire 8 km. Fishing 20 km.

Open: 15 March - 1 November.

Directions

From the N232 (Alcañiz - Vinaros/Castellón) turn off just east of Valdealgorfa (at Restaurant Las Ventas) onto A231 to Valjunquera/Valderrobres, then La Fresneda. The approach to the entrance is steep. GPS: N40:54.417 E00:03.700

Charges 2009

Per person	€ 4,50
child (2-9 yrs)	€ 4,00
pitch incl. electricity	€ 12,00

Discounts for stays over 7 days (excl. Easter and July/Aug).

ES91050 Camping Lago Park

Ctra Alhama de Aragon - Nuevalos, E-50210 Nuevalos (Zaragoza)

Tel: 976 849 038
www.alanrogers.com/ES91050

Lago Park is situated in an attractive area which receives many visitors for the Monasterio de Piedra just 3 km. distant and it enjoys pleasant views of the surrounding mountains. This site is suitable for transit stops or if you wish to visit the monasterio as it is the only one hereabouts and appears to make the most of that fact. It is not recommended for extended stays. Set on a steep hillside, the 280 pitches (260 for tourers) are on terraces. Only the lower rows are suitable for large caravans. These pitches are numbered and marked by trees, most having electricity (10A).

Facilities

The single very clean sanitary block has British style WCs. washbasins with hot water and controllable hot showers (no dividers). Restaurant/bar (June - Sept). Shop (all season). Swimming pool (late June - Sept). Play area. Gas supplies. Torches needed in some areas. Off site: Fishing 300 m. Riding 2 km.

Open: 1 April - 30 September.

Directions

From Zaragoza (120 km.) take fast A2/N11/E90 road and turn onto C202 road beyond Calatayud to Nuévalos (25 km). From Madrid, exit A2 at Alhama de Aragón (13 km). Follow signs for Monasterio de Piedra (all directions). GPS: N41:13.080 W01:47.520

Charges guide

Per person	€ 6,30
pitch incl. electricity	€ 12,20 - € 17,20

ES91040 Camping Ciudad de Zaragoza

Ctra San Juan Bautista de la Salle s/n, E-50012 Zaragoza (Zaragoza)

Tel: 876 241 495. Email: info@campingzaragoza.com
www.alanrogers.com/ES91040

Zaragoza is a popular en-route stop between the ports of Santander and Bilbao and the beaches of the Costa Brava. The city, however, has much more to offer as the former capital of Aragon and now Spain's fifth largest city. This all year site has been recommended by our Spanish agent and can be found southwest of the city centre. There are 103 touring pitches and a further 70 mobile homes for rent, as well as a small hostel. Pitches are all equipped with electricity and a water supply. On site amenities include a swimming pool, sports pitch and an attractive bar/restaurant.

Facilities

Toilet blocks have been modernised and have facilities for disabled visitors. Motorcaravan services. Bar. Restaurant. Swimming pool. Tennis. Sports pitch. Play area. Mobile homes for rent. Off site: Zaragoza city centre 4 km. (regular bus service).

Open: All year.

Directions

Follow the Autovia del Nordeste (Zaragoza ring road) southwest to leave at the junction with the N11-a. Follow signs to the city centre (Autovia de Madrid) and the site is signed to the right. GPS: N41:38.315 W00:56.485

Charges guide

Per unit incl. 2 persons	€ 15,84 - € 25,16
extra person	€ 2,89 - € 4,82

155

Menorca, steeped in history and blanketed by mystery, is an enchanting island of roughly 270 square miles in area.

The C721 highway provides the back-bone to the island, connecting modest market towns to Mahon (the main town) in the east and Ciutadella in the west.

Mahon's classic Georgian style buildings, complete with sash windows, will endear them to the British traveller. Its impressive harbour was captured by the British in 1708 during the Spanish War of Succession. In complete contrast, Ciutadella has a more Gothic feel to it. A labyrinth of tiny streets entwine the 'little city', most of which can only be accessed on foot. Monte Toro stands proudly at the centre of the island surveying all. To the south a greener lush terrain exists with long, luxurious beaches, while to the north a giant rockery erupts riddled with caves and prehistoric finds.

ES80000 Camping Son Bou

Ctra de San Jaime km 3,5, Apdo 85, Alayor, E-07730 Menorca (Menorca)

Tel: **971 372 605**. Email: **info@campingsonbou.com**   www.alanrogers.com/ES80000

Camping Son Bou was opened in 1996 and has been purpose built in local style providing a large irregular shaped pool with marvellous view across to Monte Toro and overlooked by a pine shaded, terraced bar and restaurant. The 313 large pitches are arranged in circles radiating out from the main facilities and clearly edged with stones. Natural pine tree shade covers most but the outer ring. Drinking water and refuse points are well placed. Electricity (10A) is available on nearly all pitches. The ground is hard and devoid of grass except where sprinklers operate. The beautiful island of Menorca cries out to be explored. It is peaceful and tranquil, with its characteristic dry stone walls, its low white buildings with terracotta tiled roof, its beautiful coastline, ancient monuments and pretty villages with their cycle of fiestas of religious origin. The site gets very busy with Spanish people from the mainland in high season. Earlier in the year it is quieter and greener.

Facilities

Well designed toilet block of good quality, open plan in places. Some washbasins in cabins (cold water). New bathrooms and shower. Baby room. Facilities for disabled visitors. Service wash. Shop (1/5-28/9). Bar. Restaurant. Outdoor pool (from 1/5). Tennis. Play area. Bicycle hire. English spoken. Open air cinema. Occasional barbecue with guitarist. Comprehensive activity programme. Dogs are not accepted. Off site: Riding 4 km. Village 0.75 km. with sandy beach.

Open: 5 April - 28 September.

Directions

From Mahon (Mao) follow main road to Ciutadella. Go past Alaior (bypassed) and watch for restaurant on left and sign for San Jaime/Son Bou. Continue for 3.5 km. and site on right.
GPS: N39:55.319 E04:05.468

Charges 2009

Per unit incl. 2 persons,	
car and electricity	€ 28,40 - € 33,50
extra person	€ 6,40 - € 7,75
tent and car for 2/3 persons	€ 11,40 - € 13,80

Portugal is a relatively small country occupying the southwest corner of the Iberian peninsula, bordered by Spain in the north and east, with the Atlantic coast in the south and west. In spite of its size, the country offers a tremendous variety in both its way of life and traditions.

Tourist Office

ICEP Portuguese Trade & Tourism Office,
Second Floor, 22/25a Sackville Street,
London W1S 3LY

Tel: 09063 640 610
E-mail: iceplondt@aol.com
Fax: 020 7494 1868
Internet: www.portugalinsite.com

Most visitors looking for a beach type holiday head for the busy Algarve, with its long stretches of sheltered sandy beaches, and warm, clear Atlantic waters, great for bathing and watersports. With its monuments and fertile rolling hills, central Portugal adjoins the beautiful Tagus river that winds its way through the capital city of Lisbon, on its way to the Altantic Ocean.

Lisbon city itself has deep rooted cultural traditions, coming alive at night with buzzing cafes, restaurants and discos. Moving south east of Lisbon the land becomes rather impoverished, consisting of stretches of vast undulating plains, dominated by cork plantations. Most people head for the walled town of Evora, an area steeped in two thousand years of history. The Portuguese consider the Minho area in the north to be the most beautiful part of their country, with its wooded mountain and wild coastline, a rural and conservative region with picturesque towns.

Population
10 million

Capital
Lisbon

Climate
The country enjoys a maritime climate with hot summers and mild winters with comparatively low rainfall in the south, heavy rain in the north.

Language
Portuguese, but English is widely spoken in cities, towns and larger resorts. French can be useful.

Telephone
The country code is 00 351.

Currency
The Euro (€)

Banks
Mon-Fri 08.30-11.45 and 13.00-14.45. Some large city banks offer a currency exchange 18.30-23.00.

Shops
Mon-Fri 09.00-13.00 and 15.00-19.00. Sat 09.00-13.00.

Public Holidays
New Year; Carnival (Shrove Tues); Good Fri; Liberty Day 25 Apr; Labour Day; Corpus Christi; National Day 10 June; Saints Days; Assumption 15 Aug; Republic Day 5 Oct; All Saints 1 Nov; Immaculate Conception 8 Dec; Christmas 24-26 Dec.

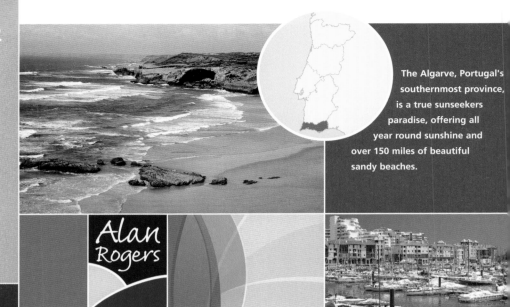

The Algarve, Portugal's southernmost province, is a true sunseekers paradise, offering all year round sunshine and over 150 miles of beautiful sandy beaches.

Alan Rogers

THE ALGARVE HAS ONE DISTRICT: FARO

The coast of the Algarve offers mile after mile of golden beaches and small sandy coves with interesting rock formations, interspersed with busy fishing ports. The capital, Faro, boasts excellent beaches, while the thriving fishing port and market centre of Lagos is one of the most popular destinations in the Algarve. Although the earthquake of 1755 caused great damage to Lagos, the streets and squares of the town have retained much of their charm. Within walking distance are some superb beaches, including Praia de Dona Ana, which is considered to be the most picturesque of all, and the smaller coves of Praia do Pinhão and Praia Camilo. Further inland and to the north, the hills mark the edge of a greener and more fertile region, brilliantly coloured by fig-trees, orange-groves and almond-trees that come into blossom in the winter. Here you will also find a series of typical villages that have successfully preserved their ancestral traditions. The walled town of Silves has a Moorish fortress, 13th century cathedral and archaeology musuem. Nearby, the narrow streets of the old spa town of Monchique wind up a steep hillside, revealing magnificent views.

Places of interest

Albufeira: popular resort, daily market, good nightlife.

Cape São Vicente: south westernmost point of Europe.

Faro: monuments, churches, museums, Gothic cathedral, good shopping centre.

Sagres: 17th century fortress.

Tavira: picturesque town, 17th and 18th century architecture.

Vilamoura: good sporting facilities including golf courses.

Cuisine of the region

Fresh fish and seafood are popular; the local speciality is *Ameijoas na Cataplana* (clams steamed in a copper pan). One of the most traditional dishes is *caldeiradas* (stew made with all kinds of different fish) and *sardinha assada* (grilled sardines). Given the abundance of trees in the region, figs and almonds are used a lot in desserts including *bolinhos de amêndoa* (small cakes made from marzipan and almond paste), which are moulded into the shape of fruits and vegetables in all kinds of different sizes.

Red text = all year opening

| 0 | 25 | 50 | 75 | 100 kms |

PO8210 Parque de Campismo Albufeira

EN125 Ferreiras - Albufeira, P-8200-555 Albufeira (Faro)

Tel: **289 587 629**. Email: **campingalbufeira@mail.telepac.pt**   **www.alanrogers.com/PO8210**

The spacious entrance to this site will accommodate the largest of units (watch for severe speed bumps at the barrier). One of the better sites on the Algarve, it has pitches on fairly flat ground with some terracing, trees and shrubs giving reasonable shade in most parts. There are some marked and numbered pitches of 50-80 sq.m. Winter stays are encouraged with many facilities remaining open including a pool. An attractively designed complex of traditional Portuguese style buildings on the hill, with an unusually shaped pool and two more for children, forms the central area of the site. It has large terraces for sunbathing and pleasant views and is surrounded by a variety of flowers, shrubs and well watered lawns, complete with a fountain. The 'á la carte' restaurant, impressive with its international cuisine, and the very pleasant self-service one; both have views across the three pools. A pizzeria, bars and a soundproofed disco are great for younger campers.

Facilities

The toilet blocks include hot showers. Launderette. Very large supermarket. Tabac (English papers). Waiter and self-service restaurants. Pizzeria. Bars. Satellite TV. Soundproof disco. Swimming pools. Tennis. Playground. Internet access. First aid post. Car wash. ATM. Car hire. Off site: Site bus service from gate to Albufeira every 45 minutes (2 km). Theme parks nearby. Beaches.

Open: All year.

Directions

From N125 coast road or N264 (from Lisbon) at new junctions follow N395 to Albufeira. Site is about 2 km. on the left. GPS: N37:06.383 W08:15.217

Charges guide

Per car and caravan	
with 2 persons	€ 23,10 - € 23,65
motorcaravan with 2 persons	€ 19,60 - € 23,15
tent and car with 2 persons	€ 22,30 - € 22,70
electricity	€ 2,90

PO8200 Orbitur Camping Valverde

Estrada da Praia da Luz, Valverde, P-8600-148 Lagos (Faro)

Tel: **282 789 211**. Email: **info@orbitur.pt**   www.alanrogers.com/PO8200

A little over a kilometre from the village of Praia da Luz and its beach and about 7 km. from Lagos, this large, well run site is certainly worth considering for your stay in the Algarve. It has 600 numbered pitches, of varying size, which are enclosed by hedges. All are on flat ground or broad terraces with good shade in most parts from established trees and shrubs. The site has a swimming pool with a long curling slide and a paddling pool (under 10s free, adults charged). This is an excellent site with well maintained facilities and good security. It attracts a good number of long-term winter visitors and is one of the better Orbitur sites.

Facilities

Six large, clean, toilet blocks have some washbasins and sinks with cold water only, and hot showers. Units for disabled people. Laundry. Motorcaravan services. Supermarket, shops, restaurant and bar complex with both self-service and waiter service in season (closed November). Takeaway. Coffee shop. Swimming pool (April - Sept) with slide and paddling pool (June - Sept). Playground. Tennis. Satellite TV in bar. Disco. Pub. Excursions. Off site: Bus service from site gate. Beach and fishing 1.5 km. Bicycle hire 3 km. Golf 10 km.

Open: All year.

Directions

From Lagos on N125 road, after 7 km. turn south to Praia da Luz. At the town follow Orbitur camping signs. The beach road is narrow and cobbled and is very challenging in a large unit.
GPS: N37:05.984 W08:43.046

Charges guide

Per person	€ 2,90 - € 5,40
child (5-10 yrs)	€ 1,50 - € 3,00
caravan and car	€ 6,80 - € 12,00
electricity	€ 2,50 - € 3,10

Off season discounts (up to 70%).

PO8220 Orbitur Camping Quarteira

Estrada da Fonte Santa, avenida Sá Cameiro, P-8125-618 Quarteira (Faro)

Tel: **289 302 826**. Email: **info@orbitur.pt**   www.alanrogers.com/PO8220

This is a large, busy attractive site on undulating ground with some terracing, taking 795 units. On the outskirts of the popular Algarve resort of Quarteira, it is 600 m. from a sandy beach which stretches for a kilometre to the town centre. Many of the unmarked pitches have shade from tall trees and there are a few small individual pitches of 50 sq.m. with electricity and water for reservation. There are 680 electrical connections. Like others along this coast, the site encourages long winter stays. There is a large restaurant and supermarket which have a separate entrance for local trade. The swimming pools (free for campers)are excellent, featuring pools for adults (with a large flume) and children (with fountains).

Facilities

Five toilet blocks provide British and Turkish style toilets, washbasins with cold water, hot showers plus facilities for disabled visitors. Washing machines. Motorcaravan services. Gas supplies. Supermarket. Self-service restaurant (closed Nov). Separate takeaway (from late May). Swimming pools (April - Sept). General room with bar and satellite TV. Tennis. Open air disco (high season). Off site: Bus from gate to Faro. Fishing 1 km. Bicycle hire (summer) 1 km. Golf 4 km.

Open: All year.

Directions

Turn off N125 for village of Almancil. In the village take road south to Quarteira. Site is on the left 1 km. after large, official town welcome sign.
GPS: N37:04.000 W08:05.000

Charges guide

Per person	€ 3,10 - € 5,50
child (5-10 yrs)	€ 1,70 - € 3,00
caravan and car	€ 6,90 - € 13,00
electricity	€ 2,50 - € 3,10

Off season discounts (up to 70%).

Check real time availability and at-the-gate prices...

www.**alanrogers**.com

Winner Alan Rogers Awards 2008

PO8202 **Camping Turiscampo**

EN125, Espiche, Luz, P-8600 Lagos (Faro)

Tel: 282 789 265. Email: info@turiscampo.com

www.alanrogers.com/PO8202

This site is being thoughtfully refurbished and updated to include most of the existing infrastructure since it was purchased by the friendly Coll family, who are known to us from their previous Spanish site. Work was still in progress when we visited but the site does show great promise and will become a quality site. The site provides 206 pitches for tourers mainly in rows of terraces, all with electricity and some with shade. They vary in size (70-120 sq.m). The upper areas of the site are being developed and are mostly destined for bungalows (which are generally separate from the touring areas). A new, elevated Californian style pool plus a children's pool have been constructed and the supporting structure is a clever water cascade and surround. There is a large sun lounger area on astroturf. One side of the pool area is open to the road. The restaurant/bar has been tastefully refurbished and Giovanni and staff are delighted to use their excellent English to provide good fare at reasonable prices (bargain menu of the day for € 6.50). The restaurant has two patios one of which is used for live entertainment and discos in season and the other for dining out. The sea is 2 km. and the city of Lagos 4 km. with all the attractions of the Algarve within easy reach. This is a very good site for families and for 'Snowbirds' to over-winter.

Facilities

The two existing toilet blocks have been refurbished and a new block added containing modern facilities for disabled campers. The site reports a further new, heated block. Hot water throughout. Facilities for children. Washing machines. Shop. Gas supplies. Restaurant/bar. Swimming pool (March - Oct) with two new terraces. Bicycle hire. Entertainment in high season on the bar terrace. Playground on sand. Adult art workshops, aqua gymnastics and miniclub (5-12 yrs) in season. Petanque. Archery. Sports field. Internet. WiFi on payment. Bungalows to rent. Off site: Bus to Lagos and other towns from Praia da Luz 1.5 km. Fishing and beach 2 km. Golf 4 km. Sailing 5 km. Boat launching 5 km. Riding 10 km.

Open: All year.

Directions

Take exit 1 from the N125 Lagos - Vila do Bispo road. The impressive entrance is about 3 km. on the right. GPS: N37:06.067 W08:43.967

Charges guide

Per person	€ 3,00 - € 5,80
child (3-10 yrs)	€ 1,60 - € 2,90
pitch incl. electricity	€ 7,90 - € 16,70
dog	€ 1,00 - € 1,50

Camping Cheques accepted.

Check real time availability and at-the-gate prices...

www.**alanrogers**.com

PO8410 Parque de Campismo de Armacão de Pera

P-8365 Armacão de Pera (Faro)

Tel: **282 312 296**. Email: **camping_arm_pera@hotmail.com**   www.alanrogers.com/PO8410

A modern site with a wide attractive entrance and a large external parking area, the 1,200 pitches are in zones on level grassy sand. They are marked by trees that provide some shade, and are easily accessed from tarmac and gravel roads. Electricity is available for most pitches. The self service restaurant, bar and well stocked supermarket should cater for most needs, and you can relax around the swimming pools. The disco near the entrance and café complex is soundproofed which should ensure a peaceful night for non-revellers. Albufeira and Portimão are within easy reach.

Facilities
Three modern sanitary blocks provide British and Turkish style WCs and showers with hot water on payment. Facilities for disabled campers. A reader reports that maintenance can be variable. Laundry. Supermarket. Self-service restaurant. Three bars (one all year). Swimming and paddling pools (May - Sept; charged per day; no lifeguard). Games and TV rooms. Tennis. Well maintained play area. ATM. Off site: Bus to town from gate. Fishing, bicycle hire and watersports nearby.
Open: All year.

Directions

Site is west of Albufeira. Turn off N125/IC4 road in Alcantarilha, taking the EN269-1 towards the coast. Site is on left before Armação de Pêra. There are sites with similar names in the area, so be sure to find the right one. GPS: N37:06.540 W08:21.180

Charges guide

Per person	€ 2,50 - € 5,50
child (4-10 yrs)	€ 1,60 - € 3,20
pitch	€ 4,00 - € 7,50
electricity (6A)	€ 2,50 - € 4,00

PO8430 Orbitur Camping Sagres

Cerro das Moitas, P-8650-998 Sagres (Faro)

Tel: **282 624 371**. Email: **info@orbitur.pt**   www.alanrogers.com/PO8430

Camping de Sagres is a pleasant site at the western tip of the Algarve, not very far from the lighthouse in the relatively unspoilt southwest corner of Portugal. With 960 pitches for tents and 120 for tourers, the sandy pitches, some terraced, are located amongst pine trees that give good shade. There are some hardstandings for motorhomes and electricity throughout. The fairly bland restaurant, bar and café/grill provide a range of reasonably priced meals. This is a reasonable site for those seeking winter sun, or as a base for exploring this 'Land's End' region of Portugal.

Facilities
Three spacious toilet blocks are showing some signs of wear but provide hot and cold showers and washbasins with cold water. Washing machines. Motorcaravan services. Supermarket. Restaurant/bar and café/grill (all Easter and June - Oct). TV room. Satellite TV in restaurant. Bicycle hire. Barbecue area. Playground. Fishing. Off site: Buses from village 1 km. Beach and fishing 2 km. Boat launching 8 km. Golf 12 km.
Open: All year.

Directions

From Sagres, turn off the N268 road west onto the EN268. After about 2 km. the site is signed off to the right. GPS: N37:01.367 W08:56.750

Charges guide

Per person	€ 2,50 - € 4,50
child (5-10 yrs)	€ 1,30 - € 2,50
caravan and car	€ 5,60 - € 10,20
electricity (6A)	€ 2,50 - € 3,10

PO8440 Parque de Campismo Quinta dos Carriços

Praia da Salema, Vila do Bispo, P-8650-196 Budens (Faro)

Tel: **282 695 201**. Email: **quintacarrico@oninet.pt**   www.alanrogers.com/PO8440

This is an attractive and peaceful, valley site with a dedicated naturist area. A traditional tiled Portuguese style entrance leads you down a steep incline into this excellent and well maintained site which has a village atmosphere. With continuing improvements, the site has been developed over the years by the Dutch owner. It is spread over two valleys (which are real sun-traps), with the 300 partially terraced pitches marked and divided by trees and shrubs (oleanders and roses). A small stream (dry when seen) meanders through the site.

Facilities
Four modern, spacious sanitary blocks, well tiled with quality fittings, are spotlessly clean. Washbasins with cold water, hot showers on payment. Washing machine. Excellent facility for disabled people. Gas supplies. Shop. Restaurant (1/3-15/10). Bar (daily in season, once a week only (1/3-15/10). TV (cable). WiFi internet. Games room. Bicycle, scooter, moped and motorcycle hire. Off site: Fishing, golf and beach 1 km. Riding 8 km. Bus service to town (not beach) from site.
Open: All year.

Directions

Turn off RN125 (Lagos-Sagres) road at junction to Figuere and Salema (17 km. from Lagos); site is signed. GPS: N37:04.447 W08:49.729

Charges guide

Per person	€ 4,90
child	€ 2,50
car and caravan	€ 11,90
motorcaravan	€ 7,25 - € 8,80
Discounts for long winter stays.	

PO8230 Camping Olhão

Pinheiros de Marim, P-8700 Olhão (Faro)

Tel: 289 700 300. Email: parque.campismo@sbsi.pt   www.alanrogers.com/PO8230

This site, with around 800 pitches, is open all year. It has many mature trees providing good shade. The pitches are marked, numbered and in rows divided by shrubs, although levelling will be necessary and the trees make access tricky on some. There is electricity for 102 pitches (6A) and a separate area for tents. Permanent and long stay units take 20% of the pitches, the touring pitches filling up quickly in July and August, so arrive early. There is some noise nuisance from an adjacent railway. The site has a relaxed, casual atmosphere. Amenities include very pleasant swimming pools and tennis courts, a reasonable restaurant/bar and a café/bar with TV and games room. All are very popular with the local Portuguese who pay to use the facilities. The large, sandy beaches in this area are on offshore islands reached by ferry and are, as a result, relatively quiet; some are reserved for naturists. This site can get very busy in peak periods and maintenance can be variable. There was a large, low season British contingent when we visited, enjoying the low prices.

Facilities

Eleven sanitary blocks are adequate, clean when seen, and are specifically sited to be a maximum of 50 m. from any pitch. One block has facilities for disabled visitors. Laundry. Excellent supermarket. Kiosk. Restaurant/bar. Café and general room with cable TV. Playgrounds. Swimming pools (April - Sept) and tennis courts (fees for both). Bicycle hire. Internet at reception. Off site: Bus service to the nearest ferry at Olhão 50 m. from site. Riding 1 km. Indoor pool 2 km. Fishing 2 km. Golf 20 km.

Open: All year.

Directions

Just over 1 km. east of Olhão, on EN125, take turn to Pinheiros de Marim. Site is back off the road on the left. Look for very large, white, triangular entry arch as the site name is different on the outside wall. GPS: N37:02.117 W07:49.350

Charges guide

Per person	€ 2,30 - € 4,10
child (5-12 yrs)	€ 1,30 - € 2,30
pitch	€ 1,75 - € 7,60
electricity	€ 2,00

Less for longer winter stays.

Check real time availability and at-the-gate prices...

www.**alanrogers**.com

With huge, sparsely populated plains dominated by vast cork plantations, which provide nearly half of the world's cork, Alentejo's main attractions include the historic city of Évora and the coastal resorts with their fine, sandy beaches.

ALENTEJO IS MADE UP OF FOUR DISTRICTS: BEJA, ÉVORA, SETÚBAL AND PORTALEGRE

One of the most impressive cities in Portugal, Évora lies on a gently sloping hill rising out of the huge Alentejo plain. A city steeped in history, it was occupied by the Romans and Moors for centuries. With its narrow streets, of Moorish origin, and white-washed houses, it also boasts one of the best-preserved Roman temples in the country plus various palaces and monuments, the majority dating from the 14th-16th centuries. One of the more extraordinary sights can be found in the Capela dos Ossos in the church of São Francisco – adorning the walls and pillars of this chamber are the bones of more than 5000 monks. On the Alentejo coast is the small peaceful town of Santiago do Cacém, which has two of the best beaches in Portugal. The nearby archaelogical site at Miróbriga includes ruins of a hippodrome, several houses (some of which have mural paintings) and a clearly defined acropolis. Further south along the coast is Porto Côvo and the larger, popular resort of Vila Nova de Milfontes, which has a little castle and ancient port.

Places of interest

Arraiolos: ancient town, 17th century castle, famous for its carpets.

Beja: provincial town founded by Julius Caesar, 13th century castle.

Borba: pretty town, noted for its marble and wine.

Elvas: ancient fortress town, 15th century aqueduct.

Estremoz: market town, medieval castle.

Odemira: quiet, characterful country town.

Reguengos de Monsaraz: charming, unspoiled village with whitewashed houses.

Vila Viçosa: attractive hillside town, 16th century convent.

Cuisine of the region

Alentejo was traditionally an important wheat-growing region (it is frequently referred to as the 'granary of Portugal'). Local specialities include *sopa de cação* (skate soup), made from fish and bread, and *ensopado de borrego* (lamb-stew). Cheeses of the region include *queijo de Serpa* and *queijos de Niza*, made from goats milk. The *queijos de Évora*, made from ewe's milk, is smaller in size with a strong, spicy flavour. *Arroz Doce* (rice pudding topped with cinnamon) is the traditional dessert for festivals and parties and is to be found all over the country.

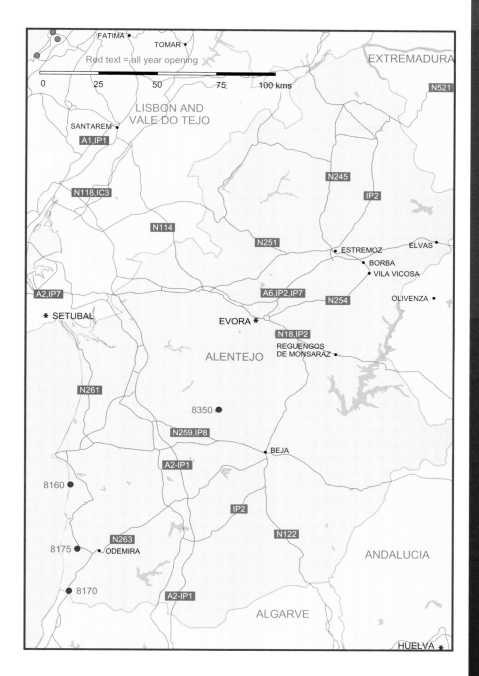

FATIMA
TOMAR

Red text = all year opening

0   25   50   75   100 kms

EXTREMADURA

N521

LISBON AND
VALE DO TEJO

SANTAREM

A1,IP1

N118,IC3

N114

N245

IP2

N251

ESTREMOZ

ELVAS

BORBA

VILA VICOSA

A2,IP7

A6,IP2,IP7

N254

OLIVENZA

SETUBAL

EVORA

N18,IP2

REGUENGOS
DE MONSARAZ

ALENTEJO

N261

8350

N259,IP8

A2-IP1

BEJA

8160

IP2

N122

N263

ANDALUCIA

8175   ODEMIRA

8170

A2-IP1

ALGARVE

HUELVA

PO8170 Parque de Campismo São Miguel

São Miguel, Odeceixe, P-7630-592 Odemira (Beja)

Tel: **282 947145**. Email: **camping.sao.miguel@mail.telepac.pt**   www.alanrogers.com/PO8170

Nestled in green hills near two pretty white villages, 4 km. from the beautiful Praia Odeceixe (beach) is the attractive camping park São Miguel. Unusually the site works on a maximum number of 700 campers, you find your own place (there are no defined pitches) under the tall trees, there are ample electrical points, and the land slopes away gently. Wooden chalet style accommodation to rent is in a separate area, but some mobile homes share the two traditional older style but clean sanitary blocks. The main building with its traditional Portuguese architecture is built around two sides of a large grassy square. It houses reception, restaurant, bars and supermarket.

Facilities

Two older style toilet blocks with British style WCs and free hot showers. Washing machines. Toilets and basins for disabled campers but no shower. Shop (June - Sept). Self-service restaurant (March - Oct). Bar, snacks and pizzeria (June - Sept). Satellite TV. Playground. Tennis (charged). Swimming pool (charged). Dogs are not accepted. Torches useful. Off site: Odeceixe 2 km. Beach, fishing and sailing 4 km. Riding 20 km.

Open: All year.

Directions

Between Odemira and Lagos on the N120 just before the village of Odeceixe on the main road well signed. GPS: N37:26.321 W08:45.341

Charges guide

Per person	€ 3,90 - € 6,00
child (5-10 yrs)	€ 2,20 - € 3,30
pitch	€ 3,90 - € 11,00
electricity	€ 3,25

Plus 7% VAT.

PO8350 Camping Markádia

Barragem de Odivelas, Apartado 17, P-7920-999 Alvito (Beja)

Tel: **284 763 141**. Email: **markadia@hotmail.com**   www.alanrogers.com/PO8350

A tranquil, lakeside site in an unspoilt setting, this will appeal most to those nature lovers who want to 'get away from it all' and to those who enjoy country pursuits such as walking, fishing or riding. There are 130 casual unmarked pitches on undulating grass and sand with ample electricity connections (16A). The site is lit but a torch is required. The friendly Dutch owner has carefully planned the site so each pitch has its own oak tree to provide shade. The open countryside and lake provide excellent views and a very pleasant environment, albeit somewhat remote.

Facilities

Four modern, clean and well equipped toilet blocks are built in traditional Portuguese style with hot water throughout. Washing machines. Motorcaravan services. Bar and restaurant (1/4-30/9). Shop (all year, bread to order). Lounge. Playground. Fishing. Boat hire. Tennis. Riding. Car wash. Dogs are not accepted in July/August. Facilities and amenities may be reduced outside the main season. Off site: Swimming and boating in the lake.

Open: All year.

Directions

From A2 between Setubal and the Algarve take exit 10 on IP8 signed Ferreira and Beja. Take road to Torrao and 13 km. later, 1 km. north of Odivelas, turn right towards Barragem and site is 3 km. after crossing head of reservoir following small signs. GPS: N38:11.220 W08:06.220

Charges guide

Per person	€ 5,20
pitch incl. electricity	€ 12,80 - € 13,50

No credit cards.

PO8160 Parque de Campismo Porto Covo

Estrada Municipal 55u, P-7520-436 Porto Covo (Setubal)

Tel: **269 905 136**   www.alanrogers.com/PO8160

This is a site in a popular, small seaside resort where a fairly large proportion of the pitches are occupied by Portuguese units. However, it has a reasonable sense of space as you pass the security barrier to reception which is part of an uncluttered and attractively designed 'village square' area with some well established apartments for rent. The pitches are somewhat small but are hedged, reasonably level, all have electricity (5A), and are shaded. The beaches are a short walk and feature steep cliffs and pleasant sandy shores.

Facilities

The toilet blocks are clean with the usual amenities including hot showers. Motorcaravan services. Restaurant (10/6-30/9). Bar with satellite TV. Shop in season. Recreation room with games and a TV. Play area. Swimming pools (10/6-30/9). Tennis. Barbecue areas. Boat trips and fishing trips organised. Off site: The village is a short walk with shops, bars and restaurants. Bus service to Lisbon 300 m. from site. Fishing 500 m. Riding 20 km. Golf 25 km.

Open: All year.

Directions

From E120-1 Cercal - Sines road (the road changes from the E120 at Tanganheira). Turn left (southwest) to Porto Covo and follow site signs. Do not be surprised to be led through a new housing estate - look for large white water tower with site logo. GPS: N37:51.161 W08:47.284

Charges guide

Per person	€ 3,40 - € 1,75
pitch incl. electricity	€ 8,15 - € 11,50

All plus 7% VAT. Reductions in low season.

PO8175 Zmar - Eco Camping Resort

Herdade a de Mateus EN393/1, San Salvador, P-7630 Odemira (Beja)

Tel: **707 200 626**. Email: **info@zmar.eu**   www.alanrogers.com/PO8175

Zmar is an exciting new project which will open in 2009. We plan to undertake a full inspection during the coming season. The site is located at Zambujeira do Mar, on the Alentejo coast. This is a highly ambitious initiative to be developed along very strict environmental lines. Renewable resources, for example, such as locally harvested timber and recyclable plastic will be used wherever possible. Solar energy will be used whenever practicable. Pitches will be around 100 sq.m. and will mostly benefit from artificial shade. Caravans and wood clad mobile homes will also be available for rent. The swimming pool complex will feature a large outdoor pool and an indoor pool area with a wellness centre. An innovative children's play park is planned with climbing nets, labyrinths and caves. There will also be a children's farm and a large play house. For adults, many sports amenities will also be available around the resort's 81 hectare park. These will include a sports field, cycle hire and tennis courts. Zmar's restaurant will be open throughout the season and will focus on local produce and traditional cuisine.

Facilities	Directions
Bar. Restaurant. Creperie. Takeaway food. Supermarket. Swimming pool. Covered pool. Wellness centre. Sports field. Games room. Children's play area and play house. Bicycle hire. Activity and entertainment programme. Mobile homes and caravans for rent. Caravan repair and servicing. Off site: Vicentina coast and the Alentejo natural park. Sines (birthplace of Vasco de Gama). Cycle and walking tracks. Sea fishing.	Leave the A2 motorway at exit 12 (Ourique) and head west on IP2 to Ourique. Then continue west on N123 to Garvao. Here take the N369 and N263 to Odemira. Continue on N393 through Boavista to Zambujeira do Mar. GPS: N37:36.253 W08:43.885

Charges 2009

Not yet set. Contact the site for further details.

Open: All year.

With its deep-rooted cultural traditions, range of leisure activities, year-round sunshine, sandy beaches, historic towns and villages, Lisbon and Vale do Tejo has something for everyone. It is also the centre of Fado, the traditional haunting folk song of Portugal.

THIS REGION IS DIVIDED INTO FOUR DISTRICTS: LEIRIA, LISBON, SANTARÉM AND SETÚBAL

(PART OF SETÚBAL ALSO FEATURES IN THE ALENTEJO REGION)

Standing on the banks of the river Tagus, Lisbon has been the capital of Portugal since 1255. Places of interest in the city include the medieval quarters of Alfama and Mouraria, with their cobbled streets and alleys, colourful buildings, markets and castles, and Belém, with its tower and the 16th century Jerónimos monastery. Lisbon also boasts an assortment of museums. Not far from the capital lies the romantic town of Sintra, which has an array of cottages, manor houses and palaces. Its mountains also form part of the Sintra-Cascais Natural Park. Along the Atlantic coast, high sweeping cliffs lead down to white sandy beaches, backed by lagoons. Europe's westernmost point, Cabo da Roca, is found here as are plenty of coastal towns and villages including Peniche, Nazaré and Óbidos, a small medieval walled town with cobbled streets, tiny whitewashed houses and balconies brimming with flowers. Further inland, at Alcobaça, Tomar and Batalha, are ancient monasteries, with castles in Leiria, Tomar and Santarém. Recreational pursuits include water sports, fishing and golf. In summer there are open air music festivals.

Places of interest

Estoril: casino, golf course and racing track.

Fátima: one of the most important centres of pilgrimage in the Catholic world.

Leiria: medieval royal castle, 16th century cathedral, Romanesque church.

Mafra: 18th century Palace-Convent, the largest Portuguese religious monument.

Santarém: castle, archaeology museum, Gothic convent and churches.

Sesimbra: picturesque small fishing town, medieval castle, the Lagoa de Albufeira is a favourite spot for windsurfers.

Setúbal: natural reserve, beaches, golf courses.

Tomar: 12th century Templars' Castle, Gothic and Renaissance churches, 15th century synagogue.

Cuisine of the region

Fish soups, stews and seafood are popular, including *sardinha assada* (grilled sardines) and *Bifes de Espardarte* (swordfish steaks). Sintra is famed for its cheesecakes, which according to ancient documents were already being made in the 12th century, and were part of the rent payments. Wine-producing regions include Azeitão, Bucelas, Carcavelos and Colares.

Caldeiradas: fish stews.

Queijadas: cheese tarts.

Pastéis de Belém: custard tarts.

Travesseiros: puff pastries stuffed with a sweet eggy mixture.

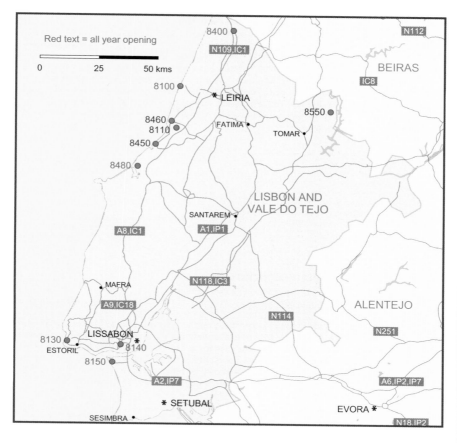

PO8550 Camping Quinta da Cerejeira

P-2240-33 Ferreira do Zêzere (Santarem)

Tel: **249 361 756**. Email: **info@cerejeira.com**

www.alanrogers.com/PO8550

This is a delightful, small, family owned new venture run by Gert and Teunie Verheij assisted by their children. It is a converted farm (quinta) and has been coaxed into a very special campsite. The pitches are on flat grass or on long terraces under fruit and olive trees. There are 18 pitches with electricity (6A) from a central server. There is a some shade and the site is full of rustic charm and craft works. It is very peaceful with views of the surrounding green hills from the charming vine-covered patio above a small swimming pool. You will notice the working well, no longer powered by a donkey but you can see where he used to circle to pump water.

Facilities

The single rustic sanitary building has seatless British style WCs with hot showers. It could be busy at peak periods. Washing machine. No facilities for disabled campers. No shop but just ask and the baker calls daily. Bar with snacks and restaurant. Children's club room. Games and rest room with satellite TV. Artistic workshops. Internet access and WiFi. Swing for children. Torches useful. Off site: Bus from town 1 km. Town has shops, bars and restaurants. Fishing 5 km. Watersports 5 km. Riding 11 km.

Open: 1 February - 30 November.

Directions

From Lisbon take A1/A23 to Torres Novas then IC3 to Tomar and N238 to Ferreira do Zezere. Take road N348 to Vila de Rei and the site is 1 km. from Ferreira do Zezere to the eastern side of town (do not go into the town).
GPS: N39:42.200 W08:16.690

Charges guide

Per person	€ 3,00 - € 3,25
pitch incl. car	€ 5,25 - € 7,75
electricity	€ 2,25

Check real time availability and at-the-gate prices...
www.alanrogers.com
169

PO8150 Orbitur Camping Costa da Caparica

Avenida Alfonso de Albuquerque, Quinta de Ste Antonio, P-2825-450 Costa da Caparica (Setubal)

Tel: **212 901 366**. Email: **info@orbitur.pt**   www.alanrogers.com/PO8150

This is very much a site for 600 permanent caravans but it has relatively easy access to Lisbon (just under 20 km.) via the motorway, by bus or even by bus and ferry if you wish. It is situated near a small resort, favoured by the Portuguese themselves, which has all the usual amenities plus a good sandy beach (200 m. from the site) and promenade walks. There is a small area for touring units which includes some larger pitches for motorcaravans. We see this very much as a site to visit Lisbon rather than for prolonged stays.

Facilities

The three toilet blocks have mostly British style toilets, washbasins with cold water and some hot showers – they come under pressure when the site is full. Facilities for disabled visitors. Washing machine. Motorcaravan services. Supermarket. Large bar/restaurant (not Nov.). TV room (satellite). Playground. Gas supplies. Off site: Bus service from site gate. Fishing 1 km. Riding 4 km. Golf 5 km.

Open: All year.

Directions

Cross the Tagus bridge (toll) on A2 motorway going south from Lisbon, immediately take the turning for Caparica and Trafaria. At 7 km. marker on IC20 turn right (no sign) – the site is at the second roundabout. GPS: N38:39.220 W09:14.330

Charges guide

Per person	€ 2,70 - € 4,80
caravan and car	€ 6,70 - € 11,30
electricity	€ 2,50 - € 3,10

PO8130 Orbitur Camping Guincho

EN 247, Lugar da Areia - Guincho, P-2750-053 Cascais (Lisbon)

Tel: **214 870 450**. Email: **info@orbitur.pt**   www.alanrogers.com/PO8130

Although this is a popular site for permanent Portuguese units with 1,295 pitches, it is nevertheless quite attractively laid out among low pine trees and with the A5 autostrada connection to Lisbon (30 km), it provides a useful alternative to sites nearer the city. This is viewed as an alternative for visiting Lisbon, not a holiday site. There is a choice of pitches (small – mainly about 50 sq.m.) mostly with electricity, although siting amongst the trees may be tricky, particularly when the site is full. Located behind sand dunes and a wide, sandy beach, the site offers a wide range of facilities.

Facilities

Three sanitary blocks, one refurbished, are in the older style but are clean and tidy. Washbasins with cold water but no hot showers. Facilities for disabled visitors. Washing machines and dryers. Motorcaravan services. Gas. Supermarket. Restaurant, bar and terrace. General room with TV. Tennis. Playground. Entertainment in summer. Chalets to rent. Off site: Bus service from gate. Excursions. Riding 500 m. Beach 800 m. Fishing 1 km. Golf 3 km.

Open: All year.

Directions

Approach from either direction on N247. Turn inland 6.5 km. west of Cascais at site sign. Travelling direct from Lisbon, the site is well signed as you leave the A5 autopista. GPS: N38:43.270 W09:28.000

Charges guide

Per person	€ 2,70 - € 4,80
child (5-10 yrs)	€ 1,40 - € 2,50
caravan and car	€ 6,70 - € 11,30
electricity	€ 2,50 - € 3,10

PO8140 Lisboa Camping Parque Municipal de Monsanto

Estrada da Circunvalacao, P-1400-061 Lisboa (Lisbon)

Tel: **217 623 100**   www.alanrogers.com/PO8140

This very large site is professionally operated by many uniformed staff, providing a quality service at a good price. The wide entrance with its ponds, fountains and the trees, lawns and flowering shrubs leading up to the swimming pool, is a most attractive feature. On sloping ground, the site's many terraces are well shaded by trees and shrubs. The 400 good pitches include 170 serviced pitches on concrete hardstandings. There is a huge separate area for tents, and 70 chalet style bungalows are for hire. Central Lisbon is 8 km. with two bus routes giving a regular service from the gate.

Facilities

Eight solar-powered toilet blocks contain quality facilities, including those for disabled people. Launderette. Motorcaravan service point. Shops, bar and restaurants. Two swimming pools (with lifeguard; May - Sept). Tennis. Minigolf. Sports field. Playgrounds. Roman theatre. Entertainment in high season. General and TV (cable) rooms. Internet café. Organised excursions. Off site: Excellent bus service from site gate. Lisbon city. Bicycle hire 2 km. Golf 5 km. Beaches 10 km. Riding 16 km.

Open: All year.

Directions

From Lisbon take A5 motorway towards Estoril and site is signed from junction 4 onto the 1C17 (huge site signs at first exit to Buraca). The site is immediately on the right. Enter to the right of the fountain on the tiled road. GPS: N38:43.480 W09:12.380

Charges guide

Per person	€ 4,50 - € 6,00
child (6-12 yrs)	€ 2,10 - € 3,00
pitch incl. electricity	€ 8,00 - € 11,00

PO8100 Orbitur Camping São Pedro de Moel

Rua Volta do Sete, P-2430 São Pedro de Moel (Leiria)

Tel: **244 599 168**. Email: **info@orbitur.pt**   www.alanrogers.com/PO8100

This quiet and very attractive site is situated under tall pines, on the edge of the rather select small resort of São Pedro de Moel. This is a shady site which can be crowded in July and August. The 525 pitches are in blocks and unmarked (cars may be parked separately) with 404 electrical connections. A few pitches are used for permanent units. Although there are areas of soft sand, there should be no problem in finding a firm place. The large restaurant and bar are modern as is the superb swimming pool, paddling pool and flume (there is a lifeguard).

Facilities

Four clean toilet blocks have mainly British style toilets (some with bidets), some washbasins with hot water. Hot showers are mostly in one block. Laundry. Motorcaravan services. Gas supplies. Supermarket. Large restaurant and bar with terrace (closed in November). Swimming pools (31/3-30/9). Satellite TV. Games room. Playground. Tennis. Off site: Bus service 100 m. Beach 500 m. Fishing 1 km.

Open: All year.

Directions

Site is 9 km. west of Marinha Grande, on the right as you enter São Pedro de Moel. GPS: N39:45.450 W09:01.600

Charges guide

Per person	€ 2,70 - € 4,80
child (5-10 yrs)	€ 1,40 - € 2,50
caravan and car	€ 6,70 - € 11,30
electricity	€ 2,50 - € 3,10

Off season discounts (up to 70%).

PO8110 Orbitur Camping Valado

Rua dos Combatentes do Ultramar 2, Valado, P-2450-148 Nazaré (Leiria)

Tel: **262 561 111**. Email: **info@orbitur.pt**   www.alanrogers.com/PO8110

This popular site is close to the old, traditional fishing port of Nazaré which has now become something of a holiday resort and popular with coach parties. The large sandy beach in the town (about 2 km. steeply downhill) is sheltered by headlands and provides good swimming. The campsite is on undulating ground under tall pine trees, has 503 pitches and, although some smallish individual pitches with electricity and water can be reserved, the bulk of the site is not marked out and units are close together during July/August. About 375 electrical connections are available.

Facilities

The three toilet blocks have British and Turkish style WCs, washbasins (some cold water) and 17 hot showers, all very clean when inspected. Laundry. Motorcaravan services. Gas supplies. Supermarket. Bar, snack bar and restaurant with terrace (Easter and June - Oct). TV/general room. Playground. Tennis. Off site: Bus service 20 m. Fishing and bicycle hire 2 km.

Open: 1 February - 30 November.

Directions

Site is on the Nazaré - Alcobaca N8-5 road, 2 km. east of Nazaré. GPS: N39:35.604 W09:01.670

Charges guide

Per person	€ 2,30 - € 4,10
child (5-10 yrs)	€ 1,20 - € 2,10
caravan and car	€ 5,10 - € 9,30
electricity	€ 2,50 - € 3,10

PO8480 Orbitur Camping Foz do Arelho

Rua Maldonado Freitas, P-2500-516 Foz do Arelho (Leiria)

Tel: **262 978 683**. Email: **info@orbitur.pt**   www.alanrogers.com/PO8480

This is a large and roomy ex-municipal site and improvements are still taking place. It is 2 km. from the beach and has a new central complex with a most impressive swimming pool and separated children's pool with lifeguard. Pitches are generally sandy with some hardstandings. They vary in size and are unmarked on two main levels with wide tarmac roads. There is some shade and all touring pitches have electricity (5/15A). The large two storey, brick-faced building contains all the site's leisure facilities but has no ramped access and there are no sanitary facilities on site for disabled campers.

Facilities

Four identical modern sanitary buildings (solar heating) with seatless British and Turkish style WCs and free showers. Washing machine. No facilities for disabled campers. Supermarket. Bar and snacks. restaurant (closed Nov). Children's club. Playground – supervision needed. Bus service. Doctor's room. Torches useful. Off site: Bus 500 m. Seaside town 2 km. Fishing 2 km.

Open: All year.

Directions

Site is north of Lisbon and west of Caldos la Rainha. From the A8 take N360 to Foz de Arelho. Site is well signed. GPS: N39:25.840 W09:12.050

Charges guide

Per person	€ 2,70 - € 4,80
caravan and car	€ 6,70 - € 11,30
electricity	€ 2,50 - € 3,10

Check real time availability and at-the-gate prices...
www.**alanrogers**.com
171

PO8400 Campismo O Tamanco

Rua do Louriçal 11, Casas Brancas, P-3105-158 Outeiro do Louriçal (Leiria)

Tel: **236 952 551**. Email: **tamanco@mac.com**   www.alanrogers.com/PO8400

O Tamanco is a peaceful countryside site, with a homely almost farmstead atmosphere; you will have chickens and ducks wandering around and there is a Burro here. The young Dutch owners, Irene and Hans, are sure to give you a warm welcome at this delightful little site. The 75 good sized pitches are separated by cordons of all manner of fruit trees, ornamental trees and flowering shrubs, on level grassy ground. There is electricity to 72 pitches and 5 pitches are suitable for large motorhomes. The site is lit and there is nearly always space available. The swimming pool is very pleasant, as is the small bar and a restaurant (with vegetarian menu options). There may also be entertainment for the children during the day. The site is extremely popular with the Dutch, mature couples and winter campers. One can fish or swim in a nearby lake and the resort beaches are a short drive. There is some road noise on pitches at the front of the site.

Facilities	Directions
The single toilet block provides very clean and generously sized facilities including washbasins in cabins, with easy access for disabled visitors. As facilities are limited they may be busy in peak periods. Hot water throughout. Washing machine. Bar/restaurant. Roofed patio with fireplace. TV room/lounge (satellite). Internet access. Swimming pool. Off site: Bus service 1 km. Lake 2 km. Beach 11 km. Market in nearby Lourical every Sunday.	From the A17 Lisboa - Porto, take exit 10 for Carrico, turn right at the roundabout and O Tomanco is on the left. GPS: N39:59.500 W08:47.310

Open: All year.

Charges 2009

Per person	€ 3,90
child (up to 10 yrs)	€ 2,10
pitch with electricity	€ 8,45 - € 10,85
dog	€ 0,80

Winter discounts up to 40%.
No credit cards.

PO8450 Parque de Campismo Colina do Sol

Serra Dos Mangues, P-2465 São Martinho do Porto (Leiria)

Tel: **262 989 764**. Email: **parque.colina.sol@dix.pt**   www.alanrogers.com/PO8450

Colina do Sol is a well appointed site with its own swimming pool and near the beach. Only 2 km. from the small town of São Martinho do Porto, it has around 350 pitches marked by fruit and ornamental trees on grassy terraces. Electricity (6A) is available. The attractive entrance with its beds of bright flowers, is wide enough for even the largest of outfits, and the surfaced roads are very pleasant for manoeuvring. There is a warm welcome and good English is spoken. The beach is at the rear of the site, with access via a gate which is locked at night. We are told that swimming in the sea requires great care when there are large waves – there is no lifeguard. The site has a well stocked supermarket, a restaurant and a bar with a delightful paved terrace beside the large clean swimming and paddling pools. This is a convenient base for exploring the Costa de Prata and for excursions to the old town of Leiria, with its crenulated walls towering high above the rock faces, and to the famous shrine of Fátima. Market in São Martinho do Porto is on Sunday.

Facilities	Directions
Two large, clean and modern toilet blocks provide British style WCs (some with bidets), washbasins, some with hot water. Dishwashing and laundry sinks are outside but covered. Motorcaravan services. Supermarket. Bar and restaurant (1/7-31/8). Satellite TV. Swimming pool (1/7-10/9). Off site: Bus from the gate to nearby towns. Shop, restaurant and bar within 200 m. Beach (no lifeguard).	Turn from EN 242 (Caldas - Nazaré) road northeast of São Martinho do Porto. Site is clearly signed. GPS: N39:31.370 W09:07.380

Open: All year, excl. 25 December.

Charges guide

Per person	€ 3,65 - € 4,30
child (4-10 yrs)	€ 1,79 - € 2,10
pitch	€ 6,92 - € 9,85
electricity	€ 2,60

Less in low seasons.

Check real time availability and at-the-gate prices...

www.**alanrogers**.com

PO8460 Camping Caravaning Vale Paraiso

EN242, P-2450-138 Nazaré (Leiria)

Tel: 262 561 800. Email: info@valeparaiso.com

www.alanrogers.com/PO8460

A pleasant, well managed site, Vale Paraiso improves every year, with the latest additions being new reception buildings and pool areas. The owners are keen to welcome British visitors and English is spoken. The site is by the main N242 road in eight hectares of undulating pine woods. There are 650 shady pitches, many on sandy ground only suitable for tents. For other units there are around 250 individual pitches of varying size on harder ground with electricity available. A large range of sporting and leisure activities includes an excellent outdoor pool and paddling pool with sunbathing areas. An adventure playground is safe with new equipment. There is a pleasant bar, innovative takeaway selling roasts and a lower level restaurant/bar. Several long beaches of white sand are within 2-15 km. allowing windsurfing, sailing, surfing or body-boarding. Animation for children and evening entertainment is organised in season. Nazaré is an old fishing village with narrow streets, a harbour and marina and many outdoor bars and cafés, with a lift to Sitio. There is much of historical interest in the area although the mild Atlantic climate is also conducive to just relaxing.

Facilities

Spotless sanitary facilities have hot water throughout. Nearly all WCs are British style. Modern facilities for disabled people. Baby baths. Washing machine and dryers. Motorcaravan services. Supermarket (1/5-30/9). Restaurant (15/5-15/9). Café/bar with satellite TV. Takeaway. Tabac. Swimming and paddling pools (March - Sept; free for under 11s). Petanque. Leisure games. Amusement hall. Bicycle hire. Safety deposit. Gas supplies. E-mail and fax facilities. Apartments and moblie homes to rent. Off site: Bus service from gate. Fishing 2 km. Boat launching 2 km. Riding 6 km. Golf 40 km.

Open: 1 January - 18 December and 28 - 31 December.

Directions

Site is 2 km. north of Nazaré on the EN242 Marinha Grande road. GPS: N39:37.131 W09:03.230

Charges 2009

Per person	€ 3,20 - € 4,50
child (3-10 yrs)	€ 1,60 - € 2,30
pitch	€ 6,00 - € 17,80
electricity (4-10A)	€ 2,70

Credit cards accepted for amounts over € 150. Camping Cheques accepted.

Beiras is the traditional name for a strip of land flanked by Portugal's two main rivers – the Douro and the Tagus. This region is made up of two contrasting areas: white sandy beaches, fishing villages and pine forests lie along the coast, while inland the mountains dominate the landscape.

BEIRAS HAS FIVE DISTRICTS: AVEIRO, COIMBRA, CASTELO BRANCO, GUARDA AND VISEU

One of Europe's oldest university towns, Coimbra was Portugal's capital from 1143 to 1255. The university, founded in 1290, has kept its academic traditions, as seen in the black-capped students, in the soulful tones of the fado de Coimbra (a traditional song sung to the sound of guitars by the students) and in the Queima das Fitas (Burning of the Ribbons), a boisterous celebration of graduating students. Coimbra also boasts a Romanesque cathedral and south of the town lies Conímbriga, with the most important Roman remains in Portugal. Surrounded by the original walls, the archaeological site features an early Christian burial ground, a set of hot springs and a museum. Further north lies Aveiro. Famous for its lagoon, the town is crisscrossed by canals where colourfully painted moliceiro boats sail. To the east lies the Serra de Estrela, the highest mountain range in the country. It is home to the textile town of Covilha, attractive villages including Gouveia, Manteigas and Seia, plus the mountain resort of Guarda. Along the coast, the pretty seaside resorts of São Martinho do Porto, Nazaré and Figueira da Foz offer fine sandy beaches, good seafood restaurants and water sports facilities.

Places of interest

Belmonte: hilltop town, castle, Romanesque-Gothic church.

Bussaco: national park founded by monks in the 6th century.

Castelo Branco: 13th century castle, medieval quarter, 16th-18th century churches.

Curia and *Luso:* spa towns.

Monsanto: historic village, 12th-century castle, 18th-century manor-houses.

Viseu: remains of Gothic walls, cathedral.

Cuisine of the region

Roast pork, lamb stew, seafood and fresh fish are popular, including *truta* (trout) from the mountains of Serra da Estrela. The famous ewe's milk cheese Queijo da Serra, is also a produced in the mountains, and can be bought at Cheese Fairs held in villages and towns throughout the region during February and March. Regional desserts include hard and sweet biscuits, pancakes and sponge cake (*ovos-moles, pão-de-ló*).

Chanfana: lamb stewed in red wine.

Leitão assado da Bairrada: roast pork.

Red text = all year opening

PO8040 Parque de Campismo da Vagueira

Gafanha da Vagueira, Gafanha da Boa Hora, P-3840-254 Vagos (Aveiro)

Tel: **234 797 526**

www.alanrogers.com/PO8040

This is a large site set 1.5 km. from the beach and 500 m. from the 'Ria da Gosta Nova' river. It is shaded under tall pine trees and has comprehensive facilities and reasonable prices. The 800 pitches are unmarked, on sand and pine needles with a large number of permanent Portuguese units which are here in high season and weekends at other times. Groups are taken in high season. All touring pitches have electricity (6A). In sympathy with the surroundings, the modern buildings have clean lines and include a restaurant and bar with a disco area outside where music is played at weekends. This complex extends into a large rectangle holding the extremely large supermarket and facilities listed below. The whole site is securely fenced and is kept remarkably clean. The rules of peace between 11 pm - 7 am are firmly applied. This is a good family site if you do not need a pool and have transport to get you to the beach. The seaside town here is a mixture of buildings and services which seem to be unsure of which future direction to take, but the beach is excellent.

Facilities

Seven modern sanitary buildings with British and Turkish style WCs and free showers. Facilities for disabled campers (unlocked). Washing machines. Bar/snacks and separate (June-Sept). Large supermarket. Children's club. Outdoor disco. Games room. Playground. Tennis (charge). Satellite TV. Internet room. Torches useful. Off site: Seaside town has shops bars and restaurants. Bus 500 m. River fishing 500 m. Watersports at beach 1.5 km. Golf and riding 1 km.

Open: All year.

Directions

Site is south of Aveiro. Take N109 south from Aveiro towards Mira. At Vagos take the N333 right turn towards Vagueira. Site is well signed at this turn and is just off the roundabout you arrive at on the beach road. GPS: N40:33.475 W08:44.710

Charges guide

Per person	€ 1,83 - € 3,65
child	€ 0,95 - € 1,85
pitch and car	€ 3,25 - € 8,50
electricity	€ 2,00

PO8050 Orbitur Camping São Jacinto

EN 327 km 20, São Jacinto, P-3800-909 Aveiro (Aveiro)

Tel: **234 838 284**. Email: **info@orbitur.pt**

www.alanrogers.com/PO8050

This small site is in the Sao Jacinto nature reserve, on a peninsula between the Atlantic and the Barrinha, with views to the mountains beyond. The area is a weekend resort for locals and can be crowded in high season – it may therefore be difficult to find space in July/Aug, particularly for larger units. This is not a large site, taking 169 units on unmarked pitches, but in most places trees provide natural limits and shade. Swimming and fishing are both possible in the adjacent Ria, or the sea, 20 minutes walk from a guarded back gate. There is a private jetty for boats and the manager will organise hire of the decorative 'Moliceiros' boats used in days gone by to harvest seaweed for the land. A deep bore-hole supplies the site with drinking water.

Facilities

Two toilet blocks, very clean when inspected, contain the usual facilities. Dishwashing and laundry sinks. Washing machine and ironing board in a separate part of the toilet block. Motorcaravan services. Shop. Restaurant, bar and snack bar (Easter and June - Oct). Playground. Five bungalows to rent. Off site: Bus service 20 m. Fishing 200 m. Bicycle hire 10 km.

Open: 1 February - 31 October.

Directions

Turn off N109 at Estarreja to N109-5 to cross bridge over Ria da Gosta Nova and on to Torreira and São Jacinto. From Porto go south N1/09, turn for Ovar on the N327 which leads to São Jacinto. GPS: N40:40.498 W08:43.377

Charges guide

Per person	€ 2,30 - € 4,10
child (5-10 yrs)	€ 1,20 - € 2,10
pitch incl. electricity	€ 7,60 - € 12,40

PO8060 Camping Costa Nova

Quinta dos Patos, Costa Nova do Prado, P-3830 Gafanha da Encarnação (Aveiro)

Tel: **234 393 220**. Email: **info@campingcostanova.com**

www.alanrogers.com/PO8060

This campsite has been recommended by our agent and we plan to undertake a full inspection in 2009. Camping Costa Nova is situated between a river (Ria de Aveiro) and the sea with direct access to a large sandy beach via a wooden walkway. The 300 grassy pitches are provided with electricity hook ups (10A). This site is ideal for those who enjoy watersports and the surroundings offer plenty of sites of interest for exploration. The site boasts a large bar/restaurant and a café with TV and internet access. English speaking visitors are welcomed and this sheltered site also attracts many for winter stays. Apartments are available for let.

Facilities

Sanitary facilities with free hot water. Laundry room. Restaurant. Bar. Takeaway food. Snack bar. Shop. Games room. Disco. TV. Play area. Internet access. Off site: Beach 500 m. Fishing.

Open: 1 February - 31 December.

Directions

On the IP5 travelling from Aveiro east towards Barra, cross the bridge. At roundabout take third exit and site is well signed. GPS: N40:35.983 W08:45.083

Charges guide

Per unit incl. electricity	€ 5,20 - € 6,30
person	€ 2,50
child (under 10 yrs)	€ 1,25

PO8070 Orbitur Camping Mira

Estrada Florestal no 1 km 2, Dunas de Mira, P-3070-792 Praia de Mira (Coimbra)

Tel: **231 471 234**. Email: **info@orbitur.pt**

www.alanrogers.com/PO8070

A small, peaceful seaside site set in pinewoods, Orbitur Camping Mira is situated to the south of Aveiro and Vagos, in a quieter and less crowded area. It fronts onto a lake at the head of the Ria de Mira, which eventually runs into the Aveiro Ria. A back gate leads directly to the sea and a wide quiet beach 300 m. away. A road runs alongside the site boundary where the restaurant complex is situated resulting in some road noise. The site has around 225 pitches on sand, which are not marked but with trees creating natural divisions. Electricity and water points are plentiful.

Facilities

The modern toilet blocks are clean, with 14 free hot showers and washing machines. Facilities for disabled visitors. Motorcaravan services. Gas supplies. Shop. Restaurant, bar and snack bar (Easter and June - Oct). TV room. Play area. Bicycle hire. Bungalows (7) to rent. Off site: Bus service 150 m. (summer only). Fishing 500 m. Indoor pool, lake swimming and riding at Mira 7 km.

Open: 1 January - 30 November.

Directions

Take the IP5 (A25) southwest to Aveiro then the A17 south to Figuera da Foz. Then take the N109 north to Mira and follow signs west to Praia (beach) de Mira. GPS: N40:27.198 W08:47.941

Charges guide

Per person	€ 2,50 - € 4,50
child (5-10 yrs)	€ 1,30 - € 2,50
caravan and car	€ 5,60 - € 10,20
electricity	€ 2,50 - € 3,10

PO8090 Orbitur Camping Gala

EN109 km 4 Gala, P-3080-458 Figueira da Foz (Coimbra)

Tel: 233 431 492. Email: info@orbitur.pt

www.alanrogers.com/PO8090

This site of around 450 pitches is on sandy terrain under a canopy of pine trees and well cared for. Some pitches near the road are rather noisy. One can drive or walk the 300 m. from the back of the site to a private beach; you should swim with caution when it is windy – the warden will advise. The site fills in July/August and units may be very close together, but there should be plenty of room at other times. Besides the beach, Coimbra and the nearby Roman remains are worth visiting.

Facilities

The three toilet blocks have British and Turkish style toilets, individual basins (some with hot water) and free hot showers. Laundry. Motorcaravan services. Gas supplies. Supermarket and restaurant/bar with terrace. Lounge. Playground. Tennis. TV. Doctor visits in season. Car wash area. Open-air pool (June-Sept). Off site: Beach 300 m. Fishing 1 km. Bicycle hire and riding 3 km.

Open: All year.

Directions

Site is 4 km. south of Figueira da Foz beyond the two rivers; turn off N109 1 km. from bridge on southern edge of Gala, look for Orbitur sign on roundabout it is then 600 m. to site.
GPS: N40:07.110 W08:51.410

Charges guide

Per person	€ 2,70 - € 4,80
child (5-10 yrs)	€ 1,40 - € 2,50
caravan and car	€ 6,70 - € 11,30
electricity	€ 2,50 - € 3,10
Off season discounts (up to 70%).	

PO8330 Camping Municipal Arganil

EN17 km 5, Sarzedo, P-3300 Arganil (Coimbra)

Tel: 235 205 706

www.alanrogers.com/PO8330

This peaceful, inland site is attractively located in the hamlet of Sarzedo, some 2 km. from the town of Arganil. A spacious and well planned site, it is of a high quality for a municipal and prices are very reasonable! Delightfully situated among pine trees above the River Alva where one can swim, fish or canoe. The 150 pitches, most with electricity (15A), are of a reasonable size, mainly on flat sandy grass terraces and most shaded by tall trees. The site is kept beautifully clean and neat and access roads are tarmac. An excellent, small restaurant has an unusual attached bar with terrace.

Facilities

Sanitary facilities are clean and well maintained, with Turkish and British style WCs, controllable hot showers, washbasins in semi-private partitioned cabins and a hairdressing area. Ramped entrances make it suitable for disabled visitors. Washing machines. Bar, restaurant and snacks. Shop (July - Sept). TV room. Tennis. Off site: Bus service 50 m. River beach and fishing 100 m. Watersports 200 m. Swimming pool in nearby Arganil. Golf 25 km.

Open: All year.

Directions

From EN17/N2 Coimbra - Sarzedo at 324.4 km. marker exit to Sarzedo (site signed). Ignore first site sign to Avelar as there is a better access 500 m. further up the road on the right, also signed.
GPS: N40:14.000 W08:05.000

Charges guide

Per person	€ 1,60 - € 1,80
pitch	€ 1,50 - € 5,20
electricity	€ 2,50 - € 2,40

PO8335 Camping Quinta Chave Grande

Casfreires, Ferreira d'Aves, P-3560-043 Sátão (Viseu)

Tel: 232 665 552. Email: chave-grande@sapo.pt

www.alanrogers.com/PO8335

Quinta Chave Grande is a quality campsite with friendly Dutch owners. It is set in a rural valley, close to many charming old villages, yet also only 25 km. from the provincial capital of Viseu, with its museums, churches and beautiful old town centre. The site occupies a large area and there are 180 unmarked touring pitches, although some are defined by trees. Electricity (6A) is available but long leads may be required. Larger units can be accommodated and there is a separate terraced area for tents. Torches are essential. For those who enjoy walking there are 8 marked walking tours starting from the campsite providing an opportunity to see some magnificent scenery.

Facilities

Two modern toilet blocks, one with private en-suite cubicles for use by families and for visitors with disabilities. Service wash available. No shop but local tradesmen visit the site. Bar (all season). Swimming pool and children's pool (1/5-1/10). Fenced play area. Organised events for children and teenagers in July/August. Tennis. Boules. Off site: Fishing 5 km. Riding 25 km. Golf 40 km. Marked walks. Good touring area.

Open: 1 April - 31 October.

Directions

From A25 (IP5) Salamanca to Viseu take N229 northeast to Sátão. Site is very well signed along road and is 12 km. northeast of Satao.
GPS: N40:49.362 W07:41.765

Charges 2009

Per person	€ 4,50
child (3-16 yrs)	€ 2,50
pitch incl. car	€ 7,00 - € 8,00
electricity	€ 2,50

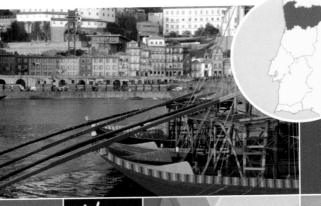

Originally inhabited by Celtics, Romans and Moors, the North is a region steeped in history. Renowned for its beautiful countryside, the River Douro winds its way past mountains, valleys, vineyards and cliffs until it reaches the sandy beaches of the Atlantic coast near the city of Porto.

THE REGION IS COMPRISED OF FIVE DISTRICTS: BRAGA, BRAGANÇA, PORTO, VIANA DO CASTELO AND VILA REAL

Situated in the north western corner of Portugal, the Costa Verde boasts lush green pine forests and unspoilt sandy beaches, dotted with picturesque seaside villages, including Caminha and Vila Nova de Cerveira. It is also renowned for its wine, being the home of Port and Vinho Verdo. Located on the banks for the River Douro, the attractive city of Porto is the centre of the Port wine trade – free tastings are offered at the wine cellars in Vila Nova de Gaia – and terraced vineyards can be found across the Douro Valley. The region is also a perfect place for walking, mountain trekking, canoeing or simply relaxing in the spa towns of Carvalhelhos, Chaves and Pedras Salgadas. Vidago has a magnificent park with swimming pools and a golf course, while the mountains of Peneda, Soajo and Gerês form the Peneda Geres National Park, an area covering 170,000 acres, with an abundance of wildlife. Vila Nova de Foz is the centre for visits to the Côa Archaeological Park, which houses one of the world's largest collections of outdoor Palaeolithic rock art, dating back 22,000 years.

Places of interest

Barcelos: medieval walled town with dungeon, ceramics museum, archaeology museum.

Bragança: medieval castle and walls, 16th century cathedral, railway museum with 19th century locomotives and carriages.

Chaves: Roman bridge, 14th century castle with Archaeology and Epigraphy Museum.

Guimarães: medieval castle and walls, palace.

Lamego: medieval castle, 12th century fortress.

Ponte de Lima: beautiful small town, Roman bridge, medieval towers, manor houses.

Viana do Castelo: town famous for its handicrafts and colourful regional costumes.

Vila do Conde: ancient medieval shipyard, famous for its manufactured lace.

Cuisine of the region

Typical dishes include *bacalhau* (dried and salted cod), *rabanadas*, *papos-de-anjo* and *barrigas-de-freiras* (sweetmeats). Porto has its own tripe dish *Tripas à moda do Porto*.

The Minho region is renowned for its *Vinhos Verdes*, whose vines are grown on trellises (being suspended high in the air on special frames). In the Douro region, the vines are grown on terraces, giving the impression of huge natural staircases leading down to the banks of the river. Both red and white wines are produced here including the famous *Vinho do Porto* (Port Wine).

Caldo verde: thick soup made with green cabbage, potatoes and spicy sausage.

Feijoada à transmontana: bean stew.

PO8020 Orbitur Camping Viana do Castelo

Rua Diogo Alvares, Cabadelo, P-4900-161 Darque (Viana do Costelo)

Tel: **258 322 167**. Email: **info@orbitur.pt**

www.alanrogers.com/PO8020

This site in northern Portugal is worth considering as it has the advantage of direct access, through a gate in the fence (locked at night) to a large and excellent soft sand beach (400 m.) which is popular for windsurfing. There are 225 pitches on undulating sand, most with good shade from pine trees and with electricity in all areas (long leads may be needed). Some flat good sized pitches are reserved for caravans and motorcaravans. As usual with Orbitur sites, most pitches are not marked and it could be crowded in July/August. A pleasant restaurant terrace overlooks the pool. A ferry crosses the river to the town centre. The site is also convenient for visiting the medieval town of Ponte de Lima (24 km), with its white-washed houses, towers and Roman bridge, and Viana do Castelo is famous for its beautiful embroideries and festival processions.

Facilities

Toilet facilities are in two blocks, both with washbasins with cold water and hot showers. Facilities for disabled campers. Laundry. Motorcaravan services. Gas supplies. Supermarket. Small restaurant with terrace and bar (all Easter and 1/6-30/9). Open-air pool (June - Sept). Reading room with TV, video and fireplace. Playground. Tennis. Medical post. Off site: Fishing 100 m. Beach 50 m.

Open: All year.

Directions

On N13 coast road driving north to south drive through Viana do Castelo and over estuary bridge. Turn immediately right off N13 towards Cabedelo and the sea. Site is the third campsite signed, the other two are not recommended.
GPS: N41:40.720 W08:49.582

Charges guide

Per person	€ 2,70 - € 4,80
child (5-10 yrs)	€ 1,40 - € 2,50
caravan and car	€ 6,70 - € 11,30
electricity	€ 2,50 - € 3,10

Off season discounts (up to 70%).

Check real time availability and at-the-gate prices...
www.**alanrogers**.com
179

PO8370 Parque de Campismo de Cerdeira

P-4840 Campo do Gerês (Braga)

Tel: 253 351 005. Email: info@parquecerdeira.com

www.alanrogers.com/PO8370

Located in the National Park of Peneda Gerês, amidst spectacular mountain scenery, this excellent site offers modern facilities in a truly natural area. The National Park is home to all manner of flora, fauna and wildlife, including the roebuck, wolf and wild boar. The well fenced, professional and peaceful site has some 600 good sized, unmarked, mostly level, grassy pitches in a shady woodland setting. Electricity is available for most pitches, though some long leads may be required. A very large timber complex, tastefully designed with the use of noble materials, granite and wood, provides a superb restaurant with a comprehensive menu. A pool with a separated section for toddlers is a welcome, cooling relief in the height of summer. There are unlimited opportunities in the immediate area for fishing, riding, canoeing, mountain biking and climbing, so take advantage of this quality mountain hospitality.

Facilities

Four very clean sanitary blocks provide mixed style WCs, controllable showers and hot water. Laundry. Gas supplies. Shop. Restaurant/bar (1/4- 6/10, plus weekends and holidays). Playground. Bicycle hire. TV room (satellite). Medical post. Good tennis courts. Minigolf. Car wash. Barbecue area. Torches useful. English spoken. Attractive bungalows to rent. Dogs are not accepted June - August. Off site: Fishing and riding 800 m.

Open: All year.

Directions

From north, N103 (Braga - Chaves), turn left at N205 (7.5 km. north of Braga). Follow N205 to Caldelas Terras de Bouro and Covide where site is clearly marked to Campo do Geres. An eastern approach from the N103 is for the adventurous but will be rewarded by magnificent views over mountains and lakes. GPS: N41:45.811 W08:11.330

Charges 2009

Per person	€ 3,20 - € 5,00
child (5-11 yrs)	€ 2,00 - € 3,20
pitch	€ 4,30 - € 9,00
electricity (6/10A)	€ 2,50 - € 3,75

camping | bungalows | restaurant | swimming pool | kayak | trekking | Btt | winter and summer sports

on national park Peneda-Gerês | Tlf. + 351 253 351 005 | www.parquecerdeira.com | PORTUGAL

PO8030 Orbitur Camping Rio Alto

EN13 km 13 Rio Alto-Est, Estela, P-4570-275 Póvoa de Varzim (Porto)

Tel: 252 615 699. Email: info@orbitur.pt

www.alanrogers.com/PO8030

This site makes an excellent base for visiting Porto which is some 35 km. south of Estela. It has around 700 pitches on sandy terrain and is next to what is virtually a private beach. There are some hardstandings for caravans and motorcaravans and electrical connections to most pitches (long leads may be required). The area for tents is furthest from the beach and windswept, stunted pines give some shade. There are arrangements for car parking away from camping areas in peak season. There is a quality restaurant, snack bar and a large swimming pool plus across the road from reception.

Facilities

Four refurbished and well equipped toilet blocks have hot water. Laundry facilities. Facilities for disabled campers. Gas supplies. Shop (1/6-31/10). Restaurant, bar, snack bar (1/5-31/10). Swimming pool (1/6-30/9). Tennis. Play area. Games room. Surfing. TV. Twice weekly evening entertainment in season. Off site: Fishing. Golf. Bicycle hire. Riding (all within 5 km).

Open: All year.

Directions

From A28 (Porto), leave at exit 18 signed Fao/Apuila. At roundabout take N13 in direction of Pavoa de Varzim/Porto for 2.5 km. At Hotel Contriz, turn right onto narrow cobbled road. Site well signed in 2 km. GPS: N41:26.702 W08:45.460

Charges guide

Per person	€ 2,90 - € 5,40
caravan and car	€ 6,80 - € 12,00
electricity (5/15A)	€ 2,50 - € 3,10

Check real time availability and at-the-gate prices...

alanrogers

PO8010 Orbitur Camping Caminha

EN 13 km 90, Mata do Camarido, P-4910-180 Caminha (Viana do Costelo)
Tel: **258 921 295**. Email: **info@orbitur.pt**

www.alanrogers.com/PO8010

In northern Portugal close to the Spanish border, this pleasant site is just 200 metres from the beach. It has an attractive and peaceful setting in woods alongside the river estuary that marks the border with Spain and on the edge of the little town of Caminha. The site is shaded by tall pines with other small trees planted to mark large sandy pitches. The main site road is surfaced but elsewhere take care not to get trapped in soft sand. Pitching and parking can be haphazard. Static units are grouped together on one side of the site. Water points, electrical supply and lighting are good. With a pleasant, open feel about the setting, fishing is possible in the estuary and swimming, either there or from the rather open, sandy beach.

Facilities

The clean, well maintained toilet block has British style toilets, washbasins (cold water) and hot showers, plus beach showers, extra dishwashing and laundry sinks (cold water). Laundry. Motorcaravan services. Supermarket. Small restaurant/bar with snacks (all Easter and 1/6-15/9). Bicycle hire. Off site: Beach 200 m. Fishing 200 m. Bus service 800 m.

Open: All year.

Directions

From the north, turn off the main coast road (N13-E50) just after camping sign at the end of the embankment alongside the estuary, about 1.5 km. south of ferry. From the south on N13 turn left at Hotel Faz de Minho at start of estuary and follow for 1 km. through woods to site.
GPS: N41:51.981 W08:51.506

Charges guide

Per person	€ 2,50 - € 4,50
pitch incl. electricity	€ 8,10 - € 13,30

PO8375 Camping Celorico de Basto

Adoufe Gemeos, P-4890-361 Celorico de Basto (Braga)
Tel: **255 323 100**. Email: **geral@celoricodebastocamping.com**

www.alanrogers.com/PO8375

Celorico de Basto is a new site, open all year and first opened in 2008. The site has been recommended by our Portuguese agent and we plan to undertake a full inspection in 2009. Celorico is an attractive small town close to Braga, and located in the Tamega river valley (a tributary of the Douro). This is excellent walking and cycling country and is also an important wine producing region – Porto is within easy access. On-site amenities here include a bar and restaurant and a small shop. Several mobile homes are available for rent. The Tamega is popular for fishing (1 km from site) and various other activities are possible in the area, including golf (19 km) and riding (30 km). Porto is a popular excursion and is Portugal's second city. The historic centre is a UNESCO world heritage site with a great wealth of fine architecture, notably the Oporto Cathedral and beautiful Romanesque church of Cedofeita.

Facilities

Shop. Bar. Restaurant. Wellness centre. Play area. TV room. Tourist information. Motor caravan services. Mobile homes for rent. Off site: Fishing 1 km. Walking and cycle tracks. Golf 19 km. Porto 70 km. (using motorway).

Open: All year.

Directions

Approaching from Porto, head east on A4 motorway as far as Amarante. From here, head north on the N210 along the Tamega valley passing Ponte Nova until you reach Celerico de Basto. From here follow signs to the site. GPS: N41:23.373 W08:00.467

Charges 2009

Contact the site for further details.

PORTUGAL
CELORICO DE **BASTO**
of life!
www.celoricodebastocamping.com
geral@celoricodebastocamping.com T. +351 255 323 100
A natural way
***
camping

Accommodation

Over recent years many of the campsites featured in this guide have added large numbers of high quality mobile homes and chalets. Many site owners believe that some former caravanners and motorcaravanners have been enticed by the extra comfort they can now provide, and that maybe this is the ideal solution to combine the freedom of camping with all the comforts of home.

Quality is consistently high and, although the exact size and inventory may vary from site to site, if you choose any of the sites detailed here, you can be sure that you're staying in some of the best quality and best value mobile homes available.

Home comforts are provided and typically these include a fridge with freezer compartment, gas hob, proper shower – often a microwave and radio/cassette hi-fi too but do check for details. All mobile homes and chalets come fully equipped with a good range of kitchen utensils, pots and pans, crockery, cutlery and outdoor furniture. Some even have an attractive wooden sundeck or paved terrace – a perfect spot for outdoors eating or relaxing with a book and watching the world go by.

Regardless of model, colourful soft furnishings are the norm and a generally breezy décor helps to provide a real holiday feel.

Although some sites may have a large number of different accommodation types, we have restricted our choice to one or two of the most popular accommodation units (either mobile homes or chalets) for each of the sites listed.

The mobile homes here will be of modern design, and recent innovations, for example, often include pitched roofs which substantially improve their appearance.

Design will invariably include clever use of space and fittings/furniture to provide for comfortable holidays – usually light and airy, with big windows and patio-style doors, fully equipped kitchen areas, a shower room with shower, washbasin and WC, cleverly designed bedrooms and a comfortable lounge/dining area (often incorporating a sofa bed).

In general, modern campsite chalets incorporate all the best features of mobile homes in a more traditional structure, sometimes with the advantage of an upper mezzanine floor for an additional bedroom.

Our selected campsites offer a massive range of different types of mobile home and chalet, and it would be impractical to inspect every single accommodation unit. Our selection criteria, therefore, primarily takes account of the quality standards of the campsite itself.

However, there are a couple of important ground rules:

- FEATURED MOBILE HOMES MUST BE NO MORE THAN 5 YEARS OLD

- CHALETS NO MORE THAN 10 YEARS OLD

- ALL LISTED ACCOMMODATION MUST, OF COURSE, FULLY CONFORM WITH ALL APPLICABLE LOCAL, NATIONAL AND EUROPEAN SAFETY LEGISLATION.

For each campsite we given details of the type, or types, of accommodation available to rent, but these details are necessarily quite brief. Sometimes internal layouts can differ quite substantially, particularly with regard to sleeping arrangements, where these include the flexible provision for 'extra persons' on sofa beds located in the living area. These arrangements may vary from accommodation to accommodation, and if you're planning a holiday which includes more people than are catered for by the main bedrooms you should check exactly how the extra sleeping arrangements are to be provided!

Charges

An indication of the tariff for each type of accommodation featured is also included, indicating the variance between the low and high season tariffs. However, given that many campsites have a large and often complex range of pricing options, incorporating special deals and various discounts, the charges we mention should be taken to be just an indication. We strongly recommend therefore that you confirm the actual cost when making a booking.

We also strongly recommend that you check with the campsite, when booking, what (if anything) will be provided by way of bed linen, blankets, pillows etc. Again, in our experience, this can vary widely from site to site.

On every campsite a fully refundable deposit (usually between 150 and 300 euros) is payable on arrival. There may also be an optional cleaning service for which a further charge is made. Other options may include sheet hire (typically 30 euros per unit) or baby pack hire (cot and high chair).

ES81030 Camping El Maset

see report page 32

Playa de Sa Riera, E-17255 Begur (Girona)

AR1 – ESTUDIO APARTAMENTO – Apartment

Sleeping: 1 bedroom, sleeps 5: 1 double, 2 single beds, sofa bed, pillows & blankets provided

Living: living/kitchen area, heating, TV, fan, shower & separate wc

Eating: fitted kitchen with hobs, coffee machine, fridge/freezer

Outside: table & chairs, sun lounger, parasol

Pets: not accepted

AR2 – MEDES 1 – Mobile Home

Sleeping: 2 bedrooms, sleeps 5: 1 double, 2 single beds, sofa bed, pillows & blankets provided

Living: living/kitchen area, heating, TV, fan, shower & separate wc

Eating: fitted kitchen with hobs, coffee machine, fridge/freezer

Outside: table & chairs, sun lounger, parasol

Pets: not accepted

Other (AR1 and AR2): bed linen and cot for rent

	AR1	AR2
Open: 6 April - 26 September		
Weekly Charge	**AR1**	**AR2**
Low Season (from)	€ 434	€ 434
High Season (from)	€ 637	€ 637

ES81800 Camping Sant Pol

see report page 41

Carrer del Doctor Fleming No.1, E-17220 Sant Feliu de Guíxols (Girona)

AR1 – GARBY – Bungalow

Sleeping: 2 bedrooms, sleesp 5: 1 double, 2 single beds, sofa bed, pillows & blankets provided

Living: living/kitchen area, heating, safe, shower & wc

Eating: fitted kitchen with hobs, microwave, coffee machine, fridge/freezer

Outside: table & chairs, parasol, BBQ

Pets: accepted

AR2 – GANX 5 – Bungalow

Sleeping: 1 bedrooms, sleeps 3: 1 double, sofa bed, pillows & blankets provided

Living: living/kitchen area, heating, safe, shower & wc

Eating: fitted kitchen with hobs, coffee machine, fridge/freezer

Outside: table & chairs, parasol, BBQ

Pets: accepted

Other (AR1 and AR2): bed linen and high chair for rent

	AR1	AR2
Open: 27 March - 10 December		
Weekly Charge	**AR1**	**AR2**
Low Season (from)	€ 378	€ 288
High Season (from)	€ 1029	€ 714

ES84800 Camping & Bungalows Sanguli

see report page 50

Prolongacion Calle, Apdo 123, E-43840 Salou (Tarragona)

AR1 – VILLA PARADISE – Bungalow

Sleeping: 2 bedrooms, sleeps 6: 1 double, 2 single beds, 2 sofa beds, pillows & blankets provided

Living: living/kitchen area, air conditioning, TV, shower & separate wc

Eating: fitted kitchen with hobs, microwave, dishwasher, fridge/freezer

Outside: table & chairs, 2 sun loungers

Pets: not accepted

AR2 – TAHITI SUITE – Bungalow

Sleeping: 2 bedrooms, sleeps 6: 1 double, 2 single beds, 2 sofa beds, pillows & blankets provided

Living: living/kitchen area, air conditioning, TV, shower & wc

Eating: fitted kitchen with hobs, microwave, oven, fridge

Outside: table & chairs, 2 sun loungers

Pets: not accepted

	AR1	AR2
Open: 27 March - 1 November		
Weekly Charge	**AR1**	**AR2**
Low Season (from)	€ 364	€ 420
High Season (from)	€ 1470	€ 1260

ES84790 Camping Playa Cambrils Don Camilo

▶ see report page 52

Ctra Cambrils - Salou km 1,5, E-43850 Cambrils (Tarragona)

AR1 – O'HARA – Mobile Home

Sleeping: 2 bedrooms, sleeps 5: 1 double, 2 single beds, sofa bed, pillows & blankets provided

Living: living/kitchen area, heating, TV, safe, shower & separate wc

Eating: fitted kitchen with hobs, microwave, coffee machine, fridge/freezer

Outside: table & chairs

Pets: not accepted

AR2 – PREMIUM – Bungalow

Sleeping: 2 bedrooms, sleeps 4: 1 double, 1 single, bunkbed, pillows & blankets provided

Living: living/kitchen area, heating, TV, shower & separate wc

Eating: fitted kitchen with hobs, microwave, coffee machine, fridge/freezer

Outside: table & chairs

Pets: not accepted

Open: 13 March - 18 October	AR1	AR2
Weekly Charge Low Season *(from)*	€ 308	€ 283
High Season *(from)*	€ 987	€ 868

ES84810 Camping Cambrils Park

▶ see report page 54

Avenida Mas Clariana s/n., E-43850 Cambrils (Tarragona)

AR1 – BONITA – Bungalow

Sleeping: 2 bedrooms, sleeps 6: 1 double, 2 single beds, 2 sofa beds, pillows & blankets provided

Living: living/kitchen area, air conditioning, TV, shower & separate wc

Eating: fitted kitchen with hobs, microwave, dishwasher, fridge/freezer

Outside: table & chairs, 2 sun loungers

Pets: not accepted

AR2 – ALOHA – Bungalow

Sleeping: 2 bedrooms, sleeps 6: 1 double, 2 single beds, 2 sofa beds, pillows & blankets provided

Living: living/kitchen area, air conditioning, TV, shower & wc

Eating: fitted kitchen with hobs, microwave, oven, fridge

Outside: table & chairs, 2 sun loungers

Pets: not accepted

Open: 3 April - 12 October	AR1	AR2
Weekly Charge Low Season *(from)*	€ 89	€ 77
High Season *(from)*	€ 195	€ 185

PO8202 Camping Turiscampo

▶ see report page 161

EN125, Espiche, Luz, P-8600 Lagos (Faro)

AR1 – BUNGALOW 5 PERSONS – Bungalow

Sleeping: 2 bedrooms, sleeps 5: 1 double, 2 single beds, bunkbed, pillows & blankets provided

Living: living/kitchen area, heating, shower & separate wc

Eating: fitted kitchen with hobs, microwave, oven, grill, coffee machine, fridge/freezer

Outside: table & chairs

Pets: not accepted

AR2 – MOBILE HOME 5/6 PERSONS – Mobile Home

Sleeping: 2 bedrooms, sleeps 5: 1 double, 2 single beds, sofa bed, pillows & blankets provided

Living: living/kitchen area, heating, shower & separate wc

Eating: fitted kitchen with hobs, microwave, oven, grill, coffee machine, fridge/freezer

Outside: table & chairs

Pets: not accepted

Other (AR1 and AR2): bed linen for rent

Open: All year	AR1	AR2
Nightly Charge Low Season *(from)*	€ 43	€ 46
High Season *(from)*	€ 100	€ 107

PO8175 Zmar - Eco Camping Resort

see report page 167

Herdade a de Mateus EN393/1, San Salvador, P-7630 Odemira (Beja)

AR1 – CHALET – Chalet

Sleeping: 2 bedrooms, sleeps 4: 1 double, 2 single beds, pillows & blankets provided

Living: living/kitchen area, air conditioning, TV, shower & wc

Eating: fitted kitchen with hobs, microwave, oven, dishwasher, fridge/freezer

Outside: table & chairs, parasol

Pets: not accepted

Open: May - December	
Weekly Charge	**AR1**
Low Season (from)	€ 450
High Season (from)	€ 1050

PO8460 Camping Caravaning Vale Paraiso

see report page 173

EN242, P-2450-138 Nazaré (Leiria)

AR1 – CHALET – Chalet	**AR2 – APARTAMENTO – Apartment**
Sleeping: 2 bedrooms, sleeps 5: 1 double, 2 single beds, bunkbed, pillows & blankets provided	**Sleeping:** 2 bedrooms, sleeps 6: 1 double, 2 single beds, bunkbed, sofa bed, pillows & blankets provided
Living: living/kitchen area, TV, fan, shower & separate wc	**Living:** living/kitchen area, heating, TV, fan, shower & separate wc
Eating: fitted kitchen with hobs, microwave, dishwasher, coffee machine, fridge/freezer	**Eating:** fitted kitchen with hobs, microwave, dishwasher, coffee machine, fridge/freezer
Outside: table & chairs, parasol	**Outside:** table & chairs, parasol
Pets: accepted	**Pets:** not accepted

Other (AR1 and AR2): bed linen and cot for rent

Open: All year		
Weekly Charge	**AR1**	**AR2**
Low Season (from)	€ 315	€ 315
High Season (from)	€ 710	€ 712

Low Cost Flights
An Inexpensive Way To Arrive At Your Campsite

Many campsites are conveniently served by a wide choice of low cost airlines. Cheap flights can be very easy to find and travellers increasingly find the regional airports often used to be smaller, quieter and generally a calmer, more pleasurable experience.

Low cost flights can make campsites in more distant regions a much more attractive option: quicker to reach, inexpensive flights, and simply more convenient.

Many campsites are seeing increased visitors using the low cost flights and are adapting their services to suit this clientele. An airport shuttle service is not uncommon, meaning you can take advantage of that cheap flight knowing you will be met at the other end and whisked to your campsite. No taxi queues or multiple drop-offs.

Obviously, these low cost flights are impractical when taking all your own camping gear but they do make a holiday in campsite owned accommodation much more straightforward. The low cost airline option makes mobile home holidays especially attractive: pack a suitcase and use bed linen and towels provided (which you will generally need to pre-book).

Pricing Tips

- Low cost airlines promote cheap flights but only a small percentage of seats are priced   at the cheapest price. Book early for the best prices (and of course you also get a better choice of campsite or mobile home)

- Child seats are usually the same costs as adults

- Full payment is required at the time of booking

- Changes and amendments can be costly with low cost airlines

- Peak dates can be expensive compared to other carriers

Car Hire

For maximum flexibility you will probably hire a car from a car rental agency. Car hire provides convenience but also will allow you access to off-site shops, beaches and tourist sights.

Travelling

When taking your car (and caravan, tent or trailer tent) or motorcaravan to the continent you do need to plan in advance and to find out as much as possible about driving in the countries you plan to visit. Whilst European harmonisation has eliminated many of the differences between one country and another, it is well worth reading the short notes we provide in the introduction to each country in this guide in addition to this more general summary.

Of course, the main difference from driving in the UK is that in mainland Europe you will need to drive on the right. Without taking extra time and care, especially at busy junctions and conversely when roads are empty, it is easy to forget to drive on the right. Remember that traffic approaching from the right usually has priority unless otherwise indicated by road markings and signs. Harmonisation also means that most (but not all) common road signs are the same in all countries.

Your vehicle

Book your vehicle in for a good service well before your intended departure date. This will lessen the chance of an expensive breakdown. Make sure your brakes are working efficiently and that your tyres have plenty of tread (3 mm. is recommended, particularly if you are undertaking a long journey).

Also make sure that your caravan or trailer is roadworthy and that its tyres are in good order and correctly inflated. Plan your packing and be careful not to overload your vehicle, caravan or trailer – this is unsafe and may well invalidate your insurance cover (it must not be more fully loaded than the kerb weight of the insured vehicle).

CHECK ALL THE FOLLOWING:

- GB sticker. If you do not display a sticker, you may risk an on-the-spot fine as this identifier is compulsory in all countries. Euro-plates are an acceptable alternative within the EU (but not outside). Remember to attach another sticker (or Euro-plate) to caravans or trailers. Only GB stickers (not England, Scotland, Wales or N. Ireland) stickers are valid in the EU.

- Headlights. As you will be driving on the right you must adjust your headlights so that the dipped beam does not dazzle oncoming drivers. Converter kits are readily available for most vehicle, although if your car is fitted with high intensity headlights, you should check with your motor dealer. Check that any planned extra loading does not affect the beam height.

- Seatbelts. Rules for the fitting and wearing of seatbelts throughout Europe are similar to those in the UK, but it is worth checking before you go. Rules for carrying children in the front of vehicles vary from country to country. It is best to plan not to do this if possible.

- Door/wing mirrors. To help with driving on the right, if your vehicle is not fitted with a mirror on the left hand side, we recommend you have one fitted.

- Fuel. Leaded and Lead Replacement petrol is increasingly difficult to find in Northern Europe.

Compulsory additional equipment

The driving laws of the countries of Europe still vary in what you are required to carry in your vehicle, although the consequences of not carrying a required piece of equipment are almost always an on-the-spot fine.

To meet these requirements we suggest that you carry the following:

- FIRE EXTINGUISHER

- BASIC TOOL KIT

- FIRST AID KIT

- SPARE BULBS

- TWO WARNING TRIANGLES – two are required in some countries at all times, and are compulsory in most countries when towing.

- HIGH VISIBILITY VESTS – now compulsory in France, Spain (required for all car passengers), Italy and Austria (and likely to become compulsory throughout the EU) in case you need to walk on a motorway.

Insurance and Motoring Documents

Vehicle insurance

Contact your insurer well before you depart to check that your car insurance policy covers driving outside the UK. Most do, but many policies only provide minimum cover (so if you have an accident your insurance may only cover the cost of damage to the other person's property, with no cover for fire and theft).

To maintain the same level of cover abroad as you enjoy at home you need to tell your vehicle insurer. Some will automatically cover you abroad with no extra cost and no extra paperwork. Some will say you need a Green Card (which is neither green nor on card) but won't charge for it. Some will charge extra for the Green Card. Ideally you should contact your vehicle insurer 3-4 weeks before you set off, and confirm your conversation with them in writing.

Breakdown insurance

Arrange breakdown cover for your trip in good time so that if your vehicle breaks down or is involved in an accident it (and your caravan or trailer) can be repaired or returned to this country. This cover can usually be arranged as part of your travel insurance policy (see below).

Documents you must take with you

You may be asked to show your documents at any time so make sure that they are in order, up-to-date and easily accessible while you travel. These are what you need to take:

- Passports (you may also need a visa in some countries if you hold either a UK passport not issued in the UK or a passport that was issued outside the EU).

- Motor Insurance Certificate, including Green Card (or Continental Cover clause)

- DVLC Vehicle Registration Document plus, if not your own vehicle, the owner's written authority to drive.

- A full valid Driving Licence (not provisional). The new photo style licence is now mandatory in most European countries).

Personal Holiday insurance

Even though you are just travelling within Europe you must take out travel insurance. Few EU countries pay the full cost of medical treatment even under reciprocal health service arrangements. The first part of a holiday insurance policy covers people. It will include the cost of doctor, ambulance and hospital treatment if needed. If needed the better companies will even pay for English language speaking doctors and nurses and will bring a sick or injured holidaymaker home by air ambulance.

An important part of the insurance, often ignored, is cancellation (and curtailment) cover. Few things are as heartbreaking as having to cancel a holiday because a member of the family falls ill. Cancellation insurance can't take away the disappointment, but it makes sure you don't suffer financially as well. For this reason you should arrange your holiday insurance at least eight weeks before you set off.

Whichever insurance you choose we would advise reading very carefully the policies sold by the High Street travel trade. Whilst they may be good, they may not cover the specific needs of campers, caravanners and motorcaravanners.

Telephone 01580 214006 for a quote for our European Camping Holiday Insurance with cover arranged through Green Flag Motoring Assistance and Inter Group Assistance Services, one of the UK's largest assistance companies. Alternatively visit our website at www.insure4campers.com.

Travelling continued

European Health Insurance Card (EHIC)

Make sure you apply for your EHIC before travelling in Europe. Eligible travellers from the UK are entitled to receive free or reduced-cost medical care in many European countries on production of an EHIC. This free card is available by completing a form in the booklet 'Health Advice for Travellers' from local Post Offices. One should be completed for each family member. Alternatively visit www.dh.gov.uk/travellers and apply on-line. Please allow time to send your application off and have the EHIC returned to you.

The EHIC is valid in all European Community countries plus Iceland, Liechtenstein, Switzerland and Norway. If you or any of your dependants are suddenly taken ill or have an accident during a visit to any of these countries, free or reduced-cost emergency treatment is available - in most cases on production of a valid EHIC.

Only state-provided emergency treatment is covered, and you will receive treatment on the same terms as nationals of the country you are visiting. Private treatment is generally not covered, and state-provided treatment may not cover all of the things that you would expect to receive free of charge from the NHS.

Remember an EHIC does not cover you for all the medical costs that you can incur or for repatriation - it is not an alternative to travel insurance. You will still need appropriate insurance to ensure you are fully covered for all eventualities.

Travelling with children

Most countries in Europe are enforcing strict guidelines when you are travelling with children who are not your own. A minor (under the age of 18) must be accompanied by a parent or legal guardian or must carry a letter of authorisation from a parent or guardian. The letter should name the adult responsible for the minor during his or her stay. Similarily, a minor travelling with just one of his/her parents, must have a letter of authority to leave their home country from the parent staying behind. Full information is available at www.fco.gov.uk.

Open All Year

The following sites are understood to accept caravanners and campers all year round. It is always wise to phone the site to check as, for example, the facilities available may be reduced.

SPAIN

Cataluña-Catalunya

ES80360	Esponellà
ES81300	Calonge
ES82280	Blanes
ES82350	Bon Repos
ES82400	Bona Vista Kim
ES83900	Vilanova Park
ES84820	Pineda de Salou
ES85020	Montblanc Park
ES85060	Serra de Prades
ES85080	Poboleda
ES85350	Cala d'Oques
ES85360	Ametlla
ES91190	Frontera
ES91225	Vall de Camprodon
ES91240	Bedurà Park
ES91400	Pedraforca

Comunidad Valenciana

ES85580	Vinaros
ES85590	Azahar
ES85600	Playa Tropicana
ES85700	Torre La Sal 2
ES85800	Bonterra
ES85850	Altomira
ES85900	Monmar
ES86120	Euro (Oliva)
ES86130	Olé
ES86150	Kiko
ES86200	Alqueria
ES86250	Kiko Rural
ES86450	Mariola
ES86750	Vall de Laguar
ES86810	Villasol
ES86830	Benisol
ES86840	Almafrá
ES86850	El Raco
ES86870	Cap Blanch
ES86900	Costa Blanca
ES87420	Marina
ES87430	Marjal
ES87540	Javea
ES87550	Moraira

Murcia

ES87440	Puerta
ES87450	Fuente
ES87480	Madriles
ES87520	El Portus (Naturist)
ES87530	Manga

Andalucia

ES87490	Sopalmo
ES87510	Cuevas Mar
ES87560	Cueva Negra
ES87620	Escullos
ES87630	Cabo de Gata
ES87650	Garrofa
ES87680	Roquetas
ES87810	El Pino
ES87820	Laguna Playa
ES87830	Almanat (Naturist)
ES87850	Rural Iznate
ES87900	Fuente de Piedra
ES88000	Marbella Playa
ES88020	Cabopino
ES88030	Buganvilla
ES88090	El Sur
ES88500	Paloma
ES88550	Tarifa
ES88570	Pinar San José
ES88580	Rosaleda
ES88590	Roche
ES88650	Playa Las Dunas
ES88710	Giralda
ES88900	Gazules
ES90780	Villares
ES90800	El Brillante
ES90810	Villsom
ES90840	Campiña
ES90850	Carlos III
ES90890	Despenaperros
ES92700	Suspiro-Moro
ES92750	Avellanos
ES92760	Reina Isabel
ES92850	Lomas
ES92890	Trevélez
ES92900	El Balcon
ES92920	Puerta La Alpujarra
ES92930	Orgiva
ES92950	Don Cactus

Extremadura

ES90270	Monfrague
ES90860	Cáceres
ES90870	Merida

Castilla La-Mancha

ES90900	El Greco
ES90960	Mirador
ES90970	Batanes

Madrid

ES90910	Aranjuez
ES92000	El Escorial
ES92100	Pico-Miel
ES92120	Monte Holiday

Castilla y León

ES90210	Fuentes Blancas
ES90245	Riaza
ES90250	Regio
ES92500	Costajan
ES92530	Picon del Conde

Galicia

ES89360	Bayona Playa
ES89380	Paxarinas
ES90240	As Cancelas

Asturias

ES89400	Cantiles
ES89650	Picos-Europa

Cantabria

ES89640	Molino
ES89730	Santillana

Pais Vasco-Euskadi

ES90300	Igueldo
ES90340	Leagi
ES90390	Gran Zarautz

La Rioja

ES92280	Berceo

Aragón

ES90600	Peña Montañesa
ES90610	Ligüerre de Cinca
ES90640	Gavín
ES91040	Ciudad de Zaragoza
ES91250	Lago Barasona

PORTUGAL

Algarve

PO8200	Valverde
PO8202	Turiscampo
PO8210	Albufeira
PO8220	Quarteira
PO8230	Olhao
PO8410	Armacao-Pera
PO8430	Sagres
PO8440	Quinta

Alentejo

PO8160	Porto Covo
PO8170	São Miguel
PO8175	Zmar
PO8350	Markádia

Lisbon & Vale do Tejo

PO8100	Sao Pedro-Moel
PO8130	Guincho
PO8140	Monsanto
PO8150	Caparica
PO8400	O Tamanco
PO8480	Foz do Arelho

Beiras & Centre

PO8040	Vagueira
PO8090	Gala
PO8330	Arganil

Porto & North

PO8375	Celorico de Basto
PO8010	Caminha
PO8030	Rio Alto
PO8370	Cerdeira

Dogs

For the benefit of those who want to take their dogs with them or for people who do not like dogs at the sites they visit, we list here the sites that have indicated to us that they do not accept dogs. If you are, however, planning to take your dog we do advise you to contact them first to check – there may be limits on numbers, breeds, etc. or times of the year when they are excluded.

Sites that do not accept dogs

SPAIN

Cataluña-Catalunya

ES80900	Cypsela
ES81010	Playa Brava
ES81030	El Maset
ES81400	Treumal
ES84200	Stel (Roda)
ES84810	Cambrils
ES85300	Playa Montroig
ES85370	Templo del Sol (Nat)
ES85400	Torre del Sol
ES91230	Solsones
ES91240	Bedurà Park
ES91430	Pirineus

Comunidad Valenciana

ES85600	Playa Tropicana
ES85900	Monmar
ES86810	Villasol

Murcia

ES87480	Madriles

Andalucia

ES87580	Tau de San José
ES88550	Tarifa

Castilla y León

ES92510	Rio Lobos

Cantabria

ES89980	Playa de Isla
ES89990	Punta Marina
ES90000	Playa Joyel

Aragón

ES91100	Fresneda

Balears

ES80000	Son Bou

PORTUGAL

Alentejo

PO8170	São Miguel

Maybe - not accepted in high season

SPAIN

Cataluña-Catalunya

ES80720	Medes
ES80800	Delfin Verde
ES81600	Cala Gogo
ES82320	Bella Terra

Comunidad Valenciana

ES85590	Azahar
ES85800	Bonterra

Andalucia

ES88030	Buganvilla
ES88500	Paloma
ES88570	Pinar San José
ES88580	Rosaleda
ES92950	Don Cactus

Cantabria

ES89930	Playa del Regaton

PORTUGAL

Alentejo

PO8350	Markádia

Porto & North

PO8370	Cerdeira

Fishing

We are pleased to include details of sites which provide facilities for fishing on site. However, it is always best to contact sites directly to check that they provide for your individual requirements.

SPAIN

Cataluña-Catalunya

ES80100	Castell Mar
ES80150	Laguna
ES80300	Nautic Almata
ES80310	Gaviota
ES80320	Riu
ES80350	Amfora
ES80400	Dunas
ES80500	Aquarius
ES80600	Ballena Alegre 2
ES80640	Bassegoda
ES80740	Illa Mateua
ES80800	Delfin Verde
ES81010	Playa Brava
ES81400	Treumal
ES81600	Cala Gogo
ES82000	Cala Llevadó
ES82280	Blanes
ES82300	Bella Terra
ES82320	Bella Terra
ES82350	Bon Repos
ES82380	Caballo de Mar
ES84200	Stel (Roda)
ES84780	Joan
ES84830	Tamarit
ES84850	Palmeras
ES84860	Torre de la Mora
ES85300	Playa Montroig
ES85330	Els Prat - Marius
ES85350	Cala d'Oques
ES85360	Ametlla
ES85370	Templo del Sol (Nat)
ES85400	Torre del Sol
ES91190	Frontera
ES91225	Vall de Camprodon
ES91420	Solana del Segre
ES91430	Pirineus

Comunidad Valenciana

ES85600	Playa Tropicana
ES85700	Torre La Sal 2
ES86120	Euro (Oliva)
ES86130	Olé
ES86150	Kiko
ES86880	Playa Paraiso
ES87430	Marjal

Murcia

ES87440	Puerta
ES87520	El Portus (Naturist)
ES87530	Manga

Andalucia

ES87650	Garrofa
ES87820	Laguna Playa
ES87830	Almanat (Naturist)
ES88550	Tarifa
ES92890	Trevélez
ES92950	Don Cactus

Castilla La-Mancha

ES90900	El Greco
ES90980	Rio Mundo

Madrid

ES90910	Aranjuez

Castilla y León

ES92570	Frias

Galicia

ES89360	Bayona Playa
ES89380	Paxarinas

Asturias

ES89440	Cascada
ES89450	Lagos-Somiedo
ES89500	Costa Verde
ES89600	Paz
ES89650	Picos-Europa

Fishing continued

Cantabria
ES89620   Isla
ES89640   Molino
ES89700   Arenas-Pechon
ES89910   Barguilla
ES89930   Playa del Regaton
ES89980   Playa de Isla
ES90000   Playa Joyel

Pais Vasco-Euskadi
ES90350   Portuondo
ES90450   Angosto

La Rioja
ES90400   Haro
ES92250   Rioja
ES92260   Cameros

Navarra
ES90430   Errota el Molino
ES90480   Urrobi

Aragón
ES90580   Baliera
ES90600   Peña Montañesa
ES90610   Ligüerre de Cinca

PORTUGAL
Alentejo
PO8350   Markádia

Beiras & Centre
PO8070   Mira

Porto & North
PO8010   Caminha

Bicycle Hire

We understand that the following sites have bicycles to hire on site or can arrange for bicycles to be delivered. However, we would recommend that you contact them directly to check as the situation can change.

SPAIN

Cataluña-Catalunya
ES80090   Salatà
ES80150   Laguna
ES80300   Nautic Almata
ES80310   Gaviota
ES80320   Riu
ES80330   Palmeras
ES80350   Amfora
ES80360   Esponellà
ES80400   Dunas
ES80500   Aquarius
ES80600   Ballena Alegre 2
ES80640   Bassegoda
ES80720   Medes
ES80740   Illa Mateua
ES80800   Delfin Verde
ES80900   Cypsela
ES81000   Inter-Pals
ES81600   Cala Gogo
ES81700   Valldaro
ES82100   Tucan
ES83400   Rupit
ES83900   Vilanova Park
ES83920   El Garrofer
ES84020   Vendrell Platja
ES84100   Playa Bara
ES84200   Stel (Roda)
ES84780   Joan
ES84820   Pineda de Salou
ES84850   Palmeras
ES85020   Montblanc Park
ES85060   Serra de Prades
ES85300   Playa Montroig
ES85330   Els Prat - Marius
ES85360   Ametlla
ES85370   Templo del Sol (Nat)
ES85400   Torre del Sol
ES85550   Eucaliptus
ES91230   Solsones
ES91400   Pedraforca
ES91440   Stel (Puigcerdá)

Comunidad Valenciana
ES85590   Azahar
ES85600   Playa Tropicana
ES85800   Bonterra
ES86115   Azul
ES86150   Kiko

ES86220   Santa Marta
ES86250   Kiko Rural
ES87420   Marina
ES87430   Marjal

Murcia
ES87440   Puerta
ES87480   Madriles

Andalucia
ES87580   Tau de San José
ES87620   Escullos
ES87630   Cabo de Gata
ES87900   Fuente de Piedra
ES88900   Gazules
ES90840   Campiña
ES92890   Trevélez
ES92900   El Balcon
ES92930   Orgiva
ES92950   Don Cactus

Extremadura
ES90270   Monfrague
ES90870   Merida

Castilla La-Mancha
ES90970   Batanes
ES90980   Rio Mundo

Madrid
ES90910   Aranjuez

Castilla y León
ES90230   Santiago
ES92500   Costajan

Galicia
ES89380   Paxarinas
ES90240   As Cancelas

Cantabria
ES89620   Isla
ES89730   Santillana
ES89910   Barguilla

Pais Vasco-Euskadi
ES90450   Angosto

La Rioja
ES90400   Haro

Navarra
ES90420   Etxarri
ES90430   Errota el Molino

Aragón
ES90600   Peña Montañesa
ES90610   Ligüerre de Cinca
ES90640   Gavín
ES91250   Lago Barasona

Balears
ES80000   Son Bou

PORTUGAL

Algarve
PO8202   Turiscampo
PO8210   Albufeira
PO8230   Olhao
PO8430   Sagres
PO8440   Quinta

Alentejo
PO8160   Porto Covo
PO8175   Zmar

Lisbon & Vale do Tejo
PO8460   Vale Paraiso
PO8480   Foz do Arelho
PO8550   Quinta Da Cerejeira

Beiras & Centre
PO8040   Vagueira
PO8070   Mira

Porto & North
PO8010   Caminha

Horse Riding

We understand that the following sites have horse riding stables on site. Where facilities are within easy reach and we have been given details, we have included this information in the individual site reports. However, we recommend that you contact the site to check that they meet your requirements.

SPAIN

Cataluña-Catalunya
ES80150   Laguna
ES80300   Nautic Almata
ES85060   Serra de Prades

Andalucia
ES92890   Trevélez
ES92900   El Balcon

Extremadura
ES90270   Monfrague

Castilla Y Leon
ES90230   Santiago

Asturias
ES89450   Lagos-Somiedo

Cantabria
ES89620   Isla
ES89700   Arenas-Pechon

Rioja
ES92250   Rioja

Aragón
ES90600   Peña Montañesa

PORTUGAL

Alentejo
PO8350   Markádia

Boat Launching

We understand that the following sites have boat slipways on site. Where facilities are within easy reach and we have been given details, we have included this information in the individual site reports. However, we recommend that you contact the site to check that they meet your requirements.

SPAIN

Cataluña-Catalunya
ES80300   Nautic Almata
ES80320   Riu
ES81010   Playa Brava
ES84850   Palmeras
ES85300   Playa Montroig
ES85330   Els Prat - Marius
ES85400   Torre del Sol

Comunidad Valenciana
ES86120   Euro (Oliva)
ES86150   Kiko
ES86880   Playa Paraiso

Murcia
ES87520   El Portus (Naturist)

Andalucia
ES87650   Garrofa
ES87820   Laguna Playa
ES88550   Tarifa

Galicia
ES89360   Bayona Playa

Cantabria
ES89700   Arenas-Pechon

Navarra
ES90430   Errota el Molino

Aragón
ES90610   Ligüerre de Cinca
ES91250   Lago Barasona

PORTUGAL

Alentejo
PO8350   Markádia

How can I cruise to
Spain overnight
with my car?

NEW
service from
Portsmouth
2009

We know a way

Take an overnight cruise from Portsmouth or Plymouth to Santander, and avoid a long drive through France. On board, enjoy fine dining, great shopping, and a peaceful night's sleep in your en-suite cabin.

In 2009, you'll be able to sail from either Portsmouth or Plymouth and enjoy the fastest, most luxurious way to Spain with your car.

CORK
PLYMOUTH
POOLE PORTSMOUTH
CHERBOURG
CAEN
ROSCOFF ST MALO

SANTANDER

brittanyferries.com 0871 244 0834

Brittany Ferries
Spain

Paying too much for your mobile home holiday?

Town and Village Index

Town and Village Index continued

The Regions of Spain and Portugal

Index by Campsite Number

Index - Campsite Region and Name

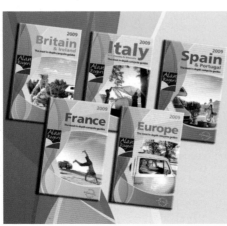

Widely regarded as the 'Bible' by site owners and readers alike, there is no better guide when it comes to forming an independent view of a campsite's quality. When you need to be confident in your choice of campsite, you need the Alan Rogers Guide.

☑ **Sites only included on merit**

☑ **Sites cannot pay to be included**

☑ **Independently inspected, rigorously assessed**

☑ **Impartial reviews**

☑ **Over 40 years of expertise**